William Mallinson is Lecturer in British History, Literature and Culture at the Ionian University, Corfu. He is a former diplomat and the author of *Cyprus: A Modern History*. (I.B.Tauris, 2005)

INTERNATIONAL LIBRARY OF TWENTIETH CENTURY HISTORY
Series ISBN: 978-1-84885-227-3
See www.ibtauriscom/ILTCH for a full list of titles

12. *Out of Austria:*
The Austrian Centre in London in World War II
Marietta Bearman, Charmian Brinson, Richard Dove, Anthony Grenville and Jennifer Taylor
978 1 84511 475 6

13. *Great Britain and the Creation of Yugoslavia:*
Negotiating Balkan Nationality and Identity
James Evans
978 1 84511 488 6

14. *Rebellion in Brunei:*
The 1962 Revolt, Imperialism, Confrontation and Oil
Harun Abdul Majid
978 1 84511 423 7

15. *London Was Ours:*
Diaries and Memoirs of the London Blitz
Amy Helen Bell
978 1 84511 592 0

16. *Myxomatosis: A History of Pest Control and the Rabbit*
Peter W.J. Bartrip
978 1 84511 572 2

17. *Serbia in the Shadow of Milosevic:*
The Legacy of Conflict in the Balkans
Janine N. Clark
978 1 84511 767 2

18. *Diplomacy Between the Wars:*
Five Diplomats and the Shaping of the Modern World:
George W. Liebmann
978 1 84511 637 8

19. *The Greater Middle East and the Cold War:*
US Foreign Policy Under Eisenhower and Kennedy
Roby C. Barrett
978 1 84511 393 3

20. *The Greek Revolution and the Making of Modern Europe: Independence, State-building and the Problem of National Identity*
Dean J. Kostantaras
978 1 84511 709 2

21. *Covert Action in the Cold War:*
US Policy, Intelligence and CIA Operations
James Callanan
978 1 84511 882 2

22. *Negotiating History:*
Resolving the Cyprus Conflict
Michalis S. Michael
978 1 84511 174 8

23. *In the Shadow of Hitler:*
Personalities of the Right in Central and:
Eastern Europe
Rebecca Haynes (ed.)
978 1 84511 697 2

24. *Creating A Socialist Yugoslavia:*
Tito, Communist Leadership and the National Question
Hilde Katrine Haug
978 1 84885 051 4

25. *The Making of the German Post-War Economy: Political Communication and Public Reception of the Social Market Economy after World War Two*
Christian L. Glossner
978 1 84885 264 8

26. *The Cyprus Referendum:*
A Divided Island and the Challenge of the Annan Plan
Chrysostomos Pericleous
978 1 84885 021 7

27. *Islam and Secularism in Turkey:*
Kemalism, Religion and the Nation State
Umut Azak
978 1 84885 263 1

28. *From Neutrality to Commitment:*
Dutch Foreign Policy, NATO and European Integration
William Mallinson
978 1 84885 344 7

29. *Britain and the Weimar Republic:*
The History of a Cultural Relationship
Colin Storer
978 1 84885 140 5

30. *Cyprus in World War II: Politics and Conflict in the Eastern Mediterranean*
Anastasia Yiangou
978 1 84885 436 9

FROM NEUTRALITY TO COMMITMENT

Dutch Foreign Policy, NATO
and European Integration

William Mallinson

BLOOMSBURY ACADEMIC
LONDON • NEW YORK • OXFORD • NEW DELHI • SYDNEY

BLOOMSBURY ACADEMIC
Bloomsbury Publishing Plc
50 Bedford Square, London, WC1B 3DP, UK
1385 Broadway, New York, NY 10018, USA

BLOOMSBURY, BLOOMSBURY ACADEMIC and the Diana logo are trademarks of Bloomsbury Publishing Plc

First published in Great Britain by I.B. Tauris 2010
Paperback edition first published by Bloomsbury Academic 2020

Copyright © William Mallinson, 2010

William Mallinson has asserted his right under the Copyright, Designs and Patents Act, 1988, to be identified as Author of this work.

For legal purposes the Acknowledgements on p. xi constitute an extension of this copyright page.

All rights reserved. No part of this publication may be reproduced or transmitted in any form or by any means, electronic or mechanical, including photocopying, recording, or any information storage or retrieval system, without prior permission in writing from the publishers.

Bloomsbury Publishing Plc does not have any control over, or responsibility for, any third-party websites referred to or in this book. All internet addresses given in this book were correct at the time of going to press. The author and publisher regret any inconvenience caused if addresses have changed or sites have ceased to exist, but can accept no responsibility for any such changes.

A catalogue record for this book is available from the British Library.

A catalog record for this book is available from the Library of Congress.

ISBN: HB: 978-1-8488-5344-7
PB: 978-1-3501-6943-2
ePDF: 978-0-8577-1278-3
ePub: 978-0-7556-3051-6

Series: International Library of Twentieth Century History, vol. 28

To find out more about our authors and books visit www.bloomsbury.com and sign up for our newsletters.

CONTENTS

List Of Abbreviations	ix
Acknowledgements	xi
Foreword	xiii
Preface	xv

INTRODUCTION   1

1 SETTING THE SCENE   5
    The Nature of Netherlands Neutrality   5
    The German Problem and the Effects of the War   10
    The Commercial Question   16
    Dutch Territorial and other Claims on Germany   17
    The Indonesian Factor   26
    The Role of National Characteristics   32
    Conclusion   34

2 EUROPEAN DEVELOPMENTS AND THE GERMAN QUESTION: THE DUTCH APPROACH   35
    Introduction   35
    The Netherlands and Europe   35
    Marshall Aid and the Dutch Dilemma   37
    Dutch Claims and Frustrations   44
    European Unity   51
    Conclusion   53

3 THE QUESTION OF SECURITY AND THE BRUSSELS TREATY ORGANISATION — 54

Introduction — 54
The Indonesian Thorn — 56
The Path to the Brussels Treaty — 59
The Brussels Treaty – a way of being heard? — 62
Conclusion — 65

4 THE NORTH ATLANTIC ROAD — 67

Introduction — 67
Lip Service – The Dutch Position on NATO — 70
The Indonesian Complication — 75
The Dutch Atlantic Attitude — 81
Conclusion — 83

5 FROM THE ATLANTIC TO EUROPE — 85

Introduction — 85
Dutch Restraint — 86
The British Information Campaign — 89
Slow Realisation of Harsh Realities and Defence Problems — 94
Trade before Ideology — 103
Germany and NATO — 105
The European Angle — 112
Conclusion — 115

6 WHOSE EUROPE? — 117

Introduction — 117
The Council of Europe – a weak beginning — 118
The Schuman Plan — 123
The Stikker Plan and the British — 131
Conclusion — 134

7 WHOSE DEFENCE? — 137

Introduction — 137
The Pleven Plan — 140
The Dutch View — 143
The British Disappointment — 151
Conclusion — 156

8 THE ROAD TO A STANDING ARMY — 158

Introduction — 158

The Resignation of the Government	159
External Pressures and Dutch Indignation	165
Stikker's Crisis	168
The British and American View	170
Conclusion	174

9 TOWARDS COMMITMENT 176
Introduction	176
Reluctant Participants	177
The Dutch Blindness	180
Germany and NATO	183
A New Enthusiasm for Europe	185
Defence – Less Enthusiasm	191
Conclusion	193

10 THE EUROPEAN ANSWER 195
Introduction	195
Germany and Commercial Precedence	195
Dutch - British Relations	197
EDC Enthusiasm – The Shining Example	199
Security through Europe	203
No Divorce because of the Children	206
Conclusion	207

11 THE LAST LAUGH 210
Introduction	210
The Dutch, Europe and the EDC	211
The German Angle	214
Between EDC and NATO	218
Back to NATO	221
Conclusion	224

12 CONCLUSIONS 225

Notes	235
Appendix: list of missing and unavailable files in the National Archives	279
Archivalia	281
Interviews	283
Bibliography	285
Index	295

LIST OF ABBREVIATIONS

BTO: Brussels Treaty Organisation

CEEC: Committee for European Economic Co-operation

ECSC: European Coal and Steel Community

EDC: European Defence Community

EPU: European Payments Union

ERP: European Recovery Programme

KVP: Catholic People's Party

OEEC: Organisation for European Economic Co-operation

PvdA: Work Party (left of Centre)

UN: United Nations

UNRRA: United Nations Relief and Recovery Agency

VVD: Party of Freedom and Democracy (liberal)

WEU: Western European Union

ACKNOWLEDGEMENTS

My thanks are due to Alan Sked for his sense of timing and objectivity. I thank Albert Kersten, official Dutch government historian, for his incisive advice on Indonesia, which is indeed worthy of being followed up in greater depth. I extend my thanks to Messrs. Robert Bos, Poulisse and other members of the Archive Department of the Royal Netherlands Ministry of Foreign Affairs, for their friendliness and co-operation. I would like to thank Mr Sierk Plantinga of the Royal Archives, for his contacts, help and sense of humour and Mrs van Anrooij for her thoughtfulness. I pay tribute to Mr Khan at the Second Chamber Archives, for his interest. My thanks go to Friso Wielenga for allowing me to access to his newspaper cuttings. I am indebted to Professor Spits for some early and important guidance. I also mention J M and W Drees for their memory, brotherhood and sense of family, K H Beyen for his memory and sense of family, Ernst van der Beugel, for his eclecticism and sense of humour, H Boon for his earnestness, Jan Hoffenaar for his powers of analysis and Dr Luns for his consistency and frankness, Anne Mackintosh of the Foreign & Commonwealth Office deserves special mention for her patience and dexterity as does Heather Yasamee of Library and Records Department for her fine balance of detailed scholarship and social understanding. I also thank Bruning of Swansea University, for her fine balance of detailed scholarship and social understanding. Last but not least I thank the Netherlands for being a country of contrasts in harmony, and Catherine and David Mallinson for their perfect mixture of tolerance, patience, understanding and aesthetic sense.

FOREWORD

The history of Western Europe since 1945 in the minds of most professional historians and students tends to be the history of the former European great powers – Britain, France and Germany (reduced for most of the period to West Germany) with an occasional condescending glance at Italy. Since there is nothing very much in the way of excitement in this story, save France's two disastrous wars of decolonisation (Vietnam and Algeria), Suez, plus the two Berlin Crises until the (re)-unification of Germany at the end of the Cold War, most of post-war Western European history could easily degenerate into a not very exhilarating history of the rise of the welfare state. What, however, rescues the period, in the eyes of some, from this potential statistical tedium, is the story of European Unification. True, in time, this also loses inspiration as it becomes mired in bureaucracy, secret deals, failing economic performance, undemocratic pressure on small states to reverse referendum results, lies about constitutional treaties and growing public apathy, but at the start of the process – the period covered in this excellent book – it was an exciting, important and fresh development in European affairs. It offered hope, a new start, a reconciliation between victors and vanquished, a way of solving the German Question, a way of consolidating US support, a means of reconstructing a continent devastated by Nazi criminality and exploitation and the necessary Allied deliverance. In short it seemed a turning point in European affairs.

The early history of efforts to launch the movement towards European cooperation, however, tends to be told, once again, merely from the viewpoint of the French, West Germans and British. Yet this does grave injustice to those who played a vital part in the story – the peoples of the Low Countries. Without the Benelux Customs Union, for example, there might never have been a European Economic Community; and without Dutch support, the proposed European Defence Community might never have got underway. William Mallinson is well aware of this, and his book is a unique example of an English-speaking historian researching the Dutch archives to paint a remarkably nuanced portrait of Dutch policy-makers in the vital days when European post-war cooperation was being born in both the military and economic spheres. He is not only aware of the international pressures they had to work under, but is equally adept in demonstrating his understanding of Dutch domestic politics and political personalities. Perhaps no other British-trained historian has managed to penetrate the surface of Dutch history in this period so well. For, to change the metaphor, Mallinson seems to know exactly how the Dutch official mind was working at this time. His book, therefore, is an essential read for all historians of post-war Europe.

The rise of the Netherlands in the seventeenth century is a relatively well-known story; its hard-fought wars with England remain alive at least in the consciousness of naval historians. The rise of Amsterdam as a world commercial centre is also known to economic historians of the eighteenth century. Yet, during the nineteenth century – certainly after the settlement of the Belgian Question – the Netherlands clung to a policy of neutrality and non-intervention in European affairs and continued this right up till 1940. The Dutch seemed content to rebuild their colonial empire in the Far East, to concentrate on world trade and to annoy nobody. However, the Germans invaded in 1940 and any belief that the wider world might be ignored came to a sorry end.

So what would happen after 1945? Would there be a return to neutrality? Would realism demand a policy of ruthlessly sticking to the defence of national interests? What in any case, would be a proper definition of these interests in post-war Europe? Naturally the Dutch, like all other nations who attempt to define their national interests, were split, causing heated debates. How a final outcome was reached is the story told by William Mallinson in this splendid book. It is well worth reading to find out what happened. I thoroughly recommend it.

Alan Sked,
Reader in International History,
London School of Economics and Political Sciences.

PREFACE

This book aims to explain why and how the traditionally independent-minded Netherlands was sucked in to the post-war Western security system and decided to support the rearmament of West Germany, despite vivid memories of the German occupation. It looks critically at how major post-war developments in Europe affected Dutch foreign policy, traditionally one of abstentionism, and considers the extent of Dutch influence in post-war Western co-operation. The Dutch attitude towards the process of German rearmament and to the Netherlands' own security needs is described and analysed.

The considerable problems the Dutch had with Britain and the United States over Indonesia and the German question, and with Britain and the 'European question', are set out and analysed, as are important aspects of Dutch-German relations, particularly the 'annexation question' and trade.

Important landmarks, and how the Dutch approached them, are dealt with. These are the Marshall Plan, the Brussels Treaty Organisation, the North Atlantic Treaty Organisation, the Council of Europe, the Schuman Plan and the Pléven Plan.

The different attitudes of two Foreign Ministers, Dirk Stikker and Willem Beyen, towards the question of European integration, are analysed. The book concludes that Beyen laid less stress on the Atlantic partnership than did Stikker, and considerably more on European integration. Its final conclusion is that the Netherlands, although it decided to be a part of an alliance, still retained sufficient independence to influence events.

Guicciardini wrote that the past has always shed light on the future, because the world has always had the same fate, and that the same things return with different colours. I think that the main characteristics of international relations revolve around human characteristics far more than around the plethora of theories that are so in vogue nowadays, more often to justify behaviour than to really co-operate. Little has changed in the Dutch spirit over the last few centuries. They still occasionally display an independent streak, even to the point of slight pedantry.

A final word on the retentive Foreign and Commonwealth Office: three of the files listed in the appendix (FO 371/96107, 96108 and 96125) are still retained under Section 3.4 of the Public Records Act, without even the title being given (The others have apparently been released recently). To retain files 58 years after they were compiled suggests slight paranoia and/or some very dirty skeletons in the cupboard. The Freedom of Information Act is still a bit of a paper tiger.

INTRODUCTION

This book sets out to explain the policy formulation behind the Dutch decision to become part of the Western security system and to support the rearmament of West Germany, and to assess the amount of leeway, or otherwise, that the Dutch had in the matter. Its starting point is that the Netherlands – that is, the area remaining after the secession of Belgium in 1831 – has never been neutral in the strict sense of the word, but has rather tried to pursue independence in its foreign policy, by playing a balancing game. It will describe and evaluate the main influences, internal and external, that led the Dutch towards direct involvement in military alliances. Finally, it will evaluate the extent to which Dutch membership of NATO has affected the country's traditionally independent stance and freedom of action.

Large and strong powers sometimes oversimplify and misunderstand the foreign policy objectives of small ones; on occasion, they even ignore them. At various times in their history, right up to today, the Dutch have been labelled obstinate, greedy, naive, religious-minded and idealistic. Quite often, the labels have been attached to explain away behaviour which the critic has not fully understood. The Dutch certainly do appear contradictory to outside observers. In the words of one eminent non-Dutch observer, the Dutch are fond of freedom, yet servile to convention, republican by nature and yet monarchy-loving, tolerant but fanatic, and both materialistic yet religious.[1] It is puzzling that a country that pursues independence in its foreign policy, despite post-war security constraints, still pays homage to the Spanish king in its national anthem,[2] an example of yet another apparent contradiction; being both traditional and progressive. Perhaps, as one respected Dutch authority has said, the Dutch are caught between dreams and reality.[3] Their foreign policy is certainly no exception; subsequent chapters will illustrate clearly numerous examples of how the Dutch, in their foreign policy formulation, have been caught between ideals and realities; more directly put, between love of law and religion on the one hand, and love of trade and money on the other.

The book will explain many apparent foreign policy contradictions. Why did the Netherlands, humiliated and badly treated by Germany, come to push for German rearmament? Why did the Dutch, on the one hand, set an example to Europe through the establishment of the Benelux Customs Union, an example that caught the imagination of the Americans yet, on the other, fight against anything that smacked of supra-nationalism? Why were they the first country to ratify the EDC treaty, when they had been against the idea at the beginning?

The book will attempt to assess the extent of external pressures. The Indonesian question, insofar as it affected Dutch foreign policy formulation, will be analysed, particularly since there is evidence that it adversely affected relations between the Netherlands and the UK and USA on the one hand, and between the UK and USA on the other.

National characteristics also play their role; did deep-seated characteristics of independence influence foreign policy formulation to a significant degree, or did pragmatic considerations on trade and security prove far stronger? Were the Dutch Foreign Ministry and Cabinet beset by major disagreements, with Dirk Stikker (Foreign Minister from 1948–1952) proclaiming both his Atlantic leanings and his Protestantism, while calling the Europeans "Federasts"? How were the Dutch able to recognise that their interests lay in co-operation and trade with Germany, while at the same time pursuing unrealistic territorial claims?

No comprehensive work dealing with Dutch foreign and security policy between 1948 and 1954 has ever been written in Britain, although certain aspects of Dutch policy have been touched on. Professor Alan Milward, for example, brings out some of the Dutch post-war economic concerns in his book *The Reconstruction of Western Europe, 1945–51*,[5] while Professor Robert Griffiths has written several papers on Dutch economic policy. On the Dutch side, Joris Voorhoeve's book *Peace, Profits and Principles*[6] provides an illuminating overview of Dutch foreign policy over a longer period, while Dr Friso Wielenga's book *West Germany, a partner from necessity: the Netherlands and the Federal Republic, 1949–1955*[7] covers bilateral relations in some depth. Dr Jan van der Harst provides a detailed account of the political, military and economic aspects of the European Defence Community in his thesis.[8]

This book, apart from drawing many different strands together, uses both the relevant Dutch and British primary sources, which no comprehensive study has yet set out to do. The resulting comparisons between the

British and Dutch viewpoints throw into relief some of the Dutch concerns in a way which would have been impossible, had only Dutch primary sources been consulted: as for the British primary sources, they occasionally throw up comments about the Dutch which may surprise some Dutch historians. The fact that several relevant files are still closed suggests that there is room for further studies on specific aspects of Dutch-British relations during the period.

The book concentrates on the diplomatic aspects, although the importance of economic and military factors is fully recognised and taken into account.

1

SETTING THE SCENE

The Nature of Netherlands Neutrality

Neutrality has often been used in describing Dutch foreign policy, particularly the foreign policy of the area that remained following the secession of Belgium in 1831. This neutrality has had to be justified at given moments. For example, Dutch neutrality in World War I was used to justify a continuation of neutrality in World War II:

> Neutrality in European conflicts is not only the Netherlands' right; it is its highest duty. It rests in the last and highest instance on the task which the Netherlands is called to fulfil and without which our continued existence as an independent state is unthinkable, because impossible.[1]

Apart from Dutch justification of their neutrality, particularly as World War II was drawing near, there was a tendency to assume that the Netherlands had always been a neutral state, especially by outside observers. Thus, when the Netherlands signed the Brussels Treaty in 1948, the British Ambassador to The Hague wrote that the Dutch had abandoned 'once and for all' a policy of neutrality.[2]

Whether one is considering a justification of Dutch neutrality, or talking about temporary policies of neutrality, one often overlooked fact cannot be avoided; the Netherlands, unlike Belgium, did not have neutrality imposed on it. *Petit-Larousse* says that Belgium's neutrality was guaranteed. While this is true, technically, use of the word 'imposed' merely reflects reality. There are of course some states which one can describe as neutral by tradition, with little chance of counter-argument; Sweden, for example has kept out of war for a considerable period; Switzerland's neutrality was guaranteed in 1815, while Austria, although only recently neutral, became so constitutionally. In assuming, on the other hand, that the Netherlands was a neutral state, one can too easily overlook some of its deeper foreign policy objectives. Therefore, before returning to the argument about the extent and nature of Netherlands neutrality, a brief sketch of its foreign policy will help to put the Dutch so-called neutrality into its proper context.

Having achieved independence in 1587, freedom to trade became the prime objective of the United Netherlands. An expanding navy contributed to the rise of the Netherlands as an important European maritime power, uninterested in territorial expansion in Europe, unlike most continental powers. J C Boogman wrote, '[....] the neutrality of the Dutch regents might be characterised as contractive, at least insofar as their territorial ambitions were concerned. In short, contraction on the side of the Netherlands as against expansion almost everywhere on the continent.'[3]

The rise of the Netherlands as an important maritime power, with substantial overseas possessions, is well-known, and its details are beyond the scope of this study. During the seventeenth century, neutrality was not part of Dutch foreign policy: the Netherlands was involved in three tough naval wars with England, and did not keep out of European alliances: following a combined English and French attack in 1672, the Dutch allied with Spain and the Holy Roman Emperor. By 1689, the situation had again changed when, until 1702, the Netherlands and England were united under one (Dutch) royal family. Although the Netherlands were involved in big power rivalries during the seventeenth century, and saw their share of wars, which were essentially naval, and fought mainly over trade, they were not interested in territorial expansion in Europe. It is hardly surprising that the Dutch, with their emphasis on overseas trade, should have produced one of the earliest treatises on maritime international law.[4]

The eighteenth century saw the beginnings of a policy of non-involvement as a factor in Dutch foreign policy, as a consequence of the power of Amsterdam as a financial centre. Naval rivalry with England was all but dead, the Dutch having realised that the English navy was top dog. By the end of the century, however, French influence, welcomed by many of the Dutch, was in the ascendant. Napoleonic excesses changed matters; following Louis Bonaparte's inability to keep control of the Netherlands, his brother annexed the country in 1810. The memory of this experience of French hegemony was, after 1815, an important factor in causing the Dutch to pursue an active policy of non-involvement. Non-involvement had always been latent in Dutch foreign policy, even if not successful.

When Dutch power was at its height, and the Netherlands was fighting its naval wars, the statesman Johan de Witt wrote:

> [...] The interest of this state lies in that peace should reign everywhere, and trade be carried on without impediments [...] the most advantageous course would be to enter into a simple treaty of commerce and navigation, without any obligation as to defence.[5]

Following the Congress of Vienna, this latent policy of non-involvement was realised, particularly after the secession of Belgium in 1831 when, despite its overseas possessions, the Netherlands was reduced to the status of a small power.

Non-involvement became the mainstay of Dutch foreign policy, even to the extent of some arguing that there was hardly any foreign policy: 'Politically, the Netherlands withdrew from the world scene. The government hardly pursued a foreign policy at all, unless it was that of abstaining from any possible commitment.'[6] The Dutch historian, E H Kossmann, wrote: 'From 1830 to 1940, Dutch national consciousness was dominated by the idea that the Netherlands constituted a haven, indeed, the world centre for justice.'[7] According to Joris Voorhoeve, in his celebrated book, *Peace, Profits and Principles*, non-alignment and non-participation in international politics and strict political neutrality became obsessions.[8] Still, however strong the degree of abstentionism in Dutch foreign policy may have been, the need to resort to an active policy was not completely ruled out. In 1862, one anonymous Dutch writer was maintaining that 'should the Great Powers go to war, then the Netherlands should maintain neutrality, to a certain degree, but that if France should violate Belgian neutrality, then the Netherlands should ally itself with England, Prussia and Belgium.'[9]

Abstentionism suited the Dutch, who were able to rebuild their East Indian Empire and trade, both of which had suffered from Napoleonic domination. Dutch non-involvement had also suited the British, who preferred to see an independent Netherlands. Whenever the Netherlands had, before 1831, been party to alliances, or considered the possibility, after 1831, their motive was to preserve their independence.

> [...] The Spaniards of the era of Philip II, the French of the Louis XIV period, the English of the seventeenth Century with their idea of Britannia rules the waves, their colossal neighbour Germany – all these have been constant threats to the independence of Holland,

and each time the Dutch have fought for their freedom more or less against their will.[10]

By 1914, Dutch abstentionism was sufficiently well-entrenched to ensure a neutral stance in World War I. It was not in the least surprising that the Dutch should have again plumped for neutrality in World War II, having witnessed, at arm's length, the horrors of World War I. As war became increasingly likely, the Dutch government, under de Geer, issued a statement fully in line with the Dutch policies of independence and non-involvement: '[...] the independent policy, as it has been followed thus far by our country, will be maintained by this cabinet fully and undiminished.'[11] True to form, the Dutch clung obstinately to their independence after the outbreak of war, in spite of Churchill's broadcast on 20 January 1940, urging them to join in the struggle against Nazi tyranny. Despite Churchill's references to them 'standing along their dykes, as they did against the tyrants of bygone days',[12] the Dutch stayed out, with the Foreign Minister, van Kleffens, arguing that the Netherlands could bring the belligerents together.[13] Even after the shock of the German invasion on 10 May 1940, de Geer urged the Dutch, ten days later, in a broadcast from London, to work with the German authorities.[14] It is not surprising that he left the cabinet on grounds of ill health. He returned to the Netherlands the following Spring,[15] a move which many of his colleagues found hard to forgive.

The Dutch government, presented with a situation which they could do nothing about, began to change their tune. In his radio broadcast on 25 November 1942, van Kleffens said that the old policy of no political agreements with any state or group of states could not be resumed.[16] By the following November, he was saying: 'It is my given conviction that [...] our pre-war policy of aloofness is stone dead.'[17] It was of course difficult to be specific, but the above statements certainly implied some future change in Dutch foreign policy. The tradition of non-involvement was, however, strong, and although van Kleffens also spoke of a future 'formation in the West with America, Canada and other British dominions as an arsenal and a vast reservoir of power,' it was not until 1948 that the Dutch finally became members, for the first time in over 100 years, of a military alliance. They had hoped that the United Nations would be enough to preserve world peace, but became disillusioned, especially when they failed in their efforts at Dumbarton Oaks to secure more than six seats on the Security Council for the smaller and middle powers.

SETTING THE SCENE 9

An explanatory memorandum written by the Foreign Ministry for the 1947–48 session of the Dutch Second Chamber brings home the nature of Netherlands neutrality:

> It is true that the Netherlands has always refused to accept a state of permanent neutrality, as still exists in Switzerland, and as Belgium and Luxembourg have recognised in the past [...] Rather, Dutch policy in the nineteenth century proceeded from the idea, that the abstention of the Netherlands from the conflicts of the big European powers must be the basis of Dutch foreign policy [...][18]

Is it accurate to say that the Dutch eventually broke with neutrality in 1948, as a result of the German invasion? The invasion certainly caused a re-evaluation and an eventual acceptance of new realities, but it was not so much neutrality that was compromised as the ability to remain completely independent and exert a measure of influence. The Dutch slowly realised that to stay aloof would only result in their being left out of the negotiations on Germany, traditionally their largest trading partner. The Dutch had managed to stay out of the war for a considerable period by using neutrality as a political tool, not because they were inherently neutral. They were successful in pursuing their independent line until the German invasion. While the invasion was the catalyst for change, it was the East-West division that eventually brought the Dutch into an alliance, coupled with their need to put their point of view and not get left on the sidelines. Previously, the Dutch brand of peace had amounted to keeping out of Europe's wars and trying to balance the external forces.

While it is indisputable that neutrality has been used by the Dutch at given moments in the past, especially to keep out of conflict, it does not appear to have been the over-riding factor in Dutch foreign policy. It is more accurate to say that neutrality was used as an intellectual tool to try to keep aloof during the First and Second World Wars. B H M Vlekke, a well-known Dutch academic, told Chatham House in 1952 that the Dutch had never been neutral, mentally or morally, before the last war. Its inclination, he said, had always been towards the West, first towards France, then Great Britain. The attitude of the latter was important because of the influence that she could exert over Dutch overseas possessions.[19] Vlekke's statements need to be qualified, for although neutrality was not enshrined in the constitution, the Dutch certainly pursued a policy akin to neutrality, albeit only evidenced when Europe was at war, while they remained aloof. Vlekke may have been trying to play to the audience. Nevertheless, it is true that the Netherlands was not officially neutral. It simply pursued its own independent line at moments of crisis in Europe. Vlekke's argument is that the Dutch had a fear of being over-dependent on any one country, and that they were always looking for a counterweight. Thus, while, for example, they accepted British naval power to protect their trading interests, Germany was their main trading partner. Dutch efforts to stay at peace eventually became synonymous with neutrality, even though the country was not constitutionally neutral.

Let us now look at the years 1945–48. Which factors actually did persuade the Dutch to drop their policy of apparent neutrality? Certainly more was involved than merely the German question alone, although this has to be considered.

The German Problem and the Effects of the War

When the Mof is poor and naked
He speaks a very modest language
But when he comes to high estate
He does evil to God and Man[20]

These words were written about the Germans in the first half of the seventeenth century by the poet Jacob Cats, and suggest that some Dutch had developed a certain antipathy towards Germans quite early on. The somewhat haughty attitude depicted in the words are not very surprising, given the Netherlands' early attachment to international law, while the Germans were going through the horrors of the Thirty Years' War.

It was not, however, until much later that the Dutch began to worry about Germany, particularly since Dutch concerns about German, or more accurately, Prussian, expansionism were offset by their experiences with France. Dutch foreign policy after 1831 was based on the need to preserve the status quo in Europe. With the large powers guaranteeing Belgium's neutrality, and Britain's interest in promoting the Netherlands' independence, mainly to contain the French, the Dutch felt reasonably secure.

This feeling of security was however tempered by distrust of the British and fear of Germany's growing economic power, both of which were exacerbated by the secession of Belgium. The widespread feeling of political and social instability throughout Europe in the 1840s in turn fuelled Dutch fears that Britain would 'grab the Dutch colonies'.[21] The Dutch sent a general to the East, under instructions to suggest measures for improving Dutch defences.²²

The Germans played on the rivalry between Antwerp and the Dutch ports, the former gaining in economic importance through the building of a railway link with Cologne in 1843. The Zollverein represented a considerable threat to Dutch commercial interests, which remained until a commercial treaty was signed in 1851.

The unification of Germany changed matters. There had already been worrying signs for the Netherlands: Ernst Moritz, in his book, *Deutschland und Europa*, written in 1803, had described the Netherlands as a 'crying mutilation of the natural boundaries of Germany.'²³ Following Prussia's annexation of Schleswig-Holstein in 1866, the Amsterdam professor and government minister, J Boscha, said that Bismarck's name had become synonymous with force, as if Attila with his Huns were standing at the Dutch frontier.²⁴ The shrewd Bismarck, hardly interested in military conquest, merely said: 'Holland annektiert sich selbst schon':²⁵ the Dutch relied heavily for their prosperity on Germany, which was their largest trading partner. In 1893, the Pan-German League proposed that the Netherlands (and Austria and German Switzerland) be incorporated into Germany.²⁶ In direct contrast to the words in the Dutch national anthem about paying homage to the King of Spain (still used today!), the words in the German anthem 'von der Maas bis an die Memel, von den Haag bis an den Belt' worried the peaceful Dutch.²⁷ But they were not prevented from being openly anti-British and pro-German during the Boer War; Abraham Kuyper, Dutch Minister – President from 1901–1905 – was even suspected of seeking an alliance with Germany.²⁸ In any case, whatever worries the Dutch had about the Prussians and the Germans at given moments, for example during the Luxembourg Affair in 1867, they were not alone in these, and the French were certainly to become consistently more anti-German than they ever were.

The Dutch attitude towards Germany was ambivalent. They could not afford to ignore the economic power of their close neighbour, but wished to preserve their independence and identity. Just before the First World War, 48 per cent of Dutch exports went to Germany, while 28 per cent of Dutch imports were from the Reich. German penetration into Dutch banking and shipping was strong, while modernisation of industry was controlled by Germans.²⁹ German economic influence led to cultural influence. Friso Wielenga sums it up succinctly: 'Given that the economic orientation towards Germany was considerably greater than towards other European powers, so was German influence in the cultural and scientific fields incontestably of more weight.'[30] The weakening of Germany following the first World War was not sufficient to radically change the Netherlands' economic relationship with Germany, particularly since trade was of supreme importance to the Dutch; in the nine years preceding World War II, for example, between 20 and 30 per cent of all Dutch imports (in value) were German, while between 15 and 20 per cent of Dutch exports went to Germany.[31] The growth of Rotterdam (which, unlike Amsterdam, had tended to be pro-German during World War I) was due to a great extent to the industrialisation of the Ruhrgebiet: in 1939, close to 23 million tons of Rotterdam's transit freight, out of a total of 57 million tons, was to and from Germany.[32]

Although Germany was the loser of World War I, it was still vital to the Dutch, who were independent enough to welcome the Kaiser as a political refugee. Although this study does not home in on the psychological aspects, it is worth referring to the words in the Dutch national anthem 'we of "Ditse" blood'. Whether etymologists and translators can all agree on the exact translation of the word 'Ditse', or not, it has German connotations, and has not been erased from the anthem.

The shock of the German invasion cannot be understated. 'Hitler's attack on the Netherlands [...] was wholly unexpected by the Dutch people, who up to the last moment had believed in the possibility of maintaining peace.'[33] Apart from the trauma of being invaded after over 100 years of peace, the suffering of the population and the damage to the economy was felt keenly in a country small in terms of both size and population. The last year of the war, when the Germans clamped down hard, was the worst. Apart from the mass deportation of Jews, and some of the population being reduced to eating tulip bulbs (boiled), the damage caused by fighting when the Allies failed to take Arnhem, was considerable. As a precaution against invasion, the Germans flooded large tracts of land. At the end of the war, more than 8 per cent of agricultural land had been flooded, one half with sea water. 2 per cent of agricultural land was rendered useless by the building of fortified zones, airports, and the laying of minefields, and a further 6 per cent because of military operations.[34] Following the railway strike, orchestrated by the Dutch government in exile, the Germans destroyed 62 per cent of the Dutch railways. In October 1944, Dutch coal mines were producing only 7,500 tons per day, about one sixth of prewar capacity.[35] Taking industrial production as 100 in 1938, it had dropped to 41 in September 1945.[36] All in all, about one third of the national wealth had been lost.[37] Given the physical and psychological damage to a small country that had tried to keep out of the war, the enormous territorial

SETTING THE SCENE 13

and financial reparations, (these will be dealt with later) which the Netherlands demanded from Germany, are understandable, even if they were not realistic.

What was the British view of the devastation? The ambassador to the Netherlands, Sir Nevile Bland, wrote in February 1946:

> Holland had not suffered as much devastation as had been expected. She was saved from a great deal of damage by the stalemate on their frontier and the rapid advance of the Allied armies elsewhere. The damage of war was only apparent in certain areas [...] But the country had been completely exhausted by the final winter of occupation and the extent of looting undertaken by the Germans was far greater than in any neighbouring country.[38]

The last months of the war were indeed hard ones. The Ambassador, who had visited the Netherlands in June 1945, before taking up residence there, wrote of 'terrible cases of malnutrition and starvation'[39]. About the same number of Dutch died as Americans in the war: the 'Economic Statistical News' of 15 May 1949 wrote that 200,000 Dutch had died during the war, of which 105,000 were Jews, adding that that represented 80 per cent of the Jewish population.[40]

The problem of collaborators was particularly large and, at times, embarrassing. 'The most intractable of the internal problems has been the treatment of the collaborators', wrote the British ambassador.[41] Paul Grey, First Secretary at the British Embassy, wrote that 203,033 Dutch people had been imprisoned, pending trial, 'many of them without hope of trial for years.'[42] An official at the British Military Mission to the Netherlands wrote:

> Many disastrous consequences result from a prolonged stay in these camps. Already in the cellars, where prisoners spend the first days, clandestine national-socialist and communist propaganda is active [...] the ultimate political consequences are far from being reassuring. A group of about one million Netherlanders, hostile in their feeling towards the 7 million, will be the ultimate result.[43]

The British were clearly worried about such consequences, and the ambassador approached the Dutch Prime Minister, Schemerhoorn, who said that when he had suggested that some of the lighter cases of collaboration might be released, the resistance groups and the communist press had led a storm of protest.⁴⁴ The Foreign Minister, van Kleffens, told the ambassador that the measure had been decided upon 'after much thought by the government in London, in order to forestall the certainty of the righteous taking the guilty into their own hands, with incalculable results but infallibly disastrous effects on public order.'⁴⁵ The Churches, wrote the ambassador, were nevertheless worried about the problem on humanitarian grounds.⁴⁶ The number of those initially imprisoned was, coincidentally, the same as those killed during the war. The problem was compounded by the purging of the judiciary, which was, of course, responsible for sentencing the prisoners. Although by February 1946, the Ambassador was writing that the worst of the crisis was over, he wondered about the outlook for the country 'when comparatively so many citizens had been in prison or under a cloud of suspicion.'⁴⁷ The measures certainly left a bitter taste, particularly since the Political Investigation Service (POD) was not known for its moderation. According to a memorandum by the British Military Mission, a member of the POD visited a camp at Laren, during which he drove about 'scattering inmates, snarling and sneering'. The POD were, he wrote, 'hated and feared by the inmates, direction and guard personnel.'⁴⁸ The police took over from the POD in October 1945.

On 1 October 1946, 44,829 men and 4437 women were still in detention.⁴⁹ There were some executions, not all of which took place immediately. For example, Ans van Dijk, a Dutch Jewess accused of betraying Jews to the Germans, was executed on 14 February 1948, following a drawn out appeals procedure.⁵⁰ The appeal of Jan Mussert, leader of the Dutch Nazis, also failed. Anti-German feeling ran very high, and in September 1946, the expulsion of Germans began. They were allowed to take 50 kilos of baggage and a maximum of 100 guilders. This led to pressure from the Churches and the Allies to put a stop to the process.⁵¹ By May 1948, there were, according to the British Ambassador, still 10,000 'political delinquents' in camps.⁵² Needless to say, there were accusations that those with influence were not arrested.⁵³ One of those not arrested was Hans Hirschfeld, later to be Dutch representative at the CEEC Paris Conference. Although a Jew, he had been exempted during the war from anti-Jewish measures by Seyss-Inquart, the Reichskommissar for the Netherlands, keeping his job as head of the Ministry of Economic Affairs, 'because of his exceptional abilities'. He was 'discharged with honour' from the Dutch Civil Service at the end of the war,⁵⁴ but was subsequently to have a glittering career.

Gerhard Hirschfeld's book *Nazi Rule and Dutch Collaboration* sums up the question neatly:

Political accommodation during the first phase of German occupation and rule had a lasting effect on wide circles of the Dutch population. A whole series of civil servants, industrialists and private individuals admitted after the war that their decision to collaborate with the German authorities was greatly influenced by events during the first months of the occupation.[55]

As Hirschfeld writes, however, there were other motives. For example, the collaboration of most of the press, while based on a desire to keep the newspapers going, was 'quite often combined with a degree of political opportunism which far exceeded what might have been deemed permissible, even under the restrictive conditions of the occupation.'[56] As regards the Dutch police's role in the deportation of Jews, Hirschfeld writes that their co-operation sprung from 'a conformist authoritarian social stance and of characteristics specific to the profession,' rather than ideological affinity.[57]

Although there certainly was a measure of collaboration, it is worth noting that on the eve of the war, there were only four (out of 100) National Socialist members of the Dutch Second Chamber. The Dutch had, in any case, little choice but to co-operate, and the relatively 'soft' treatment of the country, particularly at the beginning of the occupation, lent itself to collaboration. It is interesting, however, that there were about 200,000 Dutch members of the National Socialist Movement.

Towards the end of the war, as conditions became harsher with the forced deportation of the Jews and near starvation setting in, the Dutch naturally became increasingly alienated from their German masters. Given the background of the occupation, it is little wonder that there was such bitterness at the end of the war towards such a large section of the Dutch population, but also little wonder that the Dutch were to ask for considerable compensation. Both their hearts and their pockets had been occupied.

Immediately following the war, the level of resentment against the Germans was, then, obviously high. Dirk Stikker, Foreign Minister from August 1948 until February 1952, visited Germany in June 1944, with a British military escort. In his memoirs he wrote:

> I thought it would be a distinct pleasure to see the tables turned on the Germans, and this time to enter a factory with military show myself. For another I wanted to see with my own eyes what had happened in Germany after the Allied bombings, and how the Germans

had reacted [...] the feelings of the Germans who received us were all too well-known to me. In manner, I gave them a taste of their own medicine, cutting up rough and being properly menacing [...].[58]

Despite the emotional aspect, Stikker was realistic, and epitomised the pragmatic side of Dutch attitudes towards Germany: 'Germany naturally looms large on the Dutch horizon. From the Dutch point of view, the two principal elements in Dutch-German relations are security and trade'.[59] .In June 1945, the Dutch Prime Minister, Schemerhoorn, had faced up to the truth, when he said: 'Our foreign policy culminates in the question of our relationship with defeated Germany'.[60]

The Commercial Question

At the end of the war, a weakened, divided and occupied Germany hardly presented an immediate military threat to the Netherlands. Commercial factors assumed particular importance. *The Economist* summed matters up succinctly, if somewhat rhetorically, as follows:

And Germany? A pastoralised rump state will be no basis for entrepot trade or for the export of food [...] the truth is that nothing can finally compensate continental Europe for the loss of its largest market, and the impact of this fact is likely to be felt by the Dutch sooner than by any other people.[61]

The Dutch at first believed that Germany would no longer be the powerful economic force that it had been. In a note to the Allied governments, pressing its claims on German territory, the Foreign Minister wrote:

It should not be forgotten that Germany, as a hinterland for Netherlands economic activity, is largely lost [...] owing to a variety of factors it seems exceedingly doubtful whether Germany will again be able to absorb exports from the Netherlands comparable to prewar exports.[62]

The Economist's prediction about Dutch concerns was uncannily accurate. The idea that Germany would remain a 'pastoralised rump state' proved only temporary, and the Dutch realised that an economically strong Germany would be in their interests. Immediately after the war, however, the Dutch were obviously interested only in gaining as many reparations as possible. The Dutch, as will be seen, were frustrated in some of their objectives later on. By the Paris Agreement of 14 January 1946, it was agreed that the Netherlands would receive 3.9 per cent of confiscated German assets and 5.6 per cent of German capital equipment.[63] Clearly dissatisfied with their share, the Dutch continued to press hard for mining concessions and for large tracts of German territory. They continued to press various claims well into 1949, despite a recognised need to be more conciliatory in tone towards the Germans. These claims, to be dealt with in more detail later, were already bringing to light an element of frustration in the Dutch cabinet, vis-à-vis the Big Four. At a cabinet meeting on 27 September 1945, the Foreign Minister, van Kleffens, said that in view of the Big Four's forthcoming discussion on the Rhineland, it was important to make the Dutch standpoint on annexation known.[64] Van Kleffens continued by saying that Dutch damage amounted to 26 billion guilders (based on 1938 values). As will be seen, a large part of the Dutch case rested on the contention that since Germany would never be able to repay the Dutch adequately, territorial concessions would have to be a substitute.

1945 and 1946 were essentially years of recovery and reconstruction for the Netherlands, when commercial considerations were at the forefront. The Dutch, as they realised the need to become more involved in discussions on Germany, to press their commercial interests,   sent a series of memoranda to the Big Four, dealing with 'Allied Policy with regard to Germany'. But they met with no tangible response.[65] As will be seen, the next two years were to be characterised by Dutch attempts to make their view heard. Stikker wrote:

> [...] An even greater obstacle to the protection of legitimate Dutch interests vis-à-vis Germany than Four Power disagreement was the Great Power policy of excluding other interested powers from the decisions on Germany. This was, in fact, the vital problem for the Netherlands.[66]

Dutch Territorial and other Claims on Germany

Between 1944 and 1949, the Dutch government expended a great deal of energy in the pursuit of territorial and economic claims on Germany. The Dutch claims on parts of Germany which have been described (euphemistically) as border rectifications and (realistically) as annexations, provide a revealing insight into the problems and paradoxes of Dutch policy towards Germany in the immediate post-war years. They suggest that the Dutch experienced considerable problems in reconciling their grievances with a recognised need to be – and to be seen to be – conciliatory and cooperative internationally.

Feelings ran high: a government statement issued in October 1944 ended thus:

> The grief caused by the vindictive strangulation of the country's life, by the mass deportation of the nation's young manhood, by the starvation they have brought about, by the widespread killings and mediaeval torture, causing the deaths of thousands of good citizens, this grief may cry for justice, but one can never find adequate compensation in terms of material values.[67]

In June 1945, the Prime Minister, Schemerhoorn, said: 'The Dutch people have a score to settle in almost every sector.'[68]

The Dutch, who were to become increasingly concerned and frustrated at being left out of the Big Power decision making which affected their vital commercial interests, made their views known in July 1945. Clearly worried that the Potsdam meetings would not take their needs into account, their note (of 9 July), expressed the wish to have the 'fullest opportunity of taking part in any decisions concerning the demarcation of the Western boundaries of Germany and any part thereof.'[69] At the same time, an internal discussion paper was prepared, which set total claims at 25 billion guilders or $14.14 billion, at 1938 exchange rates. Taking into account price inflation, the figure would need to be raised by at least 75 per cent. The paper went on:

> [...] As a contribution towards making good the damage wilfully inflicted on the Netherlands by the German government [...] the Netherlands Government have decided to ask the Allied Powers to agree to the severance from Germany, and the inclusion as an integral part in Netherlands territory of 4,000 square miles, about twice the size of Northumberland, one twelfth of New York State, or one thirty-ninth of California.

The paper added that both the Allies and Germans should refrain from removing capital goods from the areas in question, so that they would retain their current value.[70]

On 17 July, the Cabinet held a meeting, at which it was decided to set up on 25 August, a 'National Commission to study the question of the possible attachment to the Netherlands of a piece of formerly German territory'.[71] At the same meeting, the Foreign Minister said that the areas would have to be cleared of Germans. He also said that Attlee had supported the annexation question in the House of Commons. Although Attlee did express support for 'all just claims',[72] there is no evidence to suggest that he knew the details or the extent of the Dutch ones. Moreover, he had been speaking in November 1944, before the Dutch government had advanced any formal claim. However, while the commission was in the process of being set up and beginning its work, the Dutch continued to exert pressure on the Allies. On 18 September, the ambassador in London, Michiels van Verduynen, wrote to the Chairman of the Council of Foreign Ministers, meeting at Lancaster House, to reiterate Dutch wishes to be involved in discussion on the Western boundaries of Germany.[73] To add to the pressure, a 'Dutch Committee for the Enlargement of Territory' had been set up in July.[74] The key figure in establishing the Committee was said to have been van Kleffens himself,[75] although he was not associated with it officially. It had a prestige address in The Hague.

On 27 September 1945, van Kleffens suggested to the Cabinet that the Netherlands should claim 7,000 square kilometres (the same as in the above-mentioned paper), equivalent to one third of the area of the Netherlands, and including 1.5 million Germans. Van Kleffens added for good measure that most of the Germans should be expelled, apart from the miners who 'would remain to work for us'.[76] The Cabinet was not unanimous on the extent of the annexations, and did not agree with van Kleffens' suggestions. Interestingly, it decided against holding a referendum on the question. The Ambassador in Paris, Tjarda van Starkenborgh Stachouwer, wrote that annexations would weaken Germany (as the French wanted), thus leaving the Netherlands subject to French economic influence.[77] The Foreign Minister from 3 July 1946, Baron van Boetzelaer van Oosterhout, (van Kleffens remained Minister without Portfolio until 1 July 1947) has also been described as being against annexation.[78] The main reason was the problem of the 1.5 million Germans. In a letter to his Ambassadors in October 1946, he wrote: 'As you know, I am personally no supporter of the annexation of German territory, together with the population.'[79] He told the Dutch Parliament: 'A considerable amount of the well earned credit which we enjoy in the world, credit based on moderation, unselfishness and on our principle to place law above power, would be lost.'[80] Albert Kersten contrasts van Boetzelaer's position with that of van Kleffens, describing the former as being against annexation, under the influence of his adviser on German affairs, Hans Hirschfeld. Van Boetzelaer believed that restoring German production capacity was a prerequisite for the economic reconstruction of Europe.[81]

The annexation question assumed such importance that on 25 and 26 October 1946, it was discussed in the General Committee of the States General, which met only rarely, to discuss matters of great national importance. It consisted of government ministers and representatives of the two chambers of parliament. Mainly as a result of this meeting and van Boetzelaer van Oosterhout's views, the territorial claims were reduced to an area of 1,750 square kilometres, comprising 119, 000 inhabitants.[82]

Although this was the claim actually put forward to the Big Four on 11 November 1946, there were still worried Dutchmen. One of the Members of Parliament, Bruins Slot, was anxious about the status of the inhabitants and their cultural assimilation. Another, Hoogcarspel, suggested that the claims represented 'annexations, which are called border corrections.'[83]

'Border corrections' was indeed the term used in the Note by the Dutch Government setting out its claims. The Note said that the Netherlands government was opposed in principle to territorial expansion through annexation, basing their claim on five considerations: a shortening of the border (from 525 kilometres to 340 kilometres); improvement of local communications; local improvement of canal and waterworks; improvements from the social and economic point of view; and redress of local anomalies. The Note went on to say: 'The government considers the [sic] compliance with their economic demands of primary importance to the economic restoration of the Netherlands – they therefore restrict their territorial claims to frontier rectifications.' The Note thus implied that the Dutch were showing moderation in their claims, and asking less than they should:

> It has become clear that the damage inflicted on the national economy has reached such proportions, that adequate compensation in the form of an allocation of German territory will not be practicable in view of the extent of the annexations which would be involved.[84]

Whatever the role played by emotion and resentment at the damage caused by the Germans, hard economic concerns lay at the core. The Dutch tried to use the 'frontier rectifications' as a bargaining counter on other economic questions, particularly on mining concessions.

> The government wish to emphasise that the two matters are closely related: therefore, should their economic demands – in particular

those concerning mining concessions – not meet with the expected approval, the Netherlands government expressly reserve the right to put forward more far-reaching claims.[85]

The tenacity of the Dutch in pursuing claims which were increasingly incompatible with the improving climate for economic co-operation in the West, and the need to bring Germany fully into the fold, not to mention the development of the Cold War and American efforts to strengthen European military co-operation, served to weaken the Dutch case. The Dutch were to end up with far less than they apparently wanted. Yet at the same time they recognised the need to appear co-operative: the Foreign Ministry Yearbook for 1949–50 stated:

> The past year, as far as Europe is concerned, was characterised by the growing conviction on every hand that close co-operation among the Western democracies is in the best means of maintaining the peace [...] Netherlands interests in the maintenance of peace are best promoted by the establishment of an effective military and economic co-operation with the countries of Europe [...] Germany also is more and more being drawn into this co-operation.[86]

Although the Dutch were tenacious, they met with resistance: the British actually suggested that the Dutch should cede some of their own territory, to correct local anomalies.[87] This led to 'furious reactions' in the cabinet, which rejected the suggestions.[88] The American Embassy in London said that the British looked 'with certain scepticism' on the Dutch claims.[89] The Head of the Dutch Military Mission to the Allied Control Commission in Berlin, Baron van Voorst tot Voorst, wrote to the Dutch Foreign Minister, Stikker, on 30 September, that the British in Berlin 'had very little sympathy for the border corrections'.[90]

The German press itself was openly against the annexations, a reflection of the degree of freedom of speech which the Germans were allowed to exercise even before the establishment of the Federal Republic, especially when the issue was one with which the British and Americans agreed. The *Liberal-demokratische Zeitung* wrote on 4 January 1948, under the heading 'Holland's Grab for West Germany' that the annexation was political, thereby criticising Dutch claims that their motives were purely economic. The *Hamburger Volkszeitung* claimed on 6 January that there were 154,770 refugees in the area, who would all be forced to leave, since they had not been there since before 1940. (The Dutch maintained that only local inhabitants would be able to stay). The *Nordwest-Zeitung* wrote on 20 January 1949 that the 'corrections were against the principles of the Atlantic Charter.'[91] Various Germans protested by letter to the Dutch Government. *Die Zeit* wrote on 20 January that the 'small-territorial imperialism of the Netherlands was no more attractive [...] than Hitler's Grossraum imperialism.'[92] At a meeting in Paris of the working group dealing with the border question, the leader of the Dutch delegation, J A Ringers, reported: 'The British delegation, supported by German information on the Hitler style, make the defence of the Dutch claims difficult.'[93] Emotion clearly played a considerable part, even in official reporting.

In the end, it is hardly surprising that the Dutch obtained far less than they had asked for: in March 1949, the Netherlands, Belgium, Luxembourg, the United States, Great Britain, and France issued a communiqué on provisional rectifications of the West German frontier, in Paris. Although the communiqué involved changes to Germany's border with Belgium, Luxembourg, the Saar (which had special status) and France, as well as with the Netherlands, amounting to a total of 135 square kilometres and a resident population of 13,500, this meant, in the case of the Netherlands, some 70 square kilometres and 10,000 inhabitants, the lion's share.[94] This was a far cry from the Netherlands' original demands, but they did not let go; while accepting the provisional rectifications, they still insisted on reserving their position.[95]

As regards the rights of the inhabitants, the communiqué stated:

> All measures will be taken with a view to safeguarding the interests of the inhabitants, as regards their status and their movable and real property. No-one will be forced to accept the nationality of the country to which the area is attached. Persons not desiring to accept this nationality will enjoy the protection afforded to persons and property by the laws of the country and no discrimination will be exercised against them. They will have the right to settle in Germany, in which case they will be allowed to take with them their movable property or selling [sic] it and being permitted to transfer the funds to Germany under the special regulations which will be prescribed. They will, on the other hand, have the right to continue to reside in the area concerned, if they so desire.[96]

This represented a considerable change from what the Netherlands government had said in 1946: 'As regards the German population in the territory to be ceded, Her Majesty's Government aim at incorporating as few

Germans as possible in the Netherlands' body politic.'⁹⁷ A referendum among the inhabitants affected was, however, never held.

On 20 April 1949, the Dutch parliament passed the necessary legislation to take over the territory, which was officially transferred on 23 April. The opposition in Germany, however, continued, led by Dr Karl Arnold, Minister-President of the Land of Nordrhein-Westfalen. On 21 July *Der Morgen* epitomised the feeling of many Germans when it quoted a prominent German, Dr Schwering, as saying that the new changes were a betrayal of the European spirit, and that the Dutch had poisoned the atmosphere by a petty foreign policy, in contrast to the generous attitude of Belgium.⁹⁸ The Belgian government had indeed embarrassed the Dutch by immediately renouncing their claim. On 15 April they had sent a message to Dr Arnold which mentioned 'the conviction that Belgium-German understanding could be helped, an understanding that is strongly sought after by the Belgium government, in a European spirit.'⁹⁹ Sentiments were strong: Arnold actually visited the Dutch First Chamber debate on the annexations, described by Stikker as 'a tactless move'.¹⁰⁰ Even the British Ambassador described the visit in particularly critical terms: '[...] methods bordering on sharp practice [...] a tactless and ill-timed visit'¹⁰¹ Although many of the Dutch were in favour of the 'border rectifications', there were plenty of dissenters. The PvdA (Socialist Party) was critical. In May 1948, a group of Dutch socialists from Groningen, led by Homer Poort, had visited German socialists, and Poort is reported to have said that 90 per cent of the Dutch were against such demands (he was referring to the annexation question).¹⁰² The figure of 90 per cent is probably exaggerated: H A Schaper, in his article on the annexation question, says that up to 1949, between 40 and 45 per cent of the population were in favour of annexation.¹⁰³ In addition, at the time of Poort's visit, the Dutch were still claiming a much larger area than was eventually agreed.

In the summer of 1949, 2 million people – 20 per cent of the Dutch population – visited the village of Elten, one of the annexed villages.¹⁰⁴ The question continued to bedevil Dutch-German relations until 1963, when almost all the territory was returned. Even to this day, the problem of the Eems-Dollart estuary, part of which the Dutch would like to be reclaimed from the sea, is still discussed by the two governments.

In conclusion, the Dutch used the question of border rectifications as a political lever to obtain what economic concessions they could. The claims had no historical basis, and were presented as just compensation for damage inflicted during the war. The specious description of what was clearly annexation as 'frontier rectifications' enabled the German press to protest vigorously, and exploit Belgian 'magnanimity'. Schaper concludes: 'The annexation question was certainly not a highpoint in Dutch diplomatic history.'[105]

The Dutch were no less persistent in their other claims than they were on the 'border rectifications' question. Clearly dissatisfied both with their share of the compensation, agreed at Paris in January 1946, and with being excluded from the Big Four's decision making on Germany, they continued to press hard for a number of concessions, principally in mining and shipping. On 1 November 1946, the Netherlands, together with Belgium and Luxembourg, submitted a memorandum to the Council of Foreign Ministers in New York, setting out their territorial and economic claims.[106] It did not meet with a response satisfactory to the Dutch. The State Department, for example, said in its reply of 8 November: 'It is not possible to give a definite reply at this time.'[107] Apart from British scepticism regarding territorial claims (and some of the desired mining concessions, to be discussed later), the Americans were concerned at what they interpreted as actions that would weaken the German economy. The US political adviser for Germany, Murphy, wrote to the Secretary of State in June 1946:

> We are in fact much concerned at increasing evidence that French, Dutch, and Belgians are aiming at a permanent, drastic reduction in the German Rhine fleet, removal of such equipment as reparations, and securing for themselves a dominant, if not monopoly, position in German import and export movements via the Rhine.[108]

The Dutch were indeed worried about the British and American attitude towards their economic concerns, particularly on the question of the use of their ports. In January 1946, some Dutch still believed that Germany would no longer be relevant as an economic power. The Minister of Commerce and Industry told a meeting of the Royal Institute of Engineers: 'Reorientation of trade will be necessary owing to the elimination of Germany [...]'[109] Yet by April, the Dutch had changed tack; officials stressed to two senior British officials of the Board of Trade that revival of trade with Germany was important. They pointed out that the ports of Amsterdam and Rotterdam were only working at about 25 per cent of their capacity, as imports and exports from Germany were being diverted to Hamburg and Bremen. They also expressed annoyance that the British Army of the Rhine was demanding payment [from the Dutch] in dollars for necessary imports from Germany.[110] The Dutch, who had depended so much on their trade with Germany before the war, now felt that their commercial interests with that country were not being properly handled by the occupying powers, particularly Britain, whose zone was adjacent to theirs. The Dutch met with resistance from the British on some of their claims, even when the British Ambassador agreed with them. For example, on the question of sheet metal in Germany belonging to a Dutch firm (Daaldorp aud Zonen), he wrote to the Control Office for Germany and Austria: 'We really think [...] the Netherlands have not been very well treated as far as this question of compensation is concerned.'[111] Clearly, there was a clash of views on the question of transit trade, with the Dutch feeling they were being ignored, which seems to have had a knock-on effect on the individual claims by companies.

The Dutch again made representations on 14 January 1947, to the Foreign Ministers' Deputies, who were meeting to prepare a peace treaty, but met with no concrete response. However, a supplementary paper, dealing with the frontier and economic claims, submitted on 25 January, enabled the Dutch to appear in London and present their case on 28 January. In the words of the State Department, 'The Dutch had an opportunity to present their views.'[112] This did not at this stage soften the American attitude. 'We face the great difficulty,' wrote Clay, the US Military Governor for Germany, to the Secretary of State, on 2 May 1947, (following a further failed attempt by the Dutch to persuade the Big Four to let them participate in decision-making on Germany, at the Foreign Ministers' Conference in Moscow),

> That the Allies, who have suffered at the hands of Germany, are extremely reluctant to deal with Germany in any way which brings a net profit to Germany [...] she is not able to finance a continuing hidden reparation programme in the form of concessions in international trade forced upon her by the Allied nations through the Occupying Powers.

Clay went on to point out that the Dutch and Belgian governments were urging that Germany use the ports of Rotterdam and Antwerp, paying foreign exchange for the service, despite the fact that Bremen and Hamburg had adequate port facilities.[113] The Dutch, together with their Benelux partners, continued to exert what pressure they could. On 26 November, they submitted a memorandum to the Big Four, stressing that they wished to be consulted on decisions on Germany. Again, they were politely rebuffed.[114]

The Dutch were to cling hard to their demands right up until the end of 1949, when those demands tended to complicate their simultaneous recognition of the need for a strong Germany. These will be dealt with in Chapter 2, which will suggest that commercial considerations weighed more heavily than concerns about military security.

The Indonesian Factor

In terms of priorities in foreign policy, the Indonesian question at least rivalled Dutch preoccupations with Germany. As such it tended to detract from calm consideration of the German problem, since it led to suspicions on the part of the Dutch as to the motives of the British and Americans, with whom they had to deal on the German problem.

'Ever since the end of the war, the domestic policies and external relationships of the Netherlands have been dominated by the situation in Indonesia,' wrote the British Ambassador in early 1950.[115] Following the transfer of sovereignty to Indonesia at a conference in the Hague on 27 December 1949, the Ambassador had written to the Foreign Secretary:

> At long last, and virtually for the first time since the war, it is possible to say that the Indonesian question has ceased to overshadow Holland's international relations in general, and to spread a cloud, although not a very black one, over Anglo-Dutch relations in particular.[116]

It is certainly time that the Indonesian problem was the Netherlands' main worry, not only in terms of the amount of time spent by the cabinet in discussing matters, but in terms of resources. For example, nearly all trained and half trained conscripts and the bulk of the Navy and Air Force were in Indonesia in 1949.[117]

There was an emotional aspect, as well; over 300,000 Dutch nationals (about 3 per cent of the population) had made their home in Indonesia, and in 1949 Dutch investments were estimated at between 1.25 to 2 billion dollars.[118] *The Economist* gives some of the flavour:

> To get out of this ill feeling that has been poisoning Anglo-Dutch relations, it is certainly necessary that there should be a frank recognition in this country of its responsibility for what happened in Indonesia in 1945 [...] Impenetrable mystery still surrounds the vital British policy decisions of September 1945, on which the subsequent course of events turned. The decision to treat Sukarno not as an

enemy but as a friend, and to recognise his government as the de facto authority in Java, was taken before a single Allied soldier had landed there – but where, when, why or on whose responsibility has never been disclosed.[119]

To gain more insight into the Dutch point of view, necessary because it explains Dutch distrust of the British and Americans, one must turn back to the confusion that ensued in the wake of the Japanese surrender, and try to pinpoint some of its causes. The Dutch appear to have been blissfully ignorant of the problems which were to appear. Cummings, Chief of the Division of North European Affairs in the State Department, wrote in 1945:

> Prior to the Japanese surrender, the attitude of the Netherlands' authorities with regard to the probable reaction of the Indonesian population to the return of the Dutch was most optimistic. Typical of this attitude is a reported statement by General van Oyen of the Netherlands' Indian Army, who stated that the people of the NEI [Netherlands East Indies], except for a few dissidents, would greatly support the former NEI government.[120]

The British ambassador echoed the Dutch attitude a few years later, albeit in rather subjective terms, when he wrote:

> The Dutch themselves have a clear conscience and cannot understand how it is possible that their motives should be so grossly misinterpreted by the other powers [...] in spite of their general high level of intelligence and culture, they cannot, in my view, be termed an imaginative people, and over Indonesia they have shown themselves genuinely incapable of appreciating the probable reactions of other races and nations.[121]

Whatever criticism some may level at the Dutch over Indonesia, British and American policy must certainly have confused them. In 1941, the British and Americans appeared, at least on the face of things, to share a common philosophy on self-determination: Article 3 of the Atlantic Charter, signed on 12 August, upheld 'the right of all people to choose the form of government under which they will live.' Attlee told an audience of West African students in London that the Charter applied to all peoples of the world.[122] Generally, the Atlantic Charter, combined with

American transpacific broadcasts, with promises of independence for the Philippines, must have raised hopes among nationalist leaders in many of the colonies.[123]

The Dutch government – in exile though it was – reacted in October 1942 in the form of a sharp statement by Foreign Minister van Kleffens, where he criticised American phrases about democracy, independence and self-determination 'as if these were constant values for all times and for all circumstances.'[124] By 6 December, Queen Wilhelmina was saying that there was no room for discrimination according to race and nationality: 'Only the ability of the individual citizens and the needs of the various groups of population will determine the policy of the government,' she said.[125] This carefully worded statement, while tempering van Kleffens' criticism, hardly suggested that the Dutch were intending to follow the apparent American policy of 'self-determination'.

In fact, the Dutch had every reason to believe that Britain and the United States would support them in regaining control over the East Indies, particularly towards the end of the War: in February 1944, Winston Churchill told the Dutch Prime Minister, Gerbrandy, that he was going to 'stand up for the Dutch Empire after the War.'[126] General MacArthur signed an agreement with van Mook, the lieutenant Governor General of the East Indies, whereby civil administration would be handed over to the latter and his officials 'as rapidly as possible' by the US Army when the time came. The American press appeared sympathetic to the Dutch. The *New York Times* of 11 July 1945 stated: 'The return of the Dutch to these islands will be welcome to the United Nations, for they were the most liberal colonial administrators. Their rule therefore was enlightened [...] they have become as necessary to Indonesia as Indonesia to them.'[127]

Although the Dutch may indeed have believed that the British and Americans would support them to the hilt, they must have been confused by events at the end of the war; they also appear to have underestimated the problems they would face with the Japanese surrender. To begin with, the Japanese had complicated matters by announcing on 7 April 1945 the setting up of a committee of enquiry into Indonesian independence. Then, following the surrender, the nationalists declared their own republic on 17 August. When a small British advance party arrived in Indonesia on 8 September 1945, they were confronted by the nationalists, who had taken matters into their own hands. Mountbatten, Supreme Commander, South East Asia, had to rearm a considerable number of Japanese troops to maintain public order.[128] He urged van Mook to negotiate with the nationalist leader Sukarno some form of agreement 'which would grant a degree of autonomy sufficient to bring Indonesian armed resistance to an end.'[129] This approach betrayed a lack of understanding of Dutch feelings about Sukarno. Some Dutch officials interpreted British neutrality as favouring the republicans.[130] On 1 October, the Dutch government issued a statement criticising 'tendencies in certain British circles to recognise the so-called Sukarno government, as the do facto government'. The statement went on to say that Sukarno had allowed himself to be the tool and puppet of the Japanese, had received a high decoration from them, had fascist tendencies and had preached hatred against the Allies.[131]

This did not deter the British. On 23 October, General Christison and Esler Denning, Mountbatten's political adviser, met with Indonesian nationalists, including Sukarno, and explained their aims of evacuating prisoners and internees, disarming the Japanese and maintaining order when necessary.[132] The Dutch grew more and more annoyed. At a meeting in Washington on 10 January 1946, the Dutch Ambassador said that the British were strengthening the hands of the Indonesian leader to the detriment of the Dutch Government's position, and constantly discussing matters with the Indonesian leaders, while rarely informing the Dutch representatives of the nature or outcome of these discussions.[133] The Americans, for their part, appeared to have had misgivings about British motives. Their Consul-General in Batavia, Foote, wrote to the Secretary of State on 10 July 1946:

> I am convinced beyond doubt British have some ulterior motive re NEI. This idea growing since 1928 when straws began pointing same direction. Since return last October, increasing number of straws all point likewise [...] nearly all British officers in Java have been openly anti-Dutch. No American could stand various insults offered to Dutch. On other hand they have been and are cordial to Indonesians.

Significantly, he carried on to say that the 12,000 British troops in Sumatra were doing nothing, and permitting the chaos to grow. Continued chaos, he said, would provide the excuse for ultimate British control.[134] However one views this polemical statement, it is worth mentioning *en passant* the commercial rivalry between the British and Americans, that had been particularly strong during the negotiations for the Mutual Aid Agreement, signed in February 1942. The Secretary of State for India, Amery, regarded Cordell Hull as 'a complete crank and a fanatic on the subject of the most favoured clause, who would try to do everything to try to get us to abandon inter-imperial preference.'[135]

Whatever the argument surrounding the actions of the British occupying forces in Indonesia, there does seem to have been a certain lack of direction. For example, at the Foreign Ministers' Conference in Moscow, Bevin had said on 16 December 1945 that with regard to Indonesia, he did 'not quite know' what his position was inasmuch as the British in Indonesia were acting under the orders of those who signed the surrender terms.[136] Yet on 24 December, he told Stalin that Her Majesty's Government were determined to withdraw from there as soon as possible.[137] The above record that Bevin 'did not quite know', which appeared in the American publication of the meeting, does not appear in the British record, which quotes Bevin as saying that:

> Since His Majesty's Government in that area were acting as agents on behalf of the Supreme Commander and were carrying out tasks allocated to them by the Military Command [the disarmament of the Japanese and the safeguarding of Allied internees], he could not agree to be answerable to a meeting of the three Powers.[138]

Two days later, he was however able to assure Molotov that the British were not expanding the British Empire.[139]

By the time the British pulled out of Indonesia (on 4 November 1946), the nationalist movement was well entrenched. Throughout 1947, the Dutch lobbied the British and Americans to help persuade the nationalists to accept Dutch power-sharing proposals.[140] The Americans did in fact try, but the Indonesians stalled.[141] The Americans were still critical of past British actions, and seemed to have supported the Dutch. The Consul-General at Batavia wrote on 2 July:

> I am and have been convinced beyond doubt that the Dutch-Indo problem would have been solved last year except for British encouragement to Indos [...] fact is British want to own or control Sumatra. They anti Dutch because think can obtain more favours from Indos than from Dutch. There appears to be no British neutrality in this situation.[142]

In August he wrote that 95 per cent of the Indonesians were 'sick of the Republic and its terrorising tactics.'[143]

At the end of 1947, American support for the Dutch position was becoming more qualified. The Acting Secretary of State wrote to the Consul-General in Batavia, on 31 December:

> NL is strong proponent of US policy in Europe. Dept believes that stability present Dutch government would be seriously undermined if NL failed to retain very considerable stake in NEI, and that the political consequences of failure present Dutch government would in all likelihood be prejudicial to US position in Western Europe. Accordingly, Dept unfavourable to any solution requiring immediate and complete withdrawal NL from Indies or any important part thereof [...] Dept favourably disposed to solution providing NL sovereignty for limited period and setting date for future independence of Indonesia.[144]

By this time, the Americans were beginning to look upon Europe as their main overseas priority, and the 'Truman Doctrine' was beginning to assume some importance, particularly with the Soviet Union's departure from the failed Four Power talks in December 1947. The failure of the Renville Agreements of 18 January 1948 and the continuing difficulty of coming to an agreement, ending up with the much criticised Dutch 'Police Action', caused a change in American policy. At the Security Council, the Americans actually supported a Soviet and Australian proposal that the Government of Indonesia be invited to take part in discussions. The Netherlands was fiercely opposed to this, on the grounds that Indonesia was not a sovereign state.

Curiously, Britain supported the Dutch position,[145] presumably because she did not wish to be seen to support moves which might detract from her own position on her colonies, particularly Malaya, where she was already involved in a protracted guerrilla war. This coming together of strange bed-fellows, particularly the Americans and Soviets, suggests how for a short while, the increasing alienation between East and West was transcended by more immediate tactical concerns.

The Indonesian problem led to increasing disillusionment on the part of the Dutch with the United Nations, on which they had set great store, and to difficulties in relations with the United States and Britain, at a time when the German question and European security were assuming greater importance. The problems caused by this major Dutch preoccupation were, as will be seen in Chapter 3, to detract considerably from Dutch thinking on their European priorities.

The Role of National Characteristics

Although it is impossible to prove that high moral principles, attachment to international law, a Calvinist tradition (even among the Catholics, who were and are the majority) and an intense dislike of totalitarianism were all-important, they certainly served to enhance the approach of the Dutch to their foreign policy concerns. Specific examples can be found, which illustrate well the need to justify in strong terms all their actions, including even the territorial claims, and to somehow combine high ideals with pragmatic economic concerns.

That the Netherlands should extol international law is hardly surprising. To understand its importance in the post-war years, it is necessary to turn back. The Dutch, depending on trade as they did, enshrined their ideas in Grotius' *Mare Liberum*, published in 1609. As Heldring points out, 'the foundation was thus laid for a typically Dutch tradition which tends to regard international law as a substitute for foreign policy.'[146] The seventeenth century statesman Johan de Witt further clarified a typically Dutch attitude when he wrote, as we have seen, that the interests of the Dutch state were peace and quiet everywhere and that commerce be carried on unimpeded.[147]

Heldring also points out that as the power of the Dutch state declined after the Congress of Vienna, the pacifist tradition became all important. The statesman Rudolf Thorbecke wrote in 1830 that the Netherlands did not take part in the envy and enmity of the great states. He went on to infer that Dutch policy, being free from lust for power, was the most impartial judge of other nations' lust for the same.[148]

Further expression was given to what Heldring terms 'moral arrogance' by Cornelis van Vollenhoven in 1913, when he justified the Netherlands' suitability for taking the lead in founding the League of Nations, by saying that the Netherlands were superior to France in prosperity, and to both France and the United States in unsuspected ('unquestioned' would be a better translation) disinterestedness.[149] In 1939, the Dutch Prime Minister, de Geer, described Dutch neutrality as a 'beacon in a dark world.'[150]

The religious characteristics of the Dutch added (and still add) an element of morality to their emphasis on international law. Although Catholics outnumber Protestants by a ratio of about four to three, the Calvinist element was always a strong factor, even among many Catholics. One has only to look at the party system in the Netherlands to understand the influence of religion in Dutch politics. Until fairly recently, and before the merger of the main denominational political parties, the Catholic People's Party has always been in the government, while the two smaller

Protestant parties have also been in coalitions. (In 1981, the three religious parties merged into the Christian Democratic Appeal). There was therefore a strong anti-communist (i.e. anti-atheist) fervour which found its expression in the Netherlands not recognising the Soviet Union until 1941. Indeed, in 1934, the Dutch had voted against the Soviet Union's inclusion in the League of Nations. Following the war, the Dutch developed more reasons for disliking communism, centred on their experience of having been occupied by a totalitarian state. As the Soviet Union's grip increased on its East European neighbours, the more the Dutch found themselves moving West.

While it is difficult to try and gauge the precise degree of influence on foreign policy exercised by national characteristics, some examples suggest it was strong during the early post-war years. The Foreign Minister, van Boetzelaer van Oosterhout, told Parliament in 1946:

> If the UN were to fail, it will not be because it was based on wrong principles, but because Mankind in its shortsightedness and unwisdom again fails to grasp the hand stretched out for its salvation, in accordance with God's plan.

Stikker, when criticising in his memoirs the idea of a European federation, alluded to the fact that of Adenauer, Schuman, de Gasperi, van Zeeland and Bech, he was the only Protestant.[151] Such statements, which clearly show that religious morals were a strong factor, were not just restricted to parliament and memoirs. When the Dutch Cabinet discussed the territorial claims on Germany, on 27 September 1945, van Kleffens, a strong proponent of the claims, said that St. Augustine, Thomas of Aquinas and Vitoria (the Spanish International law expert), had all recognised annexation as compensation in a justified war.[152] That statement, more than any, epitomised the Dutch attachment to both international law and religion, in their political life. At the Paris Peace Conference, van Boetzelaer van Oosterhout said:

> We are recognised as a people of moderation and good sense. It is however, precisely this objectivity, together with an acute sense of justice, as evidenced through our country's history by many of its prominent men, which objects to resuming international relations as if nothing had happened.[153]

This declared attachment to justice and religious morals goes some way towards explaining why the Dutch tried so hard to gain territory from Germany, and also serves to show why they felt so strongly about negotiating with Sukarno on the Indonesian question. The British ambassador wrote: 'The Calvinist streak, which is just below the surface in every Dutchman, gives them a genuine moral distaste for negotiations with such people as Sukarno [...]'[154] It is therefore important to be aware of national characteristics, particularly regarding religion and justice, and not only trade, when analysing the Dutch foreign policy perspective on the question of German rearmament and Western security.

Conclusion

These national characteristics, emphasising, as they do, justice and religion, permeate the nature of Dutch neutrality, founded on a desire to be left alone and to avoid war. They throw into relief the way the Dutch handled the German problem, particularly the territorial claims, based as they were on a curious mixture of hard nosed commercial considerations and a sense of justice. The feeling of indignation that the Dutch felt over Indonesia was enhanced, too, by this sense of justice. On the question of European co-operation, however, the Dutch were more pragmatic, and their attachment to commercial considerations, as will be seen in the next chapter, was to come to the fore, as was their preoccupation with Germany.

2

EUROPEAN DEVELOPMENTS AND THE GERMAN QUESTION: THE DUTCH APPROACH

Introduction

> Now that it was clear that a world order, based on law, would not for the time being, come to fruition, European integration offered at least the chance to realise a piece of an international legal order, on a regional level.[1]

Although this statement by Heldring seems to suggest that the Dutch were still looking at foreign policy rather idealistically and altruistically, their actions on questions relating to European integration show a pragmatic approach, based more on commercial concerns than on anything else. In fact, as will be seen, the Dutch in some respects tended to be anti-integrationist. They were also disappointed at what they saw as a lukewarm British attitude, especially since they were keen to see Britain more committed to Europe, to counterbalance French influence, which the Dutch feared, rather than to promote European federation per se. However, largely because of Benelux co-operation, some countries, but particularly the United States, seemed to assume that the Dutch were a shining example to Europe.

The Netherlands and Europe

The Dutch had, perhaps unwittingly, set an example to European federalists in co-operating with other countries. In 1943, the Netherlands, Belgium and Luxembourg signed an agreement providing arrangements to facilitate payments between the three countries and for close consultation on economic and financial policies in the future. In 1944, they entered into an agreement for the establishment of a customs union.[2] The aim of complete economic union was not achieved, but currencies were linked and Benelux certainly made an impact, in that an agreement on the unification of excise duties was eventually signed on 19 May 1949. Perhaps more important, however, was the degree of co-operation on foreign policy, particularly as a way of gaining influence at international meetings. For example, there was just one Benelux representative on the Executive Committee of the Committee of European Economic Co-operation, the Dutchman Hans Hirschfeld.[3] Moreover, it was only in conjunction with her Benelux partners that the Netherlands eventually gained entry to the big-power talks on Germany.

This kind of co-operation fired the imagination of the Americans: a week before General Marshall's famous speech of 5 June 1947, the American Secretary of State for Economic Affairs, Clayton, wrote a memorandum to Acheson, the then Undersecretary of State for Economic Affairs, advocating an aid plan for Europe 'based on a European economic federation on the order of the Belgium-Netherlands-Luxembourg Customs Union.'[4] The Americans clearly had a certain respect for Benelux's potential role vis-à-vis the German problem, as well, even though, as has been shown in Chapter 1, they were concerned at what they termed a 'hidden reparations programme'. At the end of January 1948, Marshall wrote to the Ambassador at the Hague and referred to the 'valuable contributions' that the three (Benelux) governments could make towards the future of Germany, by reason of their experience and knowledge.[5] At the end of the year, the American political adviser for Germany, Murphy, wrote to the Under Secretary of State, Lovett, to say: 'Of the Benelux countries the Dutch view of Germany is by far the most realistic and particularly during the last year the Dutch have been constructive and forward looking. This applies to a lesser extent to Belgium and Luxembourg.'[6]

But American hopes that Europe would quickly form a customs union were to be disappointed, as will be illustrated later. Their concept of European co-operation was rather different to that of Europe's, whose constituent parts, in turn, had different ideas about the extent of, and motives for, co-operation. It was General Marshall's speech and the tough negotiations on the establishment of the Organisation for European Economic Co-operation which followed it, that threw into relief the differences both between the United States and Europe, and between the European states themselves, on the question of European integration. Within those two concentric circles, the negotiations would show how the Dutch would have to creep tentatively out of their moral and legal shell to confront the Atlanticist – European dilemma, with their high expectations of Britain somewhere in between.

Marshall Aid and the Dutch Dilemma

It is hardly an understatement to say that General Marshall's announcement had a strong impact on the states of Europe, not least on the Dutch, nor that the European Recovery Programme served as a catalyst for co-operation as much as it highlighted differences between the United States and Europe, and between the states of Europe. Professor Milward's contention that American aid was intended to achieve a political, as well as an economic, purpose, also makes sense in the light of the evidence.[7] Six weeks before Marshall's announcement, the Ad Hoc Committee of the State-War-Navy Co-ordinating Committee referred to 'measures which might be undertaken, in implementation of US foreign policy, for the extension of aid, including money, food, military equipment and other forms of assistance, to foreign nations by the US.' Even more pertinently, the Committee spoke of 'urgency of need, in light of US interest.'[8] The State Department, however, was clearly sensitive to any potential American aid being interpreted as political, and the director of the Policy Planning Staff, Kennan, wrote to Acheson that steps should be taken to clarify what the press had 'unfortunately come to identify as the Truman Doctrine' and to remove 'the damaging impression that the US approach to world problems was a defensive reaction to communist pressure.'[9] However worried the State Department might have been about creating the wrong impression, the communist insurrection in Greece and the strength of the communists in France and Italy worried the Americans. All that being said, to suggest that there was a co-ordinated American conspiracy to 'take over' Europe would be incorrect. It was a case of the United States wishing to protect their interests and ideals.

Their view of Europe's troubles in 1947 appeared rather dramatic: on 27 May 1947, Clayton wrote to Acheson: 'Europe is steadily deteriorating [...] one political crisis after another [...] millions of people are slowly starving.' He went on to say that if the standard of living were lowered, there would be revolution, and ended by saying: 'The US must run this show.'[10] However exaggerated some Americans' views of Europe's problems may have been, and whatever the measure of fear of communism and revolution, there were very real economic problems, which had not been solved at Bretton Woods. Relief programmes, paid for in dollars, such as the UNRRA, were expected to end balance of payments difficulties, but did not. Clayton, in his memorandum, had also said: 'We must avoid getting into another UNRRA.'[11] The system agreed at Bretton Woods, for all its hopes, did not prevent the enormous balance of payments deficits of Western Europe in 1947.

There has been considerable debate about the seriousness of Western Europe's economic problems after the war, but particularly in 1947. Although both the level of exports and of production were rising, so too was the level of imports, and at a faster rate, thus producing a balance of payments crisis.[12] It was in the Netherlands that the problem was felt particularly keenly: for, despite the slow but steady rise in exports, their level in 1947 was still less than half that of 1938. More important, the situation was worse in that respect than in any other Western European country except Germany. In that year, only 44 per cent of Dutch imports were covered by exports.[13] Germany, which had been the Netherlands' second most important market before the war, was receiving only 7 per cent of Dutch exports in 1946.[14] To add to the balance of payments problem, the Dutch commitment to Indonesia meant a high level of defence spending.[15] The British ambassador to the Hague, Nichols, wrote: '[...] it was clear that without external aid the Dutch economy was going to collapse. The implementation of the Marshall Plan was therefore vital for Holland'.[16] This view contradicts that of Nichol's predecessor, Bland, who had written that even without American aid, the communists would not be strong enough to cause any internal disorganisation sufficiently serious to effect the economic recovery of the country.[17] Speaking at the Third Session of the Economic Commission for Europe on 28 April 1948, the Benelux delegate stated: 'Without this help, the present situation of the Netherlands would be difficult, and future prospects bleak.'[18] While the language he used was not couched in terms as dramatic as Clayton's or as certain as Nichols', and while hypotheses cannot prove that without Marshall Aid, Europe would have starved and fallen to the communists, the aid was certainly welcomed, and served as a catalyst for more co-operation between the states of Western Europe, even if it did not result in the kind of free trade area the Americans were seeking.

As for the threat of communist disruption, it does not seem to have been a real one. Back in 1945, a Foreign Office official had written:

> The Dutch Communists played an insignificant role before the war and are not expected to play a very much more important one now [...] Their leaders seem to be untrained, uneducated and more than usually irresponsible types. They have alienated what sympathy they

might have had by defending Soekarno and opposing all suggestions that Holland might annex a small strip of Germany.[19]

Even the 10.5 per cent of votes that the Communists polled in the May 1946 elections was not considered to be a serious problem by, for example, the British ambassador, Bland. He said that memories of the Resistance Movement and illusions about Soviet foreign policy had been largely removed by the passage of time. More significantly, he suggested, as we have seen, that the communists would not be strong enough to seriously affect the economic recovery of the country. He concluded his dispatch with the words:

> It is true that if acute economic distress were widespread in Holland their influence would probably increase, but I think that the sanity of the Dutch and the discipline of their strongly anti-communist Christian and Socialist trade unions would hold out and prevent the Communists from playing a decisive role.[20]

With or without communists, the Dutch generally welcomed American economic aid, although not without certain provisos.

During the CEEC meetings, which led to the setting up of the OEEC, the Dutch did not pander to American wishes although, unlike the French, they shared a common view on the need to strengthen the German economy. For example, when the bilateral agreements on the distribution of Marshall Aid were being hammered out, the Dutch joined the French, Swedes and British in refusing to contemplate an American requirement to consult the International Monetary Fund (IMF) about alterations in the exchange rates whenever the IMF felt this to be necessary. Hirschfeld felt that sovereign rights might be restricted. The British simply considered the idea unacceptable.[21] Generally, the Dutch were co-operative. The British Ambassador wrote that the Economic Co-operation Administration (ECA) in Holland [sic] had been very favourably impressed by the Dutch attitude hitherto displayed towards Marshall Aid.[22]

Despite this observation, the positive Dutch attitude towards Marshall Aid did not mean that the Dutch would go along with American wishes to help create a large customs union, unless it was in their commercial interests. Thus, while they supported the idea of a continuing OEEC,[23] and one that went beyond the immediate objectives of the Marshall Plan, they were not prepared to support French moves for a customs union with Italy and Benelux, promoted by Alphand, Head of the Economic Section at the French Ministry of Foreign Affairs, only three weeks after the CEEC began its deliberations on 12 July 1947. The Dutch continued to resist during the CEEC meetings. In the words of the American Ambassador to the Hague on 7 February 1948:

> The Netherlands government would not welcome and in fact would resist efforts either by French or American governments to enter in to Customs Union with France (alone or with Italy). Netherlands government appreciates arguments for step by step expansion Customs Union but favours as next step for Benelux (based partly on Benelux experience) broader approach including several major countries under aegis CEEC study group.[24]

Without Germany to counterbalance France, the Dutch were not prepared to support 'Fritalux'. Still, despite Dutch resistance to American and French overtures, the Netherlands ended up with a large share of Marshall Aid: calculated on exchange rates before September 1949, the country's allocation amounted to 16.1 per cent of GNP, and to 23.1 per cent of GNP at the exchange rate after September 1949. This was a considerably higher proportion than any other recipient of Marshall Aid, with the possible exception of Austria.[25]

There were three main considerations in the Dutch attitude towards European co-operation: a distrust of the French; a wish to see Germany playing a full role in European economic co-operation; and a desire to see Britain properly committed to Europe. The American ambassador wrote that one of the reasons underlying the Dutch attitude (towards a Customs Union) was sensitivity regarding French ambitions to regain a dominating 'old-fashioned' great power role. Another was the fear of the unfavourable economic consequences of a union which included a single large country.[26] Within Benelux, the Netherlands already had a large trade deficit with Belgium, which they feared could repeat itself in the case of France. In addition, Stikker, who became Foreign Minister in August 1948, was not known for his pro-French views. His memoirs are punctuated by various criticisms. The State Department wrote that the Dutch were not inclined to count too heavily on French support in a crisis and that they tended to look with disfavour on what they considered to be political and economic instability in France.[27] Willem Drees is said not to have 'fully trusted' the French.[28]

But perhaps the greatest problem in Dutch-French relations was the German one. Simply put, the Dutch wanted the German economy to be revived as soon as possible. The State Department wrote:

> The Dutch believe that an economically viable Germany is essential not only to their well-being, but to the general prosperity of Europe. Since their own economic welfare is so dependent on conditions in Germany, they are probably foremost among the European nations in advocating the integration of Germany into the Western European economic community'.[29]

When on 9 June 1947, the Dutch cabinet discussed Marshall's speech, the Trade and Industry Minister, Vos, said that the European question could never be considered without the problem of Germany.[30] A Dutch Foreign Ministry paper stated: '[...] we must strive for a successful ERP with the insertion of Germany into the West European economy.'[31] The Americans were also keen for early German involvement in economic co-operation, to the extent of selecting three German politicians to be present with representatives of the military government at the opening ceremony of the OEEC in Paris in April 1948. The French simply refused to participate at the ceremony, if Germans were present. When the French went further, and insisted that the military government signing on Germany's behalf include a statement that Germany would fulfil its obligations in respect of restrictions on her industrial production, Clay decided not to attend the ceremony.[32] As will be seen, the Dutch continued to press for German involvement in economic co-operation, despite this example of rather abrupt diplomacy on the part of the French and Americans.

British views were of particular importance to the Dutch, in the latter's ideas about European co-operation. During the CEEC negotiations in the summer of 1947, the Dutch had made quite clear their views about British participation. According to the American Ambassador to the Hague, the Dutch would not entertain the French proposals for a customs union without British participation or an indication of such participation.[33] As Wesselring wrote, a Europe without England was unattractive for the Netherlands: 'The thought of German political leadership was unacceptable, and of Italian, absurd. For the first time since 1870, France was again the leading power in Europe and the danger of French domination threatened again.'[34] The smaller Dutch needed British participation to counterbalance French and future German influence. The British government, indeed Bevin himself, made encouraging noises for a while, viewing a customs union as a defensive alliance against the Soviet Union, which had turned down Marshall Aid.[35] In January 1948, Bevin said: 'We in Britain can no longer stand outside Europe and insist that our problems and position are quite separate from those of our European neighbours.'[36] Although Bevin already had a defensive alliance in mind, the words were important for those hoping for a commitment from Britain to join in a customs union. Only a month later, on 11 February, the Foreign Office drew up a paper which concluded that the United Kingdom should take the lead in promoting and inspiring a European Customs Union.[37] British participation was, however, to prove illusory. The Cabinet was not prepared to commit Britain to a customs union, as the Foreign Office appeared to want. Sir Anthony Nutting described the British attitude towards European Unity in his book, *Europe will not Wait – a Warning and a Way Out*, in the following terms:

> Whitehall sought refuge in the cynical reflection that European unity was just a lot of Continental hot air [...] For all their internationalist preachings of the past, the Labour Party, when they took office, could scarcely have been more insular and nationalist, even blimpish, in their European policy.[38]

Despite Nutting's observations, it is important to point out, as Roger Bullen has:

> That both Labour and Conservative Governments believed that Great Britain's position as a world power of the second rank, her worldwide trading interests and her management of the Sterling Area were best protected by loose forms of association in Western Europe.[39]

Nevertheless, Britain's approach to the question of European unity certainly appeared ambivalent, if not confusing, to many in Continental Europe. Given that Britain's institutions had not undergone the battering of so many in Europe during the War, her approach, however illogical it may have seemed to many, is not difficult to explain. John Kent argues that Bevin tried to create a powerful 'Euro-African force', led by Britain as a third force, independent of the United States and the Soviet Union. When this idea proved impractical, Britain turned to pushing for a special place in an American dominated Atlantic Alliance.[40]

Britain was sceptical of European unity. 'In their approach to the future of Europe', wrote Bullen, 'the British started from the assumption that Western Europe was too weak and vulnerable to threats from without and within to contemplate a separate future.'[41] The British Government also assumed that the majority of the small states of Western Europe looked to the United Kingdom to provide leadership.[42] In this context the Council of Europe and the OEEC were useful for co-operation, where Britain could assert her leadership.

It is too easy to criticise individuals or governments for a lack of European vision, by citing the problems that arose in 1947 and 1948. Criticism, particularly the more emotional kind, however, avoids the very real complexities of an institutional, administrative, cultural, political and emotional nature that were brought to the fore. But for all the niggardly bickering, and worries about sovereignty, which the Marshall catalyst set in motion, a lot of problems were brought into the open. Although Alan Milward argues that the CEEC negotiations did virtually nothing to promote either reconstruction or integration in Western Europe,[43] it was the exposing of the real differences that enabled them to be tackled later on. One could not, after all, simply wave a magic wand.

The position of the Dutch, for all its paradoxes, was clear. On the one hand, they had made a practical effort through co-operating in Benelux, which served as an example. On the other, they were not prepared to go further without Britain committing herself. Their main aim was to sell as much to Germany as possible, but while the French, and to a certain extent the British, were prevaricating on the issue of strengthening the German economy, they were not prepared to risk what they saw as French hegemony. Although the OEEC ended up with few political teeth, it at least continued, thanks in part to Dutch insistence,[44] and was an important vehicle for enabling the Germans to regain their place. Everyone had their own idea about what European co-operation meant: the Americans hoped for a large free-trade area, the French saw a Europe in which Germany could be controlled, and the British saw an informal association of European states that, in Bevin's mind, would keep the Russians out.

As for the Dutch, they appeared torn between Europe and the Atlantic. They were unable to see beyond Benelux without some guarantee that they would not lose out to the French. Above all, they did not feel themselves to be a typically European state. The yearbook of the Dutch Foreign Ministry stated:

The Kingdom of the Netherlands is not an exclusively European State; since parts of this kingdom are situated both in America and Asia, it is at the same time directly affected by the development of political and economic relations in both these parts of the world.[15]

Here, of course, Indonesia, the Netherlands' main foreign policy preoccupation, springs to mind. The Netherlands simply did not see themselves as a typically European country. They wished to retain their independence.

While the 'European idea' still remained fairly undefined, and was clouded by specific national aims, the Dutch beavered away tenaciously at their claims.

Dutch Claims and Frustrations

The Marshall plan had been welcome to the Dutch not only as a means of solving their immediate economic problems, but because the discussions which led to the establishment of the OEEC had enabled them to stress the importance of the German economy to their and Europe's benefit. It served as a useful platform. Important to them, it gave them a voice and an official stage from which they could continue to press their claims. Their immediate concern was to gain access to the Four Power meetings on Germany. Having been rebuffed in November 1947, they continued to push for full participation. The failure of the London Conference in December 1947 and the Soviet Union's departure precipitated a change, which, combined with Dutch, and Benelux tenacity, brought them into the decision-making process, enabling the Dutch to push even harder. They stuck as doggedly as they could to unrealistic territorial claims, as has been seen, but were no less tenacious in their other claims, which they somehow fitted into their overall strategy of pushing for the strengthening of the German economy. By stressing the benefits to Europe, they were able to provide a reasonable sounding cloak for their claims.

Dr Hirschfeld was appointed Government Commissioner for the German question, and was asked by the Cabinet on 31 January 1949 to produce a paper 'dealing with the economic and political questions.'[46] Max Kohnstamm, a senior Foreign Ministry official, was extensively involved in preparing the paper, and sent a draft to Dr Boon, Secretary General of the Foreign Ministry. In his covering note, he set the tone by quoting from *Winter*, Booker T Washington's autobiography, the phrase: 'You can't keep a man in the gutter unless staying there yourself.' The paper stressed that a powerful revival of the West German economy was 'absolutely necessary', and that it was important to avoid doing 'too little, too late'. It warned against having illusions over the territorial claims, and stressed the importance of close political co-operation, solid economic integration and a readiness to make the sacrifices necessary to further European co-operation.[47]

Although, as has been seen, the Dutch had already stressed the need to integrate the German economy with that of Europe, the paper went a good deal further, in calling for the strengthening of a former enemy, about whom the Dutch were still very sensitive. The paper did indeed provoke some controversy within the Foreign Ministry: de Booy, the Dutch Ambassador to the Allied Control Council, had considerable misgivings about the paper, on which he commented in a letter to the Foreign Minister on 9 May. In a passage which shows the degree of sensitivity which the German question still aroused in some quarters in 1949, he wrote:

> Dutch policy regarding Germany is that the Netherlands will have to make itself as strong as possible against this recently hostile country, that in history has shown itself to be a very dangerous neighbour and where it is all too little evident that the people have really changed their mentality [...][48]

De Booy's other main criticism was that the paper was about policy towards West Germany alone. He wrote: '[...] it is a mistake to limit a consideration of the German question to West Germany, since it is impossible to leave East Germany out of the picture.' Although neither the Eastern nor Western parts of Germany were yet sovereign states, the Dutch had not yet come to accept that East Germany would remain part of the Eastern Block. This may appear rather naive, since de Booy wrote his criticism only two weeks before the three western occupation zones became the Federal Republic of Germany. On the other hand, the Hallstein doctrine was not yet the order of the day, and some would argue that in purely legal terms, the question was to remain unresolved for another 40 years. Hirschfeld was probably just being realistic, while de Booy was splitting hairs, to back up his disagreement with Hirschfeld's whole approach to Germany and Europe: while Hirschfeld stressed the need for European integration, De Booy went on to say that in a war, the West would have to rely on the United States. The paradox is that that was obviously true in 1949. De Booy's essential point (as he wrote) was that strengthening West Germany would give the Russians the excuse to strengthen East Germany. Events proved Hirschfeld correct: the West German economy was revitalised and there was no war.

The reason for these disagreements were that De Booy was in Berlin, and had a first hand view of the developing ideological conflict between East and West, whereas Hirschfeld was an economist with a European vision, and probably less of an Atlanticist than De Booy (or, for that matter, Stikker). In leaving out East Germany he was only being realistic. These problems were to crystallise later on, as will be seen, when security questions are discussed.

This was the background against which the Dutch continued to press their claims: for presentational purposes, outwardly, they stressed the need for Germany to play its full role in European co-operation, but inwardly there were disagreements that illustrated their dilemma over both European integration and Germany. As will be seen, and as has been hinted at, pragmatic commercial considerations outweighed security ones.

Dutch industrial production did not attain the level of 1938 until November 1947.[49] Before the war, about one fifth of Dutch trade had been with Germany, and while the balance of trade had been unfavourable to the Dutch, invisible trade had largely filled the gap,[50] Germany had been the Netherlands' most important supplier and second most important market.[51] Yet in 1946, Germany accounted for only 7 per cent of Dutch exports, the same as Switzerland, behind Benelux, Britain, Sweden and France. The correlation between the low level of Dutch exports to Germany and Dutch concern in rebuilding the German economy is obvious: at the end of 1945, German industrial production had dropped to only 25 per cent of its 1936 value, and still stood at only 44 per cent at the end of 1947.[52]

The Dutch needed the defeated country which had invaded them, although they could hardly put the problem in such stark terms. But they had lost enough, and suffered enough, to pursue their claims with considerable perseverance. While it is unnecessary to pinpoint all the Dutch grievances on trade and restitution, some of the main ones need to be mentioned, to understand the nature of the problems. The Dutch were particularly worried about the amount of German transit trade being directed via the German railways to Bremen and Hamburg, and wanted more to be routed through the Rhine ports. By 1949, Rotterdam was still handling only half the traffic it had handled in 1938.[53] The Americans, however, had considerable misgivings about Dutch efforts to gain a larger share of transit trade at German expense.[54] But the Dutch were tenacious in their various demands. For example, they were actively involved in increasing Dutch exports to Germany in a way which could easily be construed as arbitrary: in the agreed minutes of the discussions of the Mixed

Commission and the Three Western Zones of Germany, held in the Hague in March 1949, it was stated:

> This examination showed that contrary to previous forecasts, the balance of payments between the three Western Zones of Germany and the Netherlands is likely to show over the period of the Agreement a deficit position to the Netherlands of about $30 million [...] in order to improve the position, a list of additional Netherlands exports was agreed upon, by means of which it is hoped to reduce the estimated deficit by $10 million [...][55]

Trade was only part of the picture: the Dutch felt that their interests were not being adequately considered in the International Authority for the Ruhr. On 10 June 1949, the Dutch ambassador in London, Jonkheer E Michiels van Verduynen, called on a senior Foreign Office official, Sir Roger Makins, to make representations about the Ruhr. Similar representations were made in Paris and Washington. The memorandum left by the Ambassador stated:

> Since the occupation of Germany, the Netherlands interests in the coal mining and iron and steel industry have been the subject of measures, which insofar [sic] excluded a satisfactory rehabilitation of these interests [...] from the outset, all rights of Dutch shareholders in undertakings belonging to these industries have been suspended.

The memorandum also proposed that Dutch experts should visit London to discuss matters.[56] The Foreign Office reply cannot have been encouraging for the Dutch. It stated that the suggestions put forward were being considered with very[57] great care, and that the memorandum was 'so full and clear that we need not trouble you to bring over, at this stage [...] the experts.'[58] The reaction was less than enthusiastic. (The Dutch had to wait six weeks for the reply!) In a telegram to Washington on 20 August, the Foreign Office spelt out some of the main Dutch demands and gave their answers. In reply to a Dutch request that they be allowed to exchange minority interests in certain coal mines for a 50 per cent interest in the Rheinpreussen mine, the Foreign Office said: 'HMG cannot, however, agree to the consolidation of minority holdings with majority interests in advance of, or as part of, the reorganisation scheme.' The Dutch had also asked to be informed about plans for the reorganisation of the Klocknerwerke and that further measures against the concern which might prejudice Dutch interests be suspended. The Foreign Office reaction was to agree to inform the Dutch, but not to suspend further measures.[59]

Dutch dissatisfaction at what they saw as discrimination, and a feeling of being left out of important decision-making, was an important factor. For example, Benelux presented a note to the three occupying powers at the beginning of the sixth session of the Council of Foreign Ministers (23 May to 20 June 1949), asking to be kept informed of the progress of discussions and to be consulted before decisions were taken.[60]

The emphasis the Dutch placed on commercial considerations in their approach to the German problem is well illustrated in a comprehensive memorandum produced by their Foreign Ministry and presented to Parliament on 19 July 1949, entitled: 'Note on the State of Affairs with regard to the German Question.' The British ambassador wrote of the note:

> It therefore purports to be a comprehensive political document, and the fact that the contents are very largely economic shows clearly the extent to which Dutch relations with Germany, and with the Allies when German questions are under discussion, are dominated by economic and commercial considerations.[61]

Almost half the note was devoted to Dutch commercial worries, covering restitution, European economic co-operation, the border 'corrections' (the continuing problem of the Eems-Dollard-Estuary), reparations, trade traffic, shipping services and transit trade, and Dutch investment in Germany. The measure of frustration that the Dutch were still feeling showed itself in the demand 'that an end be put immediately to the factual discrimination against Dutch interests compared with those of other allies.'[62] The note was peppered with criticisms of allied policy: 'Another factor which exercises a negative influence on traffic in Dutch ports and on the Rhine, is the policy of the occupation authorities, who are diverting imports paid by themselves via German ports.' The note went on to complain that despite an agreement that the Benelux ports would play a greater role, only 10 per cent of food imports financed by the occupation authorities were handled by Benelux ports. Complaints were also made about the 'impediments to trade applied by the occupation authorities'. Another point of dissatisfaction was the fact that Dutch bank accounts in Germany were blocked.

Although a good part of the note was devoted to specific commercial questions, it also highlighted the importance the Dutch attached to Germany playing a full role in Europe. If some of the demands did not appear to promote a spirit of co-operation, the Dutch covered themselves by introducing an element of flexibility in to the note. For example, the note stated in its conclusions:

> The alarming extent of this damage would undoubtedly give the Netherlands government good ground to demand a preferential position as regards Germany in the economic field. The government believes that, at present, a demand for such a preferential position would not be a contribution towards the co-operation with other peoples which it is seeking.[63]

The Dutch were saying, albeit rather carefully, that while their claims were realistic, there were also other important considerations in their thinking on Germany. They even played down some of their claims, for example over compensation, to the extent of saying:

> Although the Netherlands government will certainly pursue compensation for past material damage, it cannot be concealed that the compensation that will finally be received will make only an extremely small contribution to the restoring of the national economy.[64]

The likelihood was that the Dutch would have to find an acceptable way of pursuing their claims in an international atmosphere where, on the one hand, co-operation among European states was improving and where, on the other, solidarity vis-à-vis the Eastern Block was increasing.

Nevertheless, the Dutch did not let go, and showed their considerable doggedness by submitting a memorandum on Dutch-German economic relations to the three occupying powers in October 1949, which again showed their frustration and dissatisfaction.[65] It complained: 'The development of the economic relations with Germany after the German capitulation has been a source of great disappointment to the Netherlands.' It dealt with the specific commercial concerns of shipping services and transit trade, capital interests (blocking of assets, the Ruhr, equalisation of burdens, prewar treaties), restitution of ships, and restitution of securities. Some of the points raised were specific enough to suggest that the Dutch were right to be dissatisfied. For example, the note stated:

> The Netherlands Embassy in Washington took up with the Department of State the question of the interpretation of the term "qualifying shares" (para 1-c). To the Netherlands Government's surprise

the Bipartite Board approved Economic Council Ordinance No 71A "to alleviate social hardships" before these discussions were concluded. This law contained a narrow interpretation of the term, unfavourable to the Netherlands' interests. According to article 6 para 102 of the above law by qualifying shares are exclusively meant shares which must be held by members of the board of directors or members of the board of management according to the statute. In practice such provisions do not occur in Germany, so that this provision is valueless.[66]

The Dutch had of course numerous other detailed claims, but it is not necessary to list them here.

However justified some of their claims may have been, and whatever dissatisfaction the Dutch showed, the note showed an important flaw in the Dutch judgment of the effects of the Netherlands-German trade agreement signed in Frankfurt on 7 September 1949. It stated that 'it offered great possibilities for a sound development of trade', but went on to say: '[...] although it may still take considerable time for the German-Netherlands trade to reach anything like the prewar level.'[67] Yet by the end of the year, Germany had leapt from the position of the Netherlands' sixth most important customer to its most important one.[68] Milward writes:

> In the first half of 1950, West German imports from the Netherlands were over 12 per cent of total imports and although this represented a wide variety of goods, some of which no doubt did not originate in the Netherlands, the difference with the comparable figure of 3.2 per cent in the first half of 1949 scarcely needs comment. Roughly half the deterioration in West Germany's trade balance with Western Europe between 1949 and 1950 was accounted for by Dutch-German trade.[69]

Although economic forecasting is always a risky business, and must have been particularly so in the volatile years after the war, the erroneous prognostication by the Dutch was hardly a small one, particularly since the two month period at the end of which the Dutch were proved wrong was certainly not a 'considerable time'. It could be that the Dutch wished to play down what looked like preferential treatment for them: after all, the agreement provided for an almost complete liberalisation of Dutch exports to Germany, but not, for the time being, the other way round.

At all events, the trade agreement seems to have had a mollifying effect on Dutch complaints. The British Ambassador wrote to the Foreign Secretary on 11 February 1950: 'Since the signing of the trade agreement between Holland and Western Germany in September last, trade has greatly increased, and complaints are correspondingly less.'[70] Nevertheless, the Ambassador saw fit to write in the same despatch: 'Germany has continued throughout 1949 to be a source of mild friction in Anglo-Dutch relations.'[71]

Although the Dutch approach to the German problem was characterised by barely concealed annoyance at what was considered to be the lackadaisical attitude of the occupation powers in relation to their demands, they saw the advantages of shrouding their complaints in repeated calls for German involvement in European co-operation, which tended to create the impression that they were in favour of European integration. Their approach to the question of European integration was however far less enthusiastic when it came down to federalism and supra-nationalist ideas, as will be seen; but Britain's lack of commitment to European unity was to help the Dutch to plump for Europe.

European Unity

The Dutch had of course recognised the importance of a strong German economy well before their note of July 1949. For example, at a cabinet meeting on 8 January 1947, the Minister of Agriculture, Mansholt, dared to say that in the long run the welfare of Germany was of primary importance.[72] A few days later, the Dutch Government had stressed the importance of some measure of German recovery, in their note of 14 January to the Big Four. The note of July 1949 on the German question concluded that bringing Germany into the West European economy was of great significance.[73] The Yearbook of the Foreign Ministry stated: 'Netherlands interests [...] are best promoted by the establishment of an effective military and economic co-operation with the countries of Europe [...] Germany also is more and more being drawn into this co-operation.'[74] 'Anxiety about Germany is one of the motives which have impelled the Dutch to support, in a cautious way, progress towards the political and economic integration of Europe,' wrote the British Ambassador in February 1950.[75] On the other hand, Stikker was known to be anti-federalist. In his memoirs, he wrote:

> But I was held back from taking an active role in European federation, as the majority of the Dutch people in an upsurge of idealism wanted at the time, precisely because I saw no indication of how

these grand ideas would fit into the pattern of world policy so long as the United States, on whose monopoly of nuclear weapons we all relied, and Great Britain and the Commonwealth had not clarified their thinking on these complex and formidable problems.[76]

Stikker put considerable emphasis, then on the Atlantic partnership. Strategic reasons apart, he seems to have had a certain emotional attachment to the Anglo-Saxon countries, which detracted from his being a European idealist. One clue as to this attachment is that he felt it necessary to point out in his memoirs (as mentioned in Chapter 1, but worth repeating here) that of Adenauer, Schuman, de Gasperi, van Zeeland and Bech, he was the only Protestant. Stikker is also known to have called the federalists 'federasts'.[77]

He was however a pragmatist, who recognised that Dutch interests could not be well served by being openly against European integration. British lack of commitment played an important role. The devaluation of sterling on 18 September 1949, the decision for which was taken without consulting fellow OEEC members, led to criticism of the British attitude towards European co-operation. The British Embassy simply informed the Dutch Ministry of Foreign Affairs the day before (a Saturday), that the devaluation would take effect the next day, adding that 'they much regretted the shortness of notice which they had been able to give the Netherlands Government'. The Dutch simply followed suit on 20 September.[78] The British devaluation led to fierce criticism in the Dutch press about Britain's commitment to Europe: 'By her unilateral action, [Britain] has flouted the idea of European economic co-operation and has given evidence of her intention to withdraw from Continental affairs in favour of an Anglo-American block [...]'[79]

'But as British hesitation and reluctance about joining Europe grew, so did continued enthusiasm for unity,' wrote Stikker.[80] The combination of British reluctance and a recognition of the use of European co-operation as a vehicle to press for German involvement began to influence Dutch thinking on Europe. The Dutch also had clear misgivings about having to negotiate directly with a strong German government over their economic claims, preferring to operate through the OEEC. Hence their insistence on early German participation in the organisation, as well as the European Payments Union and the Council of Europe. Stikker wrote:

> It was very important for us to ensure that these discriminatory measures (i.e. the Allies') would not be handled by a future German

government. This was one of the reasons which made Germany's joining the OEEC in 1949 so important to us.[81]

Conclusion

The Dutch policy towards European integration was based on trying to counter French and future German influence by pushing for British participation. As they slowly realised that Britain was unlikely to take the lead, or even involve itself substantively in European integration, they had little option but to co-operate with non-Calvinists, albeit grudgingly and with a certain amount of conceptual bickering between Atlanticists and 'Federasts'. The Dutch were generally co-operative within the OEEC, and pressed for German participation. They clearly hoped for a Germany strong enough to be a counterweight to France in continental Europe. Their insistence on German participation in European co-operation was complicated by their doggedness in sticking to unrealistic territorial claims, and tempered by the fact that one important motive for their wanting German participation in the OEEC, EPU and the Council of Europe was to pursue other claims multilaterally, rather than have to negotiate directly with a strong West German government. The Dutch were having to learn how best to combine altruism with realism. This problematic combination was to manifest itself strongly in the security question.

3

THE QUESTION OF SECURITY AND THE BRUSSELS TREATY ORGANISATION

Introduction

On 17 March 1948, the Dutch signed, for the first time in over one hundred years, a treaty committing them to a military alliance, intended ostensibly to protect the signatories from a renewed threat of German aggression. In the event of aggression, signatory states would be obliged to provide military assistance to the state under attack. On the face of it, the simple answer was that the Dutch feared both German aggression and Soviet expansionism, and therefore had no option but to break away from their old policy of non-involvement. A close examination of events, however, reveals that things were not so simple.

Until the German invasion, the Dutch had successfully kept out of Europe's wars for over one hundred years. They had watched the rivalries between France, Prussia/Germany, Britain, Russia and Austria-Hungary, which had culminated in the First World War, which they managed to keep out of. They had accepted Great Britain's protection of their main trading routes, so important to their economic well being. They had been able to run their overseas empire without any real problems. For all their occasional fear of German ambitions, the latter was their most important trading partner.

Until 1940, as has been seen, the Dutch had virtually withdrawn from the world scene, hardly pursuing a foreign policy at all, 'except to abstain from any possible commitment.'[1] Following the war, the logical assumption might have been that the Netherlands would immediately push for membership of an alliance to protect itself from any future German threat. The situation however was, first, far too confused in the immediate postwar years: Germany was impotent, creating a political and economic vacuum in Europe. The Big Powers were trying to come to an agreement on the future, and slowly drawing apart, as the countries of Eastern Europe came under Soviet influence. Secondly, it was difficult for the Netherlands to suddenly change its philosophy, based as it was on justice, religion and non-involvement, at the wave of a magic wand.

Certainly, van Kleffens, the Foreign Minister, had said in 1943, that the pre-war policy of aloofness was stone dead, and had advocated the idea of a future formation in the West with America, Canada and other British dominions.[2] Yet by the end of the war, the old school of thought seemed to be in the ascendant again, aided, perhaps, by the relative confusion of the beginnings of the Cold War. In any case, old habits die hard and, idealistic as always, some Dutchmen believed that the League of Nations could be revived after the war. Although that idea proved a non-starter, the Dutch pressed hard at Dumbarton Oaks for a system that would guarantee world peace,[3] and obviate the need for any 'regional arrangements'. It was with strong Dutch support, therefore, that Chapter One of the United Nations Charter contained the phrase (after the phrase 'to maintain international peace and security'): 'in conformity with the principles of justice and international law'. Indeed, the Dutch went further, suggesting the setting up of a panel of 'eminences grises', to pronounce on decisions of the Security Council when an appeal was addressed to them,[4] an imaginative but impractical idea which was not accepted. Although unhappy with the Charter, which in their eyes tended to discriminate against the small and middle powers, and allowed members of the Security Council the right of veto in a wide range of matters, the Dutch signed it, realising that it was better than nothing. Nevertheless, signing it did not prevent criticism: at the Paris Peace Conference in 1946, the head of the Dutch delegation, Baron van Boetzelaer van Oosterhout, said: 'the way in which the great powers have secured a privileged position in the United Nations does not augur well for the future development of that institution.'[5]

Despite Dutch attachment to international law, the United Nations system did not prove to be sufficiently strong to allow the Dutch to return to their pre-war stance of non-involvement. The period up to their signing the Brussels Pact in March 1948 was one of limbo. The attachment to morals and law was ever prevalent, as it still is, but was no longer sufficiently embedded to permit aloofness. The bitter experience of the war had taught the Dutch that morals and law were no longer a sufficient guarantee of Dutch security. The political and economic constellation of Europe had changed too much. The Dutch depended for their security on the United

States and Britain. During the period from the end of the war until the signing of the Brussels treaty, the main Dutch foreign policy preoccupations were Indonesia and the German question. In the unstable international state of affairs that prevailed at the time, the Dutch pursued them with vigour. Even though the Dutch were not key players on the emerging world stage, they pushed hard, as will be seen, to be involved in the Big Power talks. The Indonesian problem, however, detracted from their efforts in that direction. As long as this problem remained, Dutch military thinking centred on Indonesia.

The Indonesian Thorn

Even before the 'Police Action' which followed the breakdown of the Renville Agreements (see Chapter 1), American policy was changing: on 31 December 1947, the Acting Secretary of State wrote to the new American consul-general in Batavia, Livengoode, heralding a change in American policy. While pointing out, on the one hand, that the political consequences of failure by the Dutch government over Indonesia would be prejudicial to the American position in Western Europe, he ended up by advocating a solution 'providing NL sovereignty for limited period and setting date in future for independence in Indonesia.'[6]

The Renville Agreement was not destined to last beyond the end of the year. The Dutch resented the United Nations' and American pressure to negotiate with people whom they considered beyond the pale. In April 1948, the American consul-general wrote to the Secretary of State that the Dutch were accusing the Republicans of infringing the truce by infiltrating soldiers into Dutch-held areas, to conduct sabotage and propaganda.[7] In another telegram, he warned of impending chaos and the growing strength of the communists, saying that the Indonesians simply did not believe in the idea of a union between the Netherlands and the United States of Indonesia.[8] The union would, the Indonesians felt, leave a large share of political control in Dutch hands.

The situation went from bad to worse. In September, Muso (described by the State Department as an Indonesian recently returned from Moscow) launched a communist insurrection, seizing control of the city of Madiun, in central Java.[9] Hatta, the Indonesian (Republican) Prime Minister, crushed the uprising, thereby gaining more support from the Americans.

The Dutch then took the unprecedented step of sending the Foreign Minister, Stikker, to Indonesia, to meet Hatta. Matters were confused in the Netherlands and Stikker appears to have admitted as much: Livengoode wrote: 'Stikker said off record there were divisions within his own government. Admitted Catholic rightist elements thought only military action would suffice while labour opposed military action in any circumstances.'[10] Stikker's visit seems to have temporarily defused the situation. The American Ambassador to The Hague, Baruch, wrote that the Socialist Prime Minister, Drees, esteemed Stikker highly, although they were of a different political complexion. His visit, Drees told Baruch, had done much to clear the atmosphere. His government could not, on the other hand, 'consent to discussion while whole battalions armed and commanded by Republicans were daily crossing the demarcation line and murdering Dutch and Indonesians in Dutch held territory.'[11] Livengoode reported that Stikker had said, following his meeting with Hatta on 5 and 6 November, that there were 'some possibilities' and that the outlook was promising.[12]

However, the outlook was not promising, and the Americans were getting more agitated. The Acting Secretary of State sent Livengoode a telegram on 5 November which spoke for itself: 'Should events Indonesia foreshadow large scale disorder it more than possible disposition would arise not only suspend further allocations Indonesia but even question end gains to be made by allocations Netherlands present scale.'[13] Another telegram referred to the inevitability of an early breakdown in negotiations should the Netherlands maintain its position. It continued by saying that the Netherlands would receive unfavourable publicity in the United States, which might have an effect on ERP allocations.[14] Clearly, the pressure was being piled on.

The Dutch, however, did not give in, and matters reached a climax. On 2 December, Livengoode reported to the Secretary of State that he had told Stikker that his government would 'hit the ceiling', if there were any threat of a 'police action'.[15] Positions suddenly hardened: the US representative on the Committee of Good Offices of the United Nations had submitted a draft agreement on which the Netherlands and Republican government had been negotiating. In early December, the Dutch minister for Overseas Territories suddenly broke off the negotiations and returned to The Hague. This led to the Americans handing the Dutch an aidememoire, on 7 December, expressing concern about the move which, they felt, would weaken Hatta.[16] The Netherlands Government were incensed enough to demand the withdrawal of the aide memoire, a demand with which the Americans complied.[17]

Matters quickly came to a head. Hatta sent Stikker a telegram on 14 December referring to 'important concessions',[18] but it was too late. Indonesian infringements continued, and on 18 December the 'Police Action' began. Sukarno, Hatta and a number of other republican leaders were taken into custody, and the Dutch took Djodjakarta. The Americans expressed the nature of their worries in a telegram on 23 December from the Acting Secretary of State to the Acting representative at the United Nations:

> Dutch action in Indonesia appears to us as direct encouragement to spread of Communism in Southern Asia [...] jeopardy thereby presented to US co-operation Western Europe on such matters as ERP and Atlantic Pact, or on UN system for maintenance peace. We have no desire to condone or wink at Dutch action Indonesia.[19]

The Security Council called for a cease-fire, but not for a withdrawal of Dutch troops. The Dutch, having achieved at least their immediate military aim, terminated their 'action' on 31 December, at midnight. The Americans, for their part, suspended ECA aid to the Netherlands. The effect, however, was negligible, since most of the $72 million allocated had already been spent. Politically, however, the move was important, and the arms embargo that followed, (to be discussed later), even more so. Moreover, the threat of a cutting off of economic aid, or indeed simply a cutback, must have worried the Dutch, geared as they were to the Marshall Plan. The Americans were, at any rate, well aware of their politico-economic clout. Dulles wrote:

> [...] the Netherlands was in such serious economic straits, and so dependent upon the Marshall Plan aid which began to flow from the United States in 1948, that a cutting off of this aid pursuant to Security Council action would have dealt it a serious blow.[20]

The Indonesian problem was, alongside frustrations on the German question, the most contentious issue between Britain and the Netherlands. The British Ambassador wrote in early 1948:

> For Dutch relations with the world in general, and with the United Kingdom in particular, it was most unfortunate that the principal point at issue was Indonesia [...] They [...] disagree profoundly with British policy in India, Burma and Malaysia [...].[21]

Dutch feeling on the Indonesian question cannot be understated. It led to considerable press criticisms which the Ambassador saw fit to pass to the Foreign Office. The *Volkskrant* published an article on 31 December

1947, headed 'Proud Albion Became Humble in 1947', of which it is worth reproducing some extracts.

> It began in February. Trains got stuck in the snow, industries were closed owing to lack of coal. Millions of sheep froze [...] In spite of all this, the fuel crisis, which had stopped Britain's rusty machines, failed to awaken the government from its dreams [...]

Significantly, the article then referred to one hundred thousand people dying in the Indo-Pakistani war. It ended with the words '1947 has shown that Britain has become a second rate power.'[22]

The Indonesian problem is sometimes overlooked, or only mentioned en passant, when looking at the history of the postwar Netherlands in Europe. The problem nevertheless clouded relations with Britain and the United States; it also detracted for a while from European problems being seen as the Netherlands' main foreign policy priority. As regards military security, the Dutch virtually ignored pressure from Britain and the United States to build up their forces in the Netherlands, preferring to concentrate them in Indonesia. In a sense, Indonesia was the ideal – and understandable – excuse for the Dutch not to take European security too seriously. It was the Americans, with their increasing emphasis on Europe, and the pressure they exerted on the Netherlands, who helped to bring matters to a head.

The Path to the Brussels Treaty

As has been pointed out, the Netherlands' other main foreign policy priority was Germany. It would, however, be more accurate to say that the main question was its trade with Germany. As has been shown, the Dutch felt left out of decisions that affected their vital commercial interests. The territorial claims were but the tip of the iceberg. The Dutch were keen, unlike the French, to see an economically strong Germany, with whom they could restore their trade to the high pre-war levels. Apart from that, there were the questions of mining concessions and transit trade. While the Dutch sat on the sidelines, along with their Benelux neighbours, they were unable to achieve a great deal. The only way they could protect their interests was to gain entry to the Big Power talks.

Having been rebuffed in November 1947 in their efforts to gain entry to the talks, the Dutch, together with Belgium and Luxembourg, kept up the pressure. The catalyst for the breakthrough was provided by the failure of the London conference in December: the Soviet Union did not return (see

Chapter 2). The conditions for the Dutch and their partners to gain entry were now riper than before. First, the departure of the Soviets had created a vacuum: whereas before, the talks had involved the two most powerful countries in the world, they were now merely Western, and solidarity was important. Second, in January, the Benelux Economic Union passed from the planning to the practical stage – intra-Benelux trade was freed from import and export duties.[23] Third, the Americans already entertained a certain respect for the Union, feeling that it served as a good example of European economic co-operation (see Chapter 2). Fourth, the Americans were in any case looking on Europe as their main overseas priority. Fifth, the Dutch had obviously relieved the Americans over Indonesia by signing the Renville Agreement, whatever chaos resulted before the final resolution of the problem. Given American worries about Indonesia falling to the communists as a result of increased military action, admitting Benelux to the talks would clearly serve as a useful gesture.

How worried were the Dutch about their military security in 1947 and 1948? In the Indonesian context, they obviously were, with the bulk of their armed forces there. In the Netherlands themselves, however, there does not appear to have been any real concern, even after the spate of takeovers in Eastern Europe. It was more important to have the troops thousands of miles away. The Netherlands, until they signed the Brussels Treaty in March 1948, were still neutral, de facto, if not de jure. The deep tradition of non-involvement was still there, whatever wartime statements some members of the Dutch cabinet might have made.

The continuing intractability of the German problem, linked as it was to hardening attitudes between the United States and the Soviet Union, was frustrating to the Dutch who, at the beginning of 1948, had still not gained entry to the talks on Germany. Conditions for the Western democracies taking matters into their own hands were ripening. F C Spits, Chairman of the Dutch Council of the European Movement, writing in 1954, said: 'The Treaty of Brussels came to fruition under the influence of events in East Europe, where in the course of 1947, the independence of Poland, Hungary, Bulgaria and Rumania was destroyed by a rash of Communist coups d'état.'[24] Joseph Luns, Dutch Minister of Foreign Affairs, wrote in 1964:

> The Brussels Treaty came about in the extreme crisis of 1948, when the free peoples of Western Europe suddenly realised that the defeat of national socialism and fascism had not brought an end to the

THE QUESTION OF SECURITY 61

threat to peace and freedom, but that the threat came from the other side.[25]

In January 1990, he confirmed this, saying that Czechoslovakia was a strong factor in the Dutch joining the Brussels Treaty Organisation.[26] Willem Drees' sons also confirmed that he considered the Czech coup 'final proof of the bad face of Stalin'.[27] By the time of the coup in Prague, the situation was certainly ripe enough for the West to start thinking about their own security. Yet, according to Cees Wiebes and Bert Zeeman, the Central Intelligence Agency wrote after the coup: 'The Communist coup in Czechoslovakia does not reflect any sudden increase in Soviet capability.'[28] The Belgian Foreign Minister, Spaak's, comment was: 'Benes has lost the last deal of a game already decided due to concessions to the Communists.'[29]

Wiebes and Zeeman say that between 1942 and 1948, fear of Moscow was not a dominant factor.[30] In the Cabinet, the Dutch Prime Minister said on 26 February 1948 (the day after the Czech coup) that a Soviet trade delegation was in the Netherlands (adding that there were still 'many Dutch' in the Soviet Union).[31] The very fact that a Soviet trade delegation was there, following the various 'troubles' in the East European countries, hardly suggests great fear of Soviet military domination. It speaks volumes, however, for the Dutch commercial instinct and tradition. Moreover, Belgium actually signed a trade treaty with the Soviet Union in early 1948.[32] Fear of a military threat does not seem to have been an over-riding factor. The Prime Minister, Drees, told the Cabinet on 8 March, that he expected the coup in Czechoslovakia would weaken the communists in the forthcoming Dutch elections.[33] Consideration of the problem seems to have centred more on ideology than on anything else, particularly understandable in the Dutch context. Back in October 1946, van Boetzelaer had set the tone when he told the Cabinet: 'Russia probably wants no war [...]'. Significantly, however, he then alluded to the Soviet Union's political offensive.[34] The Dutch still hoped that the United Nations system of worldwide security would work, and obviate the need for regional military alliances, whatever their distaste for the ideology of the Soviet Union. It is not accurate, therefore, to say that the Dutch motive in signing the Brussels Treaty was fear of a military threat from the Soviet Union, at least certainly not the only motive, and certainly not in 1947 and early 1948. Moreover, the presence of American troops in Germany made the Dutch feel far less vulnerable than they would otherwise have felt.

Was it fear of Germany that led the Netherlands to sign the treaty? The hard evidence suggests otherwise. There was clearly no military threat for the foreseeable future. The Netherlands were actually particularly worried that the Brussels Treaty would be directed against Germany, and as such simply be an expansion of the Anglo-French Treaty of Dunkirk, intended to put paid to any threat of German aggression for 50 years (signed on 4 March 1947). The Netherlands, together with their Benelux partners, sent a joint note to Britain and France, suggesting that the 'Dunkirk method', based on mutual assistance in the case of armed aggression by Germany, was not a good base.[35] Van Boetzelaer van Oosterhout actually told the Cabinet, just after the talks on the treaty had begun, that West Germany would 'in the long run' have to be included in the treaty.[36] The Dutch were, of course, keen to see a strong German economy as soon as possible, and felt that an alliance ostensibly directed against German aggression was incompatible with the good trading relations which they sought. The Dutch, then, feared a weakened Germany. They were also frustrated at seeing decisions on Germany being formulated without their participation. As has been seen, the Dutch were keen to involve Germany in European co-operation and eventually to tie Germany in to some kind of collective security system that would detract from any further individual aggressive tendencies. Although the Dutch in the end accepted the reference to Germany in the treaty, they ensured that there was a framework for economic, social and cultural co-operation.

If anything, the Dutch were worried about the French, whom they did not consider particularly reliable (see Chapter 2); their strong moral distaste for communism influenced their thinking, since the communists were strong in France: on 18 November 1947, for example, van Boetzelaer van Oosterhout alluded at a cabinet meeting to the fact that the Communists were the largest party in France.[37] Yet more pertinently, Marshall told Bevin (on the former's farewell visit) on 17 December that both the Netherlands and Belgium were nervous of the French.[38] He was referring to their worries in the context of the Anglo-French military talks, which preceded the initiative on the Brussels Treaty.

The Brussels Treaty – a way of being heard?

Why, then, did the Dutch break away from their aloofness and sign the Brussels Treaty? Fear of the Soviet Union is not a sufficient explanation. A close examination of the events leading up to the agreement provides some clues, especially when seen in the context of the Netherlands' main European foreign policy aim – to have a say on the German question.

Following the failure of the London Four Power Conference in December 1947, Benelux again asked to be included in the talks on Germany.[39] In the meantime, the talks on Marshall Aid were going well.[40] At the end of January 1948, the French proposed a customs union of France, Italy and Benelux – the so-called FRITALUX.[41] (See Chapter 2) But the Dutch fears of French domination helped to put paid to the idea.[42]

Then came the catalyst – Bevin's speech on 22 January, in which he proposed a form of Western Union. On 26 January, van Boetzelaer van Oosterhout told the Dutch cabinet that France and Britain had approached Benelux (on 20 January), with a view to enlarging the Treaty of Dunkirk, and that the latter (i.e. Benelux) had responded, saying that they would study the proposal. Interestingly, at the same meeting, the Defence Minister, Fiévez, said that he had been to Belgium two days previously to discuss defence co-operation – Belgium and the Netherlands had decided to set up commissions to study joint procurement and joint research. The discussions were to lead to the signing of a secret treaty on 10 May.[43] According to Voorhoeve, the treaty 'never achieved much significance'. However, the political significance of any kind of formal military co-operation, beginning at the same time as Bevin's speech, and being formalised after the Netherlands had signed the Brussels Treaty, should not be played down. In its own way, it represented the first step towards breaking out of the policy of neutrality. Secret military co-operation, between two states, even if not directed against any country or countries in particular, has a practical and political significance. When Fiévez was discussing the co-operation with his Belgian counterpart, the Franco-British approach was also discussed.[44] The linkage is manifest.

Benelux met on 29–31 January, and came out in favour of Bevin's idea (there is some doubt as to whose idea it was – see Chapter 4), to the extent that Luxembourg set the wheels in motion to change its constitution, and delete the clause on neutrality.[45]

Although the Brussels Treaty was to be signed only six weeks later, the Dutch were in a hurry, and concerned at the relaxed British attitude. On 9 February, van Boetzelaer van Oosterhout told the Cabinet that at a meeting with the United Kingdom, Belgium and Luxembourg, the British had not yet prepared a draft treaty. The Prime Minister said that it was disappointing that the British had still not prepared anything.[46] At this point, the linkage with Dutch preoccupations on not having a say on the German question began to show itself clearly: at the same Cabinet meeting, the Justice Minister, van Marseveen, suggested that the British were trying to get the Dutch to take a specific position, to make it easier for them to accept Dutch pressure to be involved in the discussions on Germany. Van Boetzelaer van Oosterhout then said that the British would issue an invitation to Benelux on 19 February, to take part in economic discussions on Germany 'at ambassadorial level'.[47]

By 16 February, when the future treaty was again being discussed in the Cabinet, the Dutch were still not certain of being invited to take part in the discussions on Germany: van Boetzelaer van Oosterhout had been told by the Dutch Ambassador in London that an invitation to take part in the discussions was not yet a certainty. It seemed as if the British were 'stringing the Dutch along'. The Dutch were, of course, invited, along with their Benelux partners. The United States helped, by issuing a State Department release on 20 February, in which they 'hoped the Benelux countries would be afforded an opportunity to present their views'.[48]

There is, therefore, some evidence of linkage between the Dutch attempts to have a say on Germany and their signing the Brussels Pact. When the Big Three met in London at the end of February, simultaneous negotiations on the Brussels Pact were underway. Stikker wrote: '[...] so Benelux took advantage to press for participation in the discussions.'[49] Wiebes and Zeeman also say that the Brussels Treaty negotiations were a way for the Netherlands to have a say on Germany.[50] Thus, the Pact served as a vehicle for the Dutch to have more weight in the talks on Germany, so important to them in view of their economic grievances. Jan Hoffenaar, a Dutch Army historian, is of the opinion that influence in Europe and support on the Indonesian questions were important factors in Dutch deliberations in signing the Brussels Treaty.[51]

As mentioned, the Dutch failed to have the references to Germany deleted. They also had misgivings about getting involved in Britain's and France's wider conflicts, as the Prime Minister, Drees, pointed out to the Cabinet on 8 March. The Defence Minister, however, said that even if that were to be the case, the Netherlands would not be in a position to help.[52] French fear of Germany was still strong, while even Bevin, although by now becoming increasingly anti-Soviet, had said only a year previously that Germany was a greater danger to peace than the Soviet Union.[53]

The full significance of the important change in foreign policy which signing the Pact portended, was not really brought home to the Dutch at the time, since they were involved in more pressing concerns, such as the Indonesian problem and the OEEC talks in Paris. It was more Dutch distaste for totalitarian atheist communism and a need to protect its economic interests regarding Germany, that led to participation, rather than fear of Soviet aggression alone. Marshall Aid was of course another factor.

Dutch acceptance of Marshall Aid would have appeared inconsistent if the Dutch were to continue to remain aloof. Friendship towards America was a priority.

'The realities of the situation only became apparent to the Dutch on the signing of the Brussels Treaty and have indeed yet to be apprehended by the majority of the population [...] Public opinion took the event quietly,' wrote the British Ambassador at the time.[54] The British Military Attaché wrote that the signing of the Pact lifted morale in the army, but added later on that the Indonesian issue had remained uppermost in the minds of the majority of people.[55]

The Dutch were not prepared immediately to pour resources into defence, despite their membership of the Pact. The next few years were to be characterised by prodding from the British and Americans to increase military expenditure. The British ambassador wrote:

> Their traditional neutrality makes it hard for them to take expeditiously the planning decisions necessary to enable them to carry out their obligations under the Brussels Pact, and they are faced with the serious problem of harmonising their new commitments in the West with their existing commitments in Indonesia.[56]

Conclusion

The Dutch liked the idea of some form of Western co-operation, particularly where the British (to counter French influence) and, if possible, the Americans, were involved. They were not in favour of a purely military alliance, particularly when directed against a particular country, but had to swallow their objections. Their hostility to communism was a factor in their signing the Pact, but did not reflect any real fear of a Soviet invasion. The Prague coup certainly gave an impulse to the negotiations over the Pact, but did not lead to a belief that the Soviets were planning to invade Western Europe. The main Dutch preoccupation centred on future economic relations with Germany, which, along with their traditional distaste for military alliances, explain why they did not want Germany mentioned in the Pact. The Dutch did not regard the Pact as an essentially military expedient, but signed it to gain more access to decision-making on Germany. Events occurred very quickly: only two months after having received the invitation, the Dutch had signed the Pact. Dutch worries over Indonesia and Germany had detracted to some extent from traditional Dutch aloofness. Yet in signing the treaty, they had gained a place at the

Big Power Conference table. Once there, the Dutch committed themselves, hoping at the same time to wield more influence.

Yet although the Dutch signed the Brussels Treaty, Dirk Stikker's speech at the signing ceremony on 17 March sheds a revealing light on the Dutch kind of neutrality, based more on independence than on pure legal neutrality.

> The signature of the regional treaty concerning Western Europe marks a very important fact in the history of the Kingdom of the Netherlands. In the nineteenth century, the Netherlands followed a "policy of neutrality", or rather, since it did not involve a permanent policy of neutrality, guaranteed by the Large Powers, a policy of independence. This policy of independence was, in principle, abandoned when the Netherlands joined the League of Nations and by participation in the United Nations Organisation [...] The Western Europe Union Pact [...] puts a definite end to the possibility of remaining neutral, when one of the five partners has been the victim of aggression in Europe.[57]

Van der Harst wrote:

> However, although it is formally true that within the Western Union, Holland [sic] had given up its neutrality, in practice the membership of the new organisation meant absolutely nothing. In the first three years after the signing of the Brussels Treaty, that is from March 1948 – March 1951, the Dutch refused to build up their defence strength in Western Europe.[58]

This interpretation should be slightly tempered: a refusal to build up military strength did not necessarily imply that the new organisation meant absolutely nothing. For a country that attached supreme importance to international law, it meant a great deal, even if the significance of the treaty was not immediately brought home to the Dutch population at large. Its significance lay more in Dutch efforts to gain more influence; as such it served as a platform.

4

THE NORTH ATLANTIC ROAD

Introduction

The Brussels Treaty, notwithstanding its social and economic provisions, was essentially a regional military alliance, and as such marked the end of the Dutch policy of neutrality. Its main significance lay in the fact that it was both the kernel and the stepping-stone of the North Atlantic Treaty, which, many would argue, represented the irrevocable split between East and West. As such, the Brussels Treaty was merely a necessary staging post. With the benefit of hindsight, even before the signing of the Brussels Treaty, the final split can be seen.

Bevin played an important role in galvanising the West into taking action. As Raymond Smith shows, senior Foreign Office officials advised him to take an overtly anti-communist stance. On 18 March 1946, for example, Christopher Warner, an Under Secretary, had proposed thinking about 'defensive and counter-offensive measures' to minimise the Russian attack.[1] The Permanent Under Secretary, Sargent, shared a similar outlook. The setting up of the Russia Committee, spearheaded by the Foreign Office, added impetus to the Cold War, at least from the British side. Although Bevin was later to fall in with the British propaganda campaign, he had his initial doubts, but was persuaded to adopt a firmer line, aided, no doubt, by the rash of communist takeovers in Eastern Europe as much as by the need to counter the Soviet propaganda machine. Following a Joint Intelligence Committee Analysis on Soviet intentions in the Middle East, Bevin approved a campaign to counter Soviet propaganda in the Middle East.[2] The establishment of Information Research Department at the Foreign Office at the end of 1947 (see Chapter 5) saw the beginning of a well coordinated information campaign.

In January 1948, Bevin said that there was no prospect 'in the immediate future' of re-establishing and maintaining relations between the countries either side of the Soviet line. It would only be possible to stem the further encroachment of the Soviet tide, he said, by organising and consolidating the ethical and spiritual forces of Western civilisation. This could only be done by creating some form of union in Western Europe, whether of a formal or informal character, backed by the Americans and the Dominions. He went on to say that in the face of Soviet policy, half measures were useless. These views were conveyed to the French and Americans.[3] In the meantime, the British and French, at British instigation,[4] had approached Benelux about extending the Treaty of Dunkirk. Bevin's speech in the House of Commons followed on 22 January (see previous chapter), being followed in turn by the entry of Benelux into talks with Britain and France, on the Brussels Treaty, and with those countries and the United States, on the German problem.

Although Henderson attributes the initiative to extend the Treaty of Dunkirk to the British, it is difficult to say whether the French or British started suggesting the idea first: Bogaarts, for example, writes that at the beginning of 1947, the French suggested extending the Treaty to Belgium and the Netherlands.[5] He describes the move as a European step. On the other hand, before the Treaty had been signed, Sargent of the FO commented: 'Why should we not have a treaty with Belgium on the same lines as the one we propose to negotiate with France?'[6] Whoever first had the idea, matters had clarified by early 1948, with the Prague coup snuffing out any remaining Benelux dithering.

The idea of a North Atlantic Treaty was of course already there; Bevin was particularly keen for the Americans to be involved at an early stage, but had no alternative, in view of American hesitation, (compounded by bickering within the State Department),[7] but to 'concentrate on the European end of the system, taking upon trust the ultimate support of the US.'[8] Significantly, before the signing of the Brussels Treaty on 17 March, the Americans bowed to Bevin's request for talks between the United States, Britain and Canada.[9] (The former had also received a 'hysterical message' from the French Foreign Minister, Bidault, urging immediate consultations.)[10] The Czech coup had obviously had some effect on the West, but worry about Soviet pressure on Finland and Norway had also triggered unease. Although the (secret) tripartite talks were not to begin until 22 March, after the signing of the Brussels Treaty, the idea of a North Atlantic Pact as a bulwark against Soviet aggression, whether that aggression was conceived as spiritual, material, just plain ideological, or all three, was snowballing.

The Soviet Union grew increasingly annoyed, and some of the correspondence is revealing. Panyushkin, the Soviet Ambassador to Washington, wrote to Marshall on 6 March:

> It is not difficult to discern that this British plan is closely connected with the 'Marshall Plan', complementary to and disclosing the political aims of the American Plan in respect of Europe. Both the American plans of economic 'aid' and the British political plan of 'Western Union' set up a Western Europe as against an Eastern Europe and, consequently, lead to a political cleavage of Europe.[11]

The Soviet Union naturally played its full part in the political cleavage; whatever the rights and wrongs of the various economic measures and counter-measures that took place (such as the later monetary measures taken in West, and then East, Germany), the Berlin Blockade, that began after the talks on a North Atlantic Treaty had begun, was hardly a gesture likely to soften the attitude of Bevin and the West as a whole. The Dutch were no exception; van Kleffens, the Dutch representative at the exploratory talks, said on 6 July 1948 that before discussing the cure, the evil should first be discussed. Russia had, he said, always shown expansionist tendencies. 'Like a gas, it filled every cranny it could [...] the threat was both military and ideological [...].'[12]

Panyushkin's memorandum also showed Soviet anger at the 'secret meetings' in London on the German question:

> [...] between the representatives of the United States, Great Britain and France, designed to by-pass the Council of Foreign Ministers, in which the Soviet Union would also have participated, bearing testimony to the fact that the governments of the three powers did not baulk at complete disregard of obligations undertaken of [sic] them.

The memorandum continued:

> The fact that the representatives of only a small group of states were involved in this conference while a majority of the states which suffered most from German aggression were left outside this conference testifies to the fact that the London conference was pursuing the goal of a narrow group of creators of the Western block, which is placed vis-à-vis all the rest of the states of Europe.[13]

This statement suggests that the Soviet Union was on the face of things unaware that Benelux was now involved in the talks on Germany and that, as Stikker wrote, the Four Power Conference had become a Six Power Conference.[14] The road to NATO was characterised, then, by some strong and sometimes emotive statements by leading British, Dutch and Soviet leaders. Fear of Communism and therefore of the Soviet Union, although possibly exaggerated, cannot be discounted, particularly when one considers the effect of the coups in Eastern Europe. The Brussels Treaty Organisation was certainly a stepping-stone, created a priori with a North Atlantic system in mind. What, however, of the specific motives of the Dutch?

Lip Service – The Dutch Position on NATO?

Whatever rhetoric the Dutch used to express their distaste for communism, it was Germany that lay at the heart of their concerns in Europe; although this has already been pointed out above, it is worth stressing that concern once again. On 19 February, the American Ambassador in Paris wrote to his Secretary of State, that the three governments (Benelux) could not conceive of a regional organisation of Western Europe without their taking part in and working out the policies to be followed and the measures to be taken with respect to Germany.[15] Clearly, once the Dutch had gained access to those talks, it was obvious that they would have to cooperate within a future North Atlantic framework. They needed to appear credible. To this extent they had to pay at least lip service during the talks that led to the signing of the North Atlantic Treaty: they did not, after all, possess the military will to commit their forces, most of which were in Indonesia, to Europe. In that sense, NATO was important to them politically rather than militarily. Their position was also particularly delicate, because of the Indonesian problem, as we shall see later.

Nevertheless, in Dutch army circles, the idea of Atlantic military cooperation seems to have had a morale-boosting effect. The British Military Attaché wrote in early 1949: 'A noticeable change of outlook, which has affected the morale of the Army, resulted from the signing of the Brussels Pact, the birth of the Western Union, and the prospect of an Atlantic Pact.'[16] As will be seen later on, however, considerable tensions were to arise, owing to differences of opinion within the Dutch government as to the degree of military commitment that was considered to be really necessary.

The Dutch motive during the talks that led to the signing of the Treaty was to protect their interests vis-à-vis the German problem, even if they did not make it obvious in their attitude in the negotiations. It was hardly in their interest to rock the boat which they had been so keen on boarding. As we shall see, however, they did not simply sit through the negotiations making noises of assent. A comparison of some primary and secondary sources leads to some interesting conclusions.

Nicholas Henderson wrote his original account of the creation of the North Atlantic Treaty 'in the weeks following the signature.'[17] Although the account was not published until 1982, the fact that he was a member of the Working Party that drafted the Treaty suggests that his book can almost be treated as a 'primary secondary source'. Before looking more closely at the Dutch attitude during the talks, it is important to note that they, the Dutch, were not substantively involved until almost three months after the signing of the Brussels Pact. In the meantime, it was Britain, the United States and Canada that set the pace, during the secret tripartite talks that began at the Pentagon on 22 March. Henderson creates the impression of a cosy Atlantic club: 'Better, therefore, to proceed at the outset just between the two, bringing the Canadians in because of their special strategic position and the intimate relations which existed between her and the US and the UK.'[18] Donald McLean was, says Henderson, one of the British team at the first round of the tripartite talks.[19] It is safe to assume, therefore, that the Soviet Union knew everything. The main British aim was to obtain as much American commitment as possible. The Americans themselves came out with a series of proposals on 24 March, which Henderson described as the 'Pentagon proposals'. They called, inter alia, for an extension of the Brussels Treaty to include Norway, Sweden, Denmark, Iceland and Italy and for the issuing of invitations to a conference to conclude a security pact. The memorandum also declared that, pending the conclusion of a pact, the US Government would regard an attack upon any of the Brussels Treaty Powers as an attack against the USA, to be dealt with by the USA in accordance with Article 51 of the United Nations Charter. Owing to British pressure, the Americans made some amendments to the proposals, such as not putting pressure on the Scandinavian countries to join the Brussels Pact.[20]

By 1 April, the time of the sixth meeting, 'it was generally agreed that a treaty should be accomplished', according to the American records.[21] The records referred to the above-mentioned State Department position paper, known, nevertheless, as the 'Pentagon Paper'. This confirmed that diplomatic approaches would be made by the American government to the signatories of the Brussels Treaty 'in order to secure their approval to its extension [...] and to inform them of plans for the conclusion of a collective defence agreement for the North Atlantic Area [...]'[22]

Pressure on the Americans for greater commitment continued, mainly on the part of the British. Bevin approached the French Foreign Minister, Bidault, and the other Brussels Treaty Powers, who agreed that the British and French should approach the United States.[23] This they did, saying that it was imperative for the USA to take an initiative. Slowly but surely, the Americans began to commit themselves, notwithstanding opposition both in Congress and within the State Department itself. The so-called Vandenberg Resolution, passed by the Senate, was a step forward for the protagonists of a treaty. It also put paid to any hopes the Belgian Prime Minister, Spaak, had of propagating the idea of military co-ordination between the United States and the Brussels Treaty Powers, in place of a fully-fledged North Atlantic Treaty. Wiebes and Zeeman allude to the Belgian Foreign Minister, Spaaks', efforts to retain links between East and West, suggesting that the Dutch were far more in favour of American involvement than the Belgians.[24] The Belgians appear to have been less Atlantic-minded than the Dutch, and they were worried about unduly upsetting the Soviets. In January 1946, the British ambassador to Brussels, Knatchbull-Hugessen, had written to Bevin: 'The Belgian Minister for Foreign Affairs thought it important that any step towards a Western group should be such as to avoid arousing Russian opposition'.[25] Even after the signing of the Brussels Treaty, the Belgians were worried: Spaak told the British Ambassador that he 'had been disturbed by the reports he had received from the Belgian military representatives of the British fighting services towards [sic] the possibility of war.' Although a senior Foreign Office official wrote that the Belgians had 'got hold of the wrong end of the stick',[26] there can be little doubt that the sharper end of the British information campaign, combined with the attitude of some of the more zealous Cold War protagonists, might have been regarded as exaggerated by some Belgians. Henderson writes that Spaak unwittingly played into the hands of those American officials who were 'becoming obsessed with doubts about the wisdom and practicability of the Treaty.'[27] The difference of approach between the Dutch and Belgians helps to explain why, once the full talks began, the Benelux countries opted to have separate delegations, even if the Dutch, despite their anti-communist inclinations, refrained from being too openly anti-Soviet.

At all events, the respective positions of the protagonists were sufficiently harmonised (aided, no doubt, by the beginning of the Berlin blockade at the end of June) for substantive Seven Power talks to begin on 6 July

1948, first under the auspices of the Ambassadors' Committee, which then referred the various issues to the Seven Power Working Party.[28]

The Dutch attitude, says Sir Nicholas, 'was generally speaking, very similar to the British.'[29] Van Kleffens wished for a North Atlantic Pact that would be supplementary to, but not in substitution for, the Brussels Treaty. The American record of the relevant meeting shows that van Kleffens was pretty strong-willed and imaginative in what he said, something that Sir Nicholas does not have time to bring out. Van Kleffens is reported to have said that he:

> [...] could not conceive of the US adhering to the Brussels Pact [...] He did not think the Brussels Pact should be abolished; something else might be devised which would appeal to a greater group and be more widely acceptable. Perhaps comparison could be made with a peach; the Brussels Pact would be the hard kernel in the centre and a North Atlantic Pact the somewhat less hard mass around it.[30]

This stimulated the American representative, Lovett, to say that this was exactly the type of thing which needed discussing, in order to produce as many ideas as possible.[31] It also shows, as Sir Nicholas suggests, that the Americans were not prepared to make the running during the early stages of the talks.

The Dutch profile at the talks was not particularly low, and brought out their attachment to morals and international law as important elements of their foreign policy. Van Kleffens, for example, 'thought that the North Atlantic community was too good to be limited merely to material welfare and military security, in that it rested on a community of certain basic conceptions of the highest order.'[32] He also wanted 'appealing language' used in the preamble of a Treaty, 'like that of the American Declaration of Independence.'[33] Henderson does not bring this out.

The Dutch desire for a bulwark against communism was also brought into relief, sometimes in Cold War language. Van Kleffens had already referred to the evil of communism, 'filling every cranny it could, like a gas.'[34] Van Reuchlin, the Dutch representative on the Working Party, is reported to have said:

> [...] what we do here will perhaps have a direct effect upon the Soviet actions [...] if, for example, the countries concerned in the present talks form a weak association it undoubtedly will have a provoca-

tive effect upon the Russians, whereas a strong pact should have the opposite, or a deterrent, effect upon them.[35]

This explains Dutch concerns about having too many countries involved in a Pact. They felt it would detract from a strong position. Van Kleffens, for example, spoke about:

> The delay which might be involved in consulting other countries. Some of them, for instance Sweden, had a very cumbersome parliamentary procedure, and it would be most unfortunate if the present enthusiasm for the treaty were to be lost through interminable delays in waiting for a few countries.[36]

The Dutch, then, certainly spoke their mind at the talks during both the Ambassadors' committee meetings, and those of the Working Party. It is worth recording Sir Nicholas' description of van Kleffens:

> Van Kleffens was invariably sensitive and sensible. He had no axe to grind either for himself or his government, and he always sought to contribute by clear analysis and timely suggestion to the success of the negotiations. His Government appeared to leave him plenty of discretion. With his angular features and antique manners, it was difficult sometimes not to imagine him dressed in black brocade with white lace cuffs and broad ruff, seated at a table and looking out upon the world with calm curiosity from the chiaroscuro of some seventeenth century Dutch painting.[37]

Although this may have been Henderson's impression of Van Kleffens, it belies the latter's actual role to a certain extent. Henderson is fairly kind in his description of the Belgian representative on the Ambassadorial Committee, describing him as 'an excellent lubricant';[38] he is not so kind about the representative on the Working Party. He says that 'he sat – an inscrutable and impassive watchdog – throughout the negotiations, except for one occasion when he started barking loudly in an attempt to get the Belgian Congo included in the Pact.'[39] Of the Luxembourg representative (who sat on both the Ambassadors' Committee and in the Working Party), Henderson says that he did not allow his presence at the long afternoon meetings to interfere with the regular siesta habit which he had acquired during long residence in the East.[40]

The Working Party produced a report on 24 December 1948, which formed the body of a draft treaty, which in turn served as the basis for the negotiations that led to the signing of the treaty. According to Henderson, the Benelux representatives did not play a large part in the discussions. 'Since all documents were prepared in English,'[41] he says, 'they were not able to contribute much to the drafting'. As shall be seen, however, Henderson's contention that the Benelux representatives – and therefore, the Dutch – did not play a large part is not wholly accurate. There was of course another important factor in the Dutch having to tread very carefully – Indonesia.

The Indonesian Complication

Van Reuchlin, (the Dutch representative on the Working Party) was the 'perfect diplomat of the party [...] formal, friendly and never embarrassed – not even by the Indonesian question, which might in other, more touchy hands have spilled over and complicated the Pact talks.'[42]

The available primary sources certainly suggest that the Indonesian question did not spill over and complicate the official talks in Washington. In other diplomatic and political arenas the question was, however, very much in evidence. The Dutch were caught between trying to protect their interests in Europe (mainly their concern over the German question) and fighting a losing diplomatic battle over Indonesia. They no longer possessed the economic and military power to remain independent and maintain at the same time an enormous chunk of territory with almost 90 million inhabitants, thousands of miles away. Behind the official talks on Western security, there was therefore plenty of activity, since the Dutch needed at one and the same time to preserve their credibility as a solid anti-communist member of the new Western world and come to terms with harsh realities a long way away.

At the same time as the Working Party was drafting the basis of a North Atlantic Treaty, the Americans were coming under pressure from the Indonesians to act against the Dutch. The Acting Head of the Indonesian delegation to the United Nations, Soemitro Djojohadikoesomo, (not of course, recognised by the Dutch) wrote the following to the American acting Secretary of State, on 27 December 1948: 'We feel, however, that only by a complete suspension of all ECA allocations to the Netherlands, the government of that country, having committed an act of aggression, can be brought to order.'[43] Thus, the Netherlands found themselves in the curious position of taking part in negotiations with the Americans for an alliance, while being subjected to the withdrawal of American aid to

Indonesia and now facing the distinct possibility of a suspension of aid to themselves, coupled with an embargo on deliveries of military equipment.

Following continuing hostility in the United Nations, the Dutch representative referred to 'an unprecedented interference in the internal affairs of a state, in violation of the Charter.' He continued in a slightly more moderate vein by saying that if the resolution were adopted (it called, inter alia, for the release of the republican prisoners) the Netherlands would only carry it out to the extent that it was compatible with its responsibility for the maintenance of real freedom and order in Indonesia.[44]

The year 1949 opened with continuing pressure on the Dutch over Indonesia, at the same time as the negotiations for a North Atlantic Treaty were on their last lap. The American Consul General in Batavia wrote to the Secretary of State, Acheson, on 3 January: 'Netherlands defiance of UN has caused real world criticism that threatens future confidence in international organisation of instrument of right and justice.'[45] This world criticism of the Netherlands was particularly worrying to the State Department, which could not afford to be seen to be condoning the Dutch position; the Director of the Office of Far Eastern Affairs in the State Department, Butterworth, wrote to Bohlen, his second in command in the same office on 7 January, expressing concern about the United States' image with the 'Islamic and Asiatic countries.'[46] Indonesia was, of course, (and still is) the world's most populous Islamic state, and that could not have been lost on the Americans.

Even more germane to the Americans' worry about their country's image was the fact that Nehru announced the convening of an Asian conference to discuss Indonesia.[47] The Dutch, however, retreated only slowly. They were still not prepared to negotiate with Sukarno, because of his alleged collaboration with the Japanese, but were willing to recognise another republican, Sjahrir.[48]

At this point, the British began to get uncharacteristically worried. They had, as mentioned earlier, already supported the Netherlands in opposing an invitation to the Indonesian Republican Government to take part in talks at the Security Council. They were concerned at the knock-on effect that American threats to cease arms deliveries to the Netherlands would have on the Indonesian problem and in Malaysia, and for Western solidarity in general. The British Ambassador to Washington wrote the following on 1 February:

> So far as the Dutch are concerned, there is the danger that the Security Council may seek to impose a policy which the Dutch cannot

implement and which may force them into flouting the authority of the Security Council. This may lead to the imposition of sanctions by the Security Council, whereupon the Netherlands might withdraw from the United Nations. Any such development would be bound to weaken the position of the Netherlands in the Western Union itself. In Indonesia it will do no good to undermine the authority of the existing sovereign power at a time when an Indonesian government is in no way ready to take over power.[49]

Reading between the diplomatic lines, it seems clear that the British were urging caution, at least for nicety's sake.

British concern did not then stop; on 16 March, the Foreign and Commonwealth Secretary, Bevin, saw the American ambassador to London, Douglas, and said: '[...] the Western Union organisation should deal with the United States on a basis of oneness [...] it concerns the principle involved in our warning to the Dutch re Indonesia [...] no-one should be singled out for special action.'[50] Even Churchill, then in opposition, appears to have shared Bevin's misgivings. He had telephoned the Permanent Under Secretary at the Foreign Office less than three months previously to express his concern about the 'reckless American policy versus the Dutch', wishing to 'restrain the Americans' excessive ardour'.[51] Matters were again reaching crisis point. Four days earlier, the Dutch, under the so called 'Beel Plan',[52] had issued an invitation to the republicans to talk. The republicans, however, had problems; they felt that the Dutch would retain too much authority and that the proposed government of the United States of Indonesia would consist of Indonesians chosen by the Dutch. As an additional irritant, the main republican leaders were still exiled in Banga. Feelings were clearly running high in many quarters; the Dutch Ambassador to Washington wrote to the Secretary of State, on 18 March, that his government was annoyed at the republicans' insistence on their return to Djogjakarta. He continued:

> If, next Monday, March 21, American influence in the Security Council results in the adoption of a decision which as honest people we cannot accept, knowing that subversive influences will make it impossible to come to terms, Mr Stikker wishes you to know that this may well result in an open rupture between ourselves and the Security Council, and this when the margin is so small, and when it is difficult to see what general or Western interest should prevent adoption of the Canadian compromise. Mr Stikker furthermore

fears that public opinion would then strongly oppose Netherlands participation a few days later, in the conclusion of the Atlantic Pact, however much he and the other members of the Cabinet would desire this participation.[53]

The Foreign Office now expressed its views on the situation more directly. At the first meeting of the European Correlation Committee, held at the American Embassy in London, on 25 March, Bevin is reported to have said that 'the US should not take unilateral action against any WU country when all of the latter have the same obligations towards the UN'.[54] On 27 March – only eight days before the signing of the North Atlantic Treaty, the American ambassador wrote the following to his Secretary of State: 'Disheartening effect US action re arms has further shaken Dutch and may jeopardise WU and Atlantic Pact'. He then referred to concern about American insistence in declaring their 'possible intent' in unilaterally refusing arms assistance to one partner of the Western Union.[55] Following a call on the Secretary of State by Stikker and van Kleffens, on 31 March, the former wrote of Stikker:

> He considered any singling out of the Netherlands with regard to possible military assistance and the placing of the Netherlands on a different footing from the other member of the North Atlantic Alliance as an action which would be incomprehensible to his government and people. He asked for clarification of our position on this point. In reply, I described the Dutch action in Indonesia, relating this action to the European Recovery Programme as well as to the Military Assistance Programme. I frankly stated the reaction to be that the Dutch were wrong and that the Netherlands had been guilty of aggression. I said that this deep-rooted conviction on the part of our people has now led to a situation which gravely jeopardised the continuation of ECA assistance to the Netherlands.[56]

Thus the Americans countered Stikker's veiled threat not to sign the Treaty, with their own threats to withdraw aid. They made clear in no uncertain terms that if the Netherlands continued to defy the United Nations, Congress would cut off Marshall Plan Assistance to the Netherlands themselves.[57] Despite the concerns of the British over Dutch reactions to the pressure, some had nevertheless been fairly critical. The British ambassador to the Hague, for example, wrote:

The Calvinist streak, which is only just below the surface in every Dutchman, gives then a genuine distaste for negotiations with such people as Sukarno and Hatta, the former of whom is to them first and foremost a Quisling and the latter an opportunist [...] the combination of a long tradition of neutrality and pride in their own colonising achievements has given the Dutch a blind spot in international affairs.[58] [...] Despite the obstacles put in their path by the national character, the new Government did nevertheless make a genuine attempt to reach a peaceful settlement.[59]

The Indonesian problem had in fact made necessary general elections in the Netherlands, since the intention of establishing a United States of Indonesia under one crown entailed a constitutional reform that had to be approved by a simple majority in both Chambers of the Dutch Parliament before an election, and by two thirds majorities, following an election.

There has been some debate about how serious Stikker was in his threat not to sign the Atlantic Pact. Although Cees Wiebes and Bert Zeeman, in particular, have addressed the question in some depth,[60] the answer to the question must remain hypothetical. The likelihood that Stikker was simply bluffing is, however, fairly strong. The Dutch Cabinet seems, for example, to have been unaware of such threats: on 21 March, Lovink, the Secretary General of the Foreign Ministry, told the Cabinet that Stikker would leave on 23 March – on the Queen Mary – for New York 'where, on 4 April, the signing of the Pact would take place.'[61] Moreover, on 30 March, the Prime Minister told the Cabinet 'that he regarded the Atlantic Pact as being of great significance.'[62] Stikker was acting on his own.

The Indonesian problem was a complicating factor for the Dutch, who found the threat of arms embargoes and the suspension of aid to Indonesia completely incompatible with a spirit of co-operation. There were legal problems, too: what would the position be if one or more signatories to the North Atlantic Treaty were to accuse the Netherlands of endangering peace and security on its own territory?[63] Theoretically, Article 4 gave the NATO powers the right to move against the Netherlands! Such legal niceties did not however unduly impede the path upon which the Netherlands had embarked. In his speech in Washington on 4 April, the day upon which he signed the treaty, Stikker said:

> The Treaty we are about to sign marks the end of an illusion: the hope that the United Nations would, by itself, ensure international peace. Regretfully, we were driven to the conclusion that the Charter,

though essential, is not enough in the world as it is, to protect those vital principles for which we of the Western World who have gathered here, stand. Therefore we felt it our duty to make this Treaty. So, far from merely marking the end of an illusion it most especially marks the birth of a new hope of enduring peace.[64]

Thus, despite their anger, they signed. It is probably fair to say that they realised full well that Indonesia would have to be granted independence, and that the sooner that the Round Table conference was to get under way, the better. They were not prepared, despite some loss of face, to sacrifice their part in the Alliance for the possibility of a protracted guerrilla war, combined with international criticism.

Even after the signing of the Treaty, the Americans did not ease their pressure. On 13 April, Dulles, then the American delegate to the United Nations General Assembly, told the Italian Minister, Sforza:

We have had to cut off Marshall Plan Assistance to Indonesia and there is very considerable pressure to stop further aid to the Netherlands itself on the ground [sic] that that aid is at least indirectly assisting the Netherlands government in the pursuit of what we consider to be an unjust policy in Indonesia.[65]

Although the Indonesian problem continued, in the form of New Guinea, after Queen Juliana formally transferred sovereignty of the Netherlands East Indies on 27 December 1949, it was thereafter little more than an irritant for the Netherlands' relations with the United States and Britain. Some damage had however been done, and it was to influence the Dutch attitude towards their carrying out the military side of their NATO obligations. On 1 November 1949, the American Ambassador to The Hague, Chapin, wrote to his Secretary of state:

Undoubtedly traditional ties of friendship between Holland and US have been damaged by Indonesian problem. Embassy staff seriously concerned over latest anti-American feeling. This, however, at present remains under cover as Dutch recognise and appreciate large measure of assistance given by US to Western Europe and Holland [sic] The Dutch believe that they have been disregarded and unappreciated at the international bar.[66]

As will be seen, the Dutch were to be pressurised later on by both the British and Americans to 'pull their weight' in NATO, a situation which exists to this day (at least in the case of the British).

The Dutch Atlantic Attitude

Despite the Indonesian problem, the Dutch were able to play a full and serious role at the Washington talks. They expressed strong views about the dangers of communism, stressing at the same time the cultural aspects of the treaty; and they were clearly worried about extending full membership of the treaty to, for example, Greece and Turkey, feeling it better to restrict membership to the seven members represented at the talks, plus one or two others.[67] Importantly, there was a similarity of attitude between the Americans and Dutch, particularly where van Kleffens was concerned. When he spoke of the North Atlantic Community resting on a community of certain basic conceptions of the highest moral order, Hickerson, the American representative on the Ambassador's Committee, said that he 'had put his finger on the kernel of thinking on the working level in the State Department.'[68] Van Kleffens certainly contributed substantively to the talks, pointing out, for example, that:

> Although there was a certain parallel between the basic formula of OEEC and that of the political problems now confronting Western Europe, there was also a difference, inasmuch as it had proved to be relatively easy to get sixteen European countries around the ERP table, but not around the table of the Brussels Pact. He was certain that it was easier for Sweden, for example, to join the OEEC than the Brussels Pact.[69]

Thus, van Kleffens clearly tempered some of his more idealistic statements with incisive judgments, which may very well have influenced the talks. It is worth pointing out, for example, that van Kleffens' words take up about 15 per cent of all words recorded by the Americans at the 5th meeting of the Ambassadors' Committee at the Washington talks.[70] Despite Indonesia, the Dutch did not waver in their policy of wanting to be involved in, and indeed, pushing for, a North Atlantic Alliance. Their main motive was of course Germany. They were rudely awakened by the lack of moral and, to a certain extent, material support, over Indonesia, but did not feel it politic to match Stikker's protests with action. They would have isolated themselves and lost influence on the German question if they had done so. Intellectually, however, they contributed to the talks.

The British ambassador to the Hague wrote in 1949:

> With the advent of Marshall Aid the whole economic structure of Holland is now dependent upon influences over which she has little or no control – Economic Co-operation Administration in Washington, the Allied Control Authorities in Germany, and the Security Council and Good Offices Committee in Indonesia[71] (later called the UN Commission for Indonesia).

It is easy to understand why the Dutch were therefore Atlantic-minded, both from economic necessity (Germany) and to a certain extent, philosophically and historically. As long as Britain, and preferably the United States as well, were involved, they were prepared to co-operate. It is worth recalling Dutch suspicions of French motives in this connection (see Chapter 2), and the fact that to this day, the Dutch parliament boasts a large portrait of Winston Churchill, an Atlanticist par excellence.

The ideological fear of the Soviet Union needs to be mentioned in the Brussels Treaty context, too: during the NATO negotiations, the Western Union Foreign Ministers were of course still meeting. On 21 July 1948, the Secretary General of the Dutch Foreign Ministry and Boon, the head of the Political Section (later to be Secretary General), told the American Ambassador:

> The five Foreign Ministers agreed to exchange and co-ordinate intelligence information, to evaluate Communist activities and work out a common program to combat Communist (and other) subversive activities [...] Practically the whole of the second day [of the two day meeting] was devoted to the East-West conflict and Berlin crisis, with discussions centred on efforts to find satisfactory solution to question concerning two unknown factors; firstly, whether Soviets will embark on war and, secondly to what extent US willing to collaborate with and find means of furnishing Western Union countries with material and moral support.[72]

It is interesting that the Dutch imparted this secret information to the Americans immediately after the conclusion of the two day meeting, and shows again that some Dutch were particularly close to the Americans.

Nevertheless, it must still be pointed out that fear of the Soviet Union was not all pervasive: on 30 March 1949, only four days before the signing of the treaty, the Dutch Prime Minister, Drees, told the Cabinet that he 'considered the Atlantic Pact of great significance and also considered the Russian [sic] danger.' He also pointed out, however, that Russia [sic] was becoming careful, since the spread of its territory or its influence was accompanied by risks. Russia [sic] was, he said more interested in its influence in China.[73] Drees' relatively relaxed attitude to the need to rearm was to annoy the British later, as shall be seen.

Whatever thoughtful comments such as the above may have been made, they did not detract from the overall climate in the Netherlands, which was essentially anti-communist, at least in ideological terms. 'During the first postwar decades,' writes Leurdijk, 'Dutch moralism also found an outlet in an anti-communism comparable in holy fervour to that of John Foster Dulles [...] Dutch purism blended with the anti-totalitarian trauma developed during the years of Nazi occupation.'[74] To this should be added the dislike felt by the Dutch Socialists (and others) for Soviet communism, which they regarded as a perversion of the Socialist doctrine.

Conclusion

The signing of the North Atlantic Treaty marked the beginning of new realities for the Netherlands. However, because the Dutch were still coming to terms with these realities and were still preoccupied with the Indonesian problem, membership of the new club passed with little open debate in the Netherlands. Only the small Communist Party opposed the treaty in Parliament.[75] The British Ambassador wrote: 'The signature was welcomed by the public, but aroused little enthusiasm, and the debate on ratification in the Second Chamber was almost apathetic'.[76]

The hardening of attitudes between East and West that makes up so much of the backcloth to the formation of NATO, might suggest that the Dutch had little option, because of their strategic position, but to go along with the Cold War. At the same time, the evidence suggests that there was no strong and widespread opposition in the Netherlands to membership. The Dutch saw that it would be in their best interests to participate, since it would also provide them with an additional platform from which to influence events, particularly, as we have seen in the case of the Brussels Treaty Organisation, on the German question.

In line with tradition, the Dutch did not see their interests in a purely European alliance, and looked very much to Britain and the United States. This was consistent with their Atlantic traditions, which served as a counterweight to the strength of both French and German influence. As Vlekke wrote:

> Our tradition does not favour close association with our Eastern neighbours, but we have not forgotten that, even in the days of economic prosperity in the old Netherlands Indies, Germany was first in importance among all our trading partners [...] we are always looking for a counterweight in other quarters.[77]

Thus, within new constraints, the Dutch still tried to find counterweights: Britain's participation in the Brussels Pact and British and American participation in the Atlantic Pact represented to the Dutch not only a strengthening of security against the Soviet threat, but ensured the Netherlands' security against French and future German influence. With the impending loss of Indonesia, Dutch interests were bound to focus more on Europe, and membership of a wider alliance therefore suited them.

The Dutch role in the Alliance was clearly important. Without their having agreed to take part in the Brussels Pact, it would have been difficult to have a coherent Alliance at all. One question which is difficult to avoid asking is: did they really have any choice? The answer seems to be that they did, although it would quite clearly have been against their interests to remain aloof for, importantly, they would not have been able to exert pressure on the question of Germany, so crucial to them. Sweden, on the other hand, turned down the idea of membership point blank and even proposed a Scandinavian pact of neutrals. Henderson suggests that this was a 'historic gesture', advanced in the certainty that it would be rejected by Norway, but does not offer any evidence to support his view.[78] Sweden of course, had a more powerful and better equipped army than the Dutch, and could afford to stick to its neutrality. The Dutch were in no such position, and even if they had been, it is unlikely that they would have tried to remain outside the Alliance, although the question is of course hypothetical.

With membership of the Atlantic Alliance and the main Indonesian problem resolved by the end of 1949, the Dutch were focusing on other priorities. The British Ambassador wrote in February 1950:

> The focus of interest now shifts [from Indonesia] to the political and economic problems of Western Europe. I feel pretty sure that for political, strategic and perhaps above all for commercial reasons, Germany is likely to become the main preoccupation of the Dutch during the next year or two [...][79]

The focus did indeed shift to Europe and Germany.

5

FROM THE ATLANTIC TO EUROPE

Introduction

The Netherlands' adherence to the North Atlantic Treaty met with little opposition in the country. A number of factors combined to ensure that independence as an element of Dutch foreign policy was no longer the be all and end all. These were: a need to be involved substantively in solving the German problem and to increase Dutch influence vis-à-vis the Great Powers, in order to re-establish traditionally strong trading links with Germany; a deep dislike of totalitarian ideology, enhanced by the experience of occupation; a strong Atlantic tradition, strengthened by both the wartime experience and by the Foreign Minister, Stikker's, Atlantic preferences; and a lack of confidence in, bordering on suspicion of, France. Independence for independence's sake was no longer a viable option, although it shall be seen that this independence – or neutrality, as some call it – was from time to time to act as a check on British and American pressure to pull Dutch weight in the alliance, particularly on the question of the Netherlands' military contribution and Dutch exports to Eastern Europe.

The Berlin blockade provided symbolic proof that the Cold War was well underway. Dutch concerns shifted increasingly from Indonesia to Germany and Europe. Re-establishment of trade with Germany, the question of German rearmament, the Dutch contribution towards the Alliance's defence needs and European co-operation were the factors that contributed to push the Netherlands more and more onto the international stage. '[...] Holland cannot afford in the future to ignore the implications of world affairs,' wrote the British Ambassador in 1950. 'It is not only Indonesia which has been responsible for this change [...] but [...] a realisation that in the face of communism and the dangers inseparable from a revived Germany [...] Holland willy-nilly, must play her part.' He added (perhaps slightly patronisingly): 'From an international point of view, the Netherlands are growing up.'[1] The implication seemed to be that by joining NATO, the Netherlands were leaving adolescence behind, and that not joining the Alliance would have been childish! It would be more apposite to say that the Netherlands found themselves having to adopt to a new set of foreign policy priorities. The real question now was not whether to involve themselves or not, but to what extent, and how they should become involved, in order to gain as much commercial advantage and have as much leverage on the German question, as possible. A considerable amount of frustration continued to manifest itself, despite membership of the Brussels Treaty Organisation and of the North Atlantic Alliance. Membership did not mean that the Dutch would automatically comply with every suggestion about the build-up of their own forces, and their independent streak was to act as an occasional check on the idea of Western solidarity, as it still does today.[2]

Dutch Restraint

Despite deep-seated worry about communist ideology, the Netherlands did not put as much emphasis on the military aspects of NATO as the United States and Britain would have liked. This was in line with traditional attachment to international law and with the idea that the formation of NATO had only proved necessary because of the failure of the United Nations system to ensure international peace and security. The Dutch government looked on NATO as 'a necessary complement to the broad economic programme.'[3] The military aspect was played down. 'There was general agreement,' writes van Campen, 'that the Treaty should not be regarded as a negative phenomenon.'[4] This moderating influence on purely military measures was important to the Dutch in their trading policy towards the Eastern Block, as shall be seen. By stressing the social and economic aspects of NATO co-operation, the Dutch were able to retain some measure of their diminishing independence.

Although the Dutch were implacably anti-communist, their Foreign Ministry yearbook for 1949–50, while recognising the East West split, is tinged with restraint.

> Europe is ruled by a constantly sharpening ideological confrontation, where East and West Europe are not only separated from each other by a wall, but unfortunately are clearly opposed to each other

[...] It is no simple task for the Dutch government to determine the policy of the Kingdom in such a world.[5]

The Americans certainly took a more military and robust view of matters. Even before the North Atlantic Treaty had been ratified, and after the ending of the Berlin Blockade, an interdepartmental working group prepared a paper for the National Security Resources Board and the National Security Council, that stated: 'The present Soviet regime is essentially and implacably hostile towards the United States [...] the USSR can maintain domination of Eastern Europe by force of arms without the risk of war'. Rather ominously, the paper went on to assess American long range military capability:

> The United States will be capable of delivering effective quantities of mass destruction weapons (e.g. atomic, bacteriological and chemical agents) at ranges of 4,500 nautical miles or more by:
> 1. Inhabited aircraft – by 1951
> 2. Inhabited aircraft launching guided missiles of 100 mile range or more – by 1956–58
> 3. Guided missiles of 4,500 nautical mile range – by 1958–61
> Any war during this period will require substantially more industrial manpower, industrial facilities and raw materials than those required during World War II.[6]

The Dutch, while generally recognising the importance of the Alliance, were not in a position to immediately build up their own military contribution to the defence of Western Europe. Being a member of an alliance was one thing, but giving expression to it was quite another, and did not suit the Dutch temperament very well. The Dutch were perceived by some as being rather lackadaisical on the question of their military contributions. As will be seen later, the question of the degree of militarisation was to lead to considerable political problems both within the Netherlands and the United States, problems which are not unknown today. Even before the signing of the North Atlantic Treaty, the first signs of future problems could be perceived; during one of several visits by Field Marshal Montgomery, in his capacity as Permanent Military Chairman of the Western European Union (November 1948), there was criticism in most Dutch newspapers about his meetings with the Prime Minister, the Chiefs of Staff and the Defence Minister: although most newspapers did, according to the British Embassy, warmly welcome the visit, they regretted the lack of information. The press was particularly annoyed after the *New York Times* printed a despatch from their Hague correspondent alleging that the Field Marshal had asked the Dutch government to increase expenditure on military equipment for its land, naval and air forces.[7] Field Marshal Montgomery was, many would consider, an important public relations tool in drumming up support for increased military expenditure within the Dutch military establishment. Some sections of public opinion, however, disliked the idea of what they saw as outside interference, particularly since it appeared that the correspondent of an American newspaper knew more than they did. The British ambassador wrote in December 1948: 'I shall, however, continue to do my best to support Field Marshal Montgomery's efforts to ensure that Holland shall, with the least possible delay, have a truly national army capable of defending the line allotted to her.'[8] These grand and confident words were not, however, to become reality, with the least possible delay. Things were not quite so simple in the Netherlands.

Great Britain did its best to support and influence Dutch public opinion. On 16 June 1949, the Dutch Chief of Staff, General Kruls, gave a hard-hitting speech to the East Brabant Sector of the Netherlands Corporation for Industry and Commerce on the problems of Dutch defence and the obligations incurred by membership of Western Union. He said:

> [...] a great European power, Russia, possesses at the moment, in the East, an exceedingly powerfully armed force in a state of preparedness [...] it is said that Communism cannot succeed in maintaining itself by confining itself to a certain group of states but only by spreading itself over as wide an area as possible. If this is a fact it is only natural to assume that Russia and her satellites will by one or another means attempt to spread Communist ideology over a wider race.

The British ambassador sent this speech to his Foreign Secretary, Ernest Bevin, with the words:

> [...] it is also a suitable companion piece to Field Marshal Montgomery's address on July 15 [...] I have accordingly asked my information secretary to do what he can, without appearing to interfere in the handling of a Dutch speech in the Dutch press, to keep these two speeches in the public eye [...][9]

Given the then political climate between East and West, this kind of solidarity was obviously understandable.

Kruls was surprisingly outspoken for a servant of the Crown. He felt so strongly about the need to spend more on Dutch defence that, only ten weeks before his speech in East Brabant, he had submitted his resignation to the Queen, choosing to use the letter to express his disagreement with what he considered to be a lack of emphasis on Dutch defence. He also called for an extension of Dutch military service from 12 to 24 months.[10] Whether Kruls really meant to resign, or simply draw attention to his wish to increase Dutch commitment to defence, is a moot point. In the event, Kruls did not resign, although there was a period of uncertainty lasting into May. The Prime Minister, Drees, despite his known disinclination towards increasing defence expenditure, wrote to the Defence Minister, Schokking, on 10 May: 'I am inclined to say that it would be best to simply call on General Kruls to continue with his work.'[11]

The British Information Campaign

The topic of the British Government's overseas information campaign following the war would merit several books, and is indeed already the subject of considerable interest, as more government archives become available. Various papers have been published, such as Lyn Smith's on 'Covert British Propaganda',[12] and Raymond Smith's on British Soviet Policy.[13] There remains plenty of space for a study on the British information campaign in the Netherlands: it is important for the purposes of this study to look at the aspects of that campaign which are relevant to it.

The better to understand the considerable influence that Great Britain tried to wield in the Netherlands, and the ways in which she sought to achieve this, it is worth briefly turning back to 5 October 1945, when a meeting of the Overseas Planning Committee was held at the Ministry of Information. The brief for the meeting (at which the Foreign Office was represented) was entitled 'Plan of Propaganda for the Netherlands – Appreciation.' The aims were described as 'long term – to promote greatest possible degree of UK-NL understanding. Short term, to explain fully the reason behind Allied policy in Germany and the Far East, particularly where it has a bearing on NL'. On the Dutch attitude to the United States, the brief stated that the United States ranked next in popularity to Britain, but that there was a background of suspicion of American policy in the Pacific, 'particularly with regard to the general attitude of the US towards "Colonies".'[14] The paper stated that it was feared that the United States might 'demand economic or strategic concessions as compensation for their part in the defeat of Japan.' More pertinently, given the signs of tension that were appearing between the Allies and the Soviet Union, the paper went on:

> Politically, the Dutch feel the conflict of ideology between the Western democracies and the USSR, and tend naturally towards the West [...] The Dutch are a cultured people, knowledge of foreign languages is common, and many are widely travelled. Our publicity will therefore have to attain a high material standard both in presentation and content.[15]

Raymond Smith argues that Bevin's anti-Stalinism, combined with Foreign Office pressure, led in 1947 to the adoption of a rigid anti-Soviet stance.[16] The British spotlight therefore fell on communism whenever it reared its head in Western Europe, and a powerful publicity machine, the basis of which already existed – albeit for different reasons – in the BBC, Central Office of Information (previously the Ministry of Information) and the British Council, ground into action.

The Foreign Office's Information Policy Department (IPD), which was, in the words of a senior Foreign Office official, responsible for political propaganda abroad,[17] received quarterly reports on the countries where their staff operated. When the IPD received the report for the Netherlands for the second quarter of 1947, an official wrote on the file jacket:

> There are no language difficulties where the well educated are concerned and it is these, rather than the masses, who need convincing regarding our motives and aims. The larger, popular audiences are best reached by means of Dutch dubbed films and film strips loaned out to Dutch lecturers who have some knowledge of this country [...] Particularly interesting are the remarks on the decrease in US information. It would seem to suggest that the more affluent a country, the less need for publicity, hence our present vying with the French for influence over the minds of those who before would have been dazed with uncritical admiration by the mere display of our gold.[18]

Apart from this perhaps somewhat sinister comment about vying with the French for people's minds, the comment about the well-educated needing convincing, rather than the 'masses' is interesting in the light of the development of the information campaign. The comment on a quarterly report two years later was: 'Main efforts seem to have been spent in reaching workers in industry, particularly with anti-Communist material. To this end, the background notes in Dutch are a useful approach [...]'[19] Clearly, efforts were made to reach all sections of the Dutch population, whatever their level of education. These efforts included the Dutch government, as we shall shortly see.

The questions of the French role and of the influence of communism in the Netherlands needs further comment. Until the French communists had been dropped from the French government, suspicion of French friendliness towards the Soviet Union was strong in Britain, and was to continue even after the communists' fall from grace, because of their voting strength. It is worth reproducing what the British ambassador, Bland, wrote, in a letter entitled 'Communism in the Netherlands', at the end of 1947:

> The fact that the EVC (Unity Trade Union) are once more able to pay strikers should be carefully noted. Until very recently, they were not in a position to take this responsibility and it is doubtful if not impossible, to make the payment [...] from normal income from Dutch sources [...] It is confirmed that Blokzijl of the EVC is receiving his instructions from Paris by means of fairly constant personal contacts. Naturally there is no information concerning the source of the additional financial support which is now apparent.[20]

Of the EVC, the ambassador wrote: 'Although all concerned strenuously deny that this union is under Communist control, they deceive no one.' The above-mentioned quote about 'vying with the French for the minds of the Dutch' is easier to understand, given British suspicions about the influence of French communists, although it may not provide the whole picture.

The communist influence in the Netherlands does not appear to have been strong. The British ambassador wrote:

> [...] of all the states on the mainland of Europe, Holland [...] is perhaps the most likely to defend itself and to counter attack vigorously the onslaught of political warfare [...] their [the communists] efforts have run up against the very solid obstacles presented by the Dutch character and religious principles, and have made little headway [...] the clear cut nature of political divisions in Holland forces the Communists to be honest to a degree which they must find unwelcome [...] I think that the sanity of the Dutch and the discipline of their

strongly anti-Communist Christian and Socialist trade unions would hold out and prevent the Communists from playing a decisive role.²¹

In the same letter, he commented on the apparent successes of the communist vote in the elections of May 1946, writing: 'This would suggest that there are proportionately more Communists in Holland than, for example, the United Kingdom. In fact this is probably not so.' He was referring to the British 'first past the post' system, which did not favour minority parties, as did the Dutch system. The popularity of the communists had begun to drop even in 1945, despite their role in the wartime resistance, mainly because the Dutch quickly became suspicious. A good example is provided by the son of Willem Beyen, K H Beyen (Minister for Foreign Trade from 1978 to 1981). He recalls how, when a communist inspired dockers' strike in the summer of 1945 meant that wheat could not be unloaded in Amsterdam, a group of students who had applied for visas to visit the Soviet Union, unloaded the wheat themselves. As a result, they were refused visas by the Soviet Embassy.²² Even before the British information campaign began, communist support was, according to the British Ambassador, dropping. It is ironic that that Information Research Department (IRD)²³ of the Foreign Office – set up at the end of 1947 – began its activities at the same time as the Ambassador wrote the above-mentioned letter.

It is naturally difficult to gauge whether the political constellation in the Netherlands would have been different had there been no information campaign, since the question is a hypothetical one. Rather oddly, however, an IPD official commented on a quarterly report: 'Western Union: the COI feature articles combined with IRD material seem to be making their mark, though their effect on Dutch public opinion is not substantially stated [...]'²⁴ What was this effect? According to the ambassador's successor, Nichols, writing in 1950, the campaign did not seem to have been particularly successful:

> A small scale advance poll produced the extremely discouraging reply from four out of five of those asked that they did not wish to hear about defence. The Head of the Army Information Service agrees [...] that this does not mean – thank goodness – that we should give up trying [...].²⁵

However one views the information campaign, the Foreign Office seems to have been worried about defeatism: 'Our Information Policy Department, which is responsible for political propaganda abroad, is much disturbed at the use which may be made of the super bomb to aggravate defeatist tendencies in Western Europe [...].' It asked the Ministry of Supply for facts about the hydrogen bomb, which it could use to combat defeatism.[26] The information campaign was to continue, and to run up against the occasional problem.

As the Cold War developed, the campaign seems to have concentrated increasingly on pure anti-communism per se, as much as on promoting the idea of Western Union and a need to rearm. Communism in the Netherlands was, however, nothing like as strong as in France or Italy. Even in the immediate post-war period, with memories of the Nazi occupation very strong, there seems to have been no real possibility of the Communists coming to power. It is worth recalling here a statement from Chapter 2 by a Foreign Office official in 1945:

> The Dutch Communists played an insignificant role in Holland [sic] before the war and are not expected to play a very much more important one now [...] their leaders seem to be untrained, uneducated and more than usually irresponsible types. They have alienated what sympathy they might have had by defending Soekarno and opposing all suggestions that Holland might annex a small strip of Germany.[27]

Two years later the situation had not changed:

> [...] I think it unlikely that the creation of the Cominform will lead to any very marked change in Communist policy in Holland [...] they are not strong enough to cause any internal disorganisation in Holland sufficiently serious to affect the economic recovery of that country, with or without American aid.[28]

The British information campaign in the Netherlands seems not to have been an unqualified success, even after the Netherlands had agreed to send some men to Korea. The British ambassador wrote that the Embassy's Information Section was encountering greater resistance regarding anti-communist propaganda. He put this down mainly to 'saturation, in placing articles in the press'.[29] He also expressed concern about the way in which certain material was presented:

> Surely the time has come when we should notify the Netherlands government officially of what we are doing in this field [...] the official

in the Ministry of Foreign Affairs who is the channel through which we pass on anti-communist material intended for transmission to the Netherlands Government [...] asked if he could be informed what direct distribution had been given to such material by the embassy. The official position is that we should withhold this information from him, which seems rather absurd. I hope therefore that I may be authorised to notify the Ministry at least informally of the activities of the Information Section (and Labour Attaché).[30]

Use of the term 'rather absurd' in an official letter to another individual, as was the case, betrays a certain concern on the ambassador's part about aspects of the information campaign, at least of the anti-communist ones.

One is bound to wonder whether one of the reasons that the Dutch were slow to rearm, apart from the economic and historical reasons already mentioned, may not have been a certain resistance born of a natural tendency to be independently aloof, to outside pressure, from whatever quarter, even friendly.

Slow Realisation of Harsh Realities and Defence Problems

Whatever the amount of influence which the British (and Americans) wielded, whether through diplomatic channels or by the sheer force of Bevin,[31] the Dutch looked to Britain, despite their frustrations over the German question and Indonesia. The Berlin airlift, the arrival of American B-52s in Britain and the announcement of the first Soviet atomic explosion on 22 September 1949 certainly made Dutch membership of the Alliance a sine qua non, whatever the misgivings of some Dutch about putting too much stress on military aspects. It has already been pointed out how the Dutch character was essentially anti-communist. The Berlin airlift served to enhance their stance, rather than suddenly make them anti-communist: in February 1948, the Netherlands Institute for Public Opinion revealed that 67 per cent of the Dutch wished to oppose communism in a radical manner. The Institute added that the majority of those who wished to oppose communism by force were members of the Anti-Revolution Party, the Christian Historical Union (both Protestant), and the Catholic People's Party (87, 86 and 83 per cent respectively). 78 per cent of the members of the Party of Freedom and Democracy and even 62 per cent of the Socialists agreed that communism should be prohibited. The small Communist Party was not however banned, a sign perhaps of Dutch tolerance.[32] In fact, despite the general Dutch antipathy towards communism, the communists were a small but cohesive force, helped by the mass circulation newspaper *De Waarheid*, which had been a resistance paper. Just before the elections in July 1948, the Communist Party had ten (out of 100) seats in the Second Chamber and four (out of 50) in the First. Although the coup in Czechoslovakia was expected to lead to a dramatic fall in support for the communists, they lost only two seats in the Second Chamber and none in the First,[33] a reflection of the Dutch antipathy towards violent political swings.

The Dutch Government did not wish to annoy the Soviet Union unnecessarily. In February, it had published a memorandum on communism, which stated:

> [...] Communism in its present form must be regarded as an ideology directly opposed to the Christian ideas on humanity and social life [...] in so far as Communism has become a political reality in international life, the Government may not close its eyes to the necessity of living in peace and in the best relationship with all peoples of the world, in order to defend world peace.

The British ambassador's letter about the memorandum commented that the Dutch Government was unlikely on its own to adopt openly any very strong anti-communist line.[34] That was left to the Chief of Staff, General Kruls. As shall be seen later in this chapter, trade considerations were also rather important to the Dutch government, and tensions were to arise in that area with the Americans and British. Whatever future tensions were to come into the open later over the Dutch military commitment and their trade with the Eastern Block, the fact remained that there were genuine problems about increasing military expenditure, compounded by the fact that most Dutch felt that simple membership of the Brussels and Atlantic Pacts had reduced the fear of invasion.[35]

It is interesting to note that during the negotiations on the setting up of NATO, the Dutch do not appear to have realised the full financial implications of membership for the Dutch economy: at a cabinet meeting on 29 November 1948, the Dutch Prime Minister, Drees, told his fellow Ministers that the Pact would not entail new expenditure.[36] The fact that the bulk of the armed forces were in Indonesia already placed a severe strain on resources. The defence budget was under considerable strain; it accounted for 22 per cent of the national budget in 1949 (as against 18 per cent the previous year), compared to 20 per cent for Great Britain and only 7.25 per cent for Belgium[37] (unlike the case of Indonesia, the Congo did not pose a military problem at the time). As a proportion of national income, Dutch defence expenditure was the highest of its NATO partners, standing at 7.7 per cent, while Britain's was 7.6 per cent, Italy's 6.3 per cent, the United States' 6.4 per cent, France's 4.9 per cent, Portugal's 4.8 per cent, Norway's 4.5 per cent, Canada's 2 per cent, Denmark's 2 per cent and Luxembourg's 1 per cent.[38]

The British ambassador summed up the general feeling on rearmament in the Netherlands when he wrote in early 1950:

> Extensive propaganda was employed to build up a voluntary national reserve with a target strength of 17,000 men for defence against airborne attack and support of the armed forces and police in internal security. The response, however, has been disappointing, since the signature of the Brussels and Atlantic Pacts has reduced the fear of invasion. The present strength of the reserve is 9,000 men.[39]

The ambassador also alluded to future planning being difficult, owing to Indonesia having swallowed up 'all the available men, material and money required for defence in the West.'

It is tempting to argue that with membership of NATO and the ending of the Berlin Blockade in May 1949, the Dutch felt secure enough not to give defence expenditure in Europe as high a priority as the British and Americans would have liked. The Dutch had not yet realised all the implications of membership of the Atlantic club, such as pressure from the British and Americans to build up their armed forces and military production. It was to be a painful process. Being anti-communist was one thing. Being anti-Soviet was quite another. Dutch pluralism did not lend itself to the adoption of a policy of open hostility towards one country, in the way that the Soviet Union, the United States and Britain were able to do. Thus, although van Kleffens could, as we have seen, talk to fellow diplomats about the Soviet Union 'filling every cranny it could, like a gas', the Dutch government memorandum on communism was more restrained. This attitude continued: in May 1950, the Netherlands delegate at the Fourth North Atlantic Council, while pointing out the necessity of increasing the West's strength, added that the possibilities for negotiation must not be overlooked.[40] The views of the Prime Minister, Drees, who was a Socialist, were particularly important on the question of defence spending, as will be seen.

The North Atlantic Treaty entered into effect on 24 August, and on 17 September, the first session of the North Atlantic Council took place, in Washington. The Council established a Defence Committee, a Military

Committee, five Regional Planning Groups and a Standing Group, consisting of the United States, Great Britain and France. The latter was a subcommittee of the Military Committee, and was to come in for criticism by the Dutch later on, for not listening enough to the smaller powers. The report of the Working Group on Organisation, which was submitted to the Council, and approved on 17 September, also stated that 'appropriate machinery' would be established as soon as possible to consider the question of military production and supply.[41]

The devastating announcement on 22 September that the Soviet Union had exploded an atomic device, certainly gave impetus and a sense of urgency to NATO planning. President Truman was able to sign the Mutual Defence Assistance Act on 6 October, and the above-mentioned appropriate machinery was set up at the Second Session of the North Atlantic Council on 18 November, in the form of a Defence, Financial and Economic Committee and a Military Production and Supply Board.

These developments obviously had considerable implications for the Brussels Treaty Organisation. In Fursdon's words: '[...] it was quickly clear that relationships between the two needed clarification and co-ordination if duplication, even acrimony, were not to develop.'[42] Matters were however simplified by the fact that the area covered by the Brussels Treaty, and its membership, were contained within NATO's West European Regional Planning Group. Thus the solution adopted was for NATO's Western European Planning Group to consist of the Brussels Treaty Organisations Chiefs of Staff Committee and Permanent Committee (with the addition of American and Canadian representatives). Fursdon uses the succinct phrase 'double-hatted' role. The remaining organs remained. Thus, the Brussels Treaty Organisation continued, albeit in a truncated form.

Committed as they were to the idea of the Alliance, several factors conspired to make the immediate formulation of a totally committed military policy difficult for the Dutch: these were the burden imposed by the Indonesian problem, with its concomitant logistic and financial elements; a typically Dutch view that the Alliance should not be seen as a purely military and aggressive organisation; a feeling that the Big Three held too much sway; a creeping realisation, in some quarters, that pressure was being brought to bear on the Netherlands by the two countries, Britain and America, who had already, together and at different times, been unhelpful on the Indonesian question; and, last but not least, a slow understanding that Germany should help in the defence of Europe.

A Dutch Foreign Ministry Aide Memoire of 29 April 1949 had enunciated further arguments for not giving priority to defence expenditure:

1. The present plans for the common defence leave an important part of the Netherlands' territory unprotected, whereas the whole of the territory of the other four West European partners will be defended. This inequality of the benefits to be derived from the common defence plan, should be taken into account in distributing the cost thereof.
2. War damage from the last war was relatively higher in the Netherlands than in the other West European countries, while the destruction of Netherlands assets in Indonesia is still going on. This means that the Netherlands has, of necessity, to devote a higher percentage of its current national income to reconstruction, thus leaving a smaller percentage for consumption, including defence.
3. The Netherlands has a much higher birthrate than any of the West European countries, the net increase in population being at present around 1.5 per cent per annum. This means again, that to maintain its standard of living, a higher percentage of the Netherlands national income has to be devoted to investment.
4. Another more general adjustment which may have to be worked out would be to take into account differences of national income per capita, in such a way that a country with a high income per capita would contribute a higher percentage of its total national income than a country with a low income per capita.[43]

The British Service Attaché's report on the Netherlands Armed Forces for 1949 stated, rather sanguinely, that by mid–1951, the Netherlands would be in a position to put in the field its contribution to Western Union Land Forces, 'subject to the provision of arms by the United States'. In his covering dispatch, however, the British ambassador said, 'The cost of national defence is, as you are aware, the cause of increasing preoccupation in this country.'[44] It was not surprising that for the following year, the Military Attaché's report stated:

The year 1950 has seen little progress in the creation of a Dutch Army capable of taking its place in the Western Union Land Forces, and at the present time the Dutch have no Field Force of any sort. Plans for a Field Force of three divisions were completed by the General Staff early in the year, but the government were never willing to accept the financial burden of putting them into effect.[45]

The debate in the Dutch Cabinet about the defence contribution had already manifested itself in particularly stark terms in the shape of General Kruls. It now showed itself at inter-governmental level. A reported statement by Stikker at the meeting of the North Atlantic Council Deputies at the end of July 1950 was particularly revealing:

> Dutch Foreign Minister Stikker said he alone in Cabinet had advocated stepping up Defence Programme. He had been violently opposed by Finance Minister and otherwise apathetic Cabinet and he had received but feeble support from Defence Minister. Embassy the Hague's impression of Dutch public opinion however is that mass of people are further ahead in their concern for necessity strengthening European armed forces than such officials as Finance Minister.[46]

This apparently apologetic frankness on the part of Stikker added weight to the American Embassy in the Hague's analysis of the problem:

> Embassy the Hague reports that top Dutch officials are undecided whether to present Cabinet with revolutionary plan fundamentally altering most major postwar economic financial policies and shift to all out defence effort or speed up formation combat divisions and make additional military production effort as yet unspecified. [...] Embassy believes there is serious possibility Foreign Minister Stikker would resign from Cabinet if Netherlands response to our approach is not vigorous.[47]

The British ambassador to the Hague's view, while not departing radically from the American Embassy's, was cruelly critical: 'The slow thinking Dutch, however, only gradually learning to think internationally, did not, any more than other Western countries, immediately appreciate the degree of sacrifice and effort which the organisation of mutual defence would involve.'[48] While the Dutch may not have fully realised the implications of NATO membership, when they signed the treaty, to ascribe this to 'slow thinking' does seem to betray a rather rigid and superficial method of analysis. The more germane reasons were the previously mentioned disinclination to look at NATO as an essentially military alliance (even while pursuing membership for security reasons and to have more of a say on Germany), the logistic and financial difficulties involved in suddenly trying to transfer military resources from Indonesia, a natural inclination to put emphasis on trading interests, and a traditional habit of not making outwardly aggressive noises. The outbreak of hostilities in Korea made the situation even more critical, while bringing home more immediate realities. It was not so much 'slow thinking' or, for that matter 'growing up internationally', as having to adapt to new priorities.

'The deteriorating international situation,' the ambassador continued:

> Particularly after the outbreak of hostilities in Korea, brought to the forefront the whole question of the organisation of Western European defence. Holland's [...] own military shortcomings were glaringly exposed and for the first time it was borne in upon the Dutch Government and people that effort and sacrifices would be necessary to make good these deficiencies.[49]

The immediate effect on the man-in-the-street was more down-to-earth: 'There is certainly some anxiety amongst the people in this country lest a general war should ensue, and there has, I am told, been a small amount of stocking up on household essentials.'[50]

As the crisis developed, so did the pressure to arm. In July 1950, the Dutch Prime Minister, Drees, not known for enthusiasm on defence matters, was reported to have indicated his readiness to consider further expenditure on the armed forces and to have hinted that the Dutch were also reconsidering the possibility of offering troops to the United Nations forces in Korea.[51] The Dutch press welcomed President Truman's decision to use military measures in support of South Korea (except the communist newspaper *De Waarheid*).[52] On 8 September, the Dutch Government offered an infantry battalion. The combination of antipathy towards communism, showing 'solidarity with the West' and the stress the Dutch laid on supporting the United Nations was a strong one. Casualties amounted to 79 dead and 269 wounded, missing or captured. The United States ended up with 17,750 dead.[53]

The atmosphere of crisis had been preceded by worrying developments nearer to home: at the end of May, 50,000 men of the *Bereitschaften*[54] in the German Democratic Republic were reported to have been armed with artillery and armoured vehicles. *The Economist* commented that the force consisted in the main of ex-Waffen-SS members.[55]

Mere membership of an alliance was one thing, but lip service to that membership was no longer enough, and the time was coming for the Dutch to put their money where their mouth was. In the meantime, there were tensions, both within the Dutch Cabinet and between the Netherlands and her larger neighbours; the United States was clearly of the opinion that the Netherlands were not pulling their weight. The State Department briefing to their Deputy Representative on the North Atlantic Council, Spofford, on 21 August 1950, included the statement: 'Proposed budget for 51 seems to be definitely below Netherlands capability and rate of expenditure substantially above 1950 rather than reduction would be more appropriate.'[56] The Americans appear to have expected the Dutch immediately to translate words into action, particularly since the signature in January of the Bilateral Defence Agreement between the two countries. At the press conference held at the American Embassy on 27 January, it had been announced that a party of 30 American experts would shortly be arriving in the Netherlands, and would be attached to the Embassy. The Americans were clearly keen to get the Dutch moving.

The Americans were critical not only of the level of Dutch military expenditure, but of the allocation of resources:

We should also seek to make certain that whatever finances are now available to the NATO countries are spent in such a manner so as to yield the maximum military strength. While difficult, in view of considerations of national pride and local politics, we should discourage prestige expenditures such as [...] Dutch naval expenditures.[57]

The British concurred with the Americans; a comment on the file jacket of the Naval, Military and Air Attachés' reports on the Dutch armed forces for 1950 by a Foreign Office official, stated: The Navy is efficient and useful, but the naval base at Den Helder, which has cost so high a percentage of the budget expenditure on defence, is a white elephant. The army is, as we know already, in a very bad state. The Air force is very small, and we are told very little of its state of efficiency.[58]

As with the British, relations were to get worse rather than better, over trade and military matters. The bitterness surrounding the Indonesian question had not, it must be remembered, disappeared, and simmered just below the surface. Despite the various problems, the State Department's evaluation of American relations with the Netherlands was positive: 'The Netherlands has consistently supported the US policies and procedures, especially in relation to European defence [...]'.[59] This statement did not foresee the considerable strains that were to emerge the following year.

Relations with the United Kingdom tended at this time to centre on commercial matters, Indonesia and European co-operation.

> While the Netherlands places great reliance on Great Britain, minor differences of opinion do exist. The UN embargo on arms shipments to the Dutch East Indies, the apparent reluctance of the British to commit themselves more fully to a policy of European economic collaboration, and the arrangements made by the British with Royal Dutch Shell by which the dollar earnings of the oil company, including those from the Curaçao refineries, are placed under the control of the British Government, are constant points of irritation.[60]

Relations were, as with the Americans, to have some low points during the following two years, not only on military matters, but on European co-operation questions, as shall be seen.

The Dutch attitude towards France bears some mention here, since it tended to offset relations with the United States and Britain.

> For although the idea of French leadership in Europe makes a certain appeal in Catholic circles in Holland the majority of Dutchmen are mistrustful of French intentions and policy and doubt her ability to maintain a leading position on the continent in the face of a rapidly recovering Germany.[61]

The Americans also backed up this conclusion: '[...] they are not inclined to count too heavily on French support in a crisis [...].'[62] In January 1950, Stikker told the Minister at the American Embassy in Paris, Bohlen, that the French Government could not assume leadership on the Continent, and that the Dutch would not accept French leadership.[63]

The Dutch, and Stikker in particular, were aware that the French were not as 'Atlantic minded' as they were. An interesting insight into French views of the Americans, and an indication of French differences with the Dutch, is contained in a letter from the Dutch ambassador in France, von Voorst tot Voorst, to the Director General of the Dutch Foreign Ministry, Boon, on 9 February 1950. It reported the views of General de Lattre de Tassigny, Commander in Chief, Land Forces, Western Europe, imparted to a Dutch diplomat at a reception at the French Embassy. The former expressed alarm at 'ideas in Dutch parliamentary circles' that German rearmament would be unavoidable and should be undertaken soon. He went on to show his scepticism of the military aid from America. It was, he said, old material dating back to 1945, and the French were themselves at that moment producing weapons, which would set an example even to the Americans. He then criticised the Dutch for spending so much on their navy; for a small country like the Netherlands, it was money thrown away, which could be better spent on the army.[64] As we have seen, the Americans were also concerned at Dutch naval 'prestige' expenditures.[65]

The Dutch, then, although slowly being faced with the realities of NATO membership, displayed an independent streak, both in their reaction to British and American views on the extent and content of their military spending, and in their attitude towards the French view of Germany. Although matters had not yet come to a head on either count, there was not long to wait. In the meantime, the Dutch remained particularly independent on the question of trade with the East, which was beginning to assume considerable political importance. They were to give way only grudgingly.

Trade before Ideology

The Dutch were, as has been seen, fairly restrained in their official public statements on communism, not only because of their traditional attachment to principles of peace and a hope that the military aspects of NATO would not be stressed too much, but because of their attachment to trading principles. This attachment, juxtaposed with moves by the large NATO powers, to control exports of militarily sensitive equipment to the Eastern block, led to some criticism of the Dutch who, it appeared, manufactured goods which, for example, could be used in producing atomic energy. A report produced in early 1949 by the US Atomic Energy Commission stated that the Netherlands government had promised to reply in the near future to a questionnaire on 'atomic energy items'. It went on:

> Significant energy items produced by the Netherlands include certain categories of electrical equipment which can be manufactured by the Philips firm at Eindhoven, and small tonnages of monazite derived as a by product of tin mining in the NEI [Netherlands East Indies].[66]

It is worth pointing out here that the Dutch Government had, at the end of 1948, refused the United States permission to send three mineral engineers on a field trip to investigate monazite reserves on the islands of Billiton, Banka and Singkep. The Americans had made the proposal with the 'full knowledge and concurrence of the Government of the United Kingdom.' The American request was based on a secret Memorandum of Agreement signed on 4 August 1945 by them, the Dutch and the British. It was renewable every three years.[67] Sensitivities over Indonesia probably led to the Dutch refusal, although it would be quite in order to assume that they would have considered such a request rather heavy handed, even without the Indonesian problem.

Generally, the Americans appear to have been more worried than the Dutch about the danger of militarily sensitive material – particularly of the nuclear variety – going East. Their requests to the Dutch did not meet with automatic compliance. A Dutch government reply of 29 April 1949 illustrated their attitude:

> The Netherlands Government [...] points to the fact that it has the greatest possible interest in maintaining and expanding trade with the Eastern European countries. The Netherlands economy is dependent on dollar saving raw materials [...] Therefore the attitude of the Netherlands Government towards restricting certain exports to the Eastern Europe countries cannot be a rigid one.[68]

The Dutch wished to be their own judges of what should, and should not, be exported.

Even after the successful explosion of a Soviet atomic device at the end of September 1949, the Dutch did not automatically go the whole way towards meeting American wishes; on 15 October, Harrison, the American special representative to the Economic Co-operation Administration wrote:

> The Dutch representative [...] informed [...] his country had licensing procedure covering all exports but not prepared to agree any list at this time. Pointed out that Philips Company privately using US I-A list as guide for screening electronics exports to Soviet orbit [...] British representative suggested Netherlands Government take more positive responsibility for Philips exports. Dutch representative insisted that present trade agreements be respected.

The Dutch were not alone in their attitude: the Belgian view was that current trade agreements should not be violated, in letter or spirit.[69] The Dutch and Belgians were not only at variance with the Americans and British (the British Ambassador described the Dutch as unhelpful in the discussion on East West trade),[70] but with the French, who had produced a joint list with the British, covering militarily sensitive goods.[71] The French had, since the expulsion of the Communists from the Government in 1947, become more co-operative on security matters.

On 28 October, the Americans were still not happy. The State Department was 'of the impression' that the Netherlands and Belgium were making little effort to co-operate on trade controls.[72] The evidence suggests that the Dutch simply wished to retain control over their actions; by committing themselves to a regional agreement, they felt they would lose this control. This is borne out by the American Ambassador to The Hague, Chapin's, comments, in May 1950:

> Netherlands Government participates fully in working groups of CoCom,[73] but does not attend executive CoCom meetings. This position taken by Cabinet as being all that is needed to provide co-operation necessary for programme [...] Netherlands retention non-membership status CoCom has made it politically possible for Netherlands to participate fully in CoCom activities and take action parallel with CoCom nations despite NL November Cabinet decision not to join CoCom.[74]

The Dutch position on East West trade was, then, a clear reflection of their attitude towards the whole East-West question: they did not wish to simply be subsumed into the priorities of the Big Three. They were happy to go along with general policy, having joined NATO, thereby renouncing a policy of neutrality, but wished to retain their independence of action, and do things their way. Their sense of frustration, particularly over the German question, was to continue to manifest itself.

Germany and NATO

Although the problem of how Germany was to contribute to European defence had not been seriously tackled, other aspects of Germany's rehabilitation and role in Europe had been the subject of much negotiation, and were being solved at the same time as the NATO negotiations were in progress. The Three Power London Conference on Germany, which had begun on 26 February 1948, and had become a Six Power Conference, reached agreement on West Germany's participation in the European Recovery Programme, and set up the International Authority of the Ruhr. French attempts to exercise strong control over German decision-making on production of coal and steel were whittled away by the English and Americans. For example, the French had announced their intention of modifying the guiding principles laid down in the first session of the Conference on the Authority. The English and Americans therefore took steps to ensure that Occupation Law No 75, designed to create temporary trusteeships for the management of the coal and steel industry, and therefore to pave the way for eventual transfer back to private ownership, was promulgated before the French had any chance to radically modify its guiding principles. Milward writes:

> But there can be no doubt that Law No 75 was promulgated in order to slam the door on any French attempt to make this modification reach as far as the individual firm. There were, in short, in spite of the Assemblée Nationale's manifest discontent, still to be no French managers in the Ruhr.[75]

Other developments continued apace. The text of the Occupation Statute was agreed by the Big Three. In May, the Basic Law was announced, after which a Federal President was elected. The Chancellor, Dr Adenauer, was elected in the Bundestag (by a majority of only one vote!). With the entry into force of the Occupation Statute in September, direct military rule came to an end, and the Federal Republic came into being.

Despite Benelux's entry in 1948 into the talks on Germany, frustrations and suspicions remained vis-à-vis the Big Three after the signing of the NATO treaty. Stikker wrote: 'The German problem in particular regularly involved us in a contradiction. The Big Three had, as occupying powers, their special responsibilities, which they plainly had no intention of sharing with their NATO partners [...]'[76] At a cabinet meeting on 16 May 1949, Stikker said that he had written to his Benelux partners suggesting putting pressure on the Big Four (it is interesting that the Soviet Union was considered) to be more involved in the discussions on the German question, to be held in Paris. He said that the Soviet Embassy had stressed their readiness to involve the Benelux countries, adding that he supposed that this readiness depended on the wish to involve Poland and other countries in the discussions.[77] Soviets or no Soviets, the Netherlands did have some say in events, although not as much as they would have liked. They took part in the Paris discussions in November 1949, which led to the Petersburg Agreements.[78] 'There can be no doubt', wrote van Campen:

> That the Netherlands Government, in a general sense, supported the policies [...], but [...] they – or for that matter the Benelux as a whole – were not in a position to influence the fundamental course of events one way or another. The Government, generally speaking, were kept informed by the great powers, on one or two occasions they were offered the opportunity to state their views. But even so

the real influence of the Netherlands in these matters – the general policy of the Western Powers in the German question – was necessarily small.[79]

Although Dutch frustrations about their commercial claims vis-à-vis Germany were offset by their trade agreement with that country in September 1949 and by an improvement in their trading position (see Chapter 2), the security question was altogether a different matter, linked as it was to the sensitive question of German rearmament. Even back in March 1948, the Foreign Minister, van Boetzelaer van Oosterhout, had told the Cabinet that 'in the long run, West Germany would have to be admitted to the (Brussels) Treaty.'[80] Although the left of centre *Het Vrije Volk* still considered the Soviet threat of war to be less acute than the German one,[81] the press as a whole was slowly moving towards accepting German rearmament.

On 3 December 1949, the left-of-centre Roman Catholic *De Volkskrant* wrote: 'An undefended Germany is really a greater danger to the whole of the West than German participation in Western defence.' The editorial was headed 'Rhein or Elbe?'[82]

The conservative *NRC Handelsblad* had already written on 5 October that Germany's (and Italy's) rearmament was indispensable. On 12 December the head of the Dutch military mission to the Allied Control Commission, Vice Admiral de Booy, wrote to Stikker:

> One is very conscious, even too conscious, of the position that Germany is taking in the Cold War, and will have to take, even more strongly, in a real conflict between the East and West. Too often, one feels this to be the key factor [...] within the framework of the defence of Western Europe, one sees very well that Germany is a problem for the West.[83]

The British Ambassador wrote:

> [...] the Dutch are beginning to ask themselves who is going to be responsible for the defence of Germany – the scanty forces of the Western Union, or a new Wehrmacht. During the year there has been growing support in the Netherlands for a measure of German rearmament; but the old fear and hatred of Germany remain, and no clear-cut ideas have yet emerged upon the paradoxes created by Germany.[84]

On 17 March 1950, *Nieuwe Rotterdamse Courant (NRC)* wrote: 'The question is not whether one needs Germany's strength, but whether one can restore it in such a way as to present no threat to the West.'[85]

The British government, for its part, was not prepared to stick its neck out on the question of German rearmament, whatever the Chiefs of Staff might have thought. A Foreign Office brief prepared at the end of April 1950 shows that the British were not prepared to take the lead, and that suspicion of Germany was considerable. The brief began by recommending that the British delegation should not raise the subject of the re-establishment of German Armed Forces; if the question were raised, then the delegation was to point out that there was no need to discuss the short-term aspect. The brief continued, rather personally:

> At the same time we should be honest and recognise in our minds, although we need not say so, the full implications of our declared policy of bringing Germany into the Western system as an equal partner with equal rights. This goal will take us a long time and we may not get there, But if we do, the end of the road means German participation in all Western organisations, including the North Atlantic Treaty, and a degree of supervision, of course under the direction of a common Western military machine.

The background to the brief showed the fear that existed that Germany might 'throw in her lot with Russia' and included the significant words: 'Moreover, even if Germany does not ally herself to Russia [sic], experience teaches us that an armed Germany soon develops a truculence and arrogance which makes it impossible to deal with.'[86]

The Dutch view, at official level, was rather ambivalent. A Dutch Foreign Ministry paper of 13 May 1950, entitled 'The policy to be adopted with reference to Germany in the future and the problem of German rearmament', stated that the number of divisions required for an effective defence of Western Europe could not be contained unless Germany contributed to their formation. It went on to say, however, that the Dutch government believed that German rearmament would be premature. The paper added that discussions on the problem should take place and that Benelux should participate in a working group.[87] Prejudices and memories of the war apart, however, officials' perceptions of German views were very down to earth. Vice Admiral de Booy wrote in May:

The number of those rejecting rearmament for idealistic reasons is undoubtedly large; the 'fresh, happy war' is now out of favour for very many. Many others reject the restoration of a German army under foreign command as unworthy or impossible; others see in it a provocation to the East and an accentuation of the split between East and West.[88]

The outbreak of hostilities in Korea made the question of German rearmament more urgent, whereas before it had been more academic. The German Chancellor fuelled the debate by saying that he was concerned that Stalin had the same plan for Europe as for Korea.[89] Bevin, too, said that the following year, the Soviet Government would seek to repeat in Germany what they had done in Korea.[90] Whether or not there was a real threat of war in Europe or not, the perceived threat provided enough reason at the time to look at the rearmament question more urgently than ever. The Dutch government and press supported the American standpoint:

> The firm declaration of President Truman and the immediate decision to use military measures in support of South Korea were therefore most welcome to all newspapers (except of course the Communist newspapers) as was the prompt expression of Dutch support for the United States Government.[91]

On 22 July, the American High Commissioner in Germany said that it was 'very difficult to deny the Germans the right to defend their soil.'[92] The Americans were clearly ahead of the hesitant Europeans in pushing for German rearmament. (Following the war, it had not taken long to see off the Morgenthau Plan, which would have made Germany into an agricultural state). They could afford to be, since they had not experienced at first hand what the Europeans had. Churchill's speech in August at the Council of Europe calling for the creation of a European Army had an electrifying effect, even though he was then in opposition. Although debate as to whether he meant what he said continues to this day, the mystery is unlikely to be unravelled until his private papers have been released for general scrutiny. For the time being, we must accept Churchill's reply to Sir Anthony Nutting's question: 'I meant it for them, not for us.'[93] The false hopes that the speech raised in Europe will be discussed and analysed later. The idea of a European army had of course been well aired before Churchill's speech. In December 1949, both Leon Blum and Konrad Adenauer had called for German participation in a Federal European Army under the authority of supranational institutions.⁹⁴

Whatever the later polemics, and Britain's role in the question of European integration, to be discussed later, Churchill's statement fuelled discussion, and caused governments to look seriously at ways of permitting German rearmament. With the Americans now taking the lead in pushing for a solution, the Foreign Ministers of the Big Three met in New York on 12 – 14 September, just before the NATO Council meeting. Although the British Chiefs of Staff had put forward a long-term plan for the gradual rearmament of Germany, Bevin restricted his ideas to a German mobile police force,⁹⁵ and did not go along with the idea of integrating German troops directly into NATO. Schuman was 'shocked to hear from Dean Acheson of American proposals for a German military contribution of a possible ten divisions.'⁹⁶ When Acheson said that the plan simply entailed assigning these units to NATO, under an American general, Schuman would still not accept it.⁹⁷

Churchill's statement and the rumours of American plans led to a good deal of press comment. The Dutch press was, as has been seen, on the whole generally in favour of German rearmament, particularly if it could be harnessed in some way. The *Volkskrant* said on 2 September: 'Since both a strongly and weakly armed Germany has its dangers, there is only one way out: a European army.'⁹⁸ On 28 September *Trouw* wrote: 'In a European Army [...] the Germans can and must participate.'⁹⁹ *NRC* wrote on 27 September: 'Generally, one is however of the view that Germany's participation in West European defence is only a question of time.'¹⁰⁰ Even the left of centre *Het Vrije Volk*, wrote on 20 September that it was better to have Germans protecting the Elbe line, than Dutch troops.¹⁰¹

Dutch support for German rearmament was less qualified than British – and far ahead of the French. Back in May, Stikker had told the Americans of the strong feeling in his own parliament in favour of Germany's remilitarisation.¹⁰² The evidence suggests that the Dutch felt particularly exposed to the East. Even the Dutch Prime Minister, Drees, not known for his love of military matters, had said to his cabinet on the same day that his country signed the NATO pact, that it was of great importance, strategically, that Germany be included in the defence plan, since otherwise the defence of the Netherlands along the Ijssel line could be of little significance.¹⁰³ In other words, the help of the Germans was crucial. The problem of the Netherlands' geographical position in the Allied strategy paper for Western Europe was, as shall be seen, to show how the Netherlands were able to exercise considerable influence at the NATO Council.

In the meantime, the Dutch Foreign Minister showed a good measure of worry and frustration:

> Stikker called this morning [...] Brussels Pact Organisation had failed in its job and Council of Europe was getting nowhere. As for NATO, he felt it still in talk stage with little accomplished [...] His Government feels Germany must be brought effectively into defence of Western Europe. He was concerned about French slowness to face this need, but felt British government in last two weeks were moving towards recognition of it. He felt unified command essential and that such command could only be American.[104] (The Dutch Foreign Ministry was fully aware that the French General, De Lattre de Tassigny, Commander in Chief of Land Forces in Western Europe, was concerned at Dutch parliamentary opinion that German rearmament was unavoidable.)[105]

Stikker's frustration with the Big Three was evident, as we have seen. To try and exercise more influence, he formed an informal 'little three', which included the Canadian and Norwegian Foreign Ministers. He says in his memoirs that 'we were able to exercise [...] a considerable influence on the important decision concerning German participation in NATO.'[106] Stikker's main worry shortly before the NATO Council opened on 15 September 1950, was that the Allied Strategy paper for Western Europe (which according to Fursdon, he had only recently read) based its forward defence on the Rhine-Ijssel line.[107] The implication was that the whole of Germany, and the northern provinces of the Netherlands, would be abandoned. He expressed his concerns to Bevin on the journey to New York.[108]

The day before the Council opened, the Foreign Ministers of the 'Little Three' met Acheson. Stikker alluded to newspaper reports to the effect that the Big Three had reached 'very basic decisions' regarding European rearmament and German participation in European defence without any regard to the rest of the North Atlantic Council.[109] Although Stikker certainly suggests that the 'Little Three' exercised considerable influence, Fursdon refers to the Canadian Foreign Minister saying that it would be difficult for the Canadians to take a strong stand on 'what was essentially a European matter'. The Norwegian Foreign Minister had problems in taking the lead on the question of German rearmament, because of the continuing feeling in Norway about Germany.[110]

It was thus left to Stikker to tackle the Big Three on his own. Fursdon provides an amusing picture of Stikker seeking out the Foreign Ministers of the Big Three individually, the night before the NATO Council. Bevin had gone to bed, and female voices were heard emanating from what Stikker had assumed to be Schuman's room, which left him with Acheson, who agreed with Stikker's worries about the position of the line of defence, saying that the United States had been discussing the same thing internally.[111]

Thus, the Fifth Session of the NATO Council opened with Stikker stressing the need for a defence line as far East in Germany as possible and raising the question of more troops in Europe or possible German participation in European defence.[112] Stikker described the Rhine-Ijssel plan as 'raving lunacy'[113] He clearly influenced the British. On 16 September, Bevin wrote to Attlee:

> It is quite clear from a further analysis of the situation that the whole morale of Europe and of the Dutch in particular will be jeopardised if it is decided to defend the present Rhine-Ijssel line and thus in effect sacrifice so many people.[114]

The council agreed with Stikker's proposal that the defence line be redrawn to the East. The question of the German defence contribution, fast becoming a euphemism for German rearmament, was, of course, more vexed, particularly in view of French sensitivities. The Council simply agreed that the NATO Defence Committee would meet on 28 October to make recommendations 'as to the method by which Germany could most usefully make its contribution.' The intervening period was, as will be seen in Chapter 6, to be crucial, with Stikker's influence being eroded by French flair for innovation.

The European Angle

The Dutch, never trusting the French in large measure, and keen to involve both Britain and America in Europe, knew that they needed Germany, both to keep the Eastern block as far away as possible and because they realised the necessity of German rearmament, as well as an economically strong Germany, from which they could benefit. The question of European security simply depended on Germany, and the Dutch were more ready to admit this than the French:

The Dutch Government's policy towards Germany continued throughout 1950 to be based on considerations of political and economic realism. In spite of bitter memories of the German occupation, the Dutch Government has been in the forefront of European countries in accepting the necessity of German rearmament subject to suitable guarantees, for it was natural that the Dutch should wish to see an effective buffer between them and Soviet Russia, in addition to the prospect of support from America and the United Kingdom.[115]

The Dutch were very much in favour of Germany's economic integration into Europe, not only because of the wish to see a strong German recovery, but because the more economic involvement with the rest of Europe, then the less likelihood of military hostilities. The *Note on the German Question* of July 1949 (referred to in Chapter 2) underlined the close link between security and Germany's involvement in European co-operation:

> The undersigned [Stikker] appreciates [...] the most important aspects of the German question. These are the security question and the participation of Germany in European co-operation [...] As long as no definitive solution has been found for the German question, as long as a dividing line runs through Germany and as long as there is no real proof that the German people are working with all their heart for a democratic form of government, with a durable character, then the security question needs to be watched permanently. There is a close connection between the security question and European co-operation. The insertion of Germany, or at least the part occupied by the Western Allies, is an indispensable requirement for a strong Western Europe. Without Germany's co-operation, there is in fact no chance for a complete Western European recovery and for Western European security [...] Admission of Germany to the cultural, social, economic and political co-operation between the other European states [...] can lead in the long run to the removal of the danger of renewed German aggression.[116]

Dutch policy towards German participation in European co-operation contrasted sharply with that of the French, as Albert Kersten points out: 'The Dutch were convinced that Germany would play a decisive role in all future European co-operation, but were strongly against the fact that France strongly stressed the security aspects, in all questions relating Germany. They assumed that France's view to extending its predominance in Europe was aimed at impeding its own approach to the German question. The Dutch Government therefore pushed for the assistance of the USA and Great Britain in the defence of Western Europe, to prevent the feared insertion of their country into a Continental security block.[117]

Paradoxically, although Stikker was at first against integration whenever it touched on supranationality, he eventually came round to a more realistic view (as Kersten points out), with the nudging of the Americans. As we shall see, many Dutch were wary of supranational institutions, but realised that, in the last analysis, co-operation was infinitely preferable to isolation, whether in a NATO or a European context. If one leaves aside the supranationality aspect, and stresses the co-operation side, then the Dutch approach can be seen more clearly. By supporting Germany, they were supporting European co-operation and combating what they saw as exaggerated French influence in Europe.

> He [Stikker] doubted whether the time had come for supranational organisations. There were already far too many organisations in the world, and the best thing that the West could do was to concentrate on the practical possibilities such as the European Payments union [...] it was essential that Germany should be included [...][118]

Apart from a tacit recognition that Germany was essential to Dutch security, from a geographical standpoint, and to the national pocket, from an economic standpoint, the other reason for supporting Germany's role in European co-operation was to be able to deal indirectly with its claims, rather than have to negotiate directly with a strong German government (see Chapter 2). Stikker wrote:

> As long as there was no central German government, all these questions were discussed freely but fruitlessly with the Allied occupation authorities. It was for us of the greatest importance to ensure that these discriminatory measures were not maintained by a future central German government. This was one of the reasons that made Germany's entry to the OEEC in 1949 so important for us.[119]

As will be seen, Britain's attitude towards Europe helped the Dutch to support European integration more strongly although, as Kersten says, in defence matters, Europe's relationship with the United States, was 'sacrosanct.'[120] On 11 February 1950, the British ambassador wrote:

The focus of interest has shifted to the preparation of plans for the political and economic unity of Europe; for in this the Dutch see the only prospect of dealing with the three fold problem of Russia, Germany and their own future.[121]

Conclusions

The Dutch were more than happy to join the Brussels and Atlantic Pacts, both as a safeguard for their security interests and to keep a toehold in the decision-making process on Germany. However, although the mechanics of breaking with the previous 100 years were handled relatively simply, the implications of membership do not seem to have been taken fully into account. Thus, once the Dutch were asked to put their money where their mouth was, it became clear that their traditional policy of abstentionism and independence acted as a strong brake on the concrete action demanded by membership of the emerging Western security system. As such, Dutch moderation (at least at official level) on the question of the perceived communist threat, contrasted with the robust official attitude of the British and Americans.

Apart from some notable exceptions, the Dutch did not view the Brussels and Atlantic Pacts as purely military and offensive, and bewailed the failure of the United Nations to solve the problems of the world. The Chief of Staff, General Kruls, took a more urgent view of matters, as did Stikker, although the latter was constrained by the more relaxed attitude of the Prime Minister and Finance Minister. When Stikker was dealing directly with his counterparts in NATO, however, he certainly seems to have exercised considerable influence, particularly at the Fifth Session of the NATO Council.

Trade was also an important factor in Dutch considerations: ever mindful of their commercial interests, the Dutch were slower to go along with the British and Americans in restricting the export of certain militarily useful products to the Eastern block.

Although the above factors go a long way towards explaining the Dutch attitude towards the nascent Western security system, the picture cannot be complete without some understanding of, as well as some measure of sympathy with, the Dutch position on Indonesia. The problem is more central to Dutch concerns than many might suggest; it detracted considerably from the more immediate concerns about Western security. It preoccupied the Dutch militarily, complicated relations with the British and Americans and may well have added considerable emotion to Dutch thinking.

While the outbreak of hostilities in Korea was accompanied by strong support from the Dutch for the American viewpoint, they were relatively slow to send troops, and were still not prepared to increase their military spending, whatever paper plans were made. Such a lackadaisical attitude (at least when seen through British and American eyes at the time) may well have added spice to the British propaganda campaign. It is, however, difficult to gauge the success or otherwise of this campaign (which was to continue, as shall be seen), although one is tempted to wonder whether it intrinsically changed Dutch attitudes towards communism, the Soviet Union and the West.

The Dutch viewed the question of German rearmament more urgently than most, particularly following the outbreak of hostilities in Korea. They were close to the American viewpoint in stressing the need for German participation. They were clearly very worried about the Rhine-Ijssel defence line being used as NATO's forward line and pushed successfully to change matters. The British, while keen to involve Germany in the West, took time to make their position on German rearmament more clear-cut, and tended to leave leadership to the Americans. In short, the Dutch were happy for German troops to defend German soil, even within NATO, as long as Germany was integrated into the West. As shall be seen, their view was very different from the French one.

Following the transfer of sovereignty to Indonesia, the main priority of the Dutch was to strengthen their leverage on the German question. To that end, they pushed hard for German participation in European co-operation; in their enthusiasm to involve Germany, they were at loggerheads with the French, who were considerably more reticent, at least until the vision of Schuman, Monnet and a few others combined with French flair for innovation. Crucially, however, the Dutch sensed that by linking Germany to European co-operation, they could strengthen the toehold they had gained by joining the Brussels and Atlantic Pacts. In this way they found themselves focusing on European co-operation.

6

WHOSE EUROPE?

Introduction

In parallel with the plethora of meetings on security and the German question, enthusiasm for European co-operation was fast gaining momentum, to the point where it began to raise questions of a deep institutional significance. To understand the Dutch viewpoint, it is necessary to turn back to 1948, when the enthusiasm for European political co-operation was reaching one of several climaxes, finding its expression in the Hague Congress of the European Movement on 7–10 May 1948. As pointed out previously, Benelux provided a practical example of European co-operation, and had fired the imagination of the Americans. Not everybody had precisely the same motives; there were those who saw a future United States of Europe, with the sovereignty of individual states subsumed into a supranational federation, usually labelled federalists; and those who preferred a more step by step approach, dealing with particular sectors; they were labelled functionalists. Some Frenchmen, (and there is no doubt that the French tended to set the pace) recognised the importance of pooling Gentian coal and steel into a supranational authority, since this would make a future war highly unlikely. This view is best summed up in Schuman's statement to the Assemblée Nationale in late 1948: 'A European solution for the peace, a European solution for Germany, a European solution for the Ruhr, such is our vision of the future.'[1]

The British were expected to play a leading role in European co-operation. Given grandiose indications of support for the European ideal, particularly from Winston Churchill, it is not surprising that leadership was expected from Britain. One of Churchill's more famous European speeches was given at Zürich University on 19 September 1946, in which he called for the creation of a United States of Europe, saying:

> The structure of the United States of Europe will be such as to make the material strength of a single state less important. Small nations will count as much as large ones and gain their honour by a contribution to the common cause.²

It is cruel, but perhaps necessary, to point out that, following his election defeat, Churchill needed to keep in the public eye – later events were to show that Churchill and Britain were not as enthusiastic as they had tried to make out. To many, Churchill's ideas must have seemed later like hot air. His perceived European attitude will be discussed later.

The first big surprise for the continental Europeans came when the Labour Government turned down the invitation to the Hague Conference. However, 41 Labour members of Parliament accepted,³ in a non-official, individual capacity. Churchill, too, naturally attended. The meeting, attended by internationally known Europeans like Spaak, de Gasperi, Adenauer, Monnet, Schuman and van Zeeland, brought together, as Fursdon points out,⁴ the adversaries of a major world war of only a few years before. The atmosphere must have been both electric and emotional. The final resolution, drafted by a former French Prime Minister, Paul Ramadier, called, inter alia, for the convening of a European Assembly, and the creation of the economic and political union of Europe. The reality was to prove different. It is interesting to look at both the British and Dutch attitudes as this crucial stage in European co-operation, particularly since the Dutch, and the self-avowed Protestant, Stikker, counted on British participation in European co-operation to counter (their view of) French hegemony.

The Council of Europe – a weak beginning

The Council of Europe ended up as a relatively ineffectual talking shop, far removed from the future picture painted by Churchill. Since British commitment was so important to the other participants, particularly the Dutch, (who were generally more Anglophile than the rest of Europe, particularly with Stikker as Foreign Minister), it is worth attempting to analyse the British position.

Following the Hague Congress, the French Government took the initiative. They hardly had any choice, since the refusal of the British Government to attend the Congress showed that little would otherwise have been done. One country had to take the bull by the horns; it was not to be Britain. The French pursued the idea at the Consultative Council of the Brussels Pact, which passed it to a Committee for the Study of European Unity. 'The British Government,' wrote Milward, 'had reluctantly accepted, determined that the Council of Europe should remain entirely powerless.'[5] Whatever the rights and wrongs of the British standpoint, Britain's attitude would merit at least one fat book, which would need to include Anglo-French relations, an analysis of the British national psyche and of the psyche of those individuals responsible for not wishing to muck in with the rest. In the Committee, the British unexpectedly put forward counter-proposals 'advocating a purely consultative inter-governmental organ whose terms of reference would exclude such vital matters as defence or economic policy.'[6]

Interestingly, the Dutch government, like the British, were not at first enthusiastic about the idea of the Council of Europe. Stikker wrote in his memoirs that as long as Great Britain and the Commonwealth had not clarified their thinking, he could not see 'how these grand ideas' could fit into the pattern of world policy.[7] In August 1948, Stikker told the Cabinet that he was reserved about the idea of a 'European Assembly'. Van Schaik (the Finance Minister) referred to the idea as Utopian, while the Prime Minister, Drees, did not consider the proposal very practical, adding:

> Co-operation between the European countries must grow. It cannot be forced by plans such as the one in question. But the Netherlands cannot ignore the proposal. We do not wish to be spoilsports, although we are not enthusiastic about the proposal at the moment.[8]

At the beginning, then, the Dutch were lukewarm, and probably wary of French motives. However, unlike the British, the Dutch government modified its view. One reason lay in their keenness to see Germany involved in European co-operation: to adopt a stance of non-cooperation would have appeared inconsistent with their emerging policy of supporting the economic development of Germany within a European framework. Another lies in the importance the Dutch attached to their relations with the United States. In February 1949, Stikker referred in Parliament to the fact that the idea of a European Federation had found increasing favour 'at [sic] the other side of the Atlantic Ocean'. He alluded to the United States being a cornerstone, not only of the foreign policy of the Netherlands, but of Western Europe.[9] The third reason was that the proponents of European unity were beginning to doubt Britain's commitment. Thus, although the Dutch government were still somewhat ambiguous in pushing for a supranational solution, they opposed British suggestions that the

Assembly's members should be appointed by national governments, and that the delegations should vote en bloc according to their respective government's instructions.[10] While the negotiations were, in Milward's words 'disputatious',[11] the Dutch sided with the French on at least the above issue, thus helping to achieve a compromise between the French and British positions, whereby each government would decide the procedure to be followed in appointing the representatives of its country.[12] The British did however succeed in ensuring that the Council of Europe had no real teeth: the Assembly was completely subordinate to the Council of Ministers which, in turn, was subject to the rule of unanimity. In other words, any one country had the power of veto. The Council was born a eunuch.

Alan Sked argues in his paper on Britain and the Council of Europe that it was not simply the British who had reduced the Council of Europe to impotence, saying that the French were equally guilty. He quotes a Foreign Office official as writing: 'It is not surprising that the French Government are giving their delegates no instructions, as they have not the faintest idea what they really want themselves.' Dr Sked also admits, however, that the British must accept the lion's share of the blame for the Council of Europe being reduced to impotence.[13] On balance, it is fair to assume that had Britain been more positive, the Council would have been more than a talking shop. The Dutch certainly played their part, suggesting that a French proposal to establish both an Assembly and a Council of Ministers could be reconciled with the British view. Although Dalton, the British Chief Delegate, agreed, the powers of the Assembly were then whittled down further, writes Dr Sked.[14]

In the absence of a powerful Germany, the main battle was bound to be fought between Britain and France, both of which had an entirely different approach to the question of European unity. The British approach to the Council of Europe was epitomised by Bevin. On 29 September 1948, he told the Belgian Foreign Minister, Spaak (a European federalist per excellence) that he 'wanted to build up in the traditional British way a sort of unwritten constitution in Western Europe in which Ministers could meet and then report back to the Parliaments.'[15] This sort of vagueness was generally seen as obstructive by promoters of European co-operation. Spaak, for example, had said almost a year previously that he was 'sufficiently familiar with Anglo-Saxon psychology to realise their [the British] instinctive reluctance to follow events up to their logical consequences.'[16]

Robert Schuman wrote: 'England will only allow its integration into Europe under the force of event [...] England has an invincible prejudice against precise and rigid texts, which are the delight of continental lawyers.'[17] In his book, *Combats Inachevés*, Spaak wrote: 'Let us be fair, [...] his [Churchill's] presence at the Congress at the Hague, his proposal to create a European Army, had entertained illusions [...] she [Britain] would not even participate in partial attempts to integrate.'[18]

When the Assembly first met, it is not surprising that it was inundated with a variety of motions calling for European integration. The Committee of Ministers, however:

> Led by the British Labour government, succeeded in killing any attempt to make the Council of Europe the instrument of European political union [...] Gradually, the flame of the firing spirits dimmed in the face of compromise; compromise usually necessary because of the British government's attitude to Europe – an attitude initiated by Attlee's Labour government, but one later largely continued, to the great surprise and sadness of so many devoted Continental European federalists, by the Conservative government under Churchill.[19]

Churchill was to lose some of his popularity in both Belgium and the Netherlands, not only because of Britain's attitude towards European integration, but because of what he wrote in his memoirs published after the war. Janet Eisen, in her paper on Anglo-Dutch Relations and European Unity from 1940–48, quotes him:

> The Belgians are extremely weak and their behaviour before then was shocking. The Dutch were entirely selfish and fought only when they were attacked and then only for a few hours [...] that England should undertake to defend these countries, together with any help they may afford before the French have the Second Army in Europe, seems to me contrary to all wisdom and even common prudence.[20]

While one should not exaggerate the effect of Churchill's words, they did not help Britain's image in the Netherlands and Belgium. Churchill annoyed some Belgians even more than he annoyed some Dutch, by criticising their King for pro-German tendencies during the war. European co-operation was still the main problem in Anglo-Belgian relations. At the end of 1949, the British ambassador to Brussels wrote: 'A more serious cause for the deterioration of our position in the eyes of large numbers of leading and intelligent Belgians is the apparent uncertainty of the British attitude towards the movement for closer European integration.'[21]

The Dutch, on the other hand, were not as worried about the British attitude as the Belgians, the main reason being that the Belgians tended towards the French view of the Council of Europe.[22] The Dutch, and Stikker in particular, were, as has been suggested, particularly suspicious of the French. Thus, while the Dutch were to become increasingly exasperated with the British attitude towards European integration, as will be seen, they were not as vehement in their annoyance as the likes of Spaak.

Although annoyance with Britain was to manifest itself eloquently the following year, with the presentation of the Schuman plan by the French, there were points of contention in the meantime. As mentioned in Chapter 2, on 18 September 1949, the British Government devalued Sterling without consulting its European partners in the OEEC and the Council of Europe. The British Government gave the Netherlands Government only a day's advance warning, by delivering an Aide Memoire to the Dutch Foreign Ministry, in which they stated: 'They much regret the shortness of notice which they have been able to give the Royal Netherlands Government.'[23] The British ambassador to The Hague wrote: 'Later the devaluation of the pound without prior consultation with the OEEC States caused further criticism in the Netherlands of what they imagine to be the indifference of the United Kingdom to European unity.'[24] On 23 September the ambassador quoted a Dutch press report: '[...] by the unilateral action, [Britain] has flouted the idea of European economic co-operation and has given evidence of her intention to withdraw from Continental affairs in favour of an Anglo-American block [...].'[25] Apart from such irritations, the Dutch were critical of the degree to which the British delegation to Strasbourg introduced party politics.[26]

'It should however be emphasised,' wrote the British ambassador, 'that these criticisms are not based on ill-will, but on a genuine and widespread desire to have a firm British lead to follow.'[27] As we have seen previously, the German and Indonesian problems were a source of friction between the Dutch and British, which compounded the problem of the British attitude towards European co-operation. It is not surprising that in a debate in the Dutch Second Chamber in March 1950, reference was made to Great Britain wanting to have its cake and eat it.[28] The American Embassy in London seems to have been particularly perceptive and accurate in its view of Britain's attitude to Europe:

> The British have never accepted the concept of a political integration involving any transfer of sovereignty to a central political authority and regard as Utopian proposals for a United States of Europe. We

do not see any prospect of a change in this position [...] We feel that
the outcome of the general election will not result in any important
modification of Britain's basic attitude towards political integration.[29]

They were to be proved right.

Although the Council of Europe did not end up being what many had
wanted, the very debate it inspired kept the 'European question' well to
the fore, and gave those very federalists, particularly the French ones, the
opportunity to further develop plans which were, paradoxically, to by-pass
the institution of the Council of Europe. The Schuman plan was to bring
into relief the fundamental difference of outlook between the British and
the French and to show that when the chips were down, the Dutch preferred to stick with the Continent.

The Schuman Plan

'The French Government proposes that the entire French-German
production of coal and steel be placed under a common High Authority, in an organisation open to the participation of the other countries
of Europe.'[30] There is no doubt that Schuman's announcement startled
the world, and caught the British on the hop: when Bevin was informed
about the Schuman Plan, he is said to have flown 'into a towering rage'.[31]
As will be seen, Britain's subsequent behaviour was to be strongly criticised by many, including the Dutch. Britain's position, while not popular
with European federalists, was based on her perceived role in the world,
her lack of confidence in France and her belief that Europe could not go
it alone. For Bevin, an Atlantic solution was the only viable framework.
Following acceptance of the Schuman Plan by the Six, Bevin told Stikker
that the British 'had to try and convince the French that European unity
was not possible on a purely European basis but that it was possible on an
Atlantic basis and only on an Atlantic basis.'[32] It was, however, Britain's
own 'special relationship' with the United States that was shaken by the
way the Schuman Plan was announced, leading to a considerable outburst
of emotion from Bevin; for the French informed Acheson first and then
instructed their ambassador in London, Massigli, to inform Bevin. When
Bevin was informed, he is said by Monnet to have told Massigli: 'I think
that something has changed between our two countries.'[33] Massigli, however, provides a slightly different version:

> According to Jean Monnet [...] Bevin is said to have told me: 'I certainly think that, between our two countries, something has just

changed.' This suggestion was never made to me, but something had in fact changed: henceforth, Bevin would no longer trust Robert Schuman.[34]

Whatever the exact words spoken, Bevin was clearly very upset that he had to hear from the French ambassador something that the French had told Acheson, without Acheson informing him first. Acheson wrote:

> He was in a towering rage and at once charged that I had known of Schuman's Plan and had kept it from him. This of course, was true and I said so. But before I could explain, he rushed on to accuse me of having conspired with Schuman to create a European combination against British trade with the Continent [...] it took a long time to reduce his blood pressure to the point where discussion would replace denunciation.[35]

Pierre Melandri, commenting on Bevin's anger, justifies French secrecy by writing: 'In any case, the English, as well, had decided that secrecy was preferable when they had devalued the pound the previous autumn.'[36]

While the French solution was imaginative in its simplicity – they had certainly gone to the nub of the problem – the initiative itself was hardly unexpected. The failure of the Council of Europe to achieve integration, and the relative weakness of the International Ruhr Authority meant that the muddling could not go on forever. The straws had started to point in the same direction well before Schuman's announcement on 9 May 1950. The French needed to find a way of harnessing future German power. Dr Adenauer helped, as he was highly aware of the need for at least a bilateral solution with France. Much of the success of the plan can be put down to Adenauer's friendship with Schuman. Adenauer, in an interview in March 1950, suggested a Franco-German union as a touchstone, to which other European countries might later subscribe.[37] Thus, if the announcement of the plan was startling, the climate was ripe. Apart from French fears about an uncontrolled resurgent Germany, there were considerable worries about excess steel production.[38] Roger Bullen summed up French motives for the Schuman Plan succinctly: 'Its origin lay in the French realisation of the collapse of their efforts to prevent or successfully to delay the recovery of Germany'.[39]

The attitude of the Americans was also particularly conducive to the success of the plan. Only three days after the plan's announcement, the Economic Co-operation Administration issued a press release, part of which read:

The French proposal [...] shows real determination to achieve a high degree of economic integration among the free nations of Western Europe [...] A free, united Europe, standing together, can discourage future aggressions and lead the way to lasting peace.[40]

Shortly after, President Truman called it 'An act of constructive statesmanship in the great French tradition'.[41] Some of this can be ascribed to Acheson, whose book *Sketches from Life* brings out his admiration for Schuman. Although friendly about Bevin, he writes: 'He was a split second operator [...] he was often distracted. He could easily miss a cue and in the resulting confusion not know how to pick it up again.'[42]

What, however, of the attitude of the Dutch? One might have expected at least some initial resistance, given their worries about supranational institutions. This seems in the event to have been subsumed by the importance they attached to American policy on Europe. They knew which side of the Channel their bread was buttered on, and it was certainly not the English one. Initially, however, they did not do very much at all. On 15 May, Mansholt, the Agriculture Minister (and a convinced European) told the Cabinet that they should give their opinion on the Schuman Plan.[43] A week later, Stikker told the Cabinet that the Netherlands should participate in the plan from the beginning. The Cabinet agreed.[44]

Unlike the British, the Dutch were prepared to participate in the talks, albeit with initial reservations. On 25 May, the British Permanent representative to the OEEC, Edmund Hall-Patch wrote to Bevin:

> Spierenburg [his counterpart] told me that discussion of the French plan with Benelux Ministers yesterday was not very satisfactory [...] this renunciation of sovereignty to an ill-defined higher authority the Dutch found most unpalatable [...] Benelux Ministers were disconcerted at the nebulous nature of the French plan, and felt that much greater clarification would be necessary before discussions could be resumed.[45]

The Dutch nevertheless joined, on the understanding that they could leave the plan later if they disliked the way it emerged. The British were given assurances by Schuman's Chef de Cabinet, Clappier, that they could enter the talks, as long as supranationalism remained on the agenda. Monnet was not prepared, wrote John Young, to break the all important supranational principle, fearing 'with good reason, that the British would try to steer his plan towards merely inter-governmental co-operation.'[46]

The Dutch attitude contrasted sharply with that of the British, who were not prepared to lose one iota of sovereignty. The Dutch ambassador in London, Verduynen, reported on 12 May:

> [...] in Government circles the reaction to the Schuman proposals was cool, in the words of the "Daily Mail", they "have been received with a storm of silence" [...] Labour wonders whether Germany is really ready to take its place in an organ, in which the French remain in control.

However, he also reported a *Times* editorial as saying that the British government would have no reason and no wish to fall below the level of statesmanship set up by Mr Acheson's assurance and Mr Schuman's example.[47] The British played for time. On 19 May, Attlee told the House of Commons that the British Government would approach the French initiatives in a sympathetic spirit.[48] Monnet was at the time in London trying to persuade the British to be forthcoming.[49] Apart from British reticence, it is said that they were angry that the French had informed Acheson about the plan (and obtained his blessing) before them.[50] At all events, exchanges between the French and British continued after Monnet and his team had departed, but led to nothing concrete. On 26 May, the Dutch ambassador in Paris, van Boetzelaer, reported that the British had suggested to Schuman that they talk directly to the French about coal and steel, with Germany as an observer, 'but **not** Benelux. On the grounds of the latter, Schuman had refused.'[51] Such tactics, which could be construed as aiming at exploiting mutual suspicion between Benelux on the one hand, and France and Germany on the other, were hardly a positive step, and it is not surprising that Schuman turned down the approach point blank. On the same day, the British government sent a note to the French saying:

> It should, however, be realised that if the French Government intend to insist on a commitment to pool resources and set up an authority with certain sovereign powers as a prior condition to joining the talks, Her Majesty's Government would reluctantly be unable to accept such a condition. Her Majesty's Government would greatly regret such an outcome.[52]

Regrets or no regrets, the British Government refused on 3 June to subscribe to a press release on the plan (considering it too binding), suggesting a Ministers' conference to find a solution. The French, perhaps not surprisingly, rejected the British suggestion.[53] Thus, on 5 June, the Six met and decided to go ahead. The Dutch, for their part, were clearly not prepared, despite their Atlantic traditions, to compromise their position. 'One hoped very much,' wrote Spierenburg to Stikker, 'that England would participate in these discussions, but thought that, while England was not prepared to go along, the business had at all events to go ahead without England.'[54]

The French did try to leave the door open, agreeing with the British that the French government would:

> Lose no opportunity of engaging in exchanges of views with the British Government which will permit them during the course of discussions to take carefully into account the point of view of the British Government in order to enable the latter to participate in, or associate themselves with, the common task as soon as they feel able to do so.[55]

Such diplomatic niceties did not prevent a certain amount of emotion in some quarters, on both sides of the Channel, not to say bad feeling.

On 13 June, the Labour Party produced a brochure called 'European Unity', which declared:

> The European peoples do not want a supranational authority to impose agreements [...] in every respect we in Britain are closer to our kinsman in Australia and New Zealand on the far side of the world than we are to Europe.[56]

It is difficult to disagree with Nutting's statement that the Labour Party 'could scarcely have been more insular and nationalist, even blimpish, in their European policy.'[57] One is tempted to wonder whether the Conservative Margaret Thatcher, was an admirer of Bevin. The brochure, perhaps not surprisingly, was fiercely criticised in the United States, on the Continent,[58] and by some in Britain, including Churchill. (The latter was, of course, still in opposition, and it is interesting to note his future back-pedalling when he came to power.) Even the Vatican seems to have been particularly critical of the British government's stance: a 'reliable source' transmitted the following to the Dutch Foreign Ministry during the first half of June:

> In Vatican circles there is disappointment over Great Britain's attitude towards the Schuman Plan. It had been stated with alarm how England has worked against every attempt at European integration in an almost 'shameless' way [...] for it is feared in Rome that London has rendered a dangerous service to Moscow by keeping out of West European integration.[59]

The Vatican's attitude to the Dutch position contrasted sharply, bringing out that Stikker's plan (see following section) had attracted great interest. Another 'reliable source', this time in Paris, reported to the Dutch Prime Minister that the French believed that 'the English had hindered all attempts at integration, political and economic, for several years.'[60] The Labour brochure, although it stressed socialist principles, was not welcomed by some continental Socialists. Raymond Bifflet, an executive member of the Socialist Movement for a United States of Europe was quoted in a newspaper interview as saying: 'We have defeated the national socialism of the USSR. We have not done this to succumb to the national socialism of the English.'[61] The bad feeling was compounded by a British proposal (by the Conservatives, in the Consultative Assembly of the Council of Europe) for an international authority in which countries would have votes in proportion to their production. However, it left the way open for national vetoes. Harold MacMillan, in his support for the proposal, said in the House of Commons.

> Our people will not hand over to a supranational Authority the right to close down our pits or our steelworks. We will not allow any supranational Authority to put large numbers of our people out of work in Durham, in the Midlands, in South Wales or in Scotland.[62]

Despite Stikker's general distaste for supranationalism, and his distrust of the French, the Dutch Cabinet was clearly in favour of the Schuman Plan, and Stikker had to go along with the current. On 7 July, at a meeting of the Joint Foreign Affairs and Trade Committee, the Minister for Economic Affairs described the plan as a brilliant and sensible attempt to sweep away the historical rivalry between France and Germany, referring to it as a concrete way of achieving economic integration in Europe. Significantly, he added that the Netherlands was prepared to give up part of its sovereignty in the common interest.[63] This was in clear contrast to the British view.

This is not to say that the Dutch simply sat on the sidelines nodding. Far from it; at the talks, which began on 20 June, they actually stood out with their Belgian colleagues – against the 'great and undefined powers to be invested in the High Authority.'[64] They pushed for the powers of the Authority to be closely defined. 'Out of the interplay of views,' as Diebold says,[65] it was decided to set up a Council of Ministers, who would review the Authority's decisions, and a Common Assembly, with the power to sack the members of the Authority by a two thirds majority. These changes were accepted by the French, largely because of Benelux pressure. Thus, while the Dutch were keen to participate in the plan, for essentially economic reasons, as we shall see, and were even prepared to relinquish some sovereignty, they played an important role in shaping the eventual organs that emerged.

This evidence of Dutch influence is further supported by a letter of 12 July from Oliver Harvey in the Foreign Office to Mr Younger: 'The Belgian and Dutch delegations have continued to press for the introduction of Ministerial control.'[66] Two weeks later, the British Embassy in Paris reported details of a long talk the ambassador had had with Clappier, the French Foreign Ministers' Chef de Cabinet, about the Schuman Plan. He wrote:

> The Dutch formula continues apparently to be the main topic of discussion at present. Clappier said that under this formula, the proposed ministerial council, in addition to its consultative agencies, would retain reserved powers enabling it to give directions to the High Authority when questions arose affecting national defence, commercial policy and full employment.[67]

Importantly, the Dutch set an example to the rest of Europe in the ratification process; the Second Chamber approved the plan on 31 October 1951, before even the French Assemblée Nationale, which in turn ratified on 13 December.[68] The Second Chamber passed the motion by 62 votes to 6, with one abstention, whereas the figures for the Assemblée Nationale were 377 to 233.[69]

The State Department issued a press release on 14 December, stating: 'It is my hope (i.e. Acheson's) that other Parliaments will quickly follow the lead given by the Second Chamber of the Netherlands States General on 31 October and now by the French Assembly, and that this treaty, which has become for all of us a milestone of the first importance, will soon enter into force.'[70] The Netherlands was the second country to ratify the plan, on 19 February, 18 days after the Bundesrat gave its final approval.[71]

As mentioned above, the Netherlands had good economic grounds for supporting the plan.

> The Dutch seem to have had few economic worries about entering the community. Their coal mining industry was well established and efficient. Its costs were low [...] The Dutch steel industry is small and quite efficient, but the country is a net importer. The government stressed the advantages to the Netherlands of equal access to the community's output in times of shortage.[72]

Milward writes:

> Only in the Netherlands were the economic advantages of the steel industry indisputable. It gained safe access to imported raw materials and the new steel works at Ijmuiden, which dominated the industry, was protected from the price cutting and other discrimination which the International Steel Cartel had habitually employed against all newcomers.[73]

There was, therefore, a fair amount of opposition within the industry itself. Moreover, opposition from the industry was clearly a sensitive matter: the record of a meeting of the Council for Economic Affairs on 31 January 1951 was classified 'top secret'. More curiously, the names of those who spoke had actually been cut out of the report by Dutch weeders, when the document became available in 1981. The name of the minister who spoke was also cut out: 'Minister X said [...] industry in the Marshall countries has resisted the Schuman Plan [...] Mr X, as the representative of the Dutch steel industry, has declared that [...] there is a risk that free competition will be eliminated.'[74]

Stikker, as mentioned, had to go along with events. He, of all, must have been in a difficult position, being particularly Anglophile, yet obviously disappointed at the British government's lack of interest in the plan. 'But as British hesitation and reluctance about joining Europe grew, so did Continental enthusiasm for unity,'[75] he wrote. His position was peculiarly ambivalent. Although he had called federalists 'federasts'[76] he also declared himself to be a federalist.[77] One can but speculate, although it is possible that he was philosophically against the planned and supranational nature of the Coal and Steel Community. He was, after all, not only a banker and a director (of Heineken breweries),[78] but a founder member of the VVD (People's Party for Freedom and Democracy),[79] a party that advocated free trade. Stikker had to swallow some of his own convictions. Clearly, Britain's attitude towards Europe made it easier for him to do so, as well as his desire to keep his job.

The Stikker Plan and the British

Stikker's own European plan deserves particular mention, especially because of the timing of its announcement, a few days before the Six met in Paris to begin negotiations. Worried about the widening chasm between the OEEC and the Six, he went to Oslo at the end of May 1950, and urged speedy action to 'create a strong, balanced European market, before overproduction and unemployment will force us again to withdraw into our own shells, with a lower standard of living as a result.'[80] On 16 June ,[81] he announced his 'Plan of Action', which called for a sectoral approach to European integration, starting with the basic industries, specifically agriculture. A report by the British ambassador to The Hague makes interesting reading:

> Throughout the past week the question of integration, and the attitude of Great Britain towards participation in a greater degree of integration in Western Europe, has dominated all other topics in the press. Integration is understood here less as a return to free trading conditions within Europe and eventually throughout the world, than as some form of federal government [...] meanwhile discussions have been scheduled to begin in Paris on the Schuman proposals without British participation, and with the Netherlands Government stressing that they are not committed [...] it is also suggested [...], not for the first time, that the British have welcomed the Stikker Plan for the reason that, coming when it did, it weakened the position of the Schuman Plan. It has again been suggested that his Majesty's Government would not regret failure of the talks on the Schuman Plan, since this would give them an opportunity to put forward a plan of their own which would not entail loss of sovereignty.[82]

This of course, they did, as has been seen. The British were not, in fact, in favour of the Stikker Plan, as shall shortly be seen. Michael Wintle concludes that the plan failed because it was 'riddled with shortcomings and inconsistencies which were ruthlessly exposed during the early stages of its negotiations.'⁸³ It is not easy to avoid the feeling that the Schuman Plan inspired some people to come up with their own – rather hurriedly prepared – plans.

Stikker's plan was superseded by those of Pella and then Petsche; all were part of the general enthusiasm to arrive at a common approach to European integration, eventually ending up in the Treaties of Rome. The debate surrounding Britain's attitude did not go away:

> In all quarters, it was regarded as clear that the British would not participate in a federated Europe [...] The British Labour Government turned its back on the unity of Europe [...] Europe will continue [...] even without Britain [...] The Conservative *De Telegraaf* [...] supported the statement made by Professor Romme (leader of the Catholic Peoples' Party) that a European Federation should be established without Great Britain [...] it is clear to everybody that Britain does not want to give up the smallest particle of sovereignty. The Netherlands Labour Party was alone in expecting that the British Labour Party Government would be in favour of international co-operation, but this dream has been shattered.[84]

The Dutch Labour Party must have remembered well Bevin's introducing a resolution at the Trades Union Congress in 1927; it had call for a unified Europe.[85] The British ambassador wrote in his annual dispatch for 1950,

> More serious was the misunderstanding which arose over Great Britain's attitude to the Schuman Plan [...] The Dutch were puzzled and disappointed at Great Britain's refusal to take part [...] the urge in Dutch political circles for some form of European Federation is a factor to be reckoned with [...] an important element of disappointment because Great Britain [...] has not seemed to Dutch minds to be giving an adequate lead to Western Europe, while France appears to be aiming to establish a special position for herself in continental Europe to the exclusion of Great Britain.[86]

Britain certainly seems to have had very different views to those of the French over European integration, punctuated by what seems to have bordered on considerable hostility to French policy per se, to the extent that it is not easy to find a dividing line between Britain's attitude towards France and European integration respectively. Bevin certainly played an important role. Having already, as we have seen, 'fallen into a towering rage' when informed of the Schuman Plan, he was to be fairly acerbic in his comments of the French political scene:

> [...] he also said that he was much disturbed by the present political instability in France of which the existing ministerial crisis is a symptom. Whereas in this country the parties sink their differences in the face of a crisis in international affairs, in France the parties contrive to carry on the manoeuvres for party advantage to the detriment of the national interest.[87]

On 14 July, a meeting was held at the Treasury, attended by the top officials at the Treasury and Foreign Office. Although the meeting was called to consider guidance to be given to the British delegation to the OEEC in 'dealing with certain difficulties expected to arise', the record shows that European integration was the topic. It provides a revealing insight into British policy towards the Continent:

> On general grounds it would be most undesirable that we should do anything to hamper a rapprochement of France and Germany [...] Our general attitude ought not to be hostile, so long as the schemes do not tend to the establishment of an exclusive trading system with high protective barriers all round it. There was indeed some danger that an attempt might be made to create such a system; if so, it would be necessary for [...] us to use all our influence to prevent this result [...] our last hopes of preventing any undue concentration on the Stikker, Pella, and Petsche schemes or variants thereof would be to offer for discussion practical and attractive counter proposals.[88]

Counter proposals would indeed come, in the form of the Eden Plan but, as shall be seen, would be considered to be 'too little, too late.'

Even Stikker, for all his fear of 'federasts' and attachment to Atlanticism, supported the Schuman Plan, whatever his initial misgivings about supranationality. He covered his misgivings by agreeing to take part in the talks subject to a specific reservation that the Dutch were not committed in advance to acceptance of the Plan. Britain, on the other hand, refused to accept such a formula.[89] In some Dutch quarters, British motives were, according to the British ambassador, regarded as primarily selfish, although Stikker's concern for a lead from Britain was not unnatural in view of the Dutch wariness towards fellow Europeans.[90]

The Dutch were clearly worried by the prospect of a Europe dominated first by France and then by France and Germany, without the counterweight of Britain, and disappointed though they were, they continued to try to persuade Britain to become more involved. Stikker had to swallow his objections to a European federation of the French variety; interestingly, he was known not to like dealing with Hans Hirschfeld, the Government Commissioner for German Affairs and head of the Dutch delegation to the OEEC. The British ambassador to the Hague referred to Stikker as being so jealous of Hirschfeld, that he dealt with him through van der Beugel (Deputy Director General in the Foreign Ministry)[91] Van de Beugel himself says diplomatically that there is some truth in the contention that Stikker was jealous of Hirschfeld, mentioning the latter's predominant role in the German question.[92] This interesting little insight does suggest that tensions on the question of European integration existed within Dutch political circles, sometimes of a personal nature. In terms of parody, Stikker's 'federasts' were Catholic, pro-French dreamers, while he was a pragmatic Atlantic man, more mistrustful of the French than usual, but sad at Britain's behaviour and inability to take the bull by the horns, hoping nevertheless for the Atlantic counterweight.

Conclusions

The Dutch were swept along by the European fervour. They knew where their interests lay. For economic reasons, they opted for the Schuman Plan, and managed to change some of its proposals in the process, thereby underlining both their, and Benelux, influence. The Americans clearly had a role to play, by supporting the Schuman Plan. The Dutch co-operated in European integration from the moment the Americans expressed support. Support for European integration was fully in line with their policy of involving Germany in European integration. Although there was clearly some opposition in the Netherlands to 'Euro-fervour', it was not widespread enough to set the tone.

The British stance was ambiguous. To some, the aim of the government was to undermine, to others it appeared naive and to others simply lacking in vision. The French frustrated British efforts to water down the power of the proposed institutions of the Coal and Steel Community, forewarned perhaps by the birth of the castrated Council of Europe and the devaluation of Sterling in September 1949, without much prior warning. If the British 'Information Campaign' in the Netherlands referred to in the previous chapter had as one of its aims the convincing of the Dutch that they should not participate in the Schuman Plan, then it failed. It is difficult to forget the Foreign Office comment about 'vying with the French for the minds of the Dutch', even if the comment was made in 1947.[93] British policy towards European integration seems, at any rate, to have been particularly inconsistent, particularly given some of Bevin's statements, for example one made in early 1949: 'I would regard it as a crowning event to establish European Unity on a sound, definite and progressive basis.'[94] Bevin was clearly furious that Acheson was informed about the Schuman Plan before he was. Nutting puts his finger on 'an obsessive determination to preserve the Anglo-American Alliance as something exclusive,' adding: 'we wanted to keep the US to ourselves, like a jealous lover.'[95] Milward and Nutting refer to Britain as a nagging mother-in-law and a prim spinster respectively vis-à-vis the Franco-German European marriage. It would be more accurate to say that Britain wished to be part of the team, while refusing to accept the rules of the game in advance. In addition, the role of personalities cannot be discounted. Bevin's comments on the French, and general Foreign Office distrust of the French, played their part, as did French distrust of the British.

Personalities are not, however, sufficient to explain the differences. The nub of the disagreements lay in Britain's and France's different strategic outlooks. Bevin's idea in pushing for Western European Union in early 1948 was intended primarily as a counterweight to the Soviet Union, while the French were more interested in containing the Germans. French strategy was to use the vehicle of European integration to contain Germany, which did not accord the United States a long-term role. Stuart Croft writes:

> In January 1948, Britain was leading the movement towards a closer association of West European nations. That leadership was premised upon the movement being based upon the British ideas of union, an intergovernmental structure aimed at involving the United States and focusing on the problem of the Cold War. But by January 1949, Britain had apparently lost the leadership of Europe, and the British were widely regarded as being responsible for undermining the movement towards European unity.[96]

John Young puts things more succinctly:

> [...] both Britain and France were looking to their own interests: one to the world and the Atlantic community, the other to the German problem and European unity. These diverse interests could no

longer be contained in a single framework of activity such as Western Union.[97]

The Dutch, balancing the emotional side of their Atlanticism with their pragmatic commercialism, opted for France's, not Britain's, view of Europe, albeit not without some soul-searching. By doing so, they were able to modify some features of the French plan. On security matters, however, the Dutch had a different attitude. For in that respect, they were particularly Atlantic. Passions were to run high, as the Pléven Plan made its entry.

7

WHOSE DEFENCE?

Introduction

If the Dutch were able to go along with the Schuman Plan, despite a certain lack of confidence in France, and British standoffishness, the question of defence was a very different kettle of fish. As has been seen, the Dutch were not willing to commit large amounts of money to defence, whatever their desire for security; they already had one of the highest levels of defence spending, per head of population, in the West, owing to the Indonesian commitment. For although Indonesia had gained independence, the troops could not suddenly be made to vanish into thin air. Moreover, the problem of New Guinea remained, as a thorn in the Dutch side, and was even to be the ostensible reason for the resignation of the Dutch Cabinet in January 1951, as shall be seen in the following chapter.

Dutch defence policy was predicated firmly on the assumption that it was to be centred on an Atlantic, rather than exclusively European, concept. Although Stikker recognised the necessity of German rearmament,[1] he was not interested in an extension of the Schuman plan into the defence arena. As Kersten points out, in defence matters, the relationship between Western Europe and the United States was sacrosanct.[2] Dutch distrust, particularly Stikker's, of French motives, was also an important part of the equation, as was British distrust of the French. The American Secretary of State, Dulles, pointed out that the Dutch were opposed to the European army, precisely because they feared it would expose them to French leadership or to the possible future domination by Germany or other unknown forces, unless closely tied in with the USA and British in the North Atlantic Community.[3] Thus, when the Pléven Plan was announced, Stikker was to turn against it. Apart from that fairly predictable attitude on Stikker's part, it was to throw into relief the question of defence in the Netherlands, and lead to considerable acrimony and political instability. Paradoxically, however, the idea of a European army had been set in motion several months earlier from an unlikely source, a British politician: following the hostilities in Korea, which made the question of defence co-operation more urgent than before, Churchill latched onto the question of defence skilfully, using the platform provided by the Council of Europe. For many in Europe, Churchill, even though in opposition, was a larger than life figure, with a great deal of influence.

It is hardly surprising that he fired the imagination of Western Europeans and Americans on 11 August 1950, with his motion (co-sponsored with the past and future French Foreign Minister, Bidault, it should be remembered) to establish a European army.[4] He said: 'We should make a gesture of practical and constructive guidance by declaring ourselves in favour of the immediate creation of a European Army under a unified command and in which we should all bear a worthy and honourable part [...]'[5] The motion was passed by 89 votes to 5, with 27 abstentions.[6] It called for the formation of a European Army under a European Defence Minister, subject to proper European democratic control and acting in full co-operation with the United States and Canada.[7]

Whether Churchill meant what he said or not is still the subject of debate: the British government, for their part, were not interested. In a House of Commons debate, the Minister of Defence, Shinwell, said:

> No doubt the Right Honourable gentleman (Macmillan) with the assistance of his Right Honourable friend (Churchill) who originated this quaint and fantastic proposal, will be able to explain at some later stage [...] what he means by a European Army [...][8]

The United Kingdom's attitude was sceptical, whatever Churchill's words were meant to convey. Britain's attitude to the Pléven Plan was, as shall be seen, to be the subject of considerable anger on the Continent.

Whatever the meaning behind Churchill's words, they helped the Americans to justify the idea of German rearmament. Adenauer himself helped, by offering on 23 August, active German participation in the defence of Western Europe.[9] thereby highlighting even more the fact that the whole question of defence hinged on Germany. (Britain, it should be remembered, was, at this stage, still against the re-establishment of a German Army). It was the Americans who set the pace: on 9 September, six days before the Fifth Session of the Atlantic Council, they announced that the American troop presence in Europe would be strengthened.[10] The

British followed suit three days later,[11] although they had been considering the question before the American announcement.

On 13 September, two days before the Atlantic Council, the Big Three were still unable to agree on German participation in European defence. They did, however, agree on the formation of a German mobile police force of 30,000, to be armed with automatic weapons and tanks.[12] This was clearly also intended as a riposte to East Germany, which had over 100,000 well armed 'Volkspolizisten'. The question of a fully-fledged German army was still too sensitive a subject to be tackled head on. The British, however, were slowly being won over to the American view.[13] This left the French isolated on the question.

When the Fifth Session of the NATO Council met in Washington on 15 September 1950, the Big Three had still not agreed on the question of German troops participating in a Western European force.[14] Agreeing to precise measures proved impossible. Despite the arguments in favour of German rearmament, it was more a case of logic versus emotion. Logic called for German participation and sharing the burden, whilst emotion, especially French, was against German military rehabilitation, at least so soon after the war. Both standpoints were understandable, but could not be easily reconciled. The European idea was, however, already there, helped by the Americans in a practical way (for example, by supporting the Schuman Plan), and by Churchill, perhaps in a more rhetorical and emotional way.

While all agreed with Stikker, at the Fifth NATO Council, that the line of defence should be as far to the East as possible (see Chapter 5), German rearmament was certainly the sticking point. The Americans took the lead, pushing for German rearmament within the framework of an integrated Atlantic Army, to consist of units controlled by a central military organisation to administer, train and control these forces and headed by one single individual.[15] The idea was not far removed from Churchill's words.

The Americans, as Fursdon points out, were able to put across a solution to the Europeans about what was then 'primarily an unspeakable European problem'.[16] They were, after all, not Europeans, and therefore not as emotionally involved in their analysis of the problem. They were also particularly dominant in NATO, and Dean Acheson was 'very much in command of the meeting.'[17] The proposals were, however, too sudden to be accepted, particularly by the French. The Dutch were more amenable, particularly since they wished for German participation,[18] and, obviously a German financial contribution, which would mean they would spend less than they would otherwise have to.[19]

The French were the problem for the American plan; Spits summarises their then position as isolated.[20] It was certainly different to that of the Americans. Acheson reported on 16 September the French warning that the 'military spirit' could reawaken in Germany, as after the first war.[21] The French were in a difficult position, particularly because their position on German rearmament detracted from the Schuman Plan, the driving force of which was Franco-German reconciliation. The French were not so intransigent as to cause a breakdown of the talks; a bland Council communiqué was issued on 26 September, in which participants agreed that Germany should be enabled to contribute to the build-up of the defence of Western Europe. It requested the NATO Defence Committee to look at the ways and means of doing so.[22] The problem had been deferred.

The Pléven Plan

Despite French political instability, or perhaps because of it, the French flair for invention, as witnessed in the Schuman Plan, was now to manifest itself in the sensitive area of defence. The linkage of the Pléven Plan to the Schuman Plan is self-evident – an attempt to transcend national armies by introducing a strong element of supra-nationalism.

The Defence Committee had been asked to reconvene on 28 October. As Fursdon points out, the French, to avoid complete isolation, had to produce a solution acceptable to their partners.[23] Progress on the European Coal and Steel Community would surely suffer if the impasse were to continue. The intellectual side of French diplomacy now got to work, since it was important not to create an impression of intransigence, and thereby jeopardize the Schuman Plan. On 15 October, the Chargé d'Affaires at the American embassy in Paris was invited to the Foreign Ministry to talk to senior officials. Following the meeting, he reported back to his Secretary of State as follows:

> [...] various Ministers were considering individually possibilities of dealing with the impasse which has arisen in connection with German rearmament [...] since Germany is a member of the Council of Europe, France will not refuse to undertake a study concerning the possibility of a German contribution to the organisation of the defence of Western Europe.[24]

The French were playing for time. This clearly worried the British. Air Marshal Elliot wrote on 19 October:

Time is not on our side. We cannot afford to delay. In a few months, if not weeks, American enthusiasm will wane; the Germans will become less tractable; the Prussians will become more aggressive; the French will become more cynical and apathetic; Benelux, Scandinavia and Italy will lose heart. If we pay too much attention to French susceptibilities [...] we shall take the heart out of the Atlantic Pact and be left to console ourselves in Europe, with Portugal and Iceland.[25]

The Americans, for their part, did not wait around for the French to come up with something; on 17 October Acheson wrote to his Embassy in France:

> You may tell Mr Schuman the following: we do not consider it possible to create an effective system as far to the East in Germany as possible without the participation of German armed forces [...] we are opposed to the recreation of a German National Army and General Staff.

Significantly, the telegram continued:

> The US continues to endorse with enthusiasm the principles of the Schuman Plan for pooling the coal, iron and steel resources of Western Europe [...] we are willing to consider some application of this concept to the military field [...] we would consider sympathetically and earnestly a specific French proposal on this matter.[26]

The way the Americans linked the defence problem to the Schuman Plan so specifically indicates a certain amount of subtle pressure on the French to 'get on with their act'. It clearly put them on the spot. It highlighted American influence, particularly since the French were indeed to come up with a plan not dissimilar conceptually to the Schuman Plan, albeit criticised for being discriminatory towards Germany. American influence cannot be ignored; the French involvement in Indo-China depended heavily on American financial assistance; between January 1950 and May 1954, American financial assistance to the French war effort in Indo-China amounted to $2.6 billion, 70 per cent of the cost of the war.[27] The impetus given to the Cold War by the Korean War made a common front in Europe all the more important to the Americans.

The French were in a tight position; the Schuman Plan, so praised in Europe, was vital to French interests and to restore French credibility, so damaged by the war. It was an initiative that had transcended the chronic political instability of the Fourth Republic. As Diebold wrote: 'Not merely diplomatic strategy, but the political life of the French Government was at stake.'[28] The French were now in the international limelight; time was short, and they were under pressure to come up with a solution before 28 October. Following intensive discussions of a draft in the French Cabinet on 23 October, during which the Socialist leader, Guy Mollet, burst into tears,[29] the Assemblée Nationale passed the bill on the following day.

Whatever the highly charged atmosphere in France on the question, the plan was pragmatic enough to serve as a basis for serious discussion. The essential premise was the continuation of European integration, set in motion by the Schuman Plan. Its character, like that of the Schuman Plan, was supranational. It would include a High Authority, a Council of Ministers, a parliamentary body, a Court of Justice and a European Defence Minister. Significantly, the French rejected the possibility of German divisions, considering that this could lead to the rebuilding of a national German Army and German militarism.

Despite this evident discrimination, the deft French were able to achieve credibility with their plan. Although unanimous agreement on the plan was not achieved at the Defence Committee, which met on 28–31 October, the Americans nevertheless stressed, at their (separate) press conference 'the positive aspects.'[30] The French avoided isolation and complete disagreement by linking the plan to Churchill's and Bidault's resolution at the Council of Europe. In reality, the meeting fluffed the basic issues of German rearmament and integration of armed forces, and served more as a staging post on the road to further discussions: both the Pléven Plan and the American Plan were given to NATO's Military Committee and the Council of Deputies. The latter met on 13 November and regularly thereafter. The culmination was a cleverly contrived agreement, credited to the chairman, the American Charles Spofford, that papered over the cracks between the French view – a supranational solution which discriminated, at least for the time being, against the Germans – and the American view, which was less discriminatory, and based on an Atlantic, rather than a purely European, framework. Broadly speaking, it saw both the European Army and the NATO solution as complementary. The 'Spofford Report' was approved on 18 December by the North Atlantic Council at its sixth session in Brussels, as was the Defence Committee's report on the establishment of an integrated military force. The simultaneous approval of the idea of a Supreme Commander was also given,³¹ resulting in Eisenhower taking up the position on 2 April 1951, although he was to be particularly influential before that date.

Significantly, it was also agreed that the French would convene 'as soon as possible' a conference on the formation of a European Army. The final important decision was to authorise the Big Three to open discussions on a possible German contribution to the defence of Western Europe, the so called Petersburg Conference. Geoffrey Warner describes Spofford's solutions as ingenious. Given that it avoided a complete breakdown in the negotiations surrounding German rearmament, it was. Warner offers some evidence to suggest that the Americans, whose main aim was German rearmament, hoped that the Petersburg negotiations would prove successful, while the Paris conference would break down.³² On 10 June, however, the Petersburg negotiations were suspended, owing largely to French intransigence on the size of the German military unit. They were simply not prepared to accept the term 'division', with its militaristic connotations. In the meantime, the conference in Paris on the setting up of a European Army had finally opened on 15 February. In the end the Americans opted to support the Paris Conference, in the form of a State Memorandum approved by President Truman on 30 July 1951.³³ At the time, they saw it as the only solution left for German rearmament. What, however, of the Dutch?

The Dutch View

The (Pléven) Plan has been generally well received, especially by Catholic newspapers, but also by Liberal and Conservative papers. 'The Socialist press has been more reserved in its comment, but is still on the whole favourable;' wrote the British ambassador on 27 October 1950.³⁴ Despite press reaction, however, the Dutch Cabinet, spearheaded by Stikker, were against the whole idea. There were several reasons for this.

First, there was Stikker himself. As has been seen, he was particularly Atlantic-minded and Protestant. As Fursdon wrote: 'In his view it was a solution proposed by a set of idealists who had no idea of the practical difficulties involved.'³⁵

Second, mistrust of the French and future fears of French hegemony had been manifest for some time, '[...] the majority of Dutchmen are mistrustful of French intentions,' wrote the British ambassador in 1951.³⁶

Third, without British participation in a European Defence Community, the Dutch were not prepared to risk French and future German power, without the British counterweight. Although the Dutch, after some initial misgivings, participated in the Schuman Plan, that was because economically, Germany was more important to them than Britain. On security questions the reverse was true,[37] especially because of mistrust of the French.

Fourth, a feeling abounded that the French were being too discriminatory:

> The French Government sought on the one hand to contain Germany and keep it under control. On the other hand, the French wanted to bring Germany into a European Federation – although not as an equal partner [...] I therefore could not bring myself to believe in the European Defence Community, which was to be the next French move to retain discrimination against Germany.

Wrote Stikker.[38]

Fifth, there was the desire to have a strong military buffer between the Netherlands and the Soviet Union. The NATO idea fitted in far better with Dutch thinking than 'idealistic' supranational ones.

Sixth, there was a clear fear that the United States might support the European Defence Community simply as a way of spending less in Europe: 'I had for some time the feeling that in the back of Eisenhower's mind was the idea that the creation of the EDC would allow him to send American boys home.'[39] The evidence does not, however, lend credence to Stikker's fears. Acheson wrote: '[...] they [the Dutch] were forever afraid that membership of the European Defence Community would reduce the aid which they expected to receive from us.'[40] At a meeting with President Truman and Churchill:

> Secretary Acheson went on to explain the erroneous views held by the Dutch [...] The Dutch thought that if the European Army were set up, the United States would be less interested in Europe. As a matter of fact, of course, we would be more interested in Europe. If the European Army were set up, we would send more supplies and troops.[41]

Ernst van der Beugel affirms retrospectively that the United States would have supported Europe, had the European Army come to fruition.[42]

The Prime Minister himself, Drees, was not known for his interest in military matters (van der Beugel describes him as having a 'blind spot' on defence),[43] and he seemed quite happy to go along with Stikker's objections, although his motives, as a Socialist, were somewhat at variance with Stikker's. Apart from this, there was the feeling in the Dutch Government that Germany was having it too good. De Booy, the head of the Dutch Military Mission to the Allied Control Commission, had written in July 1950:

> [...] it is absolutely clear, that from the German side, the Korean crisis can be exploited to make capital for the wishes of the Germans, especially concerning the demands on steel production [...] German rearmament within the framework of an Atlantic Community is necessary.[44]

Stikker was particularly opposed to the supranational aspects of the Pléven Plan. On 26 October, he said in a telegram to the Dutch Embassy in Washington:

> Given that the setting up of a European Army with political organs means a completely federal state, the consequence could be [...] that strong pressure will be put on us to participate in a federal state of France, Germany, Italy and the Benelux countries. I regard participation in such a state as unacceptable to the Netherlands.[45]

De Booy, for his part, considered that the Pléven Plan had put the Germans in a difficult position:

> Adenauer has been placed in a very difficult position. One of the most prominent pillars of his foreign policy has been based on the idea of good co-operation with France, and from this, the idea of the integration of Western Europe, in which Germany will be able to hold a position of equality. This idea has now received a serious setback, since Adenauer can only see in the Pléven Plan a motion of no-confidence against Germany.[46]

The Dutch were unequivocal in their opposition. 'The new Dutch Minister of Defence made it plain that Holland did not back the Pléven Plan for a European Army', wrote the British ambassador on 7 November.[47] Stikker tried to introduce his own plan at the Council of Deputies meeting on 13 November. It entailed the setting up of a NATO High Commissioner to be responsible for all forces in Germany and for the German rearmament question, within a NATO framework. The Dutch representative at the

Council of Deputies explained his belief that the German military effort should be within a NATO framework with all 12 participants, rather than Europe alone.[48] Despite this attempt to compromise, the Dutch did not gain enough support for the plan to be accepted.

The Minister at the Dutch Embassy in Washington, De Beus, told the American Secretary of State on 29 November that Dutch participation in the Schuman Plan did not mean that they intended to accept the French concept of a European federation. They were:

> Unwilling to accept French leadership in such a group. De Beus mentioned French involvements in Indo China and North Africa and the strength of the communists in metropolitan France as being among the major reasons. The Dutch considered that they could not depend on French leadership in any defence arrangement [...] and were not willing to participate in anything less than an Atlantic group which included the UK and Scandinavians.[49]

It was Great Britain's attitude towards the Pléven Plan that fuelled Dutch fears of French hegemony. With British participation as a countervailing force to French power, Stikker may well have moderated his stance. As it was, even before the announcement of the Pléven Plan, the Labour Government was critical of Churchill's idea of a European Army. 'The message', wrote Fursdon, 'was quite clear; the United Kingdom's attitude was one of polite scepticism.'[50]

On 23 November, Stikker met Bevin at the Foreign Office and told him that he was against the European Defence Community without Great Britain. He added that although the United States might press the Netherlands to join, they would not relent. He also pressed for his 'High Commissioner compromise'. Bevin replied that the United Kingdom, with its Commonwealth ties, could not join an organisation in which the United States and Canada had no part, and put the view that a 'broad Atlantic body, including Germany', was the best solution. Both Stikker and Bevin agreed to try and persuade the French to accept the Atlantic idea instead of their own European idea.[51] Bevin subsequently sent Stikker a message, saying that he preferred a NATO solution to an EDC one.[52]

Despite the fact that there were signs of French flexibility and that the French accepted the Spofford proposals, the Dutch did not budge. They had not expected the United States to agree to continue to find a solution to the German problem on two levels – at Petersburg and in Paris. 'The American concession vis-à-vis France had not been foreseen in The

Hague,' wrote Kersten.[53] Although there was a good deal of parliamentary opposition to Stikker's policy, it was not enough, and parliament supported his line.[54] Thus, when the European Army Conference opened in Paris on 15 February 1951, the Dutch followed the British lead and sent only observers. Stikker cleverly used a Cabinet crisis (about which more will be said in the following chapter) as an excuse to remain an observer at the Conference.[55]

Although, as subsequent developments were to show, the British had no intention of ever becoming members of a European Defence Community, British policy was, at least on the face of things, more equivocal than it had been towards the Schuman Plan. The early stages of the negotiations on the European Defence Community were not in any case, clear cut, because of the Petersburg Conference, which opened before the Paris Conference – on 9 January. Its aim was to try and find a way of bringing Germany into NATO. Although the conferences were officially separate, they were clearly interdependent. At this stage, the Americans, British and Dutch were very much in favour of a NATO solution for Europe's defence. The French, of course, favoured a more European solution. This, combined with continuing French problems about the size of the German military unit, helped to bring the Petersburg Conference to an inconclusive end on 10 June. Only an interim report was produced, which was never published.[56]

A further complication to an already confused situation was the French suggestion (not Soviet, as Fursdon seems to suggest)[57] for a Four Power Conference. Perhaps as a way of testing Soviet seriousness, the three suggested a meeting of deputies, to discuss the agenda, which opened on 5 March. It adjourned on 21 June, after 74 sessions, with no agreement. The main subject had, predictably, been the question of a unified Germany. The Three were simply not prepared to accept a reunified Germany, if it were to be neutral, as the Soviet Union wished.

German reunification has been, and still is, the subject of much debate, with each side accusing the other of being responsible for the breakdown in the talks. An independent attempt to answer the question of who was responsible for the failure is outside the scope of this book, and would indeed require another. Suffice to say that there was too much suspicion for any real agreement to be reached. While some Soviet archives remain closed, it is safe to assume that Fursdon is correct in concluding that the Soviet Union was simply trying to delay the integration of European defence and isolate West Germany.[58]

In the meantime, despite the complications brought about by the Petersburg and Deputies' conferences, the Paris Conference had managed to keep going. At this point, the Americans realised that the situation needed to be clarified, particularly since, apart from the NATO forum, there was now only the Paris forum in which to pursue matters and solve the German question. Since it was proving so difficult to agree on German membership of NATO, the European Army idea was becoming increasingly attractive to the Americans. The American High Commissioner in Germany, McCloy (a European integrationist, according to Fursdon) left 'for urgent talks in the State Department on future United States and Allied policy towards Germany.'[59]

The void created by the failure of the Petersburg talks and the Deputies' meeting was filled to a certain extent by force of personality: Monnet had lunch with Eisenhower at the end of June, and appears to have convinced him of the need for a European Army. The latter told the Sub-Committee of the Senate Committee on Foreign Relations, in defence of the Paris Conference:

> When I came over here (to Europe) I disliked the whole idea of a European Army [...]. However, I have decided that it offers another chance for bringing in another link here [...] so I am going to try to help [...] but I tell you that joining Europe together is the key to the whole question.[60]

The Dutch, for their part, still remained observers. However, they now began a serious reappraisal. A paper on the Pléven Plan prepared by the Foreign Ministry on 15 June stated:

> It cannot be excluded that in the long run, the plans could well become acceptable or that their acceptance could become politically unavoidable. As long as such a situation is not in sight, there seems to be no reason for the Netherlands to give up its politically favourable position of observer.[61]

Such a situation, however, was in sight. The Paris Conference produced an interim report on 24 July, recommending a supranational European Defence Community, to operate for 50 years from its inception. Most important, however, was the compromise reached on the main sticking point for the French, the division. Following signs by the French that they were prepared to be more flexible, the Americans recommended that the basic unit should be the 'groupement' of 12 to 15,000 men. This was a masterstroke, for it avoided the use of the word 'division', with its emotional connotations. The tactical use of semiotics had come into its own.

Following these developments, the Americans, who were now setting the pace, invited Britain and France to discuss the German defence contribution. The Foreign Ministers met in Washington on 10–14 September, and issued a joint communiqué which recognised the French initiative to set up a European Defence Community as an important contribution to European unity. It also confirmed that Germany's participation in joint defence would be accompanied by a replacement of the occupation statute by a new relationship between the Three and the Federal Republic. The Seventh North Atlantic Council, held in Ottawa on 15–20 September, strengthened these developments by recognising them, although prudence did not at this stage allow more detailed discussions.

The Dutch had little chance of turning the tide, and the question was debated in the Cabinet. On 24 September, the Defence Minister, Staf, pointed out that the Americans saw the formation of a European Army as 'probably the only way to involve Germany in the defence of the West.'[62] On 8 October, following a protracted discussion in the Cabinet, Stikker agreed that the Netherlands would join the talks as a full participant, adding ominously: 'We don't want to create the impression of joining just to be obstructive.'[63] The Dutch joined the talks unenthusiastically, with the aim of doing their best to ensure that the European Army idea would not detract from NATO, which was more important to them. They – and Stikker in particular – continued to push for an Atlantic solution from within, recognising that isolation would reduce their bargaining power, and that of Benelux. On 25 October, the Benelux Prime Ministers, and Foreign, Defence and Finance Ministers met in Brussels to discuss policy at the Paris talks. The head of the Dutch delegation, Van Vredenburch, said that although the Netherlands had decided to participate, doubts still remained. Stikker stated that the creation of a European Defence Community with Belgium but without the Netherlands would be a mortal blow for Benelux.[64]

The dilemma the Netherlands found itself in is illustrated well in a paper prepared by a senior Foreign Ministry official, Max Kohnstamm. Although Kohnstamm was known to be in favour of the European Army,[65] his paper, entitled 'Contribution to the Discussion on the Pleven Plan', nevertheless brings out many of the Dutch concerns, perhaps because he knew that some of his readers had not yet been converted to the EDC:

> One can understand the enthusiasm for close co-operation with countries such as France, Germany and Italy. But the Netherlands cannot free itself from its geographical position. It can and must guard against the weakening of its bonds with the other countries of the Atlantic world. That is why the existence of the Atlantic Pact is of great importance to the Netherlands. Only within the Atlantic Pact is continental co-operation acceptable to the Netherlands.[66]

The paper went on to refer to the Netherlands' history, coming out with some particularly pertinent comments:

> The Netherlands always seeks a position for itself between the great powers. For a century of great and undisturbed prosperity, the Netherlands pursued a policy of balance of power as a neutral country between England, France and Germany. The Second World War completely changed this constellation. In this new constellation, the Netherlands will not be able to play a role on its own in the long run. As a member of a continental group forming a part of the Atlantic Community, the Netherlands will have the greatest chance of maintaining something of its nineteenth century position in the second half of the twentieth century. If it wants, the Netherlands can of course remain on the sidelines. But what then will its influence in the Atlantic Community be in the long run? How, above all, will the Netherlands rescue itself economically if it can reap the benefits of neither the Continental market not those of the Commonwealth?[67]

Significantly, Kohnstamm concluded his paper by saying that the experience gained from the discussions on the Schuman Plan showed that the elaboration of the Pléven Plan could be deeply influenced by other delegations. At the Paris conference, the Little Three generally presented a common front, coordinating their policies as much as possible. As shall be seen in Chapter 9, however, the Dutch weakened their position by bickering among themselves.

Slowly but surely, progress was made. Following a meeting in Paris on 27–30 December, of the Foreign, Defence and Finance Ministers of the six participants, a communiqué was issued which confirmed the EDC as a stage in the process of European unification, and delicately handled the vexed question of supranationality by agreeing that the assembly which the EDC proposed to establish would study the question of European organisations to replace the organisation foreseen by the draft EDC treaty.

Stikker, still not satisfied, sent a telegram to the British Foreign Secretary, Eden, which said:

> I feel most strongly that federation of small number of continental European nations can never be independent economic and political unit as the age of preponderance of these Western European countries, either singly or jointly, in world affairs, belongs to the past.[68]

He was still kicking.

The Foreign Ministers met again in Paris on 26 and 27 January 1951, making further progress, this time, in Fursdon's words on 'the vexed question of the commission, which they decided would consist of nine commissioners serving for six years.'[69] In public, Stikker now began to appear more positive. He told the Second Chamber on 8 February 1952:

> [...] I have firm confidence, and the belief, that the European Defence Community can soon become a reality [...] the road to the Defence Community is perhaps the only one left which points in the direction of a better future for Europe.[70]

He was having to sail with the wind, whatever he felt deep down. For, as shall be seen, he was to continue to snipe at the EDC, despite what he said in Parliament.

The English Disappointment

Although the Dutch had originally followed the British example of being observers at the conference, they could hardly afford the luxury of supporting the idea of a European Army from the outside, as Britain was able to do, following the election of a Conservative government in October 1951. Many Europeans, the Dutch included, had assumed that Churchill would bring Britain into the EDC talks following the defeat of the generally hostile Labour government. 'At the end of 1950', wrote the British ambassador to the Hague:

> It was still assumed that Britain would eventually form part of such an integrated Europe. It had caused considerable disappointment when Britain had stood aloof from the Schuman Plan and it was still hoped that it was not her last word on the subject [...] she [the Netherlands] could no longer stand out, and her hopes thereafter

centred on bringing Britain in with her if possible, or on leaving the way open for her later association if not.[71]

The same applied to the European Defence Community.

Some further analysis of Britain's attitude towards European integration is valid here. Before the Spofford compromise, Stikker was doing what he could to bring Germany into the defence of the West via NATO. He actually suggested to the British Ambassador that the British Labour Party bring pressure to bear on the French Socialists in the same way as the Dutch Socialists were doing. When the Foreign Office discussed this possibility with Dennis Healey, then the Secretary of the Labour Party's international department, the latter said that the Labour Party was not in a favourable position to influence the French because of the differences over European unity.[72] The Labour Government was not prepared to involve itself substantively, essentially because of what Nutting, as we have seen, describes as insularity and shortsightedness. A telegram from Bevin to the British Ambassador in Washington shows the British government's attitude more clearly:

> [...] we believe that one of the ideas underlying the French plan is that of a Continental block, which they no doubt hope will be under French leadership. It would in short be a sort of cancer in the Atlantic body [...] In allowing this European federal concept to gain a foothold within the North Atlantic Treaty Organisation, we are therefore taking a grave risk [...][73]

This kind of emotive language further underlines Bevin's suspicion, bordering on dislike, of the French.

At this point, the British had not yet accepted the 'Spofford compromise', as they were to at the NATO Council in Brussels on 18 December. On 6 December, another telegram from Bevin to the British ambassador showed British opposition to European integration:

> [...] this proposal is in effect a new Franco-American package. The French will agree to the 'Spofford compromise' [...] In return for that agreement, and as part of it, the Americans will come out publicly in favour of European integration and a European Army [...] We must not be rushed into decisions of this importance [...] The French Government have already changed their minds three or four times within the last week [...] in the midst of such uncertainty we cannot

be reasonably expected to approve a proposal of such far-reaching and fundamental character as the new Franco-American package.[74]

Even though the proposals were subsequently accepted, this did nothing to reduce British hostility towards European integration. The Permanent Under Secretary's Department[75] co-ordinated the analysis of a series of replies from European posts about European integration:

> [...] it seems that only in France and Germany can there be said to exist a deep sentiment running through the country in favour of integration. In Austria, Holland [sic] and Italy there also seems to be some emotional support for the idea, but its most influential protagonists seem to be within comparatively narrow political and social circles [...] in order to [...] have any real hope of persuading France and Germany to limit their plans to those of the Schuman Plan type, it would perhaps be desirable at the same time to find some new means of giving outward and visible favour to the Atlantic idea.[76]

The British were worried, and hoped that any weakening of the European 'federast' idea would favour the Atlantic idea. Bullen wrote: 'Any British attempt to sabotage the French proposals, the temptation being greatest with the Pléven Plan, was excluded on the grounds that it would meet with the active disapproval of the United States.'[77]

Following Churchill's return to power, the British were in a somewhat difficult position vis-à-vis their commitment to European unity. The Americans came to the rescue; they changed their stance of pressing for direct British participation to one of wanting the British to support it from the outside.[78] The back-peddling had begun. On 28 November, the Home Secretary, Sir David Maxwell Fyfe, told the Council of Europe's Consultative Assembly: 'I cannot promise that our eventual association with the European Defence Community will amount to a full and unconditional participation, because this is a matter which must be left for intergovernmental discussion elsewhere.'[79] This rather nebulous statement was followed the same evening by Eden's at the Eighth North Atlantic Council in Rome, to the effect that Britain would not participate in the EDC.[80] The effect was sufficiently dramatic to cause the President of the Strasbourg Assembly, Paul Henri Spaak, to resign.

Even members of the British Conservative delegation sent an angry letter to Churchill on 3 December,[81] some of which it is worth quoting:

> We feel obliged to bring to your attention the great and increasing difficulty of our present position as Conservative delegates to the Consultative Assembly of the Council of Europe [...] At the end of the week we shall have to listen to speeches by the Chairman of the Committees of Ministers, Dr Lange, M Schuman, Dr Adenauer, Signor de Gasperi and M van Zeeland, with a British statesman of the front rank conspicuous only by his absence. We must admit that we do not find this a very agreeable prospect [...] there are doubtless formidable reasons against our participation in a European Army at this juncture, but we do not know them [...] we must have some guidance [...] in conclusion we venture to appeal to you to take some positive action designed to restore British prestige in the Consultative Assembly, and to show that His Majesty's Government mean to play their part in the military defence and economic development of a united Europe.[82]

For their pains, the authors of the letter were treated to Churchill's views on European federation, set out in a note to the Cabinet on 29 November:

> Mr Churchill is not opposed to this but does not support integral membership of either the United Kingdom or Commonwealth [...] we help, we dedicate, we play a part, but we are not merged and do not forfeit our insular or Commonwealth-wide character [...] Our first object is the unity and the consolidation of the British Commonwealth [...] Our second, 'the fraternal association' of the English-speaking world; and third, United Europe, to which we are a separate closely – and specially – related ally and friend.[83]

To the more committed European federalists, Britain's attitude seemed confusing, not to say hostile. Even the American Under Secretary of State, Lovett, wrote that Britain appeared to want to benefit totally from the European programme, while at the same time maintaining her position that she was not totally a European country.[84]

At a meeting with the French in Paris on 17 December, Churchill said that he was 'most anxious' to help with the practical success of the plan and that 'they should be with it, but not of it'[85] Such semantic gymnastics, however, did not prevent even the Anglophile Stikker from writing in his memoirs:

In Holland there was much disappointment at the British attitude. Churchill having been the first – at Strasbourg in August 1950 – to speak about the creation of a European Army, the least that was expected was that the return of the Conservatives to power in 1951 would result in full British participation in the Paris Conference. But the United Kingdom abstained.[86]

F C Spits, the Chairman of the Dutch Council of the European Movement, headed one of the sections in his book *Towards a European Army*, simply as follows: 'England – the Great Disappointment.'[87]

Sir Anthony Nutting, Parliamentary Under Secretary of State for Foreign Affairs, then put to the Foreign Secretary, Eden, an alternative plan, to become known (Nutting makes a point of pointing out) as the 'Eden Plan'; its central plank would be 'to make the Council of Europe the parent body for all present and future European communities [...] In this way, Britain could play a part without being committed to the obligations for membership of any supranational agencies.'[88] This will be dealt with in more depth in Chapter 9. Suffice to say now that it was not to prove popular.

Complete agreement does not exist as to what Churchill had meant about British participation, in his famous speech at the Council of Europe in August 1950. If could be, that as an opposition politician, he simply wanted to gain as much publicity as possible, and was prepared to create a false impression to do so, as politicians often do. He could hardly have stood up and said that only Continental Europe must unite militarily. Should his private diaries ever be released for public inspection, the mystery may be unravelled. For the time being, however, we have his reply to a question by Sir Anthony Nutting, 'I meant it for them, not for us.'[89] The suspicion of strategic and expedient use of rhetoric cannot nevertheless be altogether dispelled.

While there can be little argument that Churchill's return to office in October excited hopes for a new British policy towards Europe (even the Historical Section of the Foreign and Commonwealth Office admits this),[90] not everybody was surprised by Britain's perceived backpedalling. The above-mentioned Dutch Foreign Ministry paper of 15 June 1951 had stated: 'That the English aversion to succumbing to a supranational organ will change under a Conservative Government, is unlikely, despite the Conservatives' evident interest in the Schuman Plan.'[91] This was to be proven to be true. 'Churchill's idea for a European Army put forward at Strasbourg in the summer of 1950 was quite different from the Pléven

Plan for a European Defence Community launched that autumn', wrote Heather Yasamee.[92] This may be true, but its very vagueness lent itself to optimistic interpretation on the part of the more federalist-minded listeners. They seem to have been unaware of, or ignored, Britain's refusal to give up any sovereignty. The Churchill government's policy towards European federation was similar in approach to that of Attlee's government. Pierre Melandri referred to Britain fearing the consequences of integration on the stature of sterling and on imperial preference.[93] The main problem was that Britain believed her world role would be weakened by European integration.

The Dutch, for their part, were still particularly suspicious of the French at the end of 1951 and well into 1952. On 11 January 1952, the Dutch Ambassador in New York, van Roijen, quoted Schuman as saying that NATO was transitory and essentially ephemeral, continuing by telling Dulles of his worry that the EDC might take a line independent of NATO with 'only one voice'.[94] He was obviously referring to France. As shall be seen, this particular attachment to NATO was to cause problems right up until the signing of the EDC treaty.

Conclusion

Geo-politically, economically, religiously and psychologically, the Netherlands were torn between the Atlantic and Continental Europe. Still apparently shocked and dazed as a result of the German invasion, and particularly because of the heavy-handed treatment that they, as a small country, had received towards the end of the war, they almost automatically jumped into the Brussels Treaty Organisation and its Atlantic extension, NATO; they sacrificed a measure of independence to have some say on the German question, and not to get left on the sidelines; they were loath to leave it to others to sort out matters that affected their vital interests.

The idea of a supra-national European Defence Community, however, was too much for a small country to swallow, at least in one gulp; all the more so, since the political climate in the Netherlands in the immediate postwar years was decidedly Atlantic and sceptical of French motives. Stikker personified this attitude. Britain's sceptical attitude also helped the Dutch to keep their distance for a while.

There were, then, a mixture of factors, many of them emotional: an old maritime tradition and dislike of standing armies, suspicion of the French, a wish to retain close links with the British and Americans, Stikker's non-Catholic attitude but, above all, a fear of being left out. In the end, the failure of the Petersburg Conference and United States influence set the tone. Kersten writes:

> America's choice in favour of a European Army caused the Dutch Government to reconsider its previously negative attitude. Most of the Officials in the Foreign Ministry now (summer 1950) realised to an increasing extent the unavoidability of a European Army and considered it advantageous following resumption of the Conference [Paris] to participate since this procedure would enable them to influence the course of the negotiations.[95]

The Dutch press was generally in favour of full Dutch participation in a European Army. The *NRC* (Right wing) wrote on 16 September 1950, even before the formal announcement of the Pleven Plan: 'Military integration is the complement of economic integration,'[96] while the *Volkskrant* (centre left) wrote on 16 February 1951:

> The fact that a German officer is sitting at a table with Western European representatives for the first time since the war, is of enormous significance. It is a shame that the Netherlands are for the time being only represented as observers.[97]

On 13 July 1951, *Trouw* (Right wing) commented: 'Perhaps the Dutch Government will at last step down from its unfortunate position and will participate as a full member of the Paris Conference, instead of as an observer.'[98] Yet still, Stikker persisted in refusing to participate.

Why was it not until October 1951 that the Dutch joined the Paris Conference as full participants? The factors set out above are not sufficient to explain what looks like a considerable degree of obstinacy on the part of Stikker. The continuing disinclination to spend money on defence, and the political instability of the government need to be looked at more closely to understand the nature of the Dutch attitude towards European defence and towards the pressure that was exercised from outside.

8

THE ROAD TO A STANDING ARMY

Introduction

When one bears in mind that the Netherlands were the first country, as shall be seen, to ratify the EDC treaty, it may strike one as odd that they were at first the most reluctant among the six to seriously entertain the idea of a supranational EDC. On the other hand, it may seem no less odd that the French, who proposed the concept (leaving aside Churchill's rather vague rhetoric), were to scupper it. Both examples highlighted the volatility and lack of clarity in international relations at the height of the Cold War, brought on by the inability to agree on what to do about Germany.

As we have seen, not everybody in the Netherlands shared Stikker's outlook on the question of defence. It is true that he held sway for quite a time; but following American support of the French position, the only way he could avoid isolation, even within Benelux, was to join in, continuing to nibble away at supranationalism from the inside.

Although the Dutch press, a group of senior Foreign Ministry officials and almost half the Second Chamber favoured the Plan from early on, Stikker's instinctive reliance on Britain and the United States, and Drees' disinclination to spend money on defence, conspired with an unstable political situation to prevent Dutch support for the French plan, in spite of American support for it. There was considerable tension between those who wanted the Netherlands to pay more for defence (both in the Netherlands and abroad), represented by the Chief of Staff, General Kruls and, of course, Stikker, and those who were more interested in putting money into the social security system, represented by the Socialist Prime Minister, Drees.

In short, until the Dutch had themselves agreed on what priority to give to defence, it was difficult to see clearly ahead. The way ahead was clouded by disagreements within the coalition (a mixture of the main religious parties, the Liberals and the Socialists). Despite the fact that technically there was relatively little parliamentary opposition to the broadly based cabinet, the problem lay within the coalition itself.

The Resignation of the Government

'After a promising start', wrote the British ambassador in early 1951:

> 1950 proved to be a difficult and frustrating year for the Dutch, for as the months went by, they found themselves assailed on all sides by increasing difficulties. The deteriorating international situation, particularly after the outbreak of hostilities in Korea, brought to the forefront the whole question of the organisation of Western European defence. Holland's own military shortcomings were glaringly exposed and for the first time it was borne in upon the Dutch Government and people that effort and sacrifices would be necessary to make good these deficiencies. Unfortunately for Holland the worsening of the international situation coincided with a deterioration in Holland's economic situation as a result of which, by the end of 1950, Holland found herself with a heavy adverse balance of payments, a big budget deficit and a rising cost of living just at the time when she must make her major rearmament effort.[1]

On 24 January 1951, the Cabinet resigned. The ostensible reason for the political crisis was, as shall be seen, the problem of New Guinea. It enabled the Dutch, however, to stall on the question of their attitude towards both European co-operation and the question of their own defence commitments within the NATO framework. Trade was their immediate preoccupation. The balance of payments deficit at the end of 1950 did not go away, and was exacerbated by German import restrictions. In March 1951, *The Economist* wrote: 'Holland realised that overnight it had, at least for the time being, lost its chief market for fruit and vegetables, and dairy produce for the duration of the economic crisis.'[2] At midnight on 26 February, a Dutch goods train was actually forbidden entry to Germany by German customs officials.[3] In February, the Netherlands trade deficit with Germany was $25 million,[4] increasing to $37 million in March.[5] 'The German difficulties are beginning to spread their contagion to neighbouring countries, especially to the Netherlands,'[6] wrote *The Economist*. The Yearbook of the Dutch Foreign Ministry for 1951–52 stated: '[...] the normalisation of Dutch trade with the Federal Republic of Germany came to a temporary end as a result of the German difficulties in the European Payments Union.'[7] The effect on the government cannot be understated, since Germany was the Netherlands' largest export market.[8] As it was, although the trade problems with Germany were resolved, the Dutch had suffered economically: 'The country which is likely to benefit most directly from the relaxation of previous restrictions on German imports is the Netherlands [...] at the end of May, it had run up an overdraft of $169,400,000 with EPU [...]'[9] The situation was indeed to change for the better later in 1951.

Given the above scenario, it is not difficult to see why the Dutch Cabinet did not give defence a high priority, whatever the views of Stikker and the Chief of Staff. It was these views that were to contribute to the fall of the Government, preceded by Stikker's resignation and Kruls' dismissal.

As mentioned, however, New Guinea was the ostensible reason for the Government's resignation:

> It [the Government] was able to survive a number of minor crises and, at the end of the year, a major crisis over the policy to be pursued in the New Guinea negotiations with the Indonesians, but the year ended with the Government in an unhappy state of helplessness and frustration.

Wrote the British ambassador.[10] The New Guinea problem merely compounded a difficult economic situation. *The Economist* wrote: 'Admittedly, it is primarily over defence that the Government has fallen, though Stikker actually resigned in the debate on Indonesian claims to New Guinea.'[11] The situation was far from clear: although, in a crucial parliamentary debate, the government won four no confidence motions, Stikker was unable to carry his own party with him. His party, the WD (Right Wing Liberal), voted against the Government on an important motion – that the Government had reversed its policy, and wished to transfer sovereignty to New Guinea without consulting Parliament.[12] Stikker's position thus became untenable and he had little option but to resign.

He wrote in his memoirs:

> I was basically in favour of the transfer of sovereignty of New Guinea to Indonesia under certain conditions, mainly because I attached far greater importance to the union than to New Guinea. But this was clearly not acceptable to my party, nor to the Cabinet.[13]

He then wrote that Oud (leader of the Liberals) had begun the crisis, and that when it was over, he, Oud, made 'many unpleasant remarks.'[14]

The question of defence, though, was the real problem, for it was hovering over the Dutch, and had already led to strong disagreements within the Cabinet, and between most members of the Cabinet and the Chief of Staff. The problems had begun with the resignation of the Minister of Defence, Schokking, in October 1950, and were to come to a head with the dismissal of the Chief of Staff on 23 January 1951. Significantly, the Prime Minister submitted his resignation to the Queen the next day. 'Three things have happened in Holland [sic] in the last few weeks', wrote *The Economist*:

> which might seem to have a common motive. General Eisenhower has called at the Hague, and well substantiated rumour has it that he was displeased; General Kruls, the Commander in Chief, has been dismissed; and the Cabinet has resigned. There is, in fact, probably no direct connexion between these events. The quarrel between Kruls and the Defence Ministry is of longer standing than the pressure for rearmament, and rumours that the rest of the General Staff were following in sympathy have to some extent been allayed by the fact that his deputy, Lieutenant General Calmeyer, has resigned only to become adviser to the Defence Minister, Dr s'Jacob.[15]

Although *The Economist* says there was probably no direct connection between the events, there is at least an indirect one between Eisenhower's visit and Kruls' dismissal: Kruls' wished to increase the Netherlands' defence commitments in line with Eisenhower's thinking, while most of the Cabinet, led by Drees, did not. In the words of the British Ambassador to the Hague, Kruls 'had formed a revised plan for a field army, due, in its turn, indirectly to the appointment of General Eisenhower.'[16] The General was certainly not happy with the Dutch attitude, although he may have been with Kruls'. At a meeting at the White House on 31 January, he is reported to have said that:

> Every country seemed to be trying hard except Holland. He could not understand Holland or the attitude of the Dutch. All they seemed interested in was a navy, which did not make any sense, when they ought to be worrying about the land defence of Holland.[17]

Naval expenditure was indeed a sensitive issue in the Netherlands. For a maritime country like the Netherlands, the naval tradition held an emotional, and therefore political, appeal, as the number of streets bearing the names of famous admirals testifies. There are still a fair number of Dutch people who are aware to this day that their navy destroyed the might of the English fleet in the River Medway in 1667.

Following the war, the majority of ministers wished to introduce drastic economies in the naval fleet. This led to the replacement of a separate minister for the Navy by a State Secretary, a position taken up by Rear Admiral Moorman on 1 May 1949.[18] This apparent reduction in the Navy's political clout was largely balanced by the popularity of Moorman in Parliament[19] and the Navy's efficiency at running its budget, which contrasted with that of the Army.[20] In the words of J W L Brouwer, in his study on the 'voice of the Navy in the Cabinet', Moorman was able to present his plans as well-arranged and feasible.[21] Moorman was even able to threaten resignation in September 1950, saying that he was not prepared to see the Army and Air Force built up at the Navy's expense.[22] It is significant that he emerged unscathed, while the Defence Minister, Sckokking, later resigned.

Despite American pressure on the Dutch to spend more on their land defence, Kruls' position was fast becoming untenable. He appears to have been stubborn in his professional life, as the manner of his departure from the scene suggests: on 23 January, he told the British Military Attaché that he had refused to resign when asked to do so by the Defence Minister. When he asked why he was being asked to resign, the Defence Minister replied that it was because his plans for the Field Army were 'wild'.[23] Kruls was dismissed that evening, while the Government resigned the following day, ostensibly because of Stikker's resignation over the New Guinea crisis. The sequence of events was more than coincidental: it was the defence issue that had weakened the cohesion of the Cabinet.

Kruls appears to have been a somewhat rigid character, who insisted on speaking his mind in public; he was more suspicious of Soviet intentions than most, and seems to have been unwavering in his efforts to have more spent on defence. His book *Peace or War*, published in 1952, shows that he was uncompromising in his views about the aims of the Soviet Union, referring to 'Moscow's attempts to rule the world'.[24] In June 1949, he had already said in public that 'it was only natural to assume that Russia and her satellites would by one or another means attempt to spread Communist ideology over a wider race.'[25] In October he referred in an interview to the training of Netherlands forces 'in an offensive spirit.'[26] An offensive spirit was not a Dutch characteristic.

THE ROAD TO A STANDING ARMY   163

As we shall see, Kruls' views were very much out of line with Drees'. It was, however, Kruls' outspokenness on matters of policy that was most annoying to the government. On 24 January, the Secretary General of the Foreign Ministry explained to the Embassy Counsellors of the NATO countries that the reports on the disagreements between Kruls and the government on the speed and the extent of the building up of the Dutch armed forces were not correct; the differences were, he said, of long standing and derived in large measure from a tendency on General Kruls' part to give public expression to his views on matters of policy.[27] Kruls had, however (see above), told the British Military Attaché that the problem was that the Defence Minister thought his plans were wild. Credence is lent to this version by the British ambassador's comments:

> There was also an unhappy lack of understanding between the Government as a whole and the chief of the General Staff, General Kruls, the latter complaining that he could get no support for his plans for reorganisation of the army while the Government, and in particular the Minister of Finance, complained that they could get no satisfactory comprehensive plan from General Kruls and no adequate assurance that any additional monies given to the army would in fact be properly spent.[28]

The real reasons for Kruls' dismissal are probably a combination of Kruls' outspokenness, particularly in public (hardly befitting a member of the armed forces) and genuine differences in policy. The government was at pains to stress this outspokenness in public as being the cause of his dismissal, and to play down differences in policy – or at least the Foreign Ministry were, even during the caretaker government that followed. They wished to avoid antagonising the United States and Britain, who agreed with the views of Kruls and Stikker, but not with Drees'.

Following Kruls' dismissal and the government's resignation, a British Foreign Office official wrote: '[...] General Kruls' plans for the Netherlands Army were much nearer to what we and General Montgomery regard as necessary if Holland is to play an effective part this year in the event of an emergency, than any previous programme.'[29] In contrast, what the British Ambassador thought about Drees is worth recording:

> Behind these difficulties lies the personality of the Prime Minister, Dr Drees. I have reported in the past [...] my efforts to make Drees appreciate the urgency and the need for Holland to make a bigger

and more willing contribution. The difficulty is that Drees is a very[30] obstinate man and he persists in the belief that there is no imminent threat of war in Western Europe. Only on Saturday 13 January, that is to say after General Eisenhower's visit, he repeated his belief that Russia did not mean to invade Western Europe and even went on to express doubts about the desirability of bringing Germany into the Western defence organisations. [...] Dr Drees is an idealist who has very much at heart his plans for the social betterment of the population and he seems to believe that the need for rearmament should not interfere with any of these plans.'[31]

This view of Drees' policies is in direct contrast to those of Kruls', whose 'appreciation of the world situation convinced him that a state of emergency existed and whose plan was based on that opinion'.[32]

Clearly, then, Kruls' resignation had a great deal to do with complete differences in outlook on the question of Dutch and, by extension, Western defence. The majority of the Cabinet did not share Kruls' or the British and American view, despite the tensions of the Cold War and the periodical visits of Eisenhower and Montgomery to the Netherlands. If anything, as shall shortly be seen, Anglo-Saxon pressure led to greater resistance on the part of the Dutch to rearm.

Stikker supported Kruls and was, by extension, identified with being in favour of the American moves to induce the Netherlands to rearm. He was, however, isolated within the Cabinet: 'Unfortunately', wrote the British ambassador:

> in all this Drees seems to be able to carry the majority of the Cabinet with him. It is understood that Stikker has opposed him but I am not yet sure how much support he had from s'Jacob, the new Minister of Defence.[33]

The Ambassador's information about Stikker opposing Drees was correct: on 22 January, at a Cabinet meeting, Stikker supported Kruls, while the Cabinet as a whole agreed to replace him.[34] As to the ambassador's uncertainty about the degree of support for Kruls from s'Jacob, the latter said at the same meeting that he had no confidence in Kruls, describing him as 'vacillating and fickle'![35] The question of defence was, then, a particularly thorny one for the Netherlands. It was made thornier by external pressures.

External Pressures and Dutch Indignation

External pressures certainly added spice to an already difficult political situation. The British and Americans began to exert pressure on the Dutch to be more committed to defence, at a time when the Dutch Government was beset by economic and foreign (the New Guinea) problems. Whether or not the pressure, or at least the methods of applying it, were timely, and contributed to an eventually more positive Dutch stance, is a matter of debate. The evidence, however suggests that the Dutch actually resisted the pressure for a while, finding it heavy-handed.

The British ambassador, Nichols', views were not, as we have seen, sympathetic to those of Drees:

> The general Cabinet attitude on rearmament, under the influence of Drees, is negative and unsatisfactory and it is small wonder that General Eisenhower was disappointed [...] this puts General Kruls, the Dutch Chief of Staff, in a very difficult position and reduces him to hoping that General Eisenhower, and the American Government behind him, will put sufficient pressure on the Dutch Government to force them into action [...] it is clearly preferable that the Netherlands Government should make up their minds as to their proper contribution now and not wait until forced by pressure from the Americans to take the appropriate steps.[36]

The Dutch government, however, did not take the 'appropriate' steps. They had already been resisting pressure on the question of extending military service from 12 to 18 months: at a Cabinet meeting on 21 August 1950, Drees had said that the Dutch government must not make any promises on the question of extending military service.[37] The pressure began. Following his visit to the Hague on 10 and 11 January, during which he had talks with Drees, s'Jacob and the Chiefs of Staff,[38] Eisenhower wrote to the American ambassador, Chapin, on 13 January. Among other things, the letter said:

> On purely official side, our impression was one of disappointment [...] We do not understand why a country of 10 million people should not plan a regular training and organisational framework which would, over years, produce additional groups of reserve divisions and necessary auxiliary troops. We believe that a twelve month period of service is not satisfactory [...][39]

The letter was accompanied by a note which stated: 'I have no objections whatsoever to your showing this letter to anyone in the government whenever you think such action desirable.'[40] Eisenhower was giving the Ambassador a blank cheque to leak the letter to whomever he thought appropriate in the Government.

On 16 January, Chapin left a copy of the letter with Stikker. The former wrote to Eisenhower:

> Because of all day Cabinet meeting and domestic political crisis, it was only this morning that I could show Stikker your letter of 13 January, leaving a copy with him. Copy will also be furnished confidentially with s'Jacob. Stikker much impressed with letter, which he felt although blunt, to the point and fair. Said copies would be furnished only to member of military sub-committee of Cabinet but letter would probably create something of a sensation. Stikker added 'personally and very confidentially, I will be indiscreet enough to say that I like the letter'.[41]

Stikker's prognostication that the letter would probably create something of a sensation was an understatement. On 19 January, Chapin wrote to Acheson:

> Fuss and furor created by General Eisenhower's visit, subsequent leak in his letter to me, Herald Tribune article referring to Drees as 'doctrinaire socialist' and New York Times story January 14 continues only slightly abated. There seems only little doubt that letter leak was through Catholic member of Cabinet Defence Council to embarrass Drees and likewise we believe General Staff collaborated in Times article.[42]

It is not easy to point the finger at any specific individual for leaking the letter to selected journalists. Jan van der Harst writes that the Cabinet sub-committee on defence discovered that the leakage of Eisenhower's letter was due to both the indiscretion of the chief of the news service of the Defence Ministry and to the American Ambassador.[43] Stikker does not mention the episode at all in his memoirs. It is most unlikely that the chief of news of a ministry would leak such a document, without being instructed to. It is also possible that there was a 'mass leakage'.

At any event, the publicity given to the defence question in the Dutch press certainly annoyed much of the Dutch cabinet. The American pressure did not stop. On 19 January the American ambassador and the head of the ECA mission wrote to the Foreign Ministry, suggesting that they increase defence expenditure by 150 million dollars in 1951, adding that they, the Americans, would help to the tune of 25 to 35 million.[44] Rather undiplomatically, they chose to suggest how the money should be allocated. The Dutch were, perhaps understandably, not happy with what could be construed by some as outside interference in the affairs of a sovereign state. On 21 January 1951, Drees told his Cabinet that American demands for increased military expenditure were unacceptable.[45] The British diplomatic view bore out the annoyance of the Dutch with the American pressure: in a letter of 20 February to the Foreign Office, Nichols wrote:

> I have seen Hall Patch's letter to Berthoud of February 12 enclosing notes of a conversation with Spierenburg. Spierenburg there talks of a joint letter by the US Ambassador here and the head of the ECA mission addressed to the Dutch Government telling them of the defence measures and internal measures which they, the Dutch Government should take; Spierenburg added that the caretaker Government are trying to obtain withdrawal of this letter. I know nothing of this letter and neither Chapin nor Hunter has mentioned it to me. But it may well be true. There have been many reports of American pressure and some of Dutch resentment, cf. what I say above about rumours of American interference, at the beginning of the governmental crisis.[46]

A week later, the ambassador wrote again, reinforcing the view that the Dutch were becoming rather annoyed:

> In the postscript of my letter to you (No 1015/36/51) of the 20 February, I referred to Spierenberg's conversation with Berthoud in which the former stated that the US Ambassador and the head of the ECA mission here had addressed a joint letter to the Dutch Government telling them of the defence measures and internal measures they should take at this juncture. I said, if you will remember, that I know nothing of this letter, but the report might well be true. Complaints were heard on many sides that outside parties were interfering in something that was not their business. It is I think true that there has been some criticism of the Americans here for exercising what is thought to be undue pressure. I don't think this criticism is really serious or widespread – it is more of a general feeling among

Dutch people that they do not wish to be dragged at the coat tails of the United States who lack expert knowledge of Europe.[47]

American pressure was a particularly sensitive issue. It is interesting that Foreign Office File WN 1015/42G, which is likely to contain further details of American pressure, has been retained under Section 3(4) of the Public Records Act 1958. The evidence of American pressure and its linkage with Kruls' dismissal is difficult to dismiss. At the same Cabinet meeting of 22 January, where it was agreed to replace Kruls with Hasselman, a reply to the letter from General Eisenhower asking for the Dutch to make more money available for defence was discussed. Drees said that the increases asked for were unacceptable and that the memorandum in question would be handled after a report by the Spierenburg Committee had been dealt with in the REA.[48] Nichols' successor, Butler, summarised the problem:

> The pressures which the United States Government felt constrained to apply in the Hague in connection with the Dutch defence programme, and the heavy hand with which they seemed occasionally to apply it, inevitably tended at times to strain the relationship between the two countries.[49]

As for Kruls, he may appear to some as a scapegoat, since his plans, although 'wild' to much of the Dutch Cabinet, were supported by the Americans and the British. As we have seen in Chapter 5, the British Ambassador supported Kruls' line. The dismissal of Kruls can be seen as a slap in the face to the British and Americans.

Stikker's Crisis

Most of the press blamed the leader of the Liberals, Oud, for the crisis that led to Stikker's resignation and the fall of the Government.[50] Predictably, the small communist faction was more outspoken:

> Mr H Gortzak, the leader of the Communist faction, declared that the Cabinet crisis was used to meet the demands of America for rearmament and war preparations. Not Mr Oud, he said, but General Eisenhower, was the cause of the falling of the previous cabinet.[51]

Whether one blames the fall of the government on the Americans, the New Guinea problem, differences within the coalition on Dutch rearmament or a combination of all three (a sensible conclusion), it left Stikker in

THE ROAD TO A STANDING ARMY   169

a delicate position. He was asked by the Queen to try and form a government. By 5 February, he had failed, because of his insistence on a 'definite defence and economic programme'.[52] The task was then given to Drees and van Schaik. Stikker still insisted on making conditions for his own return. The British ambassador supported Stikker's views: 'On the other hand the more of his conditions that he can get accepted, the better and more practical is likely to be the programme of the new Government.'[53] By 15 February, however, Stikker's continued political career was in doubt: 'According to the Secretary General [of the Foreign Ministry] it is now less certain that Stikker will be included.'[54] On 19 February, van Steenberg, the Catholic Party leader, was given the task of forming a new Government. He had failed to do so by 26 February.[55] On 28 February, the task was given to Professor Romme, the leader of the Catholic Party.

This shaky period coincided, as has been seen above, with American pressure. Some of the pressure, combined with a slow realisation by the Dutch that they would have to bite the bullet, began to tell. Information Research Department in the Foreign Office was, as we saw in Chapter 5, also particularly busy. It was during this period of caretaker government that the Dutch realised that they could not avoid for too long the question of defence. On 7 February, Drees recognised this: 'We are faced by three far reaching problems, a need for increased defence measures, economy in ordinary government expenditure and restoration of our balance of payments'.[56] It is interesting that Drees mentioned the defence problem first: on 10 March, the (caretaker) Defence Minister, s'Jacob, announced that 'military conscription would be extended from twelve to eighteen months.'[57] Just four days later a new government was announced. Drees had survived as Prime Minister and so had Stikker as Foreign Minister. Not surprisingly, perhaps, the hot seat at the Defence Ministry had changed again, with Mr Staf the new incumbent.

The new government was slightly more to the right than the previous one.[58] At any event, defence was now high on the agenda: on 17 March, Drees laid before the Second Chamber his government's policy on defence. It entailed an increase from 1,000 million to 1,500 million guilders' expenditure a year on defence over the next four years; a reaffirmation of the increase in military service from 12 to 18 months; a calling up of reserves for refresher courses; the ultimate formation of five (rather than three) army divisions; a strengthening of the Air Force; maintenance of the Navy; increased defence production; and civil defence preparations.[59]

As we shall see, words and apparent intentions were not quite the same as hard action. It was nevertheless a considerable change from the uncertainty of the previous four months. The continuing intensification of the Cold War, enhanced by the Korean War, made its contribution; Drees' statement, on the inception of his new government, included the following:

> The fighting in Korea has increased the possibility of conflicts elsewhere in the world. The Atlantic Pact countries have been faced with the necessity of taking in hand a strengthening of their defences to ensure the safety of Western Europe, which until now was protected by only weak forces. In the event of an attack on one of them, the continental countries of Western Europe, thanks to this Pact, can count not only on the co-operation of all, but also on the assistance of the United States, Great Britain and Canada.[60]

On 27 March, the British ambassador reported to the Foreign Office the Second Chamber's reaction.

> There are, I think, three conclusions to be drawn from the debate. The first is that, with the sole exception of the Communist Party, there is a general endorsement among all the main political parties in Holland of the Government's defence policy.[61]

Although neither the British nor the Americans were to profess themselves satisfied with the Dutch defence effort, as we shall shortly see, the commitment to at least spend more was a considerable victory for Stikker, and reflected a greater degree of cohesion in defence matters than had existed before. Despite the fact that Stikker's resignation had triggered the crisis, he managed to hang on to his job and ensure a more urgent attitude towards defence on the part of the Drees government.

The British and American View

Despite the Dutch commitment to increase their defence spending from 1,000 to 1,500 million guilders a year, the Americans were still not satisfied. 'The Americans for their part tried constantly to induce the Dutch Government to produce an even bigger effort [...] but they refused absolutely to go beyond the Fls 6,000 million four year programme [...]', wrote the British ambassador.[62] At a Dutch Cabinet meeting on 26 October, considerable annoyance was expressed at the American pressure to increase spending.[63]

As for the British, they appear to have had a rather low opinion of Dutch military capability. At the end of the year, there was little to show for the efforts made to date.

On November 26 Field Marshal Montgomery found the Dutch General Staff agreeing that their army was in effect useless.[64] 'The dominating theme', wrote the British Military Attaché:

> in the military hierarchy here in 1951 has been the production of 'paper' divisions ostensibly to fulfil the commitment entered into by the Government with the Standing Group of five divisions by 1954 [...] General Eisenhower's appointment as Supreme Commander in Europe and his first visit to the Hague early in 1951 concentrated attention on defence [...] these paper divisions would have satisfied the Dutch military conscience vis-à-vis the NATO obligations had it not been for periodical visits of Field Marshal Montgomery.[65]

The Military Attaché concluded that by the end of 1951, little real advance had been made in the build up of land forces. A Foreign Office official recorded on a file jacket: '[...] no good word can be found for the Army in the last year, except that the authorities have been brow-beaten by Field Marshal Montgomery into asking for a SHAPE mission, which has not yet arrived.'[66]

Apart from this feeling that the Dutch were not doing enough, fast enough, there was criticism about what were considered to be conditions imposed by the Dutch in return for their increased commitments: 'It was made quite clear by the Dutch Government that the programme could not possibly be effective unless aid was forthcoming from the United States, on a scale approximately equal in terms of money to Holland's military effort.'[67] The Americans do not appear to have been happy with the Dutch attempt at a *quid pro quo*. *The Economist* wrote:

> The most recent rearmament proposals from the Hague, suggesting Dutch production of items for the common stock in return for dollar aid has been turned down by Washington, which objects to being regarded simply as an easy source of dollars.[68]

The Dutch had, in line with their new military programme, set up a Military Production Advisory Committee. The Minister of Economic Affairs, van den Brink, said that the extent of the military production effort should not be exaggerated. Its total, he said, would in the near future still be of a modest size in comparison with civilian production on which the economic well being of the Netherlands depended.[69] The Foreign Office was still sceptical of Dutch commitment:

> Mr Herod, the NATO Production Chief, will certainly have to work upon this Dutch committee. The Dutch still seem to be hoping not to make any arms without being handsomely paid, while at the same time receiving gifts from others.[70]

This comment might however have reflected a small degree of British indignation at the fact that the Dutch appear to have been more interested in American equipment than in British.

> Holland [sic] was determined that the equipment of her army should all be American and a division's worth of British type Canadian equipment was received at the beginning of the year with rather bad grace and allocated for training purposes.[71]

According to the British ambassador, the Dutch were embarrassed, but were pressurised into accepting the gift.[72]

The Dutch were reluctant rearmers, although they were happy to see others rearm. The process was a slow and painful one. In November 1951, the British ambassador wrote to Eden:

> As you are already aware, in the early part of this year there was considerable pressure on the Dutch Government to increase their defence expenditure and when the new Government was formed in March after a prolonged Cabinet crisis, part of their programme was a provision for defence at the rate of Fls 1 500 million a year for four years [...] to sum up, the Dutch will undoubtedly make a contribution to the general defence effort [...]. Meanwhile, ministers tend to make statements both for domestic and Anglo-American consumption which seek to emphasise the extent of the Dutch defence effort, but which do not appear to be too close to the facts.[73]

The Dutch were, naturally, not very happy with British and American criticisms of their defence efforts. The Minister Plenipotentiary at the Dutch Embassy in Washington wrote an article in July 1951, which appeared in the *Denver Post*. Headed 'Netherlands Makes Sacrifices for Defence', it continued:

> In the last war the United States lost 263,000 dead, which is a terrific price to pay; but to the Netherlands with a population one fifteenth that of the United States, it also meant, by a strange coincidence, 263,000 dead; not to mention the starvation, the concentration camps, the systematic annihilation of certain groups of society [...] whereas in 1950 the total of that spending was 850 million guilders, it has risen to 1,500 million in 1951.
>
> These are not merely estimates; at the moment, military goods to the total amount of one billion guilders are under production or in preparation of production in the Netherlands, and our Government has announced that this country can produce a total of 4,500,000 guilders in military goods in the coming four years.

He also referred to the extension of military service from 12 to 18 months.[74]

The tension on defence co-ordination between the Netherlands, and the United States and Great Britain, was not to go away; nor was the tension within the Netherlands itself between the Atlanticists, and the more peaceful Continental-minded. This tension was enhanced under the surface by the disdain felt by most of the Dutch towards overt military preparations. In the Second Chamber, there was a good deal of criticism of American policy towards the Netherlands.

> The dominant theme which emerged from the speeches of members of the chamber was that Europe must be strengthened militarily and economically to make it not only secure from Russian aggression but also better able to counteract American predominance in the Western world. The Government was criticised for its half-hearted support of the idea of a European federation and for its hesitant approach to the Pléven Plan, and fears were expressed that Mr Stikker had been too much influenced by Great Britain's negative attitude.[75]

Stikker was still lukewarm towards the idea of European co-operation: 'Stikker said he rejected the line of argument which pleaded for European solidarity, or a European federation as a counterweight to the dominating influence of the United States in the North Atlantic Treaty Organisation.'[76] It is worth repeating here part of a quote by Stikker from the preceding chapter:

I feel most strongly that federation of small number of continental European nations can never be independent economic or political unit, as the age of preponderance of these Western European countries, either singly or jointly, in world affairs, belongs to the past.[76]

Many would disagree today, with the benefit of hindsight.

Conclusions

The question of Dutch participation in the European Defence Community was complicated by the Dutch attitude to strengthening its own military contribution to the NATO alliance. On the one hand, it enabled the Dutch, and Stikker in particular, to delay making a decision on Dutch participation in the Paris talks. Given the considerable debate both between different factions in the Netherlands and between the Dutch Cabinet and the Americans and British, on Dutch commitment to the Alliance, it is hardly surprising that the Dutch delayed their entry to the Paris talks. There was a considerable degree of indignation among the Dutch about what they saw as American interference. In the end, however, the Dutch began to realise that being members of an Alliance was not enough: it was necessary to spend large sums of money, at a time when many, particularly the Socialist Prime Minister, thought it better to allocate the money to the social budget. The American and British pressure to spend came at a time when the Dutch had balance of payments difficulties, and it was undoubtedly difficult for them to suddenly increase their defence expenditure, already inflated by the legacy of Indonesia. The Americans and the British do not appear to have fully understood the problems the Dutch had, both in terms of their economic priorities, or in terms of national characteristics; hence the Dutch indignation.

The government crisis in early 1951, while providing Stikker with an excuse to delay Dutch entry to the Paris talks, and maintain observer status, also served as an opportunity for the Americans and British to increase the pressure during a confused political period. One is tempted to wonder whether or not the crisis was engineered. The announcement of the new increased defence expenditure very shortly after the formation of a new Cabinet suggests that even a caretaker government was able to formulate important decisions *a priori* during a period of apparent political instability. Here, Stikker clearly played an important role. He had not, however, had everything his own way, as the dismissal of Kruls shows. That dismissal can be interpreted as a warning by the Dutch to the Americans and British, that they could only go so far in exerting pressure on the

Dutch to increase defence spending. It also shows, however, that even in the Netherlands, a military man who involved himself in sensitive political issues could find himself out of a job. As such, Kruls' dismissal was a reassertion of Dutch independence, a kind of reversion to the fact that although the Netherlands had broken with tradition and joined a military alliance, she was still independent-minded.

The year 1951 was certainly an eventful one in the Netherlands, when certain Dutch characteristics manifested themselves strongly. It is worth recording that the British ambassador wrote, after a three and a half year stay:

> The character of the Dutch today derives, in my opinion, from two main sources: the first is religious belief, in the widest and most general sense of the term, and the second a material conception of life. It might be thought there is some incompatibility here, but I do not believe this is so. The Dutchman is above all interested in security. Religion implies security in the next world, money and material advantages imply security in this [...] Two problems have dominated the political scene during my stay here. The first was Indonesia; the second was defence. To this may be added the growing importance throughout the period of the question of European integration.[78]

As we shall see in the following chapter, although the defence question still posed a problem, that of European integration came increasingly to the fore, with the Dutch failing to emulate British standoffishness, and plumping for the Continent, albeit not without difficulty.

9

TOWARDS COMMITMENT

Introduction

The end of the year [1951] saw Holland [sic] embarking a little reluctantly on the road to federation with the countries of the European Defence Community. This did not entirely conform with the pattern of European federation which Dutchmen generally and in particular the Parliamentary leaders hoped for, and hopes of bringing Britain and Scandinavia in were by no means abandoned.[1]

The year 1952 was to see the tide turn from reluctant participation in European federation (with Stikker continuing to nibble away at the 'federast' idea, while stressing Atlanticism), to a more openly pro-European stance, pioneered by a new Foreign Minister, Beyen, who as we shall see, does not appear to have been as popular with the British government as had been his predecessor.

The question of the Dutch defence contribution was still to be a touchy topic, with the Dutch army coming in for British sniping, although the intense external pressure seems to have abated. Generally, the Dutch government was more in line with parliamentary thinking on the question of security and the European Defence Community than the previous administration had been. In fact, the enthusiasm of the country as a whole towards the European Defence Community in the second half of 1952 contrasted markedly with the lukewarm attitude during the first part. The attitude of the new British ambassador, Butler, towards the Socialist Prime Minister, Drees, was also considerably more positive, as we shall see, than that of his predecessor, Nichols. It is worth remembering that in those days, the views of British ambassadors tended to carry more weight than today, when communications make it so much easier for government ministers to jump onto an aeroplane than hitherto. Until the new government was formed in September 1952, however, Stikker was still there, fighting his rearguard action, even though he had had to concede defeat and bring the Netherlands into the Paris talks, albeit with a critical attitude.²

Reluctant Participants

Although Stikker had had to bow to inevitability, he still had some influence. He showed this, by appointing an Atlanticist, Van Vredenburch, as leader of the Dutch delegation to the Paris Conference, rather than Spierenburg, a convinced European.³ Despite this, it is unlikely that Stikker entertained any real hopes of seriously damaging the European Army idea, or of bringing in Britain as a full participant: '[...] it was clear enough by the end of the year that if the EDC came into being, Holland [sic] would form part of it, with or without Britain,'⁴ he wrote in his memoirs.

Stikker's aim was rather to enhance where possible the strength of NATO which, as we have seen, he considered far more important than a European Defence Community. One of the Foreign Ministry's instructions to Van Vredenburch was to ensure 'clear guidelines on the strategic and administrative responsibility of NATO institutions vis-à-vis those of the European army.'⁵ While Stikker did not wish to try and destroy the European Army, it would clearly (in his mind) strengthen NATO, if the European Army could be weakened, since only NATO could fill the gap. Albert Kersten wrote:

> From the instructions sent to Van Vredenburch, it is clear that the Dutch government pushed for keeping military integration to a minimum. The realisation of the EDC should bring with it the smallest possible loss of national sovereignty [...] As a result of this concept, they were prepared to grant West Germany – applying the principle of equality – her own (national) defence institutions. The Dutch government hoped that their participation in the EDC negotiations would put them in a position to slow down the whole process of the federal integration of Europe.⁶

The Dutch then found unexpected help from the Belgians. For despite the Benelux idea, relations with Belgium had not been particularly good, one of the reasons being an adverse balance of payments with that country, but the other, more germane to defence sensitivities, being the Belgian relationship with the French. Kersten writes: 'The uncertainty in Holland [sic] over the aims of the Belgian government and the fact that in security questions Belgium traditionally tended towards France, seemed to restrict even probes on the question of coordination.'[7] At the preparations for the Seventh Session of the North Atlantic Council in Ottawa in September 1951, however, it emerged that the Belgian representatives had almost identical views on the level and extent of military integration as well as on the state of the Community.[8]

Despite this, the Dutch and Belgians did not adopt a common position, agreeing only to coordinate their policies. From the outside, however, they (and Luxembourg) presented a common front. Van der Harst describes the Belgians as the 'enfants terribles' of the Paris Conference.[9] The Dutch seem to have been happy to let the Belgians make the running:

> Basically, the Benelux countries, led by Paul van Zeeland, the Belgian Foreign Minister, had become worried because they could see themselves being absorbed into a Defence Community where the strength of the three larger partners, France, Italy and Germany – particularly in the economic field, would predominate. The Benelux countries would occupy a position of permanent inferiority and lack of power.[10]

This view (of Fursdon) reflected that of the British Embassy in Brussels:

> It was largely due to Belgian insistence in the final stages of the EDC negotiations that the supra-national elements of the Treaty were watered down. Moreover, Mr van Zeeland in his public pronouncements tended to advocate the 'confederal' as opposed to the 'federal' approach towards making Europe.[11]

While this may seem surprising, in view of Spaak's federal attitude, it was in fact the 'Eden proposals' to strengthen the Council of Europe, which influenced the Belgians. They were still under discussion. The Little Three fought hard for their corner during the negotiations, and it is probably because of their co-ordination that agreement was reached that there would be nine commissioners, rather than one. 'During the Conference of Ministers from 27 to 30 December, when this question was discussed,' wrote Kersten:

> Stikker found that Van Zeeland and the Luxembourg Foreign Minister, Bech, were in favour of a Commission [...] in January 1952 the number of Commissioners was fixed at nine. The Hague was satis-

fied with the general division of responsibilities between Commission and the EDC Council of Ministers.[12]

A telegram from the American ambassador in Paris, Bruce, summed matters up succinctly:

> The [Foreign] Ministers' meeting made clear complete agreement of German and French (and for all practical purposes, Italians) on the major issues involved in EDC. They agreed that EDC must from the beginning replace national armies and national budgets and must be operated as a genuine defence force and not merely as a coalition [...] in face of Benelux opposition, French and Germans maintained solid front on issue after issue [...] Belgians and Dutch were able to maintain a joint position on most issues. In substance, their position was that community should have very limited authority in initial period and would constitute little more than a coalition of national forces of the members comparable to Brussels Pact.[13]

One should not, however, exaggerate the influence of Benelux:

> The French decision to finish the negotiations before the (Eighth) NATO Council in Rome, reduced Holland's [sic] chances of influencing the draft treaty [...]. Although the EDC negotiations were not in fact completed before the NATO Council in Rome, Schuman ignored the objections of the Benelux countries.[14]

On 16 November 1951, the Minister's Conference in Paris had also confirmed the determination of France and Germany to create a supranational European Defence Community.[15] This event, followed by the Paris Agreements on 22 November, in which Germany was formally recognised as an equal partner, added impetus to the Paris Conference. 'In that agreement,' wrote Spits,

> [...] German participation in the European Army would be the condition for the restoration of Germany's sovereignty, which meant for the Little Three the disagreeable complication that, although they were not involved in these consultations, they were nevertheless more or less made responsible for the quick realisation of the European Army Treaty.[16]

The Dutch Blindness

In February, Stikker told the Second Chamber:

> [...] I have the firm confidence and the belief, that the European Defence Community can soon become a reality [...] the road of the Defence Community is perhaps the only thing left which points in the direction of a better future for Europe.[17]

Despite this public affirmation of support for the European Defence Community, the Netherlands were obsessed by the idea of a formal link between NATO and the EDC.[18] Kerstens actually wrote that this made the Dutch government blind to the reality of international relations.[19] The Dutch, but mainly Stikker, do indeed seem to have stuck blindly to the link between NATO and the EDC, almost up to the date the treaty was signed, on 27 May.

On 15 April, the Foreign Ministry sent a telegram to the Dutch ambassador in Bonn. It referred to a note from Acheson of 13 April, addressed to the Foreign Ministers of the United Kingdom, West Germany, France, Italy, Belgium, Luxembourg and the Netherlands. The note was worded strongly, and smacked of impatience:

> At the various meetings in London and Lisbon last February, I was encouraged by the progress made and was led to hope that problems of concluding the treaty for European defence community and the various contractual agreements with German Federal Republic could be speedily resolved. Since then I have been increasingly concerned by the slow progress which I believe is gravely emperiling [sic] all our plans. I therefore wish to make this appeal to you to join with me and our other colleagues in the countries concerned to make a supreme effort to conclude the various treaties and agreements in time for signature on a definite date in the near future. You are of course well aware of the risks which delay will cause in Europe. You are perhaps well aware of certain grave difficulties which will be encountered in the US with respect to congressional action if there is further delay.[20]

This was obviously strong language, but, as we shall see, it did not sway the Dutch in their obsession with NATO, despite an American proposal that both the contractual agreements and the EDC treaty be signed in the Hague:

The signing of the two sets of agreements in different places not only is awkward from the point of physical arrangements for moving Ministers back and forth on the same day or even on successive days but likewise would be a regrettable loss of an opportunity which it seems to me we should grasp to make an impressive and historic ceremony of the simultaneous signing of both sets of agreements. I therefore suggest that we consider selecting The Hague. Prominently associated as it is with ideals of peace and containing the Peace Palace where the ceremony could occur seems to me to be an ideal site. Most important however in my thinking is the necessity for setting a date, preferably May 9, and making a public announcement of that fact without delay.[21]

This did not sway the Dutch, who were particularly stubborn on the question of the duration of the EDC treaty; they felt that its duration should be the same as NATO's. This position angered both Schuman and Adenauer,[22] who saw NATO more as a temporary alliance to stave off the Soviet Union threat, whereas the EDC was, in their eyes, a vehicle for peace within Europe. Despite the American pressure, the Dutch did not budge. The above-mentioned telegram from the Foreign Ministry continued: 'The Minister's first reaction [to Acheson's message] was unfavourable, since he considers it impossible to achieve the signature regarding ratification, before the suggested date.'[23] There the telegram ended. The last-minute stubbornness of the Dutch is well revealed in a personal telegram from Stikker to his ambassador in Bonn on 7 June, ten days after the signature of the treaty, extracts of which illustrate well Stikker's views:

For your personal information, you should know that the Cabinet did not take the decision to sign the EDC treaty without concern. In particular the categorical refusal at the last Ministers' Conference to allow the Netherlands the possibility of leaving the EDC on the expiry of NATO, as long as no European federation or confederation had come about, gave rise to concern [...] Continuing distrust between France and Germany, which has expressed itself both in the EDC negotiations and elsewhere, gives few grounds thus far for the expectation that the EDC can be set up in a fruitful form of co-operation between France and Germany.[24]

The telegram went on to mention the opposition to the treaty in France and Germany and the elections in Germany the following year, when the [Social Democratic] opposition might be in power. This last minute stubbornness is well borne out by Kerstens. The Netherlands wanted the right to leave the EDC once the North Atlantic Treaty expired. Schuman tried for a compromise, whereby on expiry of the North Atlantic Treaty, provision would exist for consultations and agreements on the necessary measures. Despite Acheson's personal intervention and British pressure, Stikker did not give in and negotiated about Schuman's compromise.[25] These last minute gyrations on Stikker's part resulted in agreement that in the event of the NATO treaty ceasing to be in force or changes in NATO's membership, the EDC treaty signatories would 'examine the new situation'.[26]

The Dutch, then, succeeded in modifying certain aspects of the treaty although, as we have seen, it was the Belgians who made much of the running. An important reason for this was bickering between the Ministers of Foreign Affairs and War. This has been expressed by B P Oskam, in his study on the Dutch delegation at the negotiations: 'The negotiators from the War Ministry had much less trouble with the supranational stipulations than their colleagues at Foreign Affairs [...] this led to conflicts within the delegation which could not be hidden from the delegations of other countries.'[27] It was even suggested that the Defence Minister, Staf, wished to be master of the EDC.[28] To further complicate matters, the joint Chiefs of Staff were against the supranational elements, while the military negotiators appear to have been more amenable. The bickering was to continue after the signature of the treaty. Monnet wrote: 'Curiously enough, the military men reached agreement fairly easily on the complex organisation of an integrated command [...] but the politicians consistently confused matters [...]'[29]

Oskam lends support to the view that the military negotiators generally got on better in some cases with their counterparts in other delegations, than was the case in their own delegation. For example, The French wished to strengthen the power of the Armed Forces Committee to the cost of the Armaments Committee. The military section of the Dutch delegation supported the French.[30] Not surprisingly, the Foreign Affairs Ministry was represented on the Armaments Committee, while the Dutch Armed Forces were on the Armed Forces Committee.[31] Clearly, then, the Dutch position at the negotiations was weakened, and although, as we have seen, they worked with the Belgians, their credibility must have suffered somewhat. Whether or not they would have succeeded in shortening the duration of the EDC treaty, had they not had internal bickering, is of course open to hypothetical debate.

The Dutch (although one is tempted to say Stikker) accepted the treaty with bad grace, even though they signed it. Despite much Dutch disappointment at the British attitude (Stikker himself mentioned it),[32] distrust of the French and annoyance about having to compromise on the NATO-EDC question, they fell in with the general trend and American and British pressure. Although Britain refused to join, the United States seemed happy to use her as a tool to encourage the EDC from outside. At the last minute, Britain agreed to introduce a treaty between herself and the EDC, committing her to 'afford the party or the defence forces so attached, all the military and other aid and assistance in its power'.[33] Britain and the United States also issued a statement that 'if any action from whatever quarter threatens the integrity or unity of the Community the two Governments will regard this as a threat to their own security.'[34]

Germany and NATO

Stikker saw the EDC as an instrument of NATO, while France and the Federal Republic saw it as something in its own right, that would at a given time become part of a European federation. The fixation of both countries on a Continental European Community contrasted starkly with the conviction of the Dutch Government, that the idea of a 'third way' for a Europe between the superpowers was unrealistic.[35]

For essentially strategic reasons, the Dutch saw NATO, with its wider membership, and looser political structure, as preferable to a supranational European Army, where they felt they would be subsumed into a Franco-German marriage, as small children, with very little say. They had hoped for German membership of NATO, with Britain and the United States acting as a counterweight to any future threat from France or Germany.

To say that the Netherlands wanted Germany to rearm for its own sake would be rather simplistic. Things were more complex: the Dutch, despite a certain grudging respect for Dr Adenauer, feared that the German government would exploit the slightest sign of disunity between the European powers, even to the point of destroying the Paris Conference. This in turn, felt the Dutch, would weaken the Atlantic Alliance. The Federal Republic could then set their own terms and, if not satisfied, reunify and become neutral.[36] 'If the Dutch government wanted the rearmament of West Germany, on the grounds of its security interests, then it had to oppose the French policy of discrimination. Once the French agreed on the size of the military unit, and Germany had achieved equal (or more equal than before) status, the Dutch had less reason to oppose French policy, and concentrated on trying to strengthen NATO, this time as a counterweight to France and Germany.

Suspicion of Germany had not died down in the Netherlands, but rather been diluted by a recognition that a rearmed Germany within a strong Atlantic Alliance was the solution for Dutch security interests. Nevertheless, the Dutch watched for signs of German militarism with some care. The Dutch ambassador reported back to The Hague at the end of October 1951 about the activities of various groups. One was known as the 'Grünen Teufel' (Green Devils, parachutists) who had met in Brunswick under one of their wartime leaders, General Ramcke, who had recently been released from imprisonment for war crimes.[37] The ambassador also reported on the 'Freikorps Deutschland', led by a former SS officer, Hermann Lams and Karl Heinz Neumann, a former Nazi party official.[38] There were, said the ambassador, about 300,000 in all these organisations, less than 10 per cent of wartime strength.

More significantly, a secret note from the Dutch Prime Minister to the Cabinet spoke about the 'Bruderschaften' and some military organisations. The military organisations concentrated on such activities as helping war widows, said the note, and were therefore not dangerous. The Bruderschaften, on the other hand, wanted a strong Germany to lead Europe, and independence from the United States. It mentioned Count Kielmansegge, General Gerhard Gunther, Professor Doctor Franz Heske and General von Manteuffel, who had good contacts with the Christian Democratic Union.[39]

While the significance of such organisations should not be exaggerated, nor indeed the Dutch 'watchfulness', it should be remembered that the war had only ended six years previously, and that the Bruderschaften had played an important part in the rise of the Nazi Party. They were not all exclusively of a right-wing, nationalistic character, however. While Himmler had been a member of one, so had Karl Marx. The more traditional Bruderschaften admitted students as members only following a duel, in which a scar was administered to the cheek.

All that being said, and kept in context, it is important to note that Adenauer commanded some respect in the Netherlands. Following the debate in the Bundestag on the German contribution to the Occupation Statute, the Dutch ambassador, De Booy, wrote:

One must respect the personal preponderance of the seventy six year old Chancellor [...] over his own party and the coalition parties, as expressed in the result of two hundred and four votes against one hundred and fifty six, and respect the capacity of the German government, in contrast to, for example, the French government, to impose its political vision.[40]

On the other hand, De Booy still had worries: on 5 March he wrote: 'It would not surprise me if the current image of a politically and economically weak France were perhaps to strengthen in an undesirable way the superiority complex of the Germans vis-à-vis the French.'[41] This came at a time when the Saar problem had been (temporarily) solved at a meeting in London of the Big Three's Foreign Ministers, and at the Ninth North Atlantic Council in Lisbon from 20 to 25 February. While the German parliamentary debate referred to above had ended in a victory for Adenauer and the European Defence Community, the Bundestag had also given its views on the Saar. 'Tough words were used', wrote Fursdon.[42] The French parliamentary debate, while keeping the door open for the signature of the European Defence Community treaty, was far more equivocal. Although it gave approval to the European Army, it laid down some specific conditions, one of the more significant of which stipulated that Germany's participation in the European Defence Community 'in no way implied the entry of Germany into the North Atlantic Treaty Organisation.'[43] The Assemblée Nationale invited the government to renew its attempts to encourage other democratic countries, in particular Great Britain, to join the European Defence Community.[44] Although the Dutch and the French had no disagreements about Great Britain's membership, their positions on German membership of NATO were totally opposed to each other; the French saw German membership of NATO as a reassertion of German sovereignty and a weakening of the European Defence Community, while the Dutch saw it as a strengthening of NATO.

A New Enthusiasm for Europe

At the end of June 1952, general elections were held, at which the Catholic People's Party lost two seats, while the Party of Labour won three, which made it as strong in the Second Chamber as the former. The new British Ambassador, Sir Nevile Butler, wrote: 'Proportional representation precludes violent changes in the strength of the parties and the above [election result] was regarded as a landslide towards the moderate left and a great personal triumph for Prime Minister Drees.'[45] Following the elections, a protracted period of bargaining over ministerial posts began, that was not to end until the month of August was over.

Apart from the slide to the moderate left, (the communists lost two seats), the other main change was that Stikker was replaced as Foreign Minister by Beyen, 'a professional banker and non-Party man and Mr Luns, a career diplomat hitherto of moderate distinction, the nominee of the Catholic People's Party which, sensitive after its electoral defeat, became insistent on his constantly asserting his nominally co-equal status.'[46] Mr Luns was in fact Minister without Portfolio, and the British were to look on the twinning rather sceptically, as we shall see.

With Stikker sent off to London as ambassador, and Beyen being avowedly pro-integrationist, Dutch foreign policy underwent considerable change in the European arena. On 5 July, before a government had been formed, *The Economist* had predicted: 'Whatever happens, there will probably be some change in Holland's [sic] foreign policy. More attention to European integration is possible, although Dr Drees is known to be as sceptical about quick integration as Herr Stikker always was.'[47]

There was still a hope that Britain would join the European Defence Community, at least in early 1952. The British ambassador wrote:

> In February, Mr Staf, the Minister of Defence, was still wishing publicly to see more countries becoming members of the Defence Community, and it took the Dutch, the press in particular, long to realise or to accept the position that Britain could not join any federal institution in Europe. The reception given by the press to the Eden proposals (see Chapter 7) was anything but favourable, exactly because they made clear that Britain was thinking in terms of association with, rather than participation in, the new Europe.[48]

Whatever the ambassador wrote about press comment, the Eden proposals were not immediately dismissed by all and sundry. Indeed the British were at first optimistic – perhaps naively so – about the plan's reception. On 18 March, Eden intimated to Churchill that the French reaction to the plan was 'distinctly favourable' and that he expected the Dutch to be likewise attracted by the idea.[49] Two days later, the British ambassador in Paris wrote that Schuman welcomed the initiative, having sought for some time a method of linking the Schuman Plan with the Council of Europe.[50] As we have seen, the Belgian Foreign Minister also welcomed the plan, initially. These were however immediate reactions, perhaps enhanced by the change of government in Britain, which many on the continent hoped would be a radical departure from the Labour Government's distinctly hostile attitude towards European integration. Once the dust had settled, it seemed clear that the Eden Plan would weaken, rather than strengthen, European unity. The Italians found it illogical, fearing it would hinder the development of European federation, while Adenauer saw 'practical and theoretical difficulties'.[51]

The question of how far Britain was prepared to go in the direction of European integration is naturally open to debate, with one view holding that the French undermined the Eden Plan. John Young, for example, wrote:

> In 1952, the Eden Plan showed Britain's desire to retain close links with the continentals, but it was undermined by the opposition of Monnet and others, who were determined that nothing should interfere with their chosen supranational path and wanted to channel British association along a different course.[52]

British and French mutual suspicion was still strong. The British ambassador in Paris held the view that despite rivalry for leadership in Europe, France wanted Britain in a European system, but doubted British sincerity, considering British relations with the United States and the Commonwealth as standing in the way of full British commitment to Europe.[53] While the Eden proposals were still under discussion, some evidence does suggest that some leading Frenchmen took the proposals seriously. The French confided in the British their fear that the efficient German steel producers would bring down the price of steel when the French produced too much. This would, in turn, lead to the Coal and Steel Community countries surmounting their own difficulties by 'dumping' in traditional British markets. The French then suggested that it was in Britain's, as well as their own, interest, to be in a position to work together against such German plans.[54] When a senior Foreign Office official was made aware of these French views, he wrote: 'If this is a fair sample of the bride's pre-nuptial behaviour, the Franco-German marriage will soon be on the rocks; in which case, we should take good care not to be cited as co-respondent.'[55] This shows that matters were not as clear-cut as they may have appeared on the surface, and that the French were worried about German economic preponderance. If the British entertained any hopes, however, that the Schuman Plan would not work well, they were to be disappointed. Bullen wrote: 'The final negative assumption of British policy was that the integrationist goals of the Six were by their very ambitious nature likely to fail'.⁵⁶ Willem Beyen's son also backs up this view, saying that the British thought that 'the others would not go ahead'. He adds that the British believed themselves to be masters of Europe.⁵⁷ Dr Boon, Secretary General of the Ministry of Foreign Affairs, says that the Dutch 'found Britain's belief in her supremacy hard to understand.'⁵⁸ David Dilks restricts himself to saying of Britain's viewpoint, that the Schuman plan succeeded better than she thought it would.⁵⁹

Once the Dutch, for their part, realised that Britain was not prepared to participate in full, they 'found themselves thinking more immediately in terms of the developing community of the six.'⁶⁰ The Eden proposal was not finally killed off until 10 September, when the Six accepted a proposal from de Gasperi, the Italian Foreign Minister, that the Coal and Steel Community should undertake studies for a European Political Community, under which the separate Communities would function. This concept had been enshrined in Article 38 of the EDC treaty (also at de Gasperi's instigation), but de Gasperi was concerned at the time it might take to ratify the EDC treaty. The disappointment at what were seen by many as Britain's attempts to dilute European unity was well expressed by Spaak and Paul Reynaud, a former French Prime Minister. Spaak said that he and his friends had already waited far too long for Great Britain to get aboard the European bus and that the Eden Plan was a real half-way house arrangement which might suit Great Britain, but that half-way houses were not good enough for Europe. Reynaud spoke even more strongly, mentioning Britain's 'betrayals' of France and Europe.⁶¹ Perhaps the most detached view of Britain's attitude to European integration comes from the Atlanticist Stikker who, despite his Anglophile tendencies, wrote in his memoirs:

> Great Britain's position on European unity has always been ambiguous. Not only the role of sterling as a reserve currency but also the Commonwealth, and the special relationship with the United States [...] have not allowed the British Government to find a clear European policy. Even Churchill, when he became Prime Minister in 1951, was in no way more positive than Alllee had been in his time.⁶²

During his time as ambassador in London, however, Stikker continued to nibble away at Beyen's European policies, as shall be seen.

Stikker was certainly not popular with some European integrationists, for example de Gasperi. The Dutch ambassador in Rome told his British counterpart that de Gasperi 'did not really understand Stikker. He was a big brewer and had a business mentality which made him approach international office from quite a different angle from de Gasperi, who was a thinker and a philosopher.'[63] Significantly, the Dutch ambassador added that Beyen was much more de Gasperi's cup of tea.[64]

Although the Dutch were to continue to oppose, where they could, relinquishing their sovereignty to a European Political Authority in advance of step by step integration, the departure of Stikker from the Dutch political scene, the views of Beyen and the recognition that they could press ahead without Britain, heralded a change in Dutch foreign policy on European unity. The British Ambassador wrote: 'Economic integration being for them the primary object, they were radically opposed to resigning sovereignty to a European Political Authority unless it had evolved and included some form of European customs union and common market.'[65] Although the ambassador spoke in the same breath about the Dutch being in favour of integration, yet radically opposed to resigning sovereignty, it is possible that his conclusion was slightly influenced by a deterioration in Anglo-Dutch relations, and that he was not prepared to admit openly that this deterioration might have made it easier for the Dutch to be more openly in favour of European unity.

The problems were twofold, revolving around defence and trade. In the defence area, an element of mistrust of the British appears to have been prevalent in certain Dutch circles. It involved contingency plans for the evacuation of both British nationals and the Dutch government to Britain, in the event of the Netherlands being invaded by (presumably) communist forces. This mistrust can be inferred from a rather cryptically worded letter from the British ambassador to the Foreign Office on 30 July:

> I should record that we here believe that the Dutch [...] will not happily reconcile themselves to the contrast between our having an Anglo-Dutch plan on ice for getting our nationals home and declining to discuss with them arrangements in England to fit in with their own completed plans for the departure of their Government from the Netherlands [...] If however HMG are still strongly opposed to discussing now with the Dutch the reception of their Government, the Foreign Office might consider making use of the top secret fact which has just been brought to my notice by my Air Attaché, namely that our RAF have already plans with the Dutch for escorting Queen Juliana's plane in the event of her being compelled to leave her country by air. This disproves any Dutch impression that we are thinking exclusively about ourselves. I very much doubt whether Stikker (Foreign Minister in the caretaker government for one more month)

knows of this arrangement and it would not do for this Embassy to inform him a second time of something which his own people ought to have told him. [...] The Dutch are qualified to be our most solid supporters in Europe; I feel that this support is becoming unsteady. A new Dutch Ambassador in London is overdue, and it looks like being Stikker.[66]

This rather curious letter, while not revealing the nature of the evacuation plans in question, brought out not only Dutch annoyance at British secretiveness, but a certain lack of communication between Dutch civil servants and politicians.

The ambassador was of course correct in his prediction that Stikker was to be the new Dutch ambassador to London. Stikker was, as we have seen, one of those leaders in Continental Europe least likely to criticise British policy on European unity, and his appointment as ambassador was apt. It is worth noting in this context that Stikker had in Autumn 1951 been accused in the Second Chamber of being too much influenced by Britain's negative attitude. During the same debate, the government had been criticised for its half-hearted support of the idea of a European federation and for its hesitant approach to the Pleven Plan.[67] This was due mainly to Stikker and Drees. Stikker was to continue to stress the importance of NATO, as ambassador in London, to the detriment of the EDC. The Netherlands' increased enthusiasm for European unity coincided not only with Stikker's departure for London, but with a deterioration in relations with Britain over trade, in particular in bacon. 'On the commercial side, too, relations, although always cordial, were somewhat strained by United Kingdom import cuts.'[68] wrote the British ambassador. Although an agreement was reached in May, and the atmosphere improved, there was a stiffening in the Dutch attitude towards the end of the year, when the full effect of the cuts began to be felt. The British, too, seem to have been annoyed at the Dutch. The Foreign Office wrote:

> Up to 1952 the Dutch were inclined to fall below their commitment because of the rival attraction of the export market in Germany. It was when this market collapsed in early 1952 that they really became dependent upon the United Kingdom market. The Ministry of Food feel very strongly that the Dutch flirted with the Germans when we were short of bacon [...].[69]

These bilateral problems existed despite the British ambassador's positive view of Drees – 'a man worthy of the highest respect'[70] – which contrasted, as we have seen, with his predecessor's assessment.

More evidence of Britain not being inclined to be as close to the Dutch as hitherto is shown by the fact that Beyen did not visit Britain until the end of March 1953. Stikker told Sir Pierson Dixon, Deputy Under Secretary at the Foreign Office, that Beyen had been hurt at the British government's failure, shortly after he came into office, to respond to his suggestion that he pay a visit to London.[71] This will be discussed in the following chapter.

Relations with Germany, while hardly cordial, were becoming more important to the Dutch, principally because of trade. The difficulties with Britain brought this into relief. The Foreign Ministry Yearbook for 1951/2 stated:

> Considering the difficulties which Dutch exports to Great Britain are going through as a result of the recent import restrictions in that country, the significance of German trade is greater for the Netherlands [...] especially for Dutch exports of agricultural and horticultural products.[72]

The Yearbook for 1952/3 stated that trade relations between the two countries were of 'very great importance'. The Netherlands was Germany's largest export market; in 1952, nearly 15 per cent of Dutch exports went to Germany, while 13.5 per cent of Dutch imports came from Germany.[73] The Dutch linked their relationship with Germany closely to the European Defence Community, which they now recognised as the only practical solution for a complete normalisation of relations with that country, and the ending of the Occupation Statute, for which the Treaty made provision. The Foreign Ministry Yearbook for 1951/2 stated: '[...] the abolishing of the Occupation Statute must be seen in the closest association with the establishment of the European Defence Community.'[74] What however, of the Netherlands' own defence?

Defence – Less Enthusiasm

'Although the new Government's programme continued that laid down in 1951, progress was disappointing in so energetic and competent a people. Also the development of defence production was slow and made little impact on Dutch industry', wrote the British ambassador.[75] As we have seen, defence had never been a subject dear to the hearts of most of the

Dutch, and the rather patronising comments of the British need to be seen in this context. The Military Attaché wrote in 1953:

> After the elections in June [1952], several attempts were made to form a new Government and one was finally formed in August. From the military point of view, there was little change from the old one, and it did not alter to any significant degree the military policies which had been followed.[76]

He concluded:

> The end of 1951 found Holland [sic] with no troops they could call on in an immediate emergency. The end of 1952 finds Holland [sic] in a position to produce a semi-trained division in a short time after M day [...] All the many complex problems of the build up of an efficient corps must not yet be left to the Dutchmen – they need help and guidance for many months to come.

A Foreign Office official summarised the situation of the Dutch Armed Forces thus:

> The Netherlands Navy has maintained its efficiency [...] The Netherlands Army, though it has improved in 1952, still has no troops which could be made immediately available on D Day. The trend is certainly in the right direction however. The Air Force continues to be hampered by dependence on the Army and lack of good junior officers [...] when all services are taken into consideration, the prospects of the Dutch contributing much to the defence of Europe seem poor in the extreme.[77]

The Dutch did what was barely necessary to build up their own defences within the Alliance to avoid being seen as uncooperative. Their aim was for German troops to defend them, especially since they had little confidence in France.

> Dr Drees and his Cabinet saw and stuck firmly to the point that proper plans were of secondary importance to getting West German forces into an army which would defend the Netherlands as well as the Fatherland. The controversy (about the defence of the North and North East of Western Europe) however brought out almost too

clearly the complete absence of confidence in French policy, strategic thinking and military competence.[78]

Conclusions

The Netherlands did what it had to, to satisfy the British and Americans, but mainly the Americans, and to present a reasonably credible image on defence co-operation. Despite their general dislike of Germans, the Dutch knew that they needed them for economic reasons and because the more Germany was brought into Western European defence, the less they, the Dutch, would have to spend. This dependence on Germany was enhanced by a distrust of, and lack of confidence in, the French. Although the EDC was a French initiative, that is certainly not why the Dutch ended up supporting it. While at the beginning, the Dutch had been cynical about the Plan's chances of success at the very time that the French were promoting it, so the French, in turn, were to grow cynical, as Dutch enthusiasm grew. The main reason was that it appeared to be the only way left to harness Germany into a Western system supported by the Americans.

The bickering between the Ministries of Foreign Affairs and of War illuminated both the battle over who should take the lead on the EDC as much as the chasm between Atlanticists and Europeans. Stikker's near obsession with NATO and his last minute gyrations before the signing of the EDC treaty are worthy of note. His attitude contrasted completely with that of Schuman, for example, who described the idea of the Cold War as 'distasteful'.[79] The Eden Plan, seen by many as another British attempt to undermine the push towards European integration, was at first treated seriously by the Six. The French, in particular, appear to have seen an opportunity to co-operate with the British to offset the power of the German economy. The initial interest shown in the British plan did not last, however, and it was seen that despite Churchill's return to power, his government's antipathy towards supranationalism was similar to that of the previous Labour administration's.

It is significant that the Dutch were to be the first to ratify the EDC. It may seem odd when one considers Drees' distinctly unenthusiastic attitude towards all things military, and Stikker's dislike of supranationality and obsession with the Atlantic, that the Dutch were to prove so enthusiastic. However, the EDC was now the only realistic vehicle for Germany's participation in the defence of the West; and the sooner relations were normalised, the faster the Netherlands would return to prosperity, since a prosperous Germany meant a prosperous Netherlands. Moreover, the Dutch knew that were the EDC to fail, then German membership of NATO would be the only logical solution, whatever the French thought.

The EDC was, however, not the only important topic in Europe. European co-operation in general was becoming increasingly important, particularly in the Netherlands. The EDC was only a part of that picture. The European Coal and Steel Community had, for example, become a reality. On the face of things, most assumed that Germany would end up as part of an EDC. Until such time, however, the German question remained high on the agenda of Europe, particularly for the Americans, as has been seen. The death of Stalin in March 1953 was to complicate the issue of rearmament but, as shall be seen, the Dutch were to remain firmly anchored to Western ideology and the 'Hallstein doctrine'.[80] The year was to show, above all, how important commerce was to the Dutch. By supporting Germany in Europe, they were supporting their own prosperity.

10

THE EUROPEAN ANSWER

Introduction

The year 1953 was to be significant in that the Dutch, originally the most sceptical of the Six on the question of supranational European defence, were to work faster than other countries in ratifying the EDC treaty. The two main factors that occasioned this reversal in policy were the realisation that the EDC was the only immediate vehicle left by which Germany could be brought into Western defence (and therefore the defence of the Netherlands); and the views of the new Foreign Minister, Beyen, which were, in contrast to Stikker's, based on close European co-operation. Given Germany's increasing economic importance to the Netherlands, and France's vacillating over the EDC, the Netherlands assumed a position of considerable strategic importance for the Americans, who were worried at French instability.

With Stikker's departure from the centre stage of Dutch foreign policy, European co-operation was more important to the Dutch than hitherto. Beyen's integrationist views meant that the EDC had to be supported, since European defence co-operation was part and parcel of a Europe that went far beyond defence. The Dutch were finding increasing prosperity, and knew that Germany was the key to their continuing economic success.

Germany and Commercial Precedence

Since Germany was particularly important to Dutch economic interests, it followed that they would support German rearmament within a framework that would nip in the bud any future aggression. Now that Stikker's anti-supranational obsession had been largely eliminated – with his removal to London – the Dutch were more interested in using European co-operation as a means of enhancing their commercial and military security, rather than sniping at it. The EDC treaty provided sufficient guarantees against German aggression (indeed, removed this threat) and, more importantly, was advocated by the Americans and supported by the British, who were prepared to help, but not to participate.

The Dutch were also entering a period of increased political stability. Despite the period taken to form a new government in the summer of 1952 (or perhaps, because of it), Drees remained Prime Minister, and had come to represent a symbol of continuity. He had been Prime Minister since 1946, and enjoyed considerable respect and popularity. 'Dr Drees, the Party of Labour Prime Minister since 1946, feels father to the ten million Dutch people and to a large extent they reciprocate his feeling.'[1] This political stability was, naturally, accompanied by economic success. 'Economic developments were, on the whole, satisfactory [...] Dollar and gold reserves are now higher than at any time since the war. Industrial production rose steadily [...]'[2]

Because of the Netherlands' strong attachment to commercial principles, any defence policy that fitted into its commercial aims made sense. To support European integration – and, therefore the EDC – was to support German rehabilitation and increased exports to that country:

> Her export trade is more important to the Netherlands than to any other country in the world (46 per cent of her national income), and the fundamental basis of Dutch foreign policy is the necessity to expand it and to compensate for the loss of Indonesia. In any conflict in which her commercial interests are involved, therefore, the latter will always take precedence.[3]

Germany was the Netherlands' largest export market. 'The value of total trade between the Netherlands and the Federal Republic,' stated the Foreign Ministry Yearbook for 1953/54, 'amounted in 1953 to 2,525 million guilders, an increase of 264 million guilders vis-à-vis 1952. 14.1 per cent of all Dutch exports went to the Federal Republic, while West Germany's share of Dutch imports amounted to 15.6 per cent.'[4] Although no figures for trade with East Germany are given in the Yearbook, it nevertheless saw fit to state that trade had increased in 1953. This did not please the Americans. The British ambassador wrote that American interference in East-West trade was the one 'major irritation' in Dutch-American relations.[5] Trade was simply too important to the Dutch to allow ideology or dislike to get in their way.

While the Germans remain cordially disliked and feared possibly as much as the Russians, the old commercial relationships reasserted themselves. Increasing respect for Dr Adenauer personally was marked by a visit of Mr Beyen to Bonn towards the end of the year, the first by a Dutch Foreign Minister.[6]

This was indeed a significant event, for although in 1953, only 41 per cent of the Dutch felt friendly towards the Germans (an increase of 5 per cent over 1950), Adenauer undoubtedly commanded considerable respect in Dutch official circles. The Dutch ambassador to Bonn described Adenauer as a great statesman.[7] Given the considerable feelings of animosity that still existed, the ambassador was sticking his neck out, particularly since there was considerable annoyance in the Netherlands over the escape of seven war criminals from Breda gaol to Germany.[8] 'In 1953', wrote the British ambassador, 'Western Germany had undeniably become the country's predominant (and alarming) neighbour.'[9] Relations with Germany were based more on trade than on friendship, while those with Britain seem to have been based more on friendship and the past, than trade alone.

Dutch-British Relations

Although the British ambassador wrote that (Dutch) relations with the United Kingdom were good, this needs to be qualified, particularly since Anglo-Dutch friendship was taken for granted. Pigs, in fact, proved a point of considerable contention, and one worth bearing in mind, given Dutch sensitivity on commercial matters. Already annoyed at 'heavy handed American attempts to supervise Dutch transit trade with the Iron Curtain countries' (the British Ambassador's own words),[10] Dutch pig breeders were undergoing hardship as a result of reduced British imports of Dutch pork. The reduction of British purchases in the year 1953 (said Ambassador Stikker to Permanent Under Secretary Strang) would create great hardship for the Dutch pig breeders, who had built up their industry on a long term basis since 1948 with British encouragement. To supply British needs they had imported feeding stuffs for dollars, sold their product for sterling and subsidised their producers. The fact was that Polish bacon was cheaper than Dutch. Although the Foreign Office wrote that prospects for Dutch pig meat imports were brighter for 1954 (since the five year agreement with Poland was due to expire), the British found the Dutch had 'flirted with the Germans when they (the British) were short of bacon.'[12] This element of sour grapes cannot be ignored. Apart from irritants over trade, there seems to have been little love lost between the Dutch Chief of

Staff, Hasselman, and the Military Attaché to the British Embassy in the Hague, Colonel T C Williamson, who wrote of the former in March: 'He is still unbending and "Prussian like" [...] His inferiority complex is still manifest.' In the Autumn, the Dutch refused to allow a British observer (who was to have been the Military Attaché) to attend a military exercise, 'Grand Repulse'.[13] The Foreign Office considered the 'hand of Hasselman' to be the reason for the refusal, and was discontented that while there was no British observer, the Canadian Military Attaché had attended the exercises.[14] Although the official Dutch explanation was that the number of observers had to be kept down,[15] the reason does seem rather specious, given the attendance of the Canadian Military Attaché. Whether or not Hasselman had seen a copy of the Military Attaché's (secret) dispatch, it is logical to assume that he knew of the latter's view.

Certain British diplomats do occasionally seem to have lapsed into a slightly arrogant view of the Dutch. For example, following an announcement on 10 July that Princess Wilhelmina had 'taken the initiative for a private conference to be held in Holland shortly to which European leaders of international organisations in the spiritual field of youth movements would be invited,'[16] a Foreign Office official wrote on the file jacket: 'The House of Orange are persistent do-gooders.'[17]

As has been seen, some British diplomats, Nichols in particular, were fairly critical in their description of the Dutch, from time to time. The Secretary General of the Foreign Ministry during much of Nichol's tenure of office did not, for his part, have a particularly positive view of British ambassadors to the Netherlands, and of Nichols in particular. He refers to the 'low quality' of British Ambassadors to the Netherlands, and says that there was relief when Nichols left.[18]

There was a distinct cooling of relations between Britain and the Netherlands when Beyen took over as Foreign Minister. The British, for their part, were not keen to have talks with Beyen, who wished to have talks with the Chancellor of the Exchequer as well as the Foreign Secretary. They did not wish to be pinned down on questions of economic integration. A letter in early 1953 from the Foreign Office to the British ambassador is revealing:

> We are, as you know, coming under fairly strong pressure from a number of European countries to tell them something more about the results of the Commonwealth Conference than we were able to do at the OEEC last month. We cannot, for obvious reasons, do anything about this until we have made our first contact with the

new American Administration and it is therefore embarrassing to be confronted with individual discussions of the kind Mr Beyen evidently has in mind.[19]

Apart from showing Britain's disinclination to engage in substantive discussion with Mr Beyen, the letter shows how Britain's 'special relationship' with the United States took precedence. Revealingly, the letter continued:

> If you think that Mr Beyen will be much offended by all this, you can say that Mr Eden will be delighted to see him and give him a meal if he decided to come here this month, only in that event it will have to be primarily foreign policy, and not economic topics that form the subject of conversation.

In April, a Foreign Office official wrote that Beyen seemed 'all along to have had the idea of conferring on financial matters with the Chancellor of the Exchequer as well as of seeing the Foreign Secretary.'[20] Three days later, another official minuted: 'The trouble is that Mr Beyen has been trying to kill too many birds, foreign, political and financial, with one stone.'[21] It is clear that Beyen's views on European integration were embarrassing to the British, who had been used to Stikker's emphasis on Atlantic co-operation and aversion to 'federast' ideas. Beyen's view was that European integration would strengthen Atlantic links; this contrasted with Stikker's ideas. The former wrote: 'Better a supranational Europe without England, than a non-supranational Europe with England.'[22] Ernst van der Beugel sums up the problem bluntly: 'Beyen irritated the hell out of the British.'[23] The British ambassador referred to Beyen's disappointment that the British 'preferred to attack Europe's economic problems on a wider scale than would his own plan for integration of the six European States parties of the Coal and Steel Community.'[24] Beyen was simply too much of a European integrationist for the British.

EDC Enthusiasm - The Shining Example

Although, as shall be seen, the Dutch were to give a considerable fillip to the EDC process through ratifying before anyone else, at a time when the French were wavering, it is worth mentioning again that they knew that all would not be lost, were the EDC to fail: towards the end of the previous year, Stikker had written the following to the Foreign Ministry, after a meeting with Churchill:

Were France *not* to ratify the EDC, as Churchill feared (and even the French Ambassador gave me to understand this morning that in his opinion the current parliament would never do that), then the time could come when Germany could be brought into European defence in any form, indeed as a full member of NATO.[25]

As has been seen, Stikker was sceptical about the motives of the French. A report he had received from an (unnamed) confidential source, only three weeks before the First Chamber ratified the treaty, had concluded: 'At the moment we can describe the situation in the French parliament regarding the ratification of the EDC as hopeless [...].'[26] Although Stikker's obsession with NATO had clearly not died, and he officially supported the EDC (he hardly had any choice, having had to give it his full support in Parliament as Foreign Minister, and representing his government as Ambassador), the security provided by NATO certainly acted as a psychological umbrella for the Dutch government in its new found enthusiasm for the European Army. This confidence in NATO did not however detract from the increasing Dutch support for the EDC. *NRC* summed up the mood: '[...] this treaty seems to offer the only short term solution to involve West Germany in Atlantic defence.'[27] Another strand to Dutch support for the EDC was a fear that if it were not ratified, the Americans and Germans would work closely together. This at any rate, was the message in a letter to Stikker from a secret source, which also claimed that the United States had already discussed the matter with the Germans.[28]

Despite initial doubts, the Americans by now clearly believed that the EDC could succeed. Ernst May wrote:

> That the EDC would never materialise had been foreseen. The American and British Governments had acquiesced in the Pléven Plan on the assumption that debates in France would lead to some more practicable scheme. Within months, however, American officialdom, or at least a large part of it, had made the EDC its own. It had, moreover, become optimistic about the EDC's prospects.[29]

As the Dutch rallied solidly behind the EDC, the French were having problems. In January 1953, René Mayer was elected President of the Council following the resignation of Pinay's government. Although, as Fursdon points out, Mayer had supported the principles of the EDC, the (Gaullist) Rassemblement du Peuple Français had made their support of his candidature contingent on his negotiating additional protocols to the EDC treaty before seeking ratification. In addition, Schuman was replaced as Foreign Minister by Bidault, who began work on the additional protocols.[30] The Protocols reflected French anxieties over losing control of their armed forces and covered: the war in Indo China, where the French had a large military commitment, and were clearly worried that a European Army might not be as committed as they were; their concern that the permission of the Supreme Commander of NATO was required to transfer forces out of the EDC; the right to mobilise at national level pending the elaboration of final EDC procedures; and the rights of the French occupation forces during the transition period. This last point prompted Stikker to write from London; 'The difficulty for Germany is also free hunting and fishing rights for officers in the French Zone.'[31]

Although the Foreign Ministers of the Six's meeting in Rome at the end of February solved the problem by agreeing that the additional proposals would be interpretative texts, the French were to continue to have misgivings, as history shows. The problem was compounded by a Soviet propaganda offensive which, according to a secret memorandum written by the Canadian Foreign Ministry (available in the Dutch Foreign Ministry archives) concentrated on France (understandably).[32] To compound matters, on 18 February, a French 'national committee for the defence of French unity' was set up to fight the EDC.[33] It is not surprising that the new American Secretary of State, Dulles, said:

> If, however, there were no chance of getting effective unity, and if in particular France, Germany and England should go their separate ways, then certainly it would be necessary to give a little re-thinking to America's own foreign policy in relation to Western Europe.[34]

The Americans were however satisfied with the Dutch approach to the EDC. At a meeting at the White House on 10 March, between the American President, the Dutch Foreign Minister without portfolio (Luns), the American Under Secretary of State, and the Dutch Ambassador to Washington, the former expressed appreciation of the position which the Dutch had taken, and said he would like to see the Netherlands begin to take the leadership in early ratification.[35] They did.

In contrast to the French, the Dutch set the pace. When Beyen visited Britain in June, he told the Foreign Secretary, Selwyn Lloyd that his government had had no second thoughts about ratifying the EDC, and that it would probably be ratified without 'waiting for the others, unless the French and Germans fell for Russian manoeuvres and appeared likely to abandon EDC.'³⁶ He added that while he approved of the idea of a Four Power Conference, it should be made plain that they were not prepared to give up the EDC.³⁷

On 20 June, *The Economist* wrote:

> The Netherlands parliament has recently discussed ratification of the EDC treaty. Though there are misgivings in some quarters and an understandable perplexity at the French attitude, there is every chance that the treaty will be ratified before the Summer recess. As it is still British policy to see the defence community formed, the Dutch will be encouraged in their resolute stand.³⁸

The Economist's prediction proved correct; on 23 July the Dutch Second Chamber approved the EDC Treaty. (Whether or not *The Economist* realised that it still had to be approved by the First Chamber is a moot point). The Americans were close on ecstatic. The following day their Ambassador in The Hague wrote to Beyen: 'This successful action again confirms Netherlands' leadership in the movement for European co-operation.'³⁹ The Soviet reaction was, of course, very different. An article in Izvestia stated: 'The Dutch Chamber of Deputies, which was to have been disbanded for the Summer vacation, having been subjected to an American order, urgently concerned itself with a discussion of the "European Army" treaty'.⁴⁰ The death of Stalin in March had evidently not diminished the Soviet anti-EDC information campaign. Here, the Dutch were careful, in that they welcomed the idea of Four Power talks (that were to take place in early 1954) while remaining entirely committed to the EDC. 'In Europe,' wrote the British ambassador, 'the Soviet "new look" and propaganda caused no change in the Netherlands' attitude of caution and determination to consolidate, and if possible strengthen Western Defence, but Mr Beyen applauded the policy of seeking talks with Russia.⁴¹'

As the Dutch became the shining example of European unity, and, by extension, Western unity, (since the Americans supported the EDC), the French became increasingly difficult. When Dr Adenauer won a resounding election victory on 6 September, France's bluff began to be called. As Fursdon says, the French had had the convenient excuse to wait and see.⁴² Now the limelight was moving towards them. The mood of much of France's fear was summarised in two articles in *Le Monde*, implying that the Europe of the Six would be dominated by a strong Germany, and that the EDC would become a tool of a Bonn-Washington axis.⁴³ Generally the French were emotional, indecisive and divided on the whole issue, in stark contrast to the Dutch. The turnabout in the Dutch attitude was indeed remarkable; its answer lay in a new European fervour in the Netherlands, influenced by Beyen, in American influence, in the removal of Stikker and, most significantly, in the way the Dutch linked the EDC to their view of European federation.

Security through Europe

On 24 February, Beyen announced a proposal for a customs union of the ECSC countries, whose aim would be to establish a single market. The plan, announced as it was at the meeting of the Foreign Ministers of the Six in Rome, was overshadowed by the agreement, as we have seen, to solve the problem of the French additional protocols. Although the plan was not approved in Rome, it undoubtedly contributed to the eventual signing of the Treaty of Rome. Understandably, self-interest, essentially economic, played the strongest role in Beyen's initiative. The Dutch were not keen to go along with the European Political Authority without benefiting from it economically, in the form of a common customs union, which would guarantee them a European market for their products, making them less dependent on the vagaries of world trade. The British ambassador wrote:

> All parties in the State, excluding the Communists, support Mr Beyen's contention that some guarantee of eventual economic integration must be pressed for as part of the Political Authority. The Beyen Plan, or something like it, is part of national policy. But whereas Dr Drees and Mr Beyen and many others in all parties, whatever the French say, will have nothing to do with a Political Authority unless some such guarantees are provided for, a younger left wing section of Dr Drees' party, led by his most dynamic lieutenant, Mr Mansholt, are so impressed with the need for some new and supranational system (partly to cover the weakness of France) that they would not insist to breaking point on guarantees for economic integration, trusting that this must eventually follow.[44]

With the benefit of hindsight, the Mansholt plan for agriculture was one of the main driving forces behind the Common Agricultural policy, in turn the main pillar of the European Economic Community.

Whether Beyen was an out and out 'federast' or not, (we shall shortly see a different view to the British ambassador's), he was clearly in favour of European federation, provided that it could be made to work economically. This attitude was linked to less reliance on the Atlantic concept.

Although, apart from the emphasis on economic integration, there was no departure from Mr Stikker's foreign policy, the substitution of leisurely Mr Beyen for his active predecessor was reflected not in any diminution in the importance attached to NATO but in a loss of attention to it. 1953 saw no equivalent for the previous Stikker / Lange / Lester Pearson triumvirate.[45]

The climate had changed. In July, (following the approval by the Second Chamber of the EDC treaty), *The Economist* wrote:

> The Dutch position is both realistic and farsighted. Although the Dutch would prefer to see a far greater measure of economic integration in Europe and have initiated schemes for a European customs union and agricultural pool, they are willing to consider the EDC as a first step.[46]

Stikker's views no longer influenced Dutch policy towards European integration to any significant degree, although this did not prevent him from trying to influence policy. This led to problems with his successor at the Foreign Ministry. On 5 March Stikker wrote to Beyen, expressing doubts about the viability of pursuing European integration under French leadership.[47] Beyen's reply suggests some annoyance with Stikker:

> I must respond immediately to the position you defend in your letter of 5 March because it seems to me undesirable that any misunderstanding should arise between us on these vital points of our foreign policy [...] Finally, I should like to inform you that I am personally more optimistic that you as regards the chances of ratifying the EDC in the six parliaments.[48]

Stikker, however, was, in the words of Beyen's son, 'his own boss'[49] and it was not always easy for him to carry out the instructions of his successors at the Foreign Ministry. He displayed this tendency to ignore Beyen's views, for example, on 13 March, when he gave a lecture on 'Modern Europe'. He began by exonerating Churchill from accusations of back-peddling by saying that he (Stikker) was convinced that Churchill had meant nothing more than an allied army when he spoke of a European one. More annoyingly for Beyen, however, he said:

I must admit that personally I was rather against this plan. The setting up of a European Defence Community under a High Authority encroaches not only upon the sovereignty, and therefore the constitution of the participating powers, but also upon all their economic and social relations.[50]

Stikker's mention of his having been the only Protestant Foreign Minister of the Six bears some further discussion here, since the question of religious inclination does seem to have played a role in Dutch Foreign policy. Although Drees was not of the same political complexion as Stikker, he did, accordingly to Oskam, wish to break through the Roman (Catholic) 'private affair'. While deep analysis of the psychological and religious aspects are outside the immediate scope of this study, it is nevertheless significant that some years before his death, Beyen, who had been a non-party agnostic, was converted to Catholicism.[51] Beyen was, in the words of Ernst van der Beugel, an 'out and out European'.[52] He believed that pursuing overall horizontal integration was preferable to progressive integration, sector by sector.[53] His approach to the European Army needs to be viewed against this background.

The EDC was now seen in the Netherlands as the way to a united Europe and plans for economic integration. Scepticism about the EDC was no longer strong, and there seems to have been a belief that it would succeed. Even if it were not to, however, (and there were undoubtedly some who saw little chance for a European Army), it was still a convenient vehicle in which to pursue European integration.

Although the British ambassador, as we have seen above, thought that Beyen was against the European Political Authority, this is unlikely. Stikker clearly thought otherwise: 'According to Mr Stikker, Mr Beyen, the author of the Beyen Plan for the abolition of tariff barriers between the Six, advocated *political* integration because he thought economic integration would be ineffective without it.'[54] Bluntly put, Beyen saw economic integration as the horse, while Stikker felt that Beyen saw it as the cart, to be pulled by the political horse. The most credible answer to the relationship between political and economic integration is provided by the Dutch ambassador to Washington, van Roijen, who said at a meeting with the American Secretary of State, and other officials, that economic and political integration should be 'parallel and simultaneous'.[55] Despite these divergent, even muddled, interpretations, it is safe to assume that Beyen was simply more European than Atlantic in his outlook.

Emotionally, however, some Dutch were still torn between the European and Atlantic idea. A revealing insight into this is provided in a letter from the British ambassador to Sir Pierson Dixon at the Foreign Office on 27 May, in which he reported the views of the Deputy Secretary General at the Dutch Foreign Ministry, Ernst van der Beugel, about Drees:

> He believes personally in Beyen's ideas but realises he will have considerable difficulties in selling them [...] Van der Beugel specified that his [Drees'] fundamental anxiety is that by joining ESCS [sic] and prospectively joining EDC, the Netherlands is already imprudently throwing in her lot with the states not her natural associates: he [Drees] has a personal horror of the French, finds the Belgians very difficult, feels no real community with the Catholic Italians and of course detests the Germans. He regards the Scandinavian states and ourselves as his country's natural associates.[56]

Despite the strong undercurrent of Atlantic feelings which existed, the climate had undoubtedly changed, as even Stikker admitted. He told Sir Pierson Dixon that during his term of office the Dutch government had been unenthusiastic towards the European integration movement, but that now there was a great deal more support for it. He also described Beyen as being among the most ardent supporters of integration (for the wrong reasons, in his view).[57]

This evidence of a Dutch ambassador officially disagreeing with his Foreign Minister's reasoning is remarkable, even if it was only an aside. It shows both the difficulty Stikker had in toeing the line which he had never advocated as a politician, but also a fairly special relationship between himself and the British. At the same meeting with Dixon, Stikker said it would be a good idea if Beyen were to come to London to 'discuss all these problems frankly'.[58] As we have already seen, Stikker also said that Beyen was somewhat hurt by the British failure to respond to his suggestions that he, Beyen, pay a visit to London shortly after he came to office.[59] It is not difficult to infer that the British were not particularly interested in exchanging views with a convinced federast like Beyen.

No Divorce, because of the Children

Despite evidence that Beyen and Luns (the Foreign Minister without portfolio) did not get on, a division of duties ensured that there were no serious clashes on matters of policy. Luns was responsible for multilateral and bilateral relations outside Europe (except NATO) and Benelux relations, while Beyen covered NATO, European multilateral questions, the OEEC, ECSC and EDC. The Foreign Office view on the Dutch using two ministers for their foreign affairs seems to have been cynical, compared to the British ambassador's view. A British Foreign Office official wrote in February 1953: 'It is hardly surprising that the experiment of having twin Netherlands Foreign Secretaries should be proving unworkable.'[60] In March, an official commented: 'It is surprising that this lunatic scheme works as well as it does.'[61] Whether the scheme was lunatic or not, it involved, in Beyen's absence, Luns having to sign important documents twice, the first time as Foreign Minister *ad interim* and the second as Minister without Portfolio. The Secretary General of the Foreign Ministry was, according to the British ambassador, the real sufferer, since he had to 'dash about'.[62] Nevertheless, in contrast to the apparently more cynical Foreign Office, the ambassador wrote: 'There is no obvious issue of divergence between the two on the horizon.'[63] Moreover, in his annual review for 1953, he stated that the experiment of having two Foreign Ministers had been found to be workable.[64]

That the two ministers did not get on is however clear. Ernst van der Beugel says that he never met the two simultaneously during the whole of Beyen's four year tenure of office, referring to a 'personality problem'.[65] Beyen's son refers to humour holding them together,[66] while Luns himself says that while Beyen had a keen sense of humour, he was not devoid of it himself.[67] Van der Beugel says that the message put out to ambassadors who perceived that relations between the two were not all they could be was that there would be 'no divorce, because of the children.'[68]

It was ironic that Drees chose Beyen because, among other things, he was not a Roman Catholic. He wanted a 'neutral' minister, believing that Beyen would tend more towards the Atlantic. The irony was that Luns, a Catholic, turned out to be an Atlanticist, while Beyen was a convinced European, who later became a Catholic. Ernst van der Beugel, who helped in choosing the Foreign Ministers, stresses the irony of the whole process.[69]

Conclusions

In 1953, Dutch political stability and a favourable economic situation combined with a pro-European integrationist Foreign Minister to set an example of pragmatic European co-operation. The European Defence Community was part of the process of both European integration and of a wider East-West equation, and was supported strongly by the United States and her surrogate, Great Britain (albeit from 'outside'). While the French were dithering and having second thoughts about the EDC, the Dutch were getting on with the job of ratification. As has been seen, the Americans were particularly pleased with the efforts of the Second Chamber in being the first to ratify the EDC.

For the Dutch, the EDC proved a useful flag to wave for Europe, since they needed a strong – but controlled – Germany for their export market, and as a credible military buffer. Although Luns told the Americans that the Dutch did not tie the EDC question to political and economic integration,[70] the question was clearly linked, especially from the American perspective.

The role of the Dutch in the EDC's credibility was considerable, when contrasted with the problematic French attitude, to the point of being crucial. Had the Dutch not supported the idea, or had they delayed ratification, it is probable that the Americans would have had to reassess their policy, although this is admittedly a hypothesis. As it was, American-Dutch relations in 1953 seem to have been good, at least from the American point of view. A special report by the Psychology and Strategy Board of 11 September stated:

> American prestige in the Netherlands has reached its highest point of the post liberation in the past six months, principally as a result of gratitude for the United States' response in the flood disaster of February 1953 [...] Dutch supersensitivity on two points, however, tends to diminish deep confidence in American leadership. The loss of their Far Eastern possessions have made them unusually quick to see themselves slighted by the big powers and regarded as merely a minor European state.

'The second point of sensitivity is on East West trade control, where the Dutch are prone to complain that the United States puts less pressure on the British than on them [...]'[71] Nevertheless, the Netherlands were among the only four OEEC countries (the others being West Germany, Spain and Turkey) to receive the top ranking of 'Generally satisfactory'. In contrast, the French were placed in the column headed 'Disturbingly Unsatisfactory'.[72]

While relations with the Americans saw a considerable improvement in 1953, helped mainly by the Dutch attitude towards the EDC as much as by temporary gratitude for help in the floods, relations were generally less intense with the British, the main reason being Stikker's departure from the Hague and the increased European fervour that resulted. As regards the French, the situation on the EDC had reversed, with the

Dutch showing themselves as the solid supporters, and Stikker's predictions about the future failure of the EDC looking increasingly valid. 1954 was to prove him right.

11

THE LAST LAUGH

Introduction.
Unlike 1953, 1954 was to divert attention away from European economic integration to the question of defence; the European Defence Community, for all its specifically European federal significance, was to be part of a global power game, while the German problem remained unresolved. The year began with the Dutch being the first to ratify the EDC, yet ended with agreement on what the Dutch had originally pressed for so hard: German membership of NATO. The period in between was characterised by Soviet attempts to scupper the EDC and by the vacuum of an unarmed Germany. Perhaps understandably, Soviet propaganda was to focus on France. While the German problem remained unresolved and the EDC ratification debate dragged on, important attempts were made to stabilise the international situation. The Berlin Conference which opened on 25 January, ended in failure three weeks later with the anodyne communiqué: 'The Four Ministers have had a full exchange of views on the German question, on the problems of European security and on the Austrian question, but they were unable to reach agreement upon these matters.'[1] Soviet pressure continued and the Soviet Union even tried to join NATO on 31 March, a move that was rejected because of a Soviet condition that Germany be neutral.[2] The Geneva Conference, which opened on 26 April, reached agreement over the Korean War on 21 July. This was followed by the rejection by the Assemblée Nationale of the EDC treaty,[3] (which led to some speculation of a secret deal between Mendes – France and Molotov)[4] and finally, agreement at the London and Paris conferences respectively on the Federal Republic's entry into the North Atlantic Treaty Organisation, setting in place the European *status quo* which existed until recently.

These events had the effect of both overshadowing European economic integration and at the same time putting it into a defence context.

It did not, however, kill off the new found Dutch enthusiasm for European co-operation, but simply delayed it; the following year, once the dust had settled, Beyen, along with his Benelux partners, was to push hard for European integration. Although European integration was slowed down in 1954, it was very much part of Dutch foreign policy, particularly as regards the EDC.

The Dutch, Europe and the EDC

Although one main reason for supporting the EDC was that it appeared to be the only viable way of bringing Germany into a Western defence system, the other one, increasingly important, following Beyen's entry into the Foreign Ministry, was that it furthered the cause of European integration. *The Economist* wrote perceptively that the Netherlands had ratified the EDC 'not primarily for military reasons, but rather as a means to further European integration [...]'.[5] The two reasons, then, were always present, but under Stikker's tenure of office, the link between a supranational EDC and European integration was distasteful, while under Beyen it was a welcome development.

Stikker's and Beyen's own words about each other, or rather the paucity of them, show their differences in outlook on the European question. Beyen wrote tactfully: 'My predecessor, Mr Stikker, was a supporter of European unity but he was certainly several degrees less warm than I regarding the supranational path to reach this unity.'[6] He added that Stikker supported sectoral integration. Stikker only mentions his successor five times in his book *Men of Responsibility*. He writes: 'On the issue of unity in Western Europe, Beyen, I learned, was much nearer to the majority opinion in Parliament.'[7] While, as we have seen, Stikker spoke of 'federasts', Beyen had said at the 50th anniversary celebrations of the Dutch Chamber of Commerce in France:

> By its origin and history, Holland [...] has of all the Nordic countries remained the most Latinised [...] Let us never forget that the European countries display a complex and therefore difficult character from time to time, but always interesting, of which the common element is Latin.[8]

Stikker could never have spoken such words. It is apt that Beyen was appointed Ambassador to France upon his 'retirement', while Stikker was appointed to London. It is telling that, as we saw in Chapter 10, Beyen became a Roman Catholic.

Even with Beyen at the Foreign Ministry, the fervour for European integration seems to have diminished in 1954, although, as we have seen above, much of that fervour was channelled into the EDC. Moreover, the Dutch had set an example to the West by ratifying the EDC treaty first, thus serving the cause of European integration and pleasing the Americans. The Dutch could afford to wait, having 'done their bit', while the French began to have second thoughts. European integration, however, had certainly not been forgotten, but rather temporarily shelved. The British ambassador reported: '[...] Mr Beyen's policy that economic integration is inseparable from political integration, if temporarily in cold store, is not abandoned.'[9] Three months later he reinforced his view:

> [...] I doubt whether the Dutch as a whole have much enthusiasm in principle for schemes of supranational integration, and even the enthusiasts seem to have withdrawn into the background for the present. It is noticeable, for example, that little more has been heard in 1954 of Mr Beyen's plans for economic integration in Europe, which he canvassed at so many international meetings in the previous year when the EDC and the European Political Community were under discussion.[10]

The federalists were simply waiting in the wings.

Jan van der Harst implies that Beyen was alone in the Cabinet in his attitude towards the EDC, writing: 'With the exception of Beyen, the whole cabinet preferred a direct German participation in NATO.'[11] Although Drees was certainly lukewarm in his attitude towards the EDC, the image of Beyen being completely isolated in the Cabinet is perhaps a little exaggerated. On the general question of European integration, for example, he was supported by the Agriculture Minister, Mansholt. Moreover, although Beyen preferred an EDC solution to the direct admission of German troops into NATO,[12] as van der Harst writes, he told the Cabinet on 14 June 1954, during a French government crisis, that were the EDC not to come to fruition, then the alternative was for Germany to join NATO.[13]

The Dutch who, as we have seen, had considerable doubts about French motives, were simply to watch the French manoeuvre from one stance to the next in the drawn out ratification debate. Even Beyen, obviously less Atlantic-minded, and certainly more Francophile than Stikker ever was, wrote retrospectively that he was far from convinced that the French Parliament would ratify the EDC treaty and expressed doubts that Mendes-France supported the treaty.[14] His doubts were shared by Dean Acheson, who was to write: 'A man who looked like a man of destiny, but wasn't, Premier Mendes-France, regarded the EDC with a cold, if not hostile, eye.'[15] The Dutch were concerned about French stalling on the treaty, as were the Americans; they saw how the treaty served both their security and European interests. While Beyen was responsible for European integration, not so much stress was put on the Atlantic partnership as previously:

> United States leadership was generally distrusted as likely to be too innocent and favourable towards Germany. Attention therefore centred on the European Defence Community and the EPA, the latter being notably espoused by the small and zealous Dutch delegation to the Council of Europe, mainly of the Catholic Party.

Wrote the British Ambassador.[16]

The Netherlands were by now moving further away from Britain in their attitude towards European co-operation. Having already joined the Coal and Steel Community, and ratified the EDC treaty first, despite the initial misgivings, their attitude towards European integration was positive. Even Stikker shows this: when he met his British counterpart, Mason, in June 1954, he saw fit to tell him that Britain had not played the role in European co-operation that Western Europe had expected, and that 'Britain's refusal had placed various countries including our own, in difficulties.'[17] On a stronger note, it is worth recording what Max Kohnstamm, the former head of the German Bureau at the Dutch Foreign Ministry, said 20 years later of Britain's attitude towards European unity. Noting that Britain had refused to participate in the Schuman plan (despite 'confidential talks between senior French and British officials'), the European Defence Community and in the Common Market negotiations, he went on to say: 'Seen from the Continent, which was trying against the odds of the past to unite, some of Britain's actions seemed very near to efforts to upset this growing unity'.[18]

The above-mentioned words of the British ambassador, implying, as they do, that Dutch enthusiasm for European unity had waned, need to be qualified. The enthusiasm was still there, but was subsumed into the defence arena. Subsequent events were to show that the enthusiasm had not waned: the Benelux countries were to return to the attack in April 1955. F Roy Willis wrote, in his book: *France, Germany and the new Europe*:

> The new impetus for European integration came from the Foreign Ministers of the Benelux countries. Dutch Foreign Minister Johan

Willem Beyen, who had offered a plan for wider economic integration to the Council of Ministers of ECSC as early as February 1953, took the initiative again, before the Netherlands Council of the European Movement in April 1955, proclaiming his conviction that the time had come for the European Community to adopt comprehensive, supranational economic integration.[19]

On 20 May, he called for a Common Market.[20] The Dutch Foreign Ministry Yearbook for 1954/55 mentions 'the initiative of the Benelux countries, making it possible to put the problem of European unity back on the agenda, at the Messina Conference.'[21]

To ascribe, as the British ambassador had, the 'little more being heard of Beyen's plans' to 'the Dutch as a whole not having much enthusiasm in principle for schemes of supranational integration', was perhaps a little premature and misplaced. It was more a case of the enthusiasts using the opportunity provided by French equivocating as a breathing space, and to take stock. The fact that Beyen renewed his efforts once the European Army idea had failed backs this up. What, however, of the Federal Republic?

The German Angle

As we have seen, the Dutch needed a strong Germany for both economic and security reasons. Once they had been convinced that any future German nationalism would be subsumed into the EDC, they supported the latter strongly, although their support was tempered by a certain lack of confidence in the French, notwithstanding more cordial relations with France during Beyen's tenure of office. As for Germany, relations were not without their problems; indeed, at times, they bordered on the unfriendly, as they were until very recently. Before listing some of the problems and events that took place in 1954, some of which border on the farcical, it is well worth recording what the Dutch ambassador, Lamping, wrote to Beyen in September 1954: 'The German mentality lends itself little to compromise and alternatives, which are quickly looked upon as expressions of weakness.'

> The European concept can strike deep roots in the German psyche: with its associations with, and reminiscences of, the Holy Roman Empire, it appeals to the idealistic, sentimental, mystic expression; it satisfies the traditional German need to defend the Christian service of God and civilisation, and can, in contrast with the dangerous,

nationalistic "Wiedervereinigung" slogan of the socialists, bring an important contribution to a lasting association of Germany with the free world.[22]

Whatever the Dutch view of the German national psyche and its apparent commitment to the European ideal, there were more immediate, down-to-earth problems to be dealt with. The first was the continuing saga of the 'border corrections'. On the night of 17–18 April 1954, a group of Germans distributed pamphlets in the Netherlands calling for the return of their lost lands. The pamphlets mentioned the Atlantic Charter's stress on the right to self-determination.[23] In the same month the German ambassador, Mühlenfeld, complained about a poster at an agricultural exhibition in Utrecht caricaturing a German soldier to the point of ridicule.[24] On 24 May the German Embassy protested to the Dutch Government about crowds having damaged an embassy car in Rotterdam, during the Queen's birthday celebrations on 30 April.[25] The same note asked for more policemen to guard the diplomats' parking area. An internal Dutch Foreign Ministry memorandum of 3 June referred to a German Embassy complaint about the Second Secretary's briefcase being stolen on 13 January, in the diplomatic parking lot, despite a police guard.[26]

The dislike of Germans among some sections of the population was fuelled by the annexation question (or border correction questions, if one takes the Dutch, rather than German, perspective). The problem was still of sufficient importance to be discussed at the highest level – on 31 May, Beyen told the Cabinet that the problem would be dealt with through diplomatic channels.[27]

Diplomatic channels or not, the problem did not go away. In June, Germans crossed the border and symbolically sowed crops and grazed cattle on land that had formerly belonged to Germans and been 'allotted' to Dutch farmers. The Prime Minister, defending his government's position, referred to war damage in the Netherlands totalling 24,000 million florins.[28] On 18 August, the Dutch ambassador wrote to Beyen, enclosing an article in the *Frankfurter Algemeine Zeitung* which discussed tensions between the Germans and Dutch, referring specifically to 'behaviour on the question of returning confiscated German property.'[29] In September the Dutch were annoyed at a 'fraternising party' arranged to celebrate the freeing from gaol of former SS General Kurt Meyer.[30] The problems were naturally two-way, with the Dutch continuing to press the German government for reparations on behalf of individuals. Referring to Article 2A, Part 1, of the Reparations Agreement of Paris of 24 January 1946, they had made representations to the German Foreign Office on 28 February 1953 calling, among other things, for recompense for those who had been forced to work without payment in concentration camps. According to a Dutch Aide Memoire written at the end of June, the German reply – not given until 22 April 1954 – made clear that the government was not prepared to satisfy the Dutch requests.[31]

Another major problem was the question of the Eems-Dollard estuary. Simply put, the Dutch wanted control of the Eastern (German) side, so that they could then polderise the estuary. The Germans consistently refused. The problem – a rather sensitive one – is still 'discussed' by the two governments to this day. It has been dealt with in some detail by Friso Wielanga.[32]

Sensitivities existed in Dutch - German relations at official as well as 'street level' (the Dutch held street demonstrations against Germany every so often).[33] For example, the Dutch ambassador in Bonn wrote to Beyen and Luns in June: 'From the German side are to be noted since then[34] a revival of consciousness and a tendency to link together all outstanding Dutch - German problems.'[35] The above-mentioned Aide Memoire also brought out the disinclination of the Dutch Government to deal with the Minister President of Nordrhein-Westfalen, Dr Arnold (See Chapter 1). It stated: 'Should the Federal Republic (not Arnold) wish to speak about the border corrections, then it would best do it by informing the Embassy in the Hague, to see whether we are prepared to hold discussions.'[36]

Another particularly sensitive problem, touched on in the previous chapter, was that of seven war criminals, who had escaped from Breda gaol into Germany, in January 1953. Four were recaptured in Germany, but a Düsseldorf court refused to extradite one back to the Netherlands, because he had German nationality.[37] The Yearbook of the Dutch Foreign Ministry for 1953/4 saw fit to state:

> The course of matters regarding the extradition of the war criminals who escaped from Breda was however unsatisfactory. Only one of them has been brought back to the Netherlands and then only with the mediation of the British Occupation Authorities. From the German side, one does still not gain the co-operation which one thinks one should expect here.[38]

'The general dislike of Germany and Germans,' wrote the British ambassador:

THE LAST LAUGH 217

Persists and comes into the open from time to time, for example when German tourists behave tactlessly[39] but it is normally latent and relations between the two governments have been correct. The Netherlands Government are only too aware of the necessity of getting on with their big neighbour.[40]

Despite those words, the Dutch did not, as we have seen, suddenly drop all their claims, and the bilateral problems we have seen persisted for a while, with the Eems-Dollard question still on the agenda today. Nevertheless, trade increased:

In 1954, as well, the Netherlands remained the Federal Republic's most important trading partner with total trade turnover of Fl 3,200 million [...] 9.3 per cent of West German exports went to the Netherlands (16.7 per cent of Dutch imports), while 7.9 per cent of German imports came from the Netherlands (15.8 per cent of Dutch exports).[41]

The British ambassador, perhaps rather snidely, summed up the Dutch *raison d'être* on trade: 'In all these areas the desire for trade inclines the Netherlands Government to abstain from any action which would offend the other Governments concerned and to seek their friendship even if they do not altogether approve of them.'[42] In the case of trade with Germany, this was not true, as we have seen. More snidely, the ambassador wrote:

In practical matters such as their dealings with other countries, the Netherlands Government, like those of most small countries, are largely inspired by self interest, rather than by any ties of sentiment. It is no use expecting them automatically to support us on a particular issue in which their own interests are not endangered purely on grounds of friendship if there is any risk that their material interests or their friendship with other countries will be hurt thereby.[43]

Being attached to morals as well as money, most Dutch would have strongly disagreed with the ambassador's words. It would be more accurate to say that the Dutch were more skilful at combining their interests with their morals. In the case of their relationship with the Federal Republic, they certainly did this. They had, of course, fully accepted German rearmament within the framework of a European Defence Community. However, as worries about French commitment to the EDC began to take hold, they were seen not to have forgotten NATO as a solution for German rearmament.

Between EDC and NATO

By the end of March, it only remained for France and Italy to ratify the EDC. The Netherlands had, as we have seen, given considerable impetus, if not credibility, to the EDC by ratifying first. Fursdon wrote: '[...] Western morale received an encouraging boost when the Dutch First Chamber approved the EDC by the large majority of 36 to 4. This was a rewarding victory for Mr Beyen [...]'[44] It is worth here recalling how enthusiastic the Americans had been when the Second Chamber had ratified: 'This successful action again confirms Netherlands leadership in the movement for European co-operation.'[45] Izvestia, however, had written: 'The Dutch Chamber of Deputies, which was to have been disbanded for the Summer vacation, having been subjected to an American order urgently concerned itself with a discussion of the "European Army" Treaty.'[46] Van der Harst writes: 'At the instance of Beyen the Second Chamber [...] said it was prepared to postpone its summer recess in order to discuss the EDC Bill.'[47] The Soviet Union now concentrated on France in its anti-EDC efforts.[48] Following the failure of the Berlin Conference, the Soviet Union actually tried to join NATO, as we have seen, on condition that both halves of Germany would be neutral. The country's proposals highlighted the EDC as being dangerous for peace in Europe. Whatever its motives, the attempt to join NATO clearly had abandonment of the EDC as one of its chief aims. It is telling that, at the end of 1954, Beyen was to say that the Soviet Block had contributed nothing towards making peaceful coexistence a reality.[49] The Americans, for their part, increased their pressure on the Europeans. Having already applied economic pressure the previous summer,[50] a statement by Dulles to the North Atlantic Council in December 1953 was still having an effect. He had said that were the EDC not to become effective, it might 'never again be possible for integration to occur in freedom although it might be that West Europe would be unified as East Europe in defeat and servitude.' Although Eisenhower 'tactfully repudiated' the speech,[51] such words cannot have fallen on deaf ears.

All eyes were now turning to the French, who had two main problems: the linkage of the EDC with the Geneva Conference and Britain's commitment. They had – in their eyes at least – a valid excuse to delay ratification until an agreement on Indo-China, since so much of their military power was tied up there. On the question of British support, the French do not appear to have been sufficiently satisfied with British commitment.

Although, on 13 April, an agreement was signed in Paris on co-operation between the EDC and Britain, this was not to be enough to save the EDC. Fursdon gives a good account of the polemics, saying that Ernst van der Beugel considered that French desires were largely satisfied by a British – and American – statement accompanying the agreement.[52] Nutting, on the other hand, wrote: 'Alas, the gesture, when it came, fell too far short of what France expected to be adequate.'[53] The Gaullists were particularly critical of the British stance, since it entailed Britain's participation in the EDC Council of Ministers without its being subject to its discipline or veto.[54] To some, it looked as if Britain was prepared to accept power without responsibility.

The Dutch, for their part, were in Fursdon's words, beginning to grow increasingly upset at what they saw as a totally inward-looking selfish French attitude.[55] The NATO solution was increasingly aired, following the rejection of the EDC Treaty by the Assemblée Nationale's Foreign Affairs Commission and a subsequent political crisis leading to the fall of the Government on 12 June. On 14 June Beyen told the Cabinet that were the EDC not to come to fruition, then the alternative would be for the Federal Republic of Germany to join NATO.[56] The authoritative *NRC* wrote on 28 June (following Mendes-France's becoming the new French Prime Minister on 18 June): 'Germany's entry to the North Atlantic Treaty Organisation is the only acceptable alternative to the European Defence Community.'[57]

Confidence in France's ability to see the EDC through had never been high. As we have seen, even Beyen had doubts about Mendes-France's support for the treaty. In July the previous year, Stikker had told the American ambassador to the Hague that it was clear to him that France would never ratify.[58] Following the resolution of the war in Indo-China, a conference was held in Brussels where Mendes-France tried to obtain agreement on a French protocol to the treaty. Broadly speaking, the protocol undermined the supranational nature of the EDC, and, in Nutting's words, would have meant that integration would apply to German forces and other forces in Germany, but not to French forces outside Germany. This, said Nutting, meant a European Army for the Germans, but a French one for the French.[59] To try and introduce such fundamental changes at such a late stage was unrealistic: the Protocol was rejected. The Dutch Ambassador to Bonn wrote to the Foreign Ministry about France's isolated position.[60] Mendes-France then met Churchill, who, according to Fursdon, tried to get him to change his mind. Although Mendes-France did not, he appears to have been left with the impression that an alternative solution would be found.⁶¹

Whether Mendes-France had organised a *quid pro quo* with Moscow, whereby he would scupper the EDC in return for an end to hostilities in Indo-China, or whether he now wished for a NATO solution to the German problem, is still a matter of considerable debate. At all events, in the crucial vote in the Assemblée Nationale on 31 August, on a motion to 'move to other business' Mendes-France abstained, having announced that he would do so.

While sufficient documentary evidence has not been made available to prove that Mendes-France did a deal with the Russians, some primary sources suggest that there was a good deal of suspicion of French motives, and relations with, the Soviet Union, some of which had been manifest well before the rejection of the EDC by the Assemblée Nationale. For example, a senior Foreign Office official had written at the end of October 1950:

> The refusal on the part of the French Government to agree to implement and practise a policy towards Germany to which they have consistently paid lip service is a very serious matter. Not only does it make a coherent Western policy towards Germany almost impossible, but it creates in this country and in America the constant impression that the French are insincere.

He then listed the causes of French behaviour as: the Socialists having their eyes on the workers' vote at the approaching elections; traditional opposition to Prussian militarism; Jewish influence; and the feeling towards Russia which still existed in certain intellectual and socialist circles in France, supported by a general distrust of American policy and methods; and by the tradition of French diplomatic alliances with Russia.⁶² This distrust of French motives was strongly reflected in the American Secretary of State, Dulles', views, following the French rejection of the EDC. He wrote to Eisenhower: 'I find evidence of a rising tide of concern about Mendes-France's Russian contacts [...] He has killed EDC for now and he may be out to kill German admission to NATO.'⁶³

The Dutch, however, had genuinely hoped for an EDC solution to German rearmament. Following the abortive Brussels Conference, *De Volkskrant* had written: 'Brussels has left Mendes-France in the cold [...] Benelux knows that the EDC in NATO is eminently preferable to a German national army in NATO.'⁶⁴ At all events, the European Army was dead. As Nutting wrote: 'The EDC was a dead letter, the brain-child of a few far-sighted Frenchmen had been strangled in the cradle by their narrow nationalist compatriots, and the five nations of Europe floundered dangerously in the quicksands of confusion and despair.'[65] The floundering was not to last long. For, in the words of Ernst van der Beugel, Britain was to have 'its last big moment diplomatically.'[66]

Back to NATO

It is paradoxical, but perhaps also a sign of the volatility and emotion in international relations at the time, that the Netherlands' original preferred Atlantic solution was to be adopted by the end of the year, notwithstanding further French political gymnastics. On 1 September, Luns wrote to Lamping in Bonn saying: '[...] the most natural solution seems to be German membership of NATO, against which, however, the French will presumably raise problems.'[67] The French were, understandably, isolated. *NRC* wrote: 'France has placed herself in isolation [...]'[68] The Americans were particularly disappointed and let it be known that they might reappraise their policy. The Secretary of State told the press: 'The French negative action, without provision of any alternative, obviously imposes on the United States the obligation to reappraise its foreign policies, particularly those in relation to Europe.'[69] The British now began to increase their level of diplomatic activity. The Dutch Chargé d'Affaires in London was summoned to the Foreign Office and told that the nub of the problem was to associate Germany with the West, and to avoid the country sliding into the Soviet camp via neutralism.[70] The Dutch continued to push for German membership of NATO. *Trouw* wrote: '[...] Western co-operation, that is above all NATO [...] Germany must be involved in Western co-operation on an equal footing.'[71]

The pressure to simply do something positive increased, helped by the angry American reaction. On 7 September, the Dutch Chargé d'Affaires in Washington, de Beus, reported a current of isolationism among the American public, and a feeling that the United States was not prepared to 'go it alone'.[72] Three days later he reported that the Americans wished Germany to be a full member of NATO, without discrimination.[73]

As events were to show, the problem of German rearmament was going to be solved by using the Brussels Treaty as a vehicle for Germany to join NATO. The expanded Brussels Treaty Organisation was to be renamed Western European Union. There is still controversy as to whose idea it actually was, with Fursdon naming Eden, Stikker, MacMillan and the French. Whether one or all of these had touted the idea, it was Eden who went on a whirlwind tour of Brussels, Bonn, Rome, and Paris, to persuade the respective Foreign Ministers to accept it. His ideas were accepted, although in differing degrees, the French being the most difficult.

During Eden's tour, which began on 11 September, the Americans were also busy, not always consulting Britain in advance. When in Rome on 15 September, Eden received a telegram from Dulles informing him that he would be meeting Adenauer in Bonn that day and would like to see Eden in London. This sudden intervention also put French noses out of joint. The Dutch ambassador in Washington, van Roijen, provides the explanation for Dulles' initiative, in a telegram to Beyen on 15 September, about Dulles' impending trip to Bonn:

> Dulles is supposedly ready to promise Adenauer that Germany can count on American support [...] As was to be feared, public opinion is beginning to turn more and more sharply against France [...] one is increasingly inclined to apply 'shock treatment' to France, under the slogan that one has been patient for long enough with that country.[74]

According to the Dutch ambassador in Rome, Boon, the United States were even considering a solution without France. In a telegram to the Foreign Ministry on Eden's meetings, Boon stated: 'The fact is that the United States are at present fed up with Europe and that an alternative solution for Europe must be found, if necessary without France.'[75] Although on 17 September, according to the Dutch ambassador in Paris, van Boetzelaer, Mendes-France had now agreed to the 'Brussels Pact' solution (provided that there were sufficient 'guarantees and controls')[76], everything still depended on Paris, in the words of Lamping in Bonn, on the same day.[77] The following day, Beyen wrote to his embassy in Bonn that the 'hard American policy' could result in even the French proponents of European co-operation being 'forced into a nationalistic corner.'[78] These words clearly suggest that Beyen thought the Americans were going over the top. It is difficult to imagine Stikker using the same words.

The Americans were still disappointed at the failure of the EDC, and were hoping for a supranational solution. This is backed up by a telegram from Luns to the Dutch Foreign Ministry on 23 September:

> Yesterday, I had a discussion with Dulles, during which he said that he regarded supranational authorities for Western military co-operation with Germany as essential. Should this prove, for the moment, impossible, then America would perhaps be inclined towards accept-

ing a temporary (he spoke of a few years) solution, which included no supranational powers. However, those would have to be introduced later. Irritation with France's attitude is still manifest.[79]

This contrasts somewhat with Fursdon's account of Dulles' agreeing – albeit reluctantly – to Eden's Brussels Treaty solution, six days previously. 'Dulles admitted he saw no better solution than the one proposed by Eden [...]'[80] Fursdon was not necessarily inaccurate, however, rather, the considerable difference of emphasis in Dulles' reported views shows a certain lack of consistency in American policy towards European security, enhanced, no doubt, by the annoyance, bordering on anger, at France's behaviour. Whatever annoyance Dulles' 'initiative' might have caused the French and, to a lesser extent, the British, America's role was crucial, at least to the Dutch. The feeling was summed up by an *NRC* editorial, which stated: 'Without America, it won't work.'[81] The newspaper also praised Eden's efforts to find a way out of the European 'blind alley'.[82]

The London Conference, comprising the six ex-EDC countries, Britain, the United States and Canada, began on 28 September, When it began, the 'Brussels Treaty' solution was by no means a foregone conclusion. Eden, however, had one last trump up his sleeve, which he used with good timing. On 29 September, he announced that Britain would maintain in Europe, including Germany, the effective strength of its forces then assigned to SACEUR, and undertook not to withdraw those forces against the wishes of the Brussels Treaty Powers. Although he added two premises, relating to 'an acute overseas contingency' and 'strain on Britain's external finances', the announcement, fully supported by the Americans, led to agreement. The Occupation regime was to end, Germany (and Italy) were to join the Brussels Treaty Organisation, (to be renamed Western European Union) and the Federal Republic was to be invited to become a member of NATO.

The Dutch press welcomed the British announcement. *Trouw* spoke of the British decision as being of enormous significance,[83] while *NRC* headed an editorial 'English Statesmanship'.[84] On 23 October, the agreements were signed in Paris. Nevertheless, the French managed to keep everybody concerned on tenterhooks: although the Assemblée Nationale ratified first, it was a drawn out affair: on 23 December, the Assemblée actually rejected Article 1 of the Ratification Bill (on the establishment of Western European Union and Germany's entry into NATO). It was not until 30 December that the Article was approved, and then only by 287 to 260 votes.[85]

Eden had undoubtedly helped. Stikker wrote: 'Without Eden, the Paris Agreement of 1954, which finally opened the way for these great improvements in Western defence which were essential to our security, would never have been reached.'[86] In this connexion, it is also interesting to note that Stikker was told about Britain's 'trump card' in advance of it being played. He said that he was the only foreigner in the know beforehand, and that he had been pledged to secrecy.[87]

Conclusions

The Dutch had the last laugh. Having been against the EDC at the beginning, they found that, despite their later enthusiastic support for it, they had turned full circle, ending up supporting a solution which they had advocated. Of particular significance is the Dutch Foreign Minister van Boetzelaer's comment to the Cabinet on 8 March 1948, when discussing the Brussels Treaty, that in the long run Germany would have to be involved.[88] The obvious Dutch disappointment at the failure of the EDC was quickly overtaken by the new solution. Nevertheless, the British ambassador was perhaps exaggerating, when he wrote: 'The Dutch accepted the EDC reluctantly as the best arrangement for securing their own defence which appeared practicable at the time.'[89] With Beyen (and, of course, Luns) as Foreign Minister, the Dutch believed in the EDC as a practical answer to their own security needs and to German rearmament, despite some scepticism on Stikker's, and even Beyen's, part. Although the EDC failed, this did not stop the Dutch from actively and enthusiastically pursuing European integration the following year. The Dutch had chosen a European solution for their future, unlike Britain, which was to continue to obfuscate. At the same time, they had skilfully accepted an Atlantic solution.

12

CONCLUSIONS

> Neutrality is not a form of altruism. It is a policy by which small countries hope best to preserve their wealth, peace and identity [...] In the absence of a convenient Cold War, that means a constant polishing of a neutral image so that whenever and however the next war breaks out, aloofness is credible. A true neutral must prove constantly that it is dependent upon no one else and subject to no one else's rules or laws.[1]

Ten years after the liberation of the Netherlands from the armies of the Third German Empire, neutrality was part of Dutch history. A policy of neutrality had certainly worked up to 1940. Dutch diplomacy, according to Tamse, saw a passive policy of neutrality as offering the most security, an opinion shared by the political elite.[2] By the time of the Cold War, however, there was no neutral image for the Dutch to polish.

This book began by attempting to define the nature of Dutch neutrality, suggesting that the Netherlands have never been neutral *a priori*, but rather that a policy of abstentionism and detachment led to what could be described as a kind of *de facto* neutrality. When the Brussels Treaty was signed, Stikker himself said that the Netherlands had followed a policy of neutrality, but that it had not involved a permanent policy of neutrality guaranteed by the large powers, but rather a policy of independence.

It is worthy of note that Brierly, when discussing neutrality in his book *The Law of Nations*, does not even mention the Netherlands since, unlike Belgium, Luxembourg, Switzerland and Austria, the country was never 'neutralised'.[3] Perhaps the Netherlands is too much of a puzzle to permit a clear definition of the nature of its past neutrality. Van Kleffens provided us with a clue when he said that following the German invasion, a policy of neutrality was no longer the right way of handling a policy of independence.⁴ In other words, the Netherlands would continue to pursue its policy of independence by co-operation, rather than by abstention, as in the past. To try and define too closely so-called Dutch neutrality is dangerous, and can lead to one ending up on a semantic tightrope. All that being said, the years following the signing of the Brussels Pact were to be characterised by a continuation of an active policy of independence within new constraints, constraints that took the Dutch several years to come to terms with. The commitment that NATO membership required was to prove painful for the Dutch, who had broken with their policy of abstention to gain a voice in the German question. They were slowly but painfully made to pay for their commitment, in hard cash. Within the new constraints, the Dutch were able to pursue their foreign policy objectives with considerable stubbornness, relying where they could on finding counterweights to the future power of France and Germany. During Stikker's tenure of office, mistrust of the French was an important factor in their foreign policy and was juxtaposed with an at times almost obsessive desire to stress the Atlantic counterweight.

Emerging from the war, where their policy of neutrality had been so rudely shaken, if not destroyed, the Dutch were as a whole in a trauma. As late as 1971, Schoffer wrote: 'And the surprise attack caused a trauma, that we have perhaps still not fully got over.'⁵ Certainly, the Dutch Cabinet do not seem to have realised fully the political and economic implications of signing the Brussels Treaty. Given the extreme importance to them of Germany, they needed the platform provided by membership to pursue their interests. As we have seen, they were not interested in the military side of the treaty, and used it, rather, to gain leverage in the talks on Germany. It was frustrating for them to watch on the sidelines, as Britain, responsible for the German zone of most economic importance to them, parleyed with the other large powers. Even after the Netherlands gained entry to the talks on Germany, it was still to feel sidelined from time to time.

Viewed with hindsight, some of the Dutch claims on Germany, particularly the territorial ones, seem exaggerated and unrealistic. At the time, however, the Dutch used the territorial claims as a bargaining counter for other claims. Nevertheless, they went a little too far, as comments by the British suggest. It was certainly not a high point in Dutch diplomatic history, as Schaper, himself a diplomat, diplomatically writes.⁶ The more magnanimous Belgian attitude contrasts with that of the Dutch. On the other hand, the damage done by Germany to the Dutch people and to their economy, was considerable. Through Dutch membership of the

Brussels Treaty Organisation, the claims were given an aura of respectability, although not credibility. Van Kleffens' influence on the question, both inside and outside the Cabinet, was remarkable, and contrasted with the more realistic and conciliatory attitude of van Boetzelaer.

The Dutch were, curiously on the face of things, among the first to push for Germany's economic rehabilitation. The reasons, however, were based essentially on commercial considerations. A trading country *par excellence*, the Dutch knew instinctively that a strong German economy was vital to them, as it had always been. They jumped on any French attempt to discriminate against Germany economically, since they knew that their interests would be affected. Early assessments about the future role of Germany as a weak, mainly agricultural state, were revised early on. The Dutch pushed hard for German membership of the Council of Europe, the OEEC and the EPU on grounds of self-interest, but also because they preferred to negotiate on their claims within an international framework, rather than on a bilateral basis. Until recently, the Dutch were still inclined to avoid gratuitous contract with Germans.

Militarily, the Dutch appear to have had far less fear of a resurgent independent military Germany than the French. Their distrust of the French enhanced their emphasis on links with Britain and the United States. They were against what they saw as French designs to be the leaders of post-war continental Europe. Looking, as they did, to the Atlantic from a peripheral continental position, they were able to separate their emotions from their pockets more clearly than the French. It was, indeed, the very absence of German power that worried them, and pushed them more strongly towards the British and Americans. Given the problematic relationship between Britain and France in the immediate post-war years (and later) and the influence of Stikker, Dutch distrust of the French knew few limitations during Stikker's tenure of office.

Whatever Dutch concern about the Belgians being overly influenced by French ideas, the secret military agreement of 1948 was of considerable psychological importance. Of more obvious importance was Benelux, whose influence was considerable, not only because its three members often acted together internationally, particularly in gaining admission to the talks on Germany, but because it was praised by the Americans as an example of European co-operation. Luns, despite his Atlantic leanings, stressed the importance of Benelux in European integration.[7] Although there were from time to time clear differences of approach between the Netherlands and Belgium, for example on the border rectification question, and occasional commercial problems over transit trade and competition between the ports of Antwerp and Rotterdam, their co-operation in the European Defence Community negotiations was remarkable. Stikker's Atlanticism and self-avowed Protestantism, however, detracted to some extent from a common approach to European integration, particularly since Spaak was both Roman Catholic and a federalist. Although Stikker's ideas on European union were very different to those of Spaak, he still wrote highly of Spaak's experience and wisdom.[8] Nevertheless, within Benelux, it was mainly Spaak who carried the European integration flag. When Beyen assumed office, the Benelux combination was to prove itself effectively.

Despite Stikker's anti-supranationalism, the Schuman Plan was an opportunity that could not be missed. Initial Dutch misgivings were quickly converted to enthusiasm. By joining in the negotiations, moreover, albeit by keeping some of their options open, they were able to exert some influence over the more supranational elements of the plan. Dutch membership also shows clearly that despite Britain's refusal to participate, they were not prepared to miss out on what they considered to be a positive development. American support for the plan also weighed heavily in favour of Dutch participation.

The defence question with its emotional, ideological, strategic and financial ramifications was the most sensitive issue for the Dutch, following Indonesia's independence. The Prime Minister does not appear to have fully realised the economic implications that membership of an alliance would entail. The Dutch had a naval, rather than a military tradition, and the process of change was indeed difficult. Not only Drees, but his Finance Minister, Liftinck, put more stress on social affairs than defence spending. As Stikker himself said, he was isolated in the Cabinet on the question. In addition, despite traditional Dutch dislike of communism, the Drees Cabinet was loath to be overtly unfriendly towards the Soviet Union. The traditional policy of abstentionism and independence continued to make itself felt, albeit to a lesser degree, during the Cold War. It is significant that a Cold War warrior like Kruls was simply sacked. Although the reasons for his dismissal are complex, it is noteworthy that his support for Eisenhower's line could not save him.

The diplomatic pressure that the Americans exerted had, at least initially, a negative effect on Dutch Cabinet thinking on the defence question. The Dutch were undoubtedly annoyed at the way that the Americans acted, particularly at being advised on how to spend their money. The fall of the government in January 1951 can be attributed to the defence question as well as to New Guinea. The debate within the political and military establishment in the Netherlands was particularly lively, culminating in

Kruls' sacking. It is curious that Stikker does not choose to mention Kruls at all in his memoirs.

To look at the question of defence spending in isolation creates an unbalanced picture of Dutch commitment to the North Atlantic Alliance. The influence of the Indonesian problem needs to be taken fully into account. Apart from the severe financial constraints it placed on the Dutch budget, the question itself was highly charged, and exercised an influence on the Dutch attitude towards their commitment to the Alliance. Many of the Dutch felt betrayed by their Atlantic allies, and to immediately make the financial sacrifices that were required to build up their military strength was to expect too much. Moreover, the Dutch felt that the Germans should pay their share of the defence burden. Once Stikker had voiced his government's concern about the defence line, and it had been drawn farther East, it was obvious that German rearmament would mean that the Dutch could spend less. At any event, the Dutch certainly deserve more understanding, if not sympathy, on the question of defence spending in the early fifties.

The European Defence Community posed questions of a different kind. The Dutch clearly felt worried that they would be subsumed into a French-led Europe, and lose their links with Britain and America, hence their efforts to get the British to participate. As long as the British refused to participate fully in the EDC, the Dutch were unwilling to participate in the Paris talks. The NATO system was infinitely preferable to them, since it involved Britain and America as counterweights to French and, of course, German power. Once the Americans had come out fully in support of the EDC solution, the Dutch, although they then attended the Paris talks as full members, seem to have been obsessed with NATO, fearing that the EDC would weaken it and lead to less American commitment to Europe. The evidence suggests that their fear was exaggerated, and one is inclined to wonder whether it was Stikker's Atlanticism and suspicion of the French as much as his apparent fear of Eisenhower 'bringing his boys home' that conditioned the official Dutch attitude. Despite differences between the Minister of Defence and Foreign Affairs, Dutch influence, within Benelux, led to a Commission of nine members, but was unable to bring the duration of the EDC treaty into line with that of NATO.

One point worth noting is that although Drees and Stikker clearly differed on the level of financial commitment towards NATO, at least until the government's resignation, they tended to agree in their negative attitude towards the EDC. For despite their different political ideologies, they were both psychologically more Atlantic and Scandinavian-oriented than

Continental European. This 'unholy' alliance certainly proved a stubborn force when it emerged at the international negotiating table.

The arrival of Beyen at the Foreign Ministry marked an important change in Dutch Foreign policy, some would say drastic. Beyen really was an 'out and out' European, whatever semantic gymnastics some employed about him being lukewarm towards the idea of political integration, as opposed to economic integration. His approach contrasted even with Monnet's,[9] in that it called for broad (horizontal) economic integration, whereas Monnet advocated sectoral (vertical) integration. Beyen's own words answer the semantic conundrum:

> Think it is of essential importance if we want to preserve our 'way of life' that Europe should retain not only its political independence but above all its identity. I do not think we can hope to achieve this unless we can make and keep Europe economically strong and politically united. I am convinced neither one nor the other objective can be attained on the basis of what is called 'intergovernmental co-operation' between European states. A close and more durable bond I consider essential, a bond of 'supranational' character.[10]

More succinctly, Samkalden wrote: 'It is no secret that the Netherlands European policy was strongly activated when Mr J W Beyen became Foreign Minister in the summer of 1952. He had clear opinions and did not hide them.'[11] On the EDC question, Beyen was positive, although even he had some doubts that the French would ever ratify. Nevertheless, his attitude was important and very much in line with what the Americans wanted. At a time when the French were having major difficulties, the Netherlands' ratification of the EDC treaty was remarkable and put the country firmly in the forefront of European unity. Stikker remained sceptical, but his influence had of course diminished considerably, with his ambassadorship in London. As we have seen, Beyen did not find him helpful on the question of European integration.

A distinct cooling of relations between Britain and the Netherlands accompanied Beyen's arrival at the Foreign Ministry, essentially because Beyen's views on European unity contrasted markedly with those of Britain. Although there were some trade problems, as we have seen, on pigs and milk, and some on the exchange of information on military evacuation plans, the British disinclination to talk to Beyen for several months after his taking up his position, particularly on matters of substance, is notable. The British did not wish to be pinned down by Beyen on the degree of their commitment to European integration. Luns confirms that Beyen was not 'over popular with the United Kingdom'.[12] Even Stikker was surprised at the British attitude towards European integration for, although he was certainly no supranationalist, he favoured certain kinds of economic integration, saying he was a 'functionalist'. Generally, the Dutch were disappointed at Britain's attitude.

In Churchill's own words, Britain was 'with, but not of'. Such semantic wriggling was interpreted by many as a lack of genuine commitment to European integration. 'Mr Schuman and his colleagues' wrote Dilks, 'were in effect starting with a broad conception, not lacking in nobility and grandeur, requiring a commitment of principle from the outset. This was inimical to British practice and mental habits'.[13]

The Schuman Plan succeeded despite Britain's refusal to participate. The EDC failed for a number of reasons, only one of which may have been Britain's refusal to participate. The others were the reduced tension that followed the death of Stalin, the ending of major French commitment in Indo-China, the incipient plans for the development of a French nuclear capability and French worries about whether France would be able to hold its own in intra-European trade, if the European Political Community and Dutch liberalisation plans came to fruition.

Following the French rejection, Britain was, to a certain extent, able to make amends for its negative attitude towards European unity. Although the Americans were quick to move following the EDC's death, Eden certainly took a bold initiative. Nevertheless, the American attitude was crucial. Dulles' threat about an 'agonising reappraisal' of American policy, were the EDC to fail, had an effect. Van der Beugel wrote:

> But the 'agonising reappraisal' threat had one beneficial result. It is my firm opinion that the United Kingdom would never have taken the initiative for the Western Union Treaty through which German rearmament was ultimately solved. Neither would, without this threat, the French Assembly have accepted the provisions of this Treaty in December 1954.[14]

The French doubts about the EDC diverted attention away from less highly charged, but nevertheless important, economic matters, of which the Beyen Plan is an example. Following resolution of the German rearmament problem, Beyen renewed the pressure: 'The Dutch Minister of Foreign Affairs, Dr Beyen, together with his Belgian colleague, Paul-Henri Spaak, played a prominent role with regard to the preparations of the [Messina] conference.'[15] Brugmans wrote: 'The Dutchman Beyen introduced his plan for economic integration for the second time and, in the midst of general scepticism, the Spaak Committee was founded, which prepared the Treaty of Rome'.[16]

It is ironic that the Roman Catholic Luns was an Atlanticist (as he himself confirms),[17] and that it was Beyen who turned out to be the exponent of European integration. Despite this, it would be inaccurate to refer to Luns as being lukewarm towards European integration. He was certainly not opposed to the EDC, saying that the United States would have supported it and not pulled their troops out of Europe.[18] Although Luns and Beyen did not work well together, the lines of demarcation between their functions were sufficiently defined as to avoid undue problems. Luns, however, clearly put more stress on Atlantic co-operation, particularly on NATO, than did Beyen, who saw European integration as the Netherlands' main foreign policy priority. His attitude gives the lie to the alleged importance the Dutch attach to balancing the forces, in their foreign policy:

> It is occasionally suggested that we have to face a choice between Atlantic and European co-operation. I do not agree. Our choice has already been made. We are firmly committed to Atlantic unity which remains the very cornerstone of our foreign policy. We are also committed to the European ideals that have found expression in the Treaties of Rome and Paris on which the Common Market was built.[19]

Although in defence, the Atlantic trend in the Netherlands was by and large satisfied in the end, the European one, spearheaded by Beyen, also carried the day. In a stable and pluralistic society like that of the Netherlands, differing views are the order of the day, which explains the difficulty (and danger) of trying to define too closely whether the Dutch are Atlantic or European. For they are both, and the post-war history of the Netherlands shows that both trends can exist side by side (as the pillars of Dutch society do), stimulating each other to healthy but rarely vicious, debate. Between 1948 and 1954, January and February 1951 were the months where the solidarity of Dutch politics was sorely tested. It survived. It is tempting to conclude that the Netherlands proved itself to be a country of contrasts in harmony, and that the Dutch were able to surmount the internal problems raised by Indonesia, German rearmament and European integration by recourse to a special kind of Dutch phlegmatism, enshrined in an old proverb: 'Ben je boos, pfluck je een roos. Steek'em op je hoed, en morgen ben je weer goed.' (If you're angry, pick a rose. Stick it in your hat, and next day you're happy again.) The final conclusion, however, is short, and typically Dutch: the last words in Stikker's memoirs: 'Freedom, peace and justice.'[20] But then, do we not all say that?

NOTES

Introduction
1. De Baena, Duke, *The Dutch Puzzle*, The Hague, 1966, p.16.
2. The exact words are '...have always paid homage to the King of Spain'. Although this is obviously no longer the case, it is interesting that the Dutch include the phrase in their national anthem, whatever interpretation we might put on the words.
3. Heldring, J. L., 'Between Dreams and Reality', in J H Leurdijk (ed.), *The Foreign Policy of the Netherlands*, Alphen aan den Rijn, 1978.
4. Clayton to Acheson, 27 May 1947, FRUS 1947, vol. III, Memorandum 840.50 Recovery/5-2747, p.230.
5. Milward, Alan S., *The Reconstruction of Western Europe*, 1945–51, London, 1984.
6. Voorhoeve, Joris C., *Peace, Profits and Principles - A Study of Dutch Foreign Policy* The Hague, 1979.
7. Wielenga, Dr.Friso, *West Duitsland: Partner uit Noodzak - Nederland en de Bondsrepubliek 1949–1955*, Utrecht, 1984.
8. Van der Harst, Dr. Jan, *European Union and Atlantic Partnership: Political, Military and Economic Aspects of Dutch Defence, 1948-1954, and the Impact of the European Defence Community*, doctoral thesis, Florence, 1987.

Chapter 1
1. Telders, B. M., quoted in Van den Bosch, Amry, *Dutch Foreign Policy since 1815 – A Study in Small Power Politics*, The Hague, 1959, p.282.
2. Nichols to Bevin, 4 February 1949, PRO - F0371/79546, file Z1093/1011/29, *Annual Review for 1948*.
3. Boogman, J. C., quoted in J L Heldring, op. cit., p 308. The word 'contraction' is an exaggeration.
4. Hugo Grotius, Mare Liberum, Amsterdam, 1609.
5. Heldring, J. L. .op. cit., p.308.

6   Ibid., p.310.
7   Kossmann, E. H., *In Praise of the Dutch Republic: some Seventeenth Century Attitudes*, An inaugural lecture delivered at University College, London, 13 May 1963, p.17.
8   Voorhoeve, Joris J. C., *Peace, Profits and Principles - A Study of Dutch Foreign Policy*, The Hague, 1979, p.31.
9   Van den Bosch, Amry, op. cit., p.272.
10 De Baena, Duke, *The Dutch Puzzle*, The Hague, 1966, p.97.
11 Amry van den Bosch, op. cit., p.280.
12 Ibid., p.281.
13 Ibid., p.282.
14 Bosmans: J., in D.r J. Charité (ed.), *Biografisch Woordenboek van Nederland*, vol. III, The Hague, 1989, p.183.
15 Amy van den Bosch op. cit., p.288.
16 Ibid., p.289.
17 Ibid., p.290.
18 MBZ file 999.1 - Verdrag van Brussel; ratificatie WEU door Nederland 1948 Omslag 19, 18/3/48 - 2/4/48, doos 5, Explanatory Memorandum no. 3, Session 1947-8.
19 Vlekke, B. H. M., 'A Dutch View of the World Situation', *Journal of the Royal Institute of International Affairs*, vol. XXVII, 1952.
20 Van den Bosch, Amry, op. cit., p.272.
21 Boogman, J. C., 'Britain and the Netherlands', in Bromley J. S. and Kossmann E H (eds.), Oxford - Netherlands Historical Conference, London, 1960, p.201.
22 Ibid., Significantly, the 'Dutch' army general was a German, Friedrich von Gagern, says Boogman.
23 Amry van den Bosch, op. cit., p.272.
24 Ibid., p.273.
25 Ibid., p.275.
26 Fisher, H.A.L., *A History of Europe*, vols. I and II, London, 1960 (first published 1935),vol. II, p.1158.
27 These words are not sung today.
28 Op. cit., Van den Bosch, Amry, p.274.
29 Wielenga, Friso, *West-Duitsland: partner mit noodzaak - Nederland en de Bondsrepubliek 1949-1955*, Utrecht, 1989, p.26.
30 Ibid., p.26.
31 Stikker, Dirk U., *Men of Responsibility*, London, 1966, p.203.
32 Nichols to Bevin, 9 February 1950, PRO - F0371/89321, file WN 1011/1, *Annual Review for 1949*.

33 Schokking, J. J., 'The Netherlands in a Changing World', *Journal of the Royal Institute of International Affairs*, vol. XXIII, 1947.
34 Note by Royal Netherlands Ministry of Foreign Affairs, 9 July 1945, MBZ - File 912.13, Duitsland West, Grenscorrecties - nederlandse standpunt, 1945-6, deel 1, MAP 1912.
35 Schokking, J. J., op. cit., p.352.
36 D. P. E (full name unknown), 'A Note on the Dutch Economic Situation', *The World Today*, (Royal Institute of International Affairs), vol. IV, no. 1, January - December 1948, p.121.
37 Van den Bosch, Amry, op. cit., p.292.
38 Bland to Bevin, 20 February 1946, PRO-FO/371/60225, file Z1572, *Annual Report 1945*.
39 Bland to Churchill, 4 June 1945, PRO - F0371/49445, file Z6788, *letter*.
40 Bland to Bevin, 7 June 1946, PRO - FO371/60236, file Z5358, *letter* enclosing translation of article by Dr. S. Kleerekoper.
41 Op. cit., *Annual Report 1945*.
42 Grey to Hoyer Miller, 14 August 1945, PRO - F0371/49435, file Z9668, *letter* enclosing copy of letter of 11 August 1945 from himself to Bland.
43 Russel to Head of British Military Mission, 6 August 1945, PRO - F0371/49435, file Z10314, *memorandum* BMN/5003/G.
44 Bland to Bevin, 11 September 1945, PRO-F0371/49435, file Z 10700, *letter*.
45 Bland to Harvey, 3 November 1945, PRO-F0371/49435, file Z 12516, *letter*.
46 Ibid.,
47 Op. cit., *Annual Report* 1945.
48 Bland to Harvey, 11 September 1945, PRO - F0371/49435, file Z10700, *letter* enclosing *memorandum* by British Military Mission.
49 M D Bogaarts, *De Periode van net Kabinet Beel, 3 Juli 1946 - 7 Augustus 1948* Parlamentare Geschiedenis van Nederland, Deel II, Thesis defended (successfully) at the Catholic University of Nijmegen on 30 November 1989, The Hague, 1989, vol. C, p.1633.
50 Ibid., vol. A, p.160.
51 Ibid., vol. C, pp.1729-1733.
52 Nichols to Foreign Office, PRO - F0371/73256, file Z 4128, *Weekly Summary*, 5-12 May 1948.
53 Op. cit., *Annual Report* 1945.
54 Hirschfeld, Gerhard, *Nazi Rule and Dutch Collaboration - The Netherlands under German Occupation, 1940 - 1945*, Oxford, 1988, p.325. Wim Klinkenberg, in his book *Prins Bernhard - een politieke biografie, 1911 - 1986* (Haarlem 1979, revised 1986) describes Hirschfeld as 'pro-German' (p.194), 'the pre-war friend of the Nazis' (p.219) and an 'Abwehr' (German intelligence) collaborator' (p.539).

Hans Hirschfeld's own wartime memoirs do not make us any the wiser as to Klinkenberg's sensitive allegations. Hirschfeld criticises both the British and the Germans, the former for only agreeing to deliver arms to the Netherlands in return for rubber and tin from the Netherlands' East Indies, and the latter for torpedoing Dutch merchant shipping. He negotiated with the Germans over Dutch neutrality at the beginning of the war.

55 Ibid., p.315.
56 Ibid., p.316.
57 Ibid., p.318.
58 Op. cit., Dirk U. Stikker, p.204.
59 Ibid., p.204.
60 Schaper,H.A., 'The Security Policy of the Netherlands', in Leurdijk, J. H., (ed.) *The Foreign Policy of the Netherlands*, Alphen aan den Rijn, 1978, p.97.
61 *The Economist*, 16 February 1946, 'Rebuilding Holland'.
62 Op. cit., Note by Royal Netherlands Ministry of Foreign Affairs, 9 July 1945.
63 Denis Brogan, 'The Inter-Allied Reparations Agency', *The World Today*, (Royal Institute of International Affairs), vol V, no. 1, January to December 1949, p.268.
64 Minutes of the Dutch Council of Ministers, 27 September 1945, Dutch State Archives, MR 388.
65 Op. cit., Stikker, Dirk U., p.214.
66 Ibid., p.213.
67 Annex A to Dutch Government *Memorandum*, 5 November 1946, MBZ, file 912.13, Duitsland West, Grenscorrecties-nederlandse standpunt 1945–6, deel II, 1946, MAP 1913.
68 Op. cit., Schaper, H.A., 'The Security Policy of the Netherlands'.
69 Michiels van Verduynen to Chairman of Council of Foreign Ministers, Lancaster House, 18 September 1945, MBZ File 912.13, Duitsland West, Grenscorrecties-nederlandse standpunt 1945-6, deel I, 1945-46 MAP 1912, *letter 7032*.
70 Ibid., *enclosure to Note* of 9 July 1945.
71 Dutch Council of Ministers, 17 July 1945, Dutch State Archives, MR 388, *minutes*.
72 Schaper, H.A., 'Dutch Annexation Plans after 1945', *Internationale Spectator*, May 1985, volume 39-5, p.261.
73 Michiels van Verduynen to Chairman of Council of Foreign Ministers, 18 September 1945, op. cit.,
74 Op. cit., H.A. Schaper, 'Dutch Annexation Plans after 1945', p.262.
75 Ibid.,
76 Op. cit., Dutch Council of Ministers, 17 July 1945, *minutes*.
77 Op. cit., Schaper, H.A., 'Dutch Annexation Plans after 1945', p.265.

78 Ibid.,
79 Op. cit., Van Boetzelaer van Oosterhout to Ambassadors, 20 October 1946, MBZ file 912.13, 1945-46.
80 Van Boetzelaer van Oosterhout to General Committee of the Second Chamber, 23 October 1946, archives of the Second Chamber of the States General, file M 20.45, *memorandum*.
81 Kersten, A. E, .in Dr. J. Charité (ed.) Biografisch Woordenbock van Nederland, part III, The Hague, 1939, p.59.
82 Stikker, Dirk U., *Memoires*, Rotterdam and The Hague, 1966, p.182.
83 Meeting of General Committee of the States General, 24 and 25 October 1946, archives of the Second Chamber of the States General, file 19-20.45, *minutes*.
84 Op. cit., Dutch Government *Memorandum* of 5 November 1946.
85 Ibid.,
86 *Yearbook of the Dutch Foreign Ministry for 1949–50*, p.9. Quote translated in Amry van den Bosch, op. cit., p.302.
87 Op. cit., Schaper, H. A., 'Dutch Annexation Plans after 1945', p.269.
88 Ibid., p.270.
89 Acheson to State Department, 20 November 1946, FRUS 1946, vol. II, *telegram*, Secdel 1177, 740.00119 - Council/ 11-2046, p.1213.
90 Van Voorst tot Voorst to Stikker, 30 September 1948, MBZ file 912.13, Duitse reacties op Nederlandse eisen tot grenscorrecties part 1, 1946-48, MAP 1960, *letter* 14900/2210.
91 MBZ File 912.13, Duitse reacties op Nederlandse eisen tot grenscorrecties, part I, 1949, MAP1961.
92 Schaper, H. A., 'Dutch Annexation Plans after 1945', op. cit., p.269.
93 Ibid., p.269.
94 Van Campen, S.I. P., *The Quest for Security - some Aspects of Netherlands Foreign Policy, 1945 - 50*, The Hague, 1958, appendix 15.
95 Op. cit., Schaper, H. A., 'Dutch Annexation Plans after 1945', p.269.
96 Op. cit., Van Campen, S. I. P.
97 Op. cit., Stikker, Dirk U., p.207.
98 MBZ File 912.13, Duitse reacties op Nederlandse eisen tot grenscorrecties, deel II, 1949, MAP 1961.
99 MBZ file 912.13, Duitse reacties op Nederlandse eisen tot grenscorrecties, deel III, 1949, MAP 1962.
100 Op. cit., Dirk U. Stikker, p.212.
101 Op. cit., Nichols to Bevin, 9 February 1950, *Annual Review* for 1949.
102 *De Telegraaf*, 9 May 1948,' Hollander gegen Annexionen', in MBZ File 912.13, Duitse reacties op Nederlandse eisen tot grenscorrecties, deel I, 1946–8, MAP 1960.

103 Op. cit., H. A. Schaper, 'Dutch Annexation Plans after 1945', p.263.
104 *Die Welt*, 14 December 1949, in MBZ File 912.13, Duitse reacties op Nederlandse eisen tot grenscorrecties, deel III, 1949, MAP 1962.
105 Op. cit., H. A. Schaper, 'Dutch Annexation Plans after 1945', p.272.
106 Nichols to Attlee, 4 August 1949, PRO-F0371/76637, file 78, *despatch no. 268*, translation of memorandum.
107 Riddleberger, 1 November 1946, FRUS 1946, vol. II, *memorandum* 740.00119, Council 11-146, p.963.
108 Murphy to Secretary of State, 30 June 1946, FRUS 1946, vol. V, *telegram*, 840.811/6-3046, p.266.
109 Vos to General meeting of Royal Institute of Engineers, 19 January 1946, PRO-FO371/60205, file Z 955/29/29, *speech*.
110 Bland to Foreign Office, 10 April 1946, PRO-FO 371/60201, file Z 3478/144/29, *telegram* no. 81.
111 Reay to Hampshire, Control Office for Germany and Austria, 2 September 1946, PRO-FO371/60205, File Z 7340/291/29, *letter*.
112 Op. cit., Stikker, p.214.
113 Clay to Secretary of State, 2 May 1947, FRUS 1947, vol. II, telegram, 862.51/5247, p.916.
114 Op. cit., *Despatch no. 268*.
115 Op. cit. Nichols to Bevin, 9 February 1950, *Annual Review for 1949*.
116 Nichols to Bevin, 11 February 1950, PRO-F0371/89335, file WN1053/1, *despatch*.
117 Chancery, British Embassy, to Foreign Office, 9 February 1949, PRO-FO 371/79599, file 1193, *covering letter* to Service Attaché's note.
118 Op. cit., Amry van den Bosch., p.297.
119 *The Economist*, 18 June 1949, pp.1124 - 1125.
120 Gumming, 8 October 1945, FRUS 1945, vol. VI, *memorandum*, 856D00/10-845, p.1158.
121 Op. cit., Nichols to Bevin, 4 February 1949, *Annual Review for 1948*.
122 Thorne, Christopher, *Allies of a Kind: the United States, Great Britain and the War against Japan* 1941–45, Oxford and New York, 1979, p.61.
123 Kahin, George McT., 'The US and the Anti-colonial Revolution in South East Asia, 1945–50', Yonosuke Nagai and Akira Irye (eds.), *The Origins of the Cold War in Asia* New York, 1977, pp.345-6.
124 Von Albertini, Rudolf, 'The Decolonisation of the Dutch East Indies', in Tony Smith (ed.), *The End of the European Empire. Decolonisation after World War II*, Lexington 1975, p.173.
125 Ibid., p.173.
126 Op. cit., Thorne, Christopher, p.460.

127 Ibid., p.102.
128 Op. cit., Kahin, George McT., p.341.
129 Op. cit., Thorne, Christopher, p.682.
130 Van Bijland to van Kleffens, 21 December 1945, Collection 304, M Boon, doos 9, *letter*.
131 Cumming, FRUS 1945, vol. VI, op. cit., p.1160.
132 Winant to Secretary of State, 7 November 1945, FRUS 1945, vol. VI, *telegram* 856E.00/11-745, p.1170.
133 *Record of Conversation*, 10 January 1946, FRUS 1946, vol. VIII, 856E.00/1-1046, p.793.
134 Foote to Secretary of State, 10 July 1946, FRUS 1946, vol. VIII, telegram 856E.00/7-1046, pp.832-833.
135 Op. cit., Christopher Thorne, p.102.
136 Bevin to Conference of Foreign Ministers, 16 December 1945, FRUS 1945, vol. II, p.614.
137 Ibid., Bevin to Stalin, 24 December 1945, *Record of Conversation*, p.776.
138 Bullen, Roger and Pelly, M. E., (eds.) *Documents on British Policy Overseas* series I, volume II, Conference and Conversations 1945: London, Washington and Moscow, no. 289, U 1374/20/70, London 1985, p.724.
139 Ibid., no. 300, U 1374/20/70 p.752.
140 Douglas to Secretary of State, 4 June 1947, FRUS 1947, vol.VI, *telegram* 856E.01/6-447, p.939.
141 Secretary of State to Foote, 17 June 1947, FRUS 1947, vol. VI, *telegram* 856E.01/6-1747, p.950.
142 Foote to Secretary of State, 2 July 1947, FRUS 1947, vol. VI, *telegram* 855D.00/7-247, p.969.
143 Foote to Secretary of State, 1 August 1947, FRUS 1947, vol. VI, *telegram*, 856.E.00/8-147, p.1005.
144 Acting Secretary of State to Foote, 31 December 1947, FRUS 1947, vol. VI, *telegram* 501.BC Indonesia /12-3147, p.1006.
145 *UN Yearbook for 1947-48*, p.365.
146 Op. cit., Heldring, J. L., in Leurdijk, J. H.,(ed.), p.309.
147 Op. cit., Voorhoeve, Joris J. C., op. cit., p.42.
148 Ibid., p.51.
149 Heldring, J. L., in Leurdijk, J. H.(ed.), op. cit., pp.310 - 311.
150 Ibid., p.311.
151 Stikker, Dirk U., op. cit., p.177.
152 Dutch Council of Ministers, 27 September 1945, Dutch State Archives, MR388, *minutes*.

153 Baron van Boetzelaer van Oosterhout, 1 August 1946, FRUS 1946, vol III, p.69.
154 Op. cit., Nichols to Bevin, *Annual Review for 1948*.

Chapter 2

1 Heldring, J. L., *De Nederlandse Buitenlandse Politiek na 1945*, Baarn, 1978, p.31.
2 Van den Bosch, Arnry, *Dutch Foreign Policy since 1815 - A study in Small Power Politics*, The Hague, p.303.
3 Milward, Alan S., *The Reconstruction of Western Europe 1945–51*, Cambridge, 1987, p.65.
4 Clayton to Acheson, 27 May 1947, FRUS 1947, vol III, Memorandum 840.50 Recovery/5-2747, p.230.
5 Marshall to US Embassy, The Hague, 29 January 1948, FRUS 1948, vol. II, *telegram*, 740.00119 Council / 1 -1948 p.48.
6 Murphy to Lovett, 13 December 1948, FRUS 1948, vol.II, *letter* 711.00/12-1348, pp.1338 - 1339.
7 Milward, op. cit., p.56.
8 *Report* of Special Ad Hoc Committee of the State-War-Navy Co-ordinating Committee, 21 April 1947, FRUS 1947, Vol III, SWNCC Files, Series 360, p.204.
9 Kennan to Acheson, 23 May 1947, FRUS 1947, vol III, *letter* 840.50 Recovery/5-2347, p.229.
10 Clayton to Acheson, 27 May 1947, op. cit.,
11 Ibid.,
12 Alan Milward argues in *The Reconstruction of Western Europe, 1945–51*, that the economic crisis in Western Europe in 1947 was not as serious as some would have it. He presents a compelling argument, based on an exhaustive study of wide-ranging data. Nevertheless, the Netherlands certainly had more of a problem than most, because it depended heavily on trade, particularly with Germany.
13 Nichols to Bevin, 4 February 1949, PRO FO 371, file Z 1093/1011/29, *Annual Review for 1948*.
14 DPE (full name unknown), A Note on the Dutch Economic Situation, *The World Today*, (Royal Institute of International Affairs), vol. IV, no. 1, p.120. According to Stikker's memoirs, between 1930 and 1934, between 15 and 20% of Dutch exports went to Germany.
15 Milward, op. cit., p.490.
16 Nichols to Bevin, *Annual Review for 1948*, op. cit.,
17 Bland to Bevin, 8 December 1947, PRO F0 371, file Z 10694/101/4, *letter*.

18   MBZ File, DGEM Archive, 050, Plan Beyen (Customs Union), Jacket 66, Jan 1953 - June 1954, *Record of meeting*, 28 April 1948.
19   A. Rumbold, 2 November 1945, PRO FO 371/47988, file N 14948/10674/38, *comment on file jacket*.
20   Bland to Bevin, 8 December 12-17, PRO F0371, File Z 10304/101/G, letter.
21   Milward, op. cit., p.116.
22   Nichols to Bevin, *Annual Review for 1940*, op. cit.,
23   Van Campen, S. I. P., *The Quest for Security - some Aspects of Netherlands* Foreign Policy, 1945–50, The Hague, 1958, p.156.
24   Baruch to Secretary of State, 7 February 1948, FRUS 1948, vol. III, telegram 840.50 Recovery/ 2-748, p.379.
25   Milward, op. cit., p.97.
26   Baruch to Secretary of State, 7 February 1948, op. cit.,
27   State Department Policy Statement, 1950, FRUS 1950, vol. III, 611.58/8-2250, p.1528.
28   J. M. and W. Drees (Willem Drees' sons) The Hague, 9 January 1990, *interview*.
29   State Department Policy Statement, op. cit.,
30   Minutes of the Dutch Council of Ministers, 9 June 1947, Dutch State Archives.
31   MBZ file 912.13, Duitsland West, part III, 1947-8, MAP 1914.
32   Milward, op. cit., pp.178-9.
33   Baruch to Secretary of State, 7 February 1948, op. cit.,
34   Wesselring, H. L., 'Vier Eeuwen Frans-Nederlandse betrekkingen: het soortelijk gericht van de geschiedenis', *Internationale Spectator*, vol. 42, no. 12, December 1988, p.795.
35   Milward, op .cit., pp.235-6.
36   Inverchapel (British Ambassador to US) to Marshall, 13 January, FRUS 1948, vol. III, 840.00/1-1348.
37   Milward, op. cit., p.246.
38   Nutting, Rt. Hon Anthony, *Europe will not wait - a warning and a way out*, London 1960, p.4.
39   Bullen, Roger, 'Britain and Europe 1950-1957', Serra, Enrico, (ed.), *The Relaunching of Europe and the Treaties of Rome*, European Community Liaison Committee of Historians, vol. 3, Brussels, Milan and Baden-Baden, 1987, p.318.
40   Kent, John, 'Bevin's Imperialism and the Idea of Euro-Africa, 1945–49', in Dockrill, Michael and Young, John W. (eds.), *British Foreign Policy 1946–56*, London 1989, p.47.
41   Bullen, op. cit., p.318.
42   Ibid., p.317.

43 Milward op. cit., p.39.
44 Van Campen, S.I.P. op. cit., p.156.
45 *Yearbook of the Netherlands Foreign Ministry for 1949.*
46 Hirschfeld to Boon, 1 February 1949, MBZ file 912.230, Duitsland-Nederlandse Verlangens t-a-v Geallieerde Politiek in Duitsland, Nota Hirschfeld, deel I, January 1949 - May 1949, *memorandum.*
47 Ibid.,
48 Ibid., De Booy to Stikker, 9 May 1948, *letter*
49 D. P. E, *The World Today*, op. cit., p.121.
50 Ibid., p.123.
51 Ibid., p.119.
52 *Note on the State of Affairs with Regard to the German Question* - presented to the Second Chamber by the Foreign Minister on 19 July 1949, p.12.
53 Nichols to Bevin, 9 February 1950, PRO-FO 371, file WN 10.11/1, *Annual Review for 1949.*
54 Clay to Marshall, 2 May 1947, FRUS 1947, vol. II, *telegram*, 862.51/5-247, p.915.
55 Agreed *Minutes* of the Discussions to the Mixed Commission and the Three Western Zones of Germany, 24-26 March 1949, FO 371-76927, file CE 1678.
56 Makins, 10 June 1949, PRO FO 371/76927, *record of conversation.*
57 The word 'very' tends to be frowned upon by Foreign and Commonwealth Office drafting experts, when used in official written communications.
58 Sir Ian Kirkpatrick to Jonkheer E. Michiels van Verduynen, 22 July 1949, FO 371/76927, *letter.*
59 Ibid., Bevin to certain diplomatic posts, 20 August 1949, *savingram* 2746.
60 *Note* on the State of Affairs etc., op. cit., p.8.
61 Nichols to Attlee, 4 August 1949, PRO-FO 371/76637, file 78, *despatch* no. 268.
62 *Note* on the State of Affairs, etc., p.24.
63 Ibid., p.24
64 Ibid., p.16.
65 van Campen, S.I.P., op. cit., appendix 16.
66 Ibid.,
67 Ibid.,
68 Ibid., p.142.
69 Milward, op. cit., p.431.
70 Nichols to Bevin, 11 February 1950, FO 371-89335, File WN 1053/1, *despatch.*
71 Ibid.,
72 Dutch Council of Ministers, 8 January 1947, MR389, *minutes.*
73 *Note* of the State of Affairs etc., op. cit., p.24.
74 Yearbook of the Netherlands Foreign Ministry for 1949, p.9.

75 Nichols to Bevin, *Annual Review for 1949*, op. cit.,
76 Stikker, Dirk U., *Men of Responsibility*, London, 1966, p.177.
77 Heldring, J. L., 'Between Dreams and Reality', in Leurdijk, J. L.(ed.), *The Foreign Policy of the Netherlands*, The Hague, 1978, p.312. Van der Beugel, Ernst, The Hague, 8 January 1930, *interview*.
78 British Embassy, The Hague, to Dutch Ministry of Foreign Affairs, 17 September 1949, PRO-FO 371/79578, File Z 6261/1118/29, *aide mémoire*.
79 Nichols to Attlee, 23 September 1949, PRO-FO 371/79578, file Z 6261/1118/29, *letter* E331.
80 Stikker, op. cit., p.188.
81 Ibid., p.183.

Chapter 3

1 Heldring, J. L., 'Between Dreams and Reality', in Leurdijk J. H. (ed.), *The Foreign Policy of the Netherlands*, Alphen aan den Rijn, 1978, p.310.
2 Van den Bosch, Amry, *Dutch Foreign Policy since 1815 - A Study in Small Power Politics*, The Hague, 1959, p.291.
3 Ibid., p.293.
4 Ibid., p.294.
5 Van Boetzelaer van Oosterhout, 1 August 1946, Paris Peace Conference, *verbatim record*, FRUS 1946, vol III, CFM files, p.69.
6 Acting Secretary of State to Consul General, Batavia, 31 December 1947, FRUS 1947, vol. VI, *telegram* 501.BC Indonesia/12-3147, p.1006.
7 Consul-General, Batavia, to Secretary of State, 8 April 1948, FRUS 1948, vol. VI, *telegram* 501.BC Indonesia/4-848, p.139.
8 Consul General, Batavia, to Secretary of State, 21 July 1948, FRUS 1948, vol. VI, *telegram* 501.BC Indonesia/7-2148, pp.285-7.
9 State Department, FRUS 1948, vol .VI, *memorandum* 761.00/10-1348, p.644.
10 Consul General, Batavia to Secretary of State, 1 November 1948, FRUS 1948, vol. VI, *telegram* 501.BC Indonesia/11-148, p.393.
11 Baruch to Secretary of State 10 November 1948, FRUS 1948, vol. V, *telegram* 856e.00/11-1048, p.477.
12 Consul General, Batavia to Secretary of State, 11 November 1948, FRUS 1948, vol. VI, *telegram* 501.BC lndonesia.11-1148, p.481.
13 Acting Secretary of State to Consul General, Batavia, 5 November 1948, FRUS 1948 Vol. VI, *telegram* 501.BC lndonesia/11-548, p.463.
14 Ibid.,
15 Consul General Batavia, to Secretary of State, 2 December 1948, FRUS 1948, vol. VI, *telegram* 501.BC Indonesia/12-248, p.508.

16 FRUS 1948, vol. VI, 6 December 1948, *aide mémoire*, 501.BC Indonesia/12/748, p.537.
17 FRUS 1948, vol. VI, 6 December 1948, Ibid., p.542.
18 Acting American Representative at United Nations (Jessup) to Secretary of State, 14 December 1948, FRUS 1948, vol. VI, *telegram* 501.BC Indonesia.12-1448, p.561.
19 Acting Secretary of State to Acting American Representative at United Nations (Jessup) 23 December 1948, FRUS 1948, vol. VI, *telegram* 501.5B Indonesia/12-2348, p.597.
20 Dulles, John Foster, *War or Peace*, New York, 1957, p.54.
21 Gage to Attlee, 27 January 1948, PRO-FO 371/3256, file 275, *despatch* no. 65.
22 Gage to Kirkpatrick, 8 January 1948, PRO FO 371/73256, file Z 275/275/29, *letter* enclosing translation of article of 31 December 1947 in *De Volkskrant*.
23 Voorhoeve, Joris J. C., *Peace, Profits and Principles - A Study of Dutch Foreign Policy*, The Hague, 1979, p.155.
24 Spits, F. C., *Naar een Europees Leger*, The Hague, 1954, p.11.
25 Luns, J. M. A. H, .'De Westeuropese Unie als Katalysator', in *Internationale Spectator*, vol. XVIII, no.19, 8 May 1964, p.228.
26 Joseph Luns, Brussels, 11 January 1990, *telephone interview*.
27 Drees, J. M. and W., The Hague, 9 January 1990, *interview*.
28 Wiebes and Zeeman,' Nederland, Belgie en de Sovjet-dreiging' (1942-48), *Internationale Spectator*, September 1987, p.474.
29 Ibid., p.474.
30 Ibid., p.468.
31 Dutch Council of Ministers, 26 January 1948, Dutch State Archives MR 390, *minutes*. The Prime Minister was probably referring to Dutch businessmen, although there may well have been some prisoners of war.
32 Wiebes, Cees and Zeeman, Bert, op. cit., p.274.
33 Dutch Council of Ministers, 8 March 1948 Dutch State Archives, MR 390, *minutes*.
34 Ibid., 14 October 1946. Schaper also wrote that an anti-German stance would endanger the whole process of European co-operation (Schaper, H. A., ' Het Nederlandse Veiligheidsbeleid in de Jaren 1945-1948', *Internationale Spectator*, vol. 32, No.5, May 1978.
35 Kennan to Secretary of State 19 February 1948, FRUS 1948, vol. III, *letter*, p.7.
36 Dutch Council of Ministers, 8 March 1948, Dutch State Archives, MR 390, *minutes*.
37 Ibid., 18 November 1947, MR 389.

38 17 December 1947, FRUS 1947, Vol III, *Memorandum of conversation* by FO (Frank Roberts), Anglo-US-French Conversations, CFM files: lot M-88, box 104, p.818.
39 Dutch Council of Ministers, 5 January 1948, Dutch State Archives, MR 390, *minutes*.
40 Ibid., 12 January 1948.
41 Ibid., 19 January 1948.
42 Voorhoeve, Joris J. C., op. cit., p.156.
43 Ibid., p.156; see also Jan van der Harst, *European Union and Atlantic Partnership: Political, Military and Economic Aspects of Dutch Defence 1948 - 1954, and the Impact of the European Defence Community*, Chapter 1.1, July 1987, Florence.
44 Dutch Council of Ministers, 26 January 1948, Dutch State Archives, MR 390, *minutes*.
45 Ibid., 2 February 1948.
46 Ibid., 9 February 1948.
47 Ibid.,
48 Stikker, Dirk U., *Men of Responsibility*, London 1966, p.214.
49 Ibid., p.214.
50 Wiebes and Zeeman, op. cit., p.477.
51 Jan Hoffenaar, The Hague, 9 January 1990, *interview*.
52 Dutch Council of Ministers, 8 March 1948, Dutch State Archives, MR 390, *minutes*.
53 Young, John W., *Britain, France and the Unity of Europe, 1945 - 51*, Leicester, 1984, p.55.
54 Nichols to Bevin, 4 February 1949, PRO-FO 371/79546, file Z1093/1011/29, *Annual Review for 1948*.
55 *Note* by Military Attaché, British Embassy, 9 February 1949, PRO FO 371/79599, file 1193.
56 Nichols to Bevin, op. cit., *Annual Review for 1948*.
57 Stikker, 17 March 1948, MBZ file 999.1 - Verdrag van Brussel; ratificatie WEU door Nederland 1948, Omslag 19, 18/3/48 - 2/4/48, Doos 5, *speech*.
58 Van der Harst, Jan, op. cit., p.5.

Chapter 4

1 Smith, Raymond, 'A climate of opinion: British officials and the development of British Soviet policy 1945–7', in *International Affairs*, Vol. 64, No 4, Autumn 1988, p.636.
2 Ibid., p.642.
3 Henderson, Sir Nicholas, *The Birth of NATO*, London, 1982, pp.3-4.
4 Ibid., p.4.

5   Bogaarts, M. D., 'De Periode van het Kabinet Beel, juli 1946 - augustus 1948'; Parlemeniaire Geschiedenis van Nederland, Deel II, thesis defended on 30 November 1989 at Catholic University of Nijmegen; the Hague, 1989, p.382.
6   Note by Harvey of discussion with Baron Gruben, (political director, Belgian Ministry of Foreign Affairs, 10 February 1947, PRO FO 371/67651, file no. 249/4, *comment on file jacket* by Sargent.
7   Henderson, op. cit., p.10.
8   Ibid., p.8-10.
9   Ibid., p.12.
10 Ibid., p.11.
11 Panyushkin to US Secretary of State, Washington, 6 March 1948, FRUS 1948, vol. II, *memorandum* 740.00 119 Council/3-648, p.352.
12 Van Kleffens, 6 July 1948, Second Meeting of Washington Exploratory Talks, FRUS 1948, vol III, *minutes*, 840.20/7-648, p.154.
13 Panyushkin to US Secretary of State, op. cit., p.354.
14 Stikker, *Men of Responsibility*, London 1966, p.214.
15 Caffery to Secretary of State, 19 February 1948, FRUS 1948, vol. III, *telegram* 840.00/2-1948, p.28.
16 Military Attaché's *annual note*, British Embassy, 9 February 1949, PRO FO 371/79599, file no. 1193.
17 Henderson, op. cit., p.vii.
18 Ibid., p.14.
19 Ibid., p.15; Donald McLean was spying for the Soviet Union.
20 Ibid., pp.17-18.
21 6th meeting on security between the US, UK and Canada, 1 April 1948, FRUS 1948, vol. III, *minutes*, 840.00/3-1748, p.72.
22 Ibid.,
23 Henderson, op. cit., pp.22-23.
24 Wiebes, Cees and Zeeman, Bert, 'Nederland, Belgie en de Sovjetdreiging (1942-48)', in *Internationale Spectator*, September 1987, p.473.
25 Rendel to Crosthwaite, 17 May 1948, PRO FO 371/72921, file Z 4151/118/4/9, *letter.*
26 Crosthwaite to Rendell, 25 May 1948, ibid.,
27 Henderson, op. cit., p.22.
28 Ibid., p.35.
29 Ibid., p.39.
30 5th meeting of Ambassadors' Committee, 9 July 1948, FRUS 1948, vol. III, *minutes*, 840.20/7-748, p.169.
31 Ibid.,
32 5th meeting of Ambassadors' Committee, *minutes*, op. cit., p.178.

NOTES

33 10th meeting of Ambassadors' Committee, 22 December 1948, FRUS 1948, vol. III, *minutes*, 840.20/12-2248, p.325.
34 2nd meeting of Ambassadors' Committee, 6 July 1948, FRUS 1948, vol. III, *minutes*, 840.20/7-648, p.154.
35 3rd meeting of Ambassadors' Committee, 15 July 1948, FRUS, vol. III, *minutes*, 840.20/7-1548, p.185.
36 9th meeting of Ambassadors' Committee, 13 December 1948, FRUS 1948, vol. III, *minutes*, 840.20/12-1348, p.320.
37 Henderson, op. cit., p.42.
38 Ibid., p.42.
39 Ibid., p.57.
40 Ibid., p.57.
41 Ibid., p.56.
42 Ibid., p.57.
43 Djojohadikoesomo to American Acting Secretary of State, 27 December 1948, FRUS 1948, vol. VI, *memorandum* 501.BC Indonesia/12-2748, p.611.
44 *United Nations Yearbook*, 1948-9, pp.219-220.
45 Livengood to Secretary of State, 3 January 1949, FRUS 1949, vol. VII, pt. 1, *telegram* 501.BC Ind/1-349, p.119.
46 Butterworth to Bohlen, 7 January 1949, FRUS 1949, vol. VII, pt 1, *memorandum* 856d.00/1-749, p.136.
47 Livengood to Secretary of State, 3 January 1949, FRUS 1949 vol. VII, pt. 1, ibid., p.119.
48 Livengood to Acting Secretary of State, 12 January, FRUS vol. VII, pt. 1, *telegram* 501.BC lnd/1-1249, p.136.
49 Franks to US Secretary of State, 1 February 1949, FRUS vol. VII pt. 1, *memorandum*, 501.BC lnd/2-149, p.198.
50 Douglas to Secretary of State, 16 March 1949, FRUS 1949, vol. IV, *telegram*, 840.00/3-1649, p.230.
51 Kirkpatrick to Bevin, 24 December 1948, PRO FO 371/69788, file F 18566/5/22, *memorandum*.
52 Beel was the High Representative of the Dutch Crown in Indonesia. He was considered to be a bit of a hardliner by the Americans.
53 Van Kleffens to American Secretary of State, 18 March,1948, FRUS 1949, vol. VII pt. 1, *memorandum* 501.BC lnd/3-1849, p.329.
54 *Minutes* of 1st meeting of European Correlation Committee London, 25 March 1949, FRUS 1949, vol. IV, 840.00/4-2249 p.244.
55 Douglas to Secretary of State, 27 March 1949, FRUS 1949, vol. IV, *telegram* 840.20/3-2749 p.253.

56 31 March 1949, FRUS 1949, vol. IV, *Memorandum of Conversation*, 840.50 Recovery/3-3149, p.259.
57 Kahin, George McT, 'The US and the Anti-colonial Revolution in South East Asia, 1945-50', Yonosuke Nagai and Akire Iriye (eds.) *The Origins of the Cold war in Asia*, NewYork, 1977, p.354.
58 Nichols to Bevin, 4 February 1949, PRO FO 371/17693, File □ 1093/1011/29, *Annual Review for 1948*.
59 Ibid.,
60 Wiebes, Cees and Zeeman, Bert, 'Stikker, Indonesia and the North Atlantic Treaty', in Blom et al (eds.) *Contributions and articles on the history of the Netherlands*, part 100, No. 2, Zeist, 1985, pp.225-251.
61 Dutch Council of Ministers, 21 March 1949, Dutch State Archives, MR392, *minutes*.
62 Ibid., 30 March 1949.
63 Van Campen, S. I. P., *The Quest for Security - Some Aspects of Netherlands Foreign Policy 1945-50*, The Hague, 1958, p.110.
64 Ibid., p.109.
65 Dulles to Sforza, 13 April 1949, FRUS 1949, vol. IV, *memorandum of conversation*, US/A/1.1/802, p.549.
66 Chapin to Secretary of State, 1 November 1949, FRUS 1949, vol. VII, pt. 1, *telegram* 856d1.00/11-149, p.559.
67 Henderson, op. cit., p.59.
68 5th Meeting of Ambassadors' Committee, 9 July 1948, FRUS 1948, vol. III, *minutes*, 840.20/7-748, p.178.
69 4th meeting of Ambassadors' Committee July 1948, FRUS 1948, vol. III, *minutes*, p.167.
70 I have calculated this from the minutes of the meeting, as reproduced in FRUS 1948, vol. III. Laughter, sniggering, belching etc. are of course not usually recorded.
71 Nichols to Bevin, op. cit.,
72 Baruch to Secretary of State, 21 July 1948, FRUS 1948, vol.III, *telegram* 840.00/7-2148, p.194.
73 Dutch Council of Ministers, 30 March 1949, Dutch State Archives, MR392, *minutes*.
74 Heldring, J. L., 'Between Dreams and Reality', in Leurdijk, J. □., (ed), *The Foreign Policy of the Netherlands*, Alphen aan den Rijn, 1978, p.312.
75 Van Campen, op. cit., p.109.
76 Nichols to Bevin, 9 February 1950, PRO F0371/89321, file WN 1011/1, *Annual Review for 1949*.

77 Vlekke, B. M., 'A Dutch View of the World Situation', in *Journal of the Royal Institute of International Affairs*, vol. XVIII, Chatham House, London, 1952, pp.418.
78 Henderson, op. cit., p.84.
79 Nichols to Bevin, 11 February 1950, PRO F0371/89335, file WN 1053/1, *letter*.

Chapter 5

1 Nichols to Bevin, 9 February 1950, PRO FO 371/89321, file WN 1011/1, *Annual Review for 1949*.
2 The British (and probably the Americans) exerted considerable diplomatic pressure on the Dutch to accept cruise missiles on their territory in the late seventies and early eighties. Those weapons were never stationed on Dutch territory; by the time the Dutch were outwardly ready to accept them, the US and the USSR had come to an agreement on medium and long range nuclear missiles reduction.
3 Van Campen, S.I.P., *The Quest for Security - Some Aspects of Netherlands Foreign Policy, 1949-50*, The Hague, 1958, p.116.
4 Ibid.,
5 *Yearbook of the Royal Netherlands Ministry of Foreign Affairs*, 1949/50, p.1.
6 Steelman to Secretary of State, 17 June 1949, *letter* enclosing Inter-departmental Working Group Paper of 1 June 1949, FRUS 1949, vol. I, S/P-NSC files in Lot 62D1, NSC 33 Series, pp.339-40.
7 Nichols to Bevin, 18 November 1948, PRO FO 371/73257, file Z9414/275/29, *letter* no. 63 enclosing Weekly Summary for 11-17 November 1948.
8 Nichols to Bevin, 24 December 1948, PRO FO 371/73257, file Z10641/275/29, *letter*. no.716.
9 Nichols to Bevin, 21 July 1949, PRO FO 371/79600, File 1194, *letter* no. 248.
10 Kruls to Her Royal Highness Queen Wilhelmina, 2 April 1949, Drees Collection, no. 376, Dutch State Archives.
11 Drees to Schokking, 10 May 1949, ibid.,
12 Smith, Lyn, 'Covert British Propaganda: the Information Research Department 1947-77', *Millenium: Journal of International Studies*, Spring 1980, vol. 9, no. 1.
13 Smith, Raymond, 'A Climate of Opinion: British Officials and the Development of British Soviet Policy 1945-7', *International Affairs*, Autumn 1988, vol. 64, no. 4; although the Netherlands is not focused on, it is worth reading Pronay's and Wilson's (eds.), *The Political Re-education of Germany and her Allies after World War II* (London and Sydney 1985) and Hearnden, Arthur (ed.) *The British in Germany*, London 1978.

14 See Chapter I.
15 Overseas Planning Committee, meeting of 5 October 1945, PRO FO 371/49402, file 49, *paper* no. 62 of 24 September 1945.
16 Smith, op. cit.,
17 Makins to Howe (Minister of Supply), 16 February 1950, PRO FO 953/627, file P1013/1G, *letter.*
18 PRO FO 953/72, file PW4448, *Quarterly Report*, April - June 1947, comment on file jacket, undated.
19 PRO FO 953/610, file PW766, *Quarterly Report*, April to June 1949, comment on file jacket by J. A. Forward, undated.
20 Bland to Bevin, 8 December 1947, PRO FO 371/67851, file Z 10694/101/29G, *despatch*. One sheet on this file is closed until 2023.
21 Ibid.,
22 Beyen, K. H., The Hague, 6 January 1990, *telephone interview.*
23 IRD - Information Research Department, set up in the Foreign Office in 1947, essentially to combat Soviet propaganda. Said by some to have been wound up in 1977.
24 PRO FO 953/610, file PW 294, six monthly *Report*, July to September 1948, comment on file jacket by J. A. Forward, 11 March 1949.
25 Nicholls to Carter, 29 April 1950, PRO FO 953/940, file PG 12916/4, *letter.*
26 Makins to Howe (Ministry of Supply) 16 February 1950, PRO FO 953/627, file PI 013/1G, *letter.*
27 PRO FO 371/47988, file N14948/10674/38, *minute* on file jacket by A. Rumbold, 2 November 1945.
28 Bland to Bevin, 8 December 1947, op. cit.,
29 Nichols to Troutbeck, 23 January 1951, PRO FO 953/1143, file PG 1294/1, *letter.*
30 Ibid.,
31 Avi Schlaim 'Britain, the Berlin Blockade and the Cold War', *International Affairs*, Winter 1983/84, vol. 60. no.1.
32 PRO FO 371/73268, file Z1530/1055/29/G, extract from *Dutch Press Review*, 12 February 1948.
33 Nichols to FO, 8 July 1948, PRO FO 371/73256, file Z5567/275/29, *letter.*
34 Gage to Bevin, 11 February 1948, PRO FO 371/73268, file Z 1363/1055/29/G, *letter.*
35 *Annual Review for 1949*, op. cit.,
36 Dutch Council of Ministers, 29 November 1948, Dutch State Archives, MR391, *minutes.*
37 *The Economist*, 8 January 1949, p.49.
38 *The Economist*, 22 April 1950, p.861.

39 *Annual Review for 1949*, op. cit.,
40 Secretary of State to Acting Secretary of State 16 May 1950, FRUS 1950, vol. III, 396.1 LO/5-1650, *telegram*, p.105.
41 *Report of Working Group on Organisation*, North Atlantic Council, 1st Session, 17 September 1949, FRUS, vol. IV, 1949, 740.5/2-1951, p.337.
42 Fursdon, Major General Edward, *The European Defence Community*: a History, Macmillan, London, 1980, p.46.
43 Dutch Foreign Ministry *Aide Mémoire* of 29 April 1949, no. 74408 - 7060 GS, J. H. Van Roijen, Collection 282, 2.21.183, Doos 10, Dutch State Archives.
44 Nichols to Bevin, 13 February 1950, PRO FO 371/89382, file WN 1192/1, *despatch*.
45 *Military Attaché's Report for 1950*, PRO FO 371/96116, file WN 1193/1 and 2.
46 Secretary of State to certain diplomatic posts, 26 July 1950, FRUS 1950, vol. III, 700.00 (S)/7-2650, *telegram*, p.142. Lieftinck, the Socialist Finance Minister tended to share Drees' views on defence expenditure.
47 Secretary of State to certain diplomatic posts 31 July 1950, FRUS 1950, vol. III, 700.00 (S)/7-3150, *telegram*, p.164.
48 Nichols to Bevin, 16 February 1951, PRO FO 371/96098, file WN1011, Annual Review for 1950.
49 Ibid.,
50 Nichols to Younger, 17 July 1950, PRO FO 371/89330, file WN 1024/1, *letter*.
51 Secretary of State to certain diplomatic posts, 28 July 1950, FRUS 1950, vol. III, 700.00 (S)/7-2850, *telegram*, p.151.
52 Nichols to FO 29 June 1950, PRO FO 371/89329, file WN 1023/4, *savingram*.
53 *Yearbook of the United Nations*.
54 Bereitschaften: a form of para-military police.
55 *The Economist*, 27 May 1950, p.1159.
56 Secretary of State to Spofford, 21 August 1950, FRUS 1950, vol. III 740.5/8-2150, *telegram*, p.230.
57 State Department *paper* (Office of European Regional Affairs), 3 May 1950, FRUS 1950, vol I, 396.1 LO/5-350, p.86.
58 PRO FO 371/96116, file WN/1193/1 and 2, *Comment on file jacket* by M. D. Butler.
59 Department of State *policy statement* 25 August 1950, FRUS 1950, vol. III, 611.56/8-2250, p.528.
60 Ibid.,
61 *Annual Review for 1950*, op. cit.,
62 Department of State *policy statement*, op. cit.,
63 7th Meeting of Policy Panning Staff, 24 January 1950, FRUS 1950, vol. III, *minutes*, 840.00 R/1-2450, p.618.

64 Van Voorst tot Voorst to Dr. Boon, 9 February 1950, MBZ file 912.12 Frankrijk-Verhouding, Deel II, Map 9988, Doos 28, 1950–54, *letter.*
65 State Department *paper* (Office of European Regional Affairs), 3 May 1950, FRUS 1950, vol. I, 396.1 LO/5-350, p.86.
66 Lilienthal to McMahon, 18 February 1949, FRUS 1949, vol. I, *letter* enclosing report by Director of Production of US Atomic Energy Commission (undated), p.433, Department of State Atomic Energy files.
67 Acting Secretary of State to van Kleffens, 13 April 1948, FRUS 1948, vol. I, pt. I, Dept of State Atomic Energy files, *note*, p.705.
68 *Statement* by (Dutch) Commissioner for ERP (Hirschfeld) 29 April 1949, FRUS 1949, vol. V, 656.6031/5-1249, p.110.
69 Harrison to Hoffman, 15 October 1949, FRUS 1949, vol. V, ECA telegram Files, Lot W-130, *telegram*, p.151.
70 *Annual Review for 1949*, op. cit.,
71 *(Dutch) Commissioner for ERP (Hirschfeld)*, 28 April 1949, FRUS 1949, vol. V, statement, 656.6031/5-1249, p.110.
72 Secretary of State to US Embassy, the Hague, 28 October 1949, FRUS 1949, vol. V, 840.50, Recovery 10-2149, *telegram*, p.163.
73 CoCom - Coordinating Committee (for Multi-lateral Export Controls), set up in 1949 to control exports of militarily sensitive equipment to Eastern Block countries. Said by some to have been based at an American Embassy building in Paris. Wound up in 1994, to reflect the alleged end of the Cold War, and replaced by the Wassenaar Arrangement, which now includes, *inter alia*, the Russian Federation.
74 Chapin to Secretary of State, 9 May 1950, FRUS 1950, vol. IV, 450.603/5-950, *telegram*, p.115.
75 Alan S. Milward, *The Reconstruction of Western Europe 1945-51*, Methuen, London 1987, p.153.
76 Stikker, Dirk U., *Men of Responsibility*, John Murray, London, 1966, p.290.
77 Dutch Council of Ministers, 16 May 1949, Dutch State Archives, MR392, *minutes.*
78 Van Campen, op. cit., p.131.
79 Ibid., p.131-2.
80 Dutch Council of Ministers, 8 March 1943, Dutch State Archives, MR390, *minutes.*
81 *Het Vrije Volk*, 23 November 1949, editorial.
82 *De Volkskrant*, 3 December 1949, editorial.
83 van Voorst tot Voorst to Minister for Foreign Affairs, 12 November 1949, MBZ file 921.1-Duitsland West-Duitse Herbewapening 1950 – 53, *letter* 2539-G/3412.

84 *Annual Review for 1949*, op. cit.,
85 *NRC*, 17 March 1950, editorial.
86 DBPO series II, vol. III, no. 38, Brief for the UK delegation, no. 15 (C2837/2514/18), 26 April 1950, pp.138-141.
87 Netherlands Foreign Ministry, 13 May 1950, MBZ file 921.1-Duitsland West-Duitse Herbewapening 1950 – 53, *memorandum*.
88 De Booy to Netherlands Foreign Ministry, 8 May 1950, MBZ file 921.1 Duitsland West-Ambassade Bonn 1950, Herbewapening, *letter*, 4503/829.
89 Fursdon, op. cit., p.68.
90 DBPO, Series II, volume III, p.VIII.
91 Nichols to FO 29 June 1950, PRO FO 371/89329, file WN1023/4, *savingram*.
92 Fursdon, op. cit., p.68.
93 Ibid., p.77.
94 Van der Harst, Jan, *European Union and Atlantic Partnership: Political, Military and Economic Aspects of Dutch Defence, 1948–1954, and the Impact of the European Defence Community*, Florence 1987, p.25.
95 DBPO series II, vol. III, p.VIII.
96 Fursdon, op. cit., p.78.
97 Ibid.,
98 *De Volkskrant*, 2 September 1950, editorial.
99 *Trouw*, 28 September 1950, editorial
100 *NRC*, 27 September 1950, editorial.
101 *Het Vrije Volk*, 20 September 1950, editorial.
102 US delegate to Tripartite Meeting of Foreign Ministers, to Acting Secretary of State, 13 May 1950, FRUS 1949, vol. III, 396.1 Lo/5-1250, *telegram*, p.1056.
103 Dutch Council of Ministers, 4 April 1949, Dutch State Archives, MR392., *minutes*.
104 Katz to Secretary of State, 6 September 1950, FRUS 1950, vol. III, 740.5/9-850, *telegram*, p.269.
105 Van Voorst tot Voorst to Dr. Boon, 9 February 1950, MBZ, File 912.12 Frankrijk-Verhouding Deel II, Map 9988, Doos 28 1950–54, *letter*.
106 Stikker, op. cit., p.290.
107 Jebb to Younger, 12 September 1950, *telegram* 982 (C5851/27/18) enclosing *telegram* from Secretary of State. See also *Documents on British Policy Overseas*, Series II, vol III, 'German Rearmament, September – December 1950', Roger Bullen and M.E. Pelly(eds.) assisted by H. J. Yasamee and G. Bennet, London, 1989, no. 10, p.28.
108 Fursdon op. cit., p.79.
109 *Memorandum of Conversation* by Assistant Secretary of State, 14 September 1950, FRUS 1950, vol. III 740.5/9-1540, p.303.

110 Fursdon, op. cit., p.79.
111 Ibid., p.79.
112 Secretary of State to Acting Secretary of State, 16 September 1950, FRUS 1950, vol. III, 740.5/9-1650, *telegram*, p.308.
113 Stikker at 5th Session of North Atlantic Council 15 September 1950, *Documents on British Policy Overseas* op. cit., Calendar to no. 29 (COJA 115 Telegraphic (WU1198/402) of 16 September.
114 Jebb to Younger, 16 September 1950, *telegram* 1062 (C5912/27/18) DBPO Series II, vol. III, no. 30, p.66.
115 *Annual Review for 1950*, op. cit.,
116 *Note* on The situation regarding the German Question, presented by the Dutch Foreign Minister to the Second Chamber of the States General on 19 July 1949, Archives of the Second Chamber of the States General, pp.23-24.
117 Kersten, Albert E., ' Niederlaendische Regierung, Bewaffnung Westdeutschlands und EVG', *Die Europaeische Verteidigungsgemeinschaft: Stand und Probleme der Forschung Militaergeschichstliches Forschungsamt* (ed.) Boppard am Rhein, 1985, p.192.
118 Nichols to Bevin 10 May 1950, PRO FO 371/39348, file WN 1113/1, *despatch*.
119 Stikker, op. cit., p.183.
120 Kersten, op. cit., p.194.
121 Nichols to Bevin, 11 February 1950, PRO FO 371/89335, file WN 1053/1, *despatch*.

Chapter 6

1 Fursdon, Major General Edward, *The European Defence Community: A History*, Macmillan, London, 1980, p.55.
2 Ibid., p.14.
3 MBZ file 913.010, Congress van Europa te Den Haag 1948, DGES, Inventarisnummer 2/214, Doos 480.
4 Fursdon, op. cit., p.15.
5 Milward, Alan S., *The Reconstruction of Western Europe*, 1945-51, Cambridge University Press, Cambridge, 1987, p.393.
6 Fursdon, op. cit., p.17.
7 Stikker, Dirk U., *Men of Responsibility*, John Murray, London, 1966, p.177.
8 Dutch Council of Ministers, 23 August 1948, MR391, *minutes*.
9 Van Campen, S.I.P., *The Quest for Security - Some Aspects of Netherlands Foreign Policy 1945 –50*, Den Haag, 1958, p.120.
10 Ibid., p.118.
11 Milward, op. cit., p.393.
12 Van Campen, op. cit., p.118.

NOTES 257

13 Sked, Alan, *Britain and the Council of Europe*, unpublished paper given to the Annual Conference of the Association of Contemporary Historians, London School of Economics and Political Science, 1983. A very good paper. Being a busy type, Sked probably forgot to submit the paper for publication.
14 Ibid.,
15 Bevin, 29 September 1948, Paris, PRO FO 371/72921, file no. Z7912/118/4/G, *record of conversation*.
16 Rendel (signature illegible, Rendel assumed) to Sargent, 27 December 1947, PRO FO 371/72921, file no. 118, *letter* 184/5/47.
17 Schuman, Robert, *Pour L'Europe*, Paris, 1963, pp.113-115.
18 Spaak, Paul Henri, *Combats Inachevés*, Paris, 1969, vol II, p.47.
19 Fursdon, op. cit., p.18.
20 Eisen, Jane, t'Anglo Dutch Relations and European Unity 1940 – 1948', in Occasional *Papers in Modern Dutch Studies*, University of Hull, 1980.
21 Rendel to Bevin, 21 November 1949, PRO FO 371/79008, file no Z7563/1055/4, *despatch*.
22 A. Montague Browne, 2 October 1948, PRO FO 371/72921, file Z7912/118/4/G, *comment on jacket*.
23 British Embassy, *Aide Mémoire* to Netherlands Foreign Ministry, 17 September 1949, PRO FO 371/79578, file Z6261/1118/29.
24 Nichols to Bevin, 9 February 1950, PRO FO 371/89321, file WN 1011/1 *Annual Review for 1949*.
25 Nichols to Attlee, 23 September 1949, PRO FO 371/79578, file Z62G2/1118/kd, *letter* E331.
26 Nichols to Bevin, 11 February 1950, PRO FO 371/89335, file WN 1053/1, *despatch*.
27 *Annual Review for 1949*, op. cit.,
28 Van Campen, op. cit., p.125.
29 Holmes to State Department, 2 February 1950, FRUS 1950, vol. III 740.00/2-250, *despatch*, p.769.
30 Diebold, William, Jr, *The Schuman Plan - A Study in Economic Co operation*, New York, 1959, inside cover.
31 Acheson, Dean, *Sketches from Life*, London, 1961, p.44.
32 Bullen, Roger, 'An Idea enters Diplomacy: the Schuman Plan, May 1950', in Bullen, R., Van Strandman, Pogge and Polonsky, A. B.(eds.) *Ideas into Politics: Aspects of European History 1880 – 1950*, London, 1984, p.198.
33 Monnet, Jean *Mémoires*, London, 1978, p.305.
34 Massigli, René, *Une Comédie des Erreurs*, 1943 – 1958, Paris, 1978, p.188.
35 Acheson, op. cit., p.44.

36 Melandri, Pierre, *Les Etats Unis face à L'Unification de L'Europe 1945 – 1954*, Paris 1980, p.277.
37 Fursdon, op. cit., p.56.
38 Ibid., p.54.
39 Bullen, op. cit., p.194.
40 ECA Information Office, Press Release, 12 May 1950, MBZ file 602 - DGEM Archives - Plan Schuman 1950 – 52, Inventarisnummer 1212, Doos 200.
41 Fursdon, op. cit., p.58.
42 Acheson, op. cit., p.44.
43 Minutes of the Dutch Council of Ministers, 15 May 1950, MR 394.
44 Ibid., 22 May 1950.
45 Hall-Patch to Bevin, 25 May 1950 DBPO no. 43, CE2500/2141/181, telegram no. 248, p.91.
46 Young, John W., *Britain, France and the Unity of Europe*, 1945–51, Leicester University Press, 1984, p.154.
47 Van Verduynen to Stikker, 12 May 1950, *letter* 18072/1200 MBZ file 996.1 - EGKS Plan Schuman; algemeen, deel I, 1950 -15/6/50, doos 6.
48 Van Verduynen to Stikker, 19 May 1950, *letter* 18.475/1255, ibid.,
49 Fursdon, op. cit., p.61; Milward, p.400; Diebold, p.49
50 Fursdon, op. cit., p.61.
51 Van Boetzelaer to Dutch Foreign Ministry, 26 May 1950 Telegram 5706, MBZ file 996.1, EGKS - Plan Schuman; algemeen, deel I, 1950 -15/6/50, doos 6.
52 British Government to French Government, note 26 May 1950, ibid.,
53 Michels van Verduynen to Dutch Foreign Ministry, 3 June 1950, *telegram* 5931, ibid.,
54 Spierenburg to Stikker, 29 May 1950, *letter*, ibid.,
55 Fursdon, op. cit., p.62.
56 MBZ file 913.100 - DGES-Algemene beschouwingen over Europese eenheid, 1946-54.
57 Nutting, Rt. Hon. Sir Anthony, Europe will not wit-a warning and a way out, London, 1960, p.4.
58 Diebold, op. cit., p.56; see also Belgian adverse reaction, Eppsteiner to Makins, 28 July 1950, PRO FO371/88960, file no WB1051/5, *letter and memorandum*.
59 *Confidential Source* to Dutch Foreign Ministry, first half of June 1950, *Report* MBZ file 996.1, EGKS Plan Schuman, algemeen, deel I, 1950-15.6.50, doos 6.
60 *Confidential source* to Dutch Prime Minister, 1 July 1950, *Report*, U25322b-C42 -P2/PS 6, MBZ file 996.1 - Plan Schuman; algemeen, deel III, 1/7/50 - 31/12/50, doos 6.

NOTES

61 Harinxma thoe Slooten to Stikker, 21 October 1950, *letter* 17.852/2452, ibid.,
62 Diebold, op. cit., pp.58-59.
63 *Record of Meeting* Joint Foreign Affairs and Trade Committee, 7 July 1950, MBZ file 996.1 Plan Schuman, algemeen, deel III, 1/7/50 -31/12/50, doos 6.
64 Fursdon, op. cit., p.409.
65 Diebold, op. cit., p.63.
66 Harvey to Younger, 12 July 1950, *Documents on British Policy Overseas*, series II, vol. I: 'The Schuman Plan, the Council of Europe and Western European Integration, 1950 – 52', Bullen, Roger and Petty, M. E.(eds.) assisted byYasamee, H. J. andBennett, G., *telegram* no. 268, file CE 3567/2141/181, no.138, p.256.
67 Hayter to Stevens, 25 July 1950, ibid., *letter,* file CE 3868/2141/181, no 149, p.274.
68 Diebold, op. cit., p.83.
69 Ibid.,
70 State Department *Press Release* no. 1089, 14 December 1951, MBZ file DS3.1, Plan Schuman, algemeen, deel V, 1/7/51-31/12/51, doos 7.
71 Diebold, op. cit., p.83.
72 Diebold, op. cit., p.106.
73 Milward, op. cit., pp.416-417.
74 *Record of Meeting* of Council of Economic Affairs, 31 January 1951, MBZ file 996.1, Plan Schuman, algemeen, deel IV, 1/1/51-30/6/51, doos 7.
75 Stikker, op. cit., p.188.
76 See Chapter 2; Ernst van der Beugel, The Hague, 8 January 1990, *interview.*
77 Van Campen, op. cit., p.126
78 Milward, op. cit., p.194.
79 Approximately comparable to the right wing of the British Liberal Party, but in a Dutch way.
80 Milward, op. cit., p.446.
81 Stikker writes in his memoires (p.164) that he introduced his plan to the OEEC on 10 June, while Milward cites 16 June.
82 Nichols to Bevin, 6 March 1950, PRO FO 371/89329,fFile WN 1023/1, *despatch* no.73.
83 Griffiths, R. T, 'The Abortive Dutch Assault on European Tariffs, 1950-2'; in Wintle, Michael (ed.) and Vincent, Paul (co-ed.), *Modern Dutch Studies*, London, 1988, p.187.
84 Garran to FO, 21 November 1950, PRO FO 371/89329, file WN 1023/7, *savingram* 92.

85 Bogaarts, M. D., *De Periode van het Kabinet Beel, juli 1946 – augustus 1948*, Parlementaire Geschiedenis van Nederland, Deel II, thesis defended 30 November 1989, Catholic University of Nijmegen, Part C, p.363
86 Nichols to Bevin, 16 February 1951, PRO FO 371/96098, file WN 1011, *Annual Review for 1950*.
87 Strang to Harvey, 6 July 1053, *Documents on British Policy Overseas*, series II, vol.I, op. cit., file WF 1019/32, no.136, p.253.
88 Ibid., 14 July 1950, *Record of Meeting*, T232/194, no. 141, p.261.
89 Ibid., *calendar* to no. 67, p.124.
90 Ibid., *calendar* to no. 184, p.349.
91 Butler to Dixon, 27 May 1953, PRO FO 371/107612, file WN 1153/7, *letter*.
92 Ernst van der Beugel, The Hague, 8 January 1990, *interview*.
93 See Chapter 5, Section 3.
94 *Speech*, 25 January 1949, PRO FO 953, file P 963.
95 Nutting, op. cit., p.5.
96 Croft, Stuart, 'British policy towards Western Europe, 1947-9: the best of possible worlds?', *International Affairs*, vol. 64, no. 4, Autumn 1988, p.626.
97 Young, John W., op. cit., p.149.

Chapter 7

1 Van der Harst, Jan, *European and Atlantic Partnership: Political, Military and Economic Aspects of Dutch Defence 1948-54, and the Impact of the European Defence Community*, Florence, July 198, p.232.
2 Kersten, Albert E., ' Niederlaendische Regierung, Bewaffnung Westdeutschlands und EVG', in *Die Europaeische Verteidigungsgemeinschaft. Stand und Probleme der Forschung*, Militaergeschichtliches Forschungsamt (ed.), Boppard-am-Rhein, 1985, p.194.
3 Warner, Geoffrey, 'The United States and the Rearmament of West Germany, 1950-4', *International Affairs*, vol. 61, no. 2, Spring 1985, London, 1985, p.282.
4 Spits, F. C., Hague, 1954, p.27.
5 Fursdon, Edward, *The European Defence Community* : A History, London 1980, p.75.
6 Spits, op. cit., p.27.
7 Fursdon, op. cit., p.76.
8 Ibid., p.77.
9 Ibid., p.80.
10 Spits, op. cit., p.39.
11 Ibid., p.40.
12 Ibid., p.42.
13 Fursdon, op. cit., p.78.

14 Ibid., p.78.
15 Ibid., p.82.
16 Ibid., p.82
17 Ibid., p.82.
18 Kersten, op. cit., p.195
19 Van der Harst, op. cit., p.238.
20 Spits, op. cit., p.44.
21 Secretary of State to Acting Secretary of State, 16 September 1950, FRUS 1950, vol. III, *telegram* 740.5/9-1650, p.313.
22 Fursdon, op. cit., p.85.
23 Ibid., p.86.
24 Bohlen to US Secretary of State, 15 October 1950, FRUS 1950, vol. Ill, *telegram* 762A 5/10-1550, p.377.
25 Elliot, 19 October 1950, *Documents on British Policy Overseas*, series II, vol. III, 'German Rearmament September - December 1950', Bullen, Roger and Petty, M.E. (eds.), assisted by. Yasamee, H. J and. Bennett, G, no. 73, p.174, file CAB 21/1897, *memorandum*.
26 US Secretary of State to US Embassy Paris, 17 October 1950, FRUS vol. III, *telegram* 762A.5/10-1750, p.384.
27 Van der Harst.op. cit., p.235.
28 Diebold, William Jnr.,*The Schuman Plan*, New York, 1959, p.71.
29 Fursdon, op. cit., p.88.
30 Ibid., p.91.
31 Ibid., p.99.
32 Warner, op. cit., p.281.
33 Fursdon, op. cit., p.121.
34 Nichols to FO, 27 October 1950, PRO FO 371/89329, file WN 1023/5, *telegram* no. 81 Saving.
35 Fursdon, op. cit., p.110.
36 Nichols to Attlee, 16 February 1951, PRO FO 371/96098, *Annual Review for 1950*.
37 Van der Beugel, ErnstThe Hague, 8 January 1990, *interview*.
38 Stikker, Dirk U., *Men of Responsibility*, London, 1966, pp.299-300.
39 Ibid., p.303.
40 Acheson, Dean, *Present at the Creation*, London, 1969, p.643.
41 US Delegation, *minutes* of 4th formal meeting of President Truman and Prime Minister Churchill, the White House, 8 January 1952, FRUS 1952-54, vol. V, (Truman Library, David D. Lloyd files), no. 344, p.794.
42 Van der Beugel, Ernst, The Hague, 8 January 1990, *interview*.
43 Ibid.,

44 De Booy to MFA, 27 July 1950, MBZ file 921.1 - Duitsland West; Militaire Aangeelegenheden, deel 1 - 1949 - 31/10/50, *letter* 9281-G/1605.
45 Stikker to Dutch Embassy Washington, 26 October 1950, MBZ file 921.311 - Plan Pléven 'Europa Leger', 1950 and 1951, *telegram* 14166.
46 De Booy to MFA, 7 November 1950, ibid., *letter* 14897/2680.
47 Nichols to Attlee, 7 November 1950, PRO FO 371/89329 File WN 1023/6, *telegram* no. 85 saving.
48 Spofford to US Secretary of State, 21 November 1950, FRUS 1950, vol. III, *telegram* 740.5/11-2150, p.475.
49 *Memorandum of Conversation* by Perkins, 29 November 1950, FRUS 1950, vol. III, 740.5/11-2950.
50 Fursdon, op. cit., p.77.
51 Bevin to Nichols, 23 November 1950, *Documents on British Policy Overseas*, series II vol III, 'German Rearmament, September- December 1950', Bullen, Roger and Petty, M.E.(eds.) assisted by Yasamee, H. J.and Bennett, G., no. 114, p.289, file WV 1195/461, *letter*.
52 Gevers to Boon, 25 November 1950, MBZ file 921.1 - Duitsland (West) Militaire Aangelegenheden, deel I, 1946-54 *letter* enclosing *memorandum of conversation* of 23 November 1950.
53 Kersten, op. cit., p.201.
54 Ibid., p.200.
55 Ibid., p.201.
56 Fursdon, op. cit., p.115 and Spits, op. cit., p.78.
57 Fursdon nevertheless writes (p.119) 'Thus the repeated Russian proposals for Four Power talks on Germany held a certain attraction in France [...]' Spits writes (p.79) 'The French offer to hold a Four Power meeting has a long history [...]'.
58 Fursdon, op. cit., p.120.
59 Ibid., p.117.
60 Ibid., p.119.
61 *Paper* prepared by DEU/WS Department, June 1950, Dutch Ministry of Foreign Affairs, MBZ file 921.311 Plan Pléven – 'Europa Leger' 1950 and 1951.
62 Dutch Council of Ministers, 24 September 1951, Dutch State Archives, MR 395, *minutes*.
63 Ibid., 8 October.
64 *Record of meeting*, 25 October 1950, MBZ file 999.0 Benelux; Beschouwingen in Benelux in Beneluxverband 1951-53, EDG Archives, 1950–54, omslag 16, doos 5, 10/51 - 1/53.
65 Op. cit., van der Harst, p.243 and Kersten, p.201.

66 Dutch Foreign Ministry *position paper* by Max Kohnstamm, undated, (but probably December 1951) photocopy no. 37550 (A121) MBZ file 921.311 - Pléven – 'Europe Leger' 1950 and 1951.
67 Ibid.,
68 Stikker to Dutch Ministry of Foreign Affairs, 5 January 1952, MBZ file 999.4A, NATO-EDG, 1952, *telegram.*
69 Fursdon, op. cit., p.136.
70 Ibid., p.137.
71 Butler to Eden, 13 February 1952 PRO FO 371/101898, file WN 1011/1, *Annual Review for 1951.*
72 Jebb to Attlee (from Secretary of State), 29 September 1950, *Documents on British Policy Overseas,* series II, vol. III, op. cit., no 50, p.120, file WU1198/451, *telegram* 1255.
73 Bevin to Franks, 29 November 1950, ibid., no. 119, p.305, file WV 1195/481, *telegram* 5318.
74 Bevin to Franks, 6 December 1950, ibid., no. 129, p.341, file WV 1198/661, *telegram* 5486.
75 It is likely that the Permanent Under Secretary's Department was responsible for liaison with the Secret Intelligence Service.
76 Barnes, 20 July 1951, *Documents on British Policy Overseas* Series II, vol I, 'The Schuman Plan, the Council of Europe and Western European Integration, 1950-52', Bullen, Roger and Petty, M.E. (eds.), assisted by Yasamee, H. J.and Bennett, G., no. 347, p.656, *memorandum.*
77 Bullen, Roger, 'Britain and Europe 1950–1957', in *The Relaunching of Europe and the Treaties of Rome,* European Community Liaison Committee of Historians, vol. 3, Serra, Enrico (ed.), Brussels, Milan and Baden-Baden, 1987, p.321.
78 Fursdon, op. cit., p.128.
79 Nutting, Anthony, *Europe will not wait - a warning and a way out,* London, 1950 p.40.
80 Ibid., p.40.
81 Ibid., p.41.
82 Julian Amery, Tufton Beamish, Robert Boothby, Dick Harden, Christopher Hollis, Charles M Radclyffe and Priscilla Tweedsmuir to Churchill, 3 December 1951, DBPO, Series II, vol I, (WU 10712/62), no. 406, pp.769-770, *letter.*
83 DBPO Series II, vol.II, note to the Cabinet, calender to no.406, p.770.
84 FRUS 1953, vol III, p.419 in Pierre Melandri, 'The Rôle of European Unification in the Foreign policy of the United States', in Poidevin, Raymond (ed.), *Origins of European Integration, March 1948 - May 1950,* Brussels, Milan, Paris, Baden-Baden, 1986, p.39.

85 DBPO, Series II, vol. I, record of meeting, Paris, 17 December 1951 (Zp28/8), no 418, p.796.
86 Stikker, op. cit., p.302.
87 Spits, op. cit., p.136.
88 Nutting, op. cit., p.42.
89 Fursdon, op. cit., p.77.
90 Yasamee, H. J., 'Anthony Eden and Europe', *Occasional Papers*, no 1, London, November 1987, pp.40-41.
91 MFA *position paper* (Kohnstamm) op. cit.,
92 Yasamee, Ibid., p.40.
93 Melandri, Pierre, *Une Comédie des Erreurs, 1943-1956*, Paris, 1978, p.38.
94 Secretary of State to US Embassy, The Hague, 11 January 1952, FRUS, vol. V, 1952–4, *telegram* 740.5/1-1152, p.580.
95 Kersten, op. cit., p.204.
96 *NRC*, 16 September 1950, *editorial*.
97 *De Volkskrant*, 16 February 1951, *editorial*.
98 *Trouw*, 13 July 1951, *editorial*.

Chapter 8

1   Nichols to Attlee, 16 February 1951, PRO 371/96098 WN 1011/1, *Annual Review for 1950*.
2   *The Economist*, 10 March 1951 p.537.
3   Ibid.,
4   Ibid., 17 March 1951, p.629.
5   Ibid., 21 April 1951, p.949.
6   Ibid., 17 March 1951, p.629.
7   *Yearbook* of the Royal Netherlands Ministry of Foreign Affairs for 1951/52, p.88.
8   Ibid., p.83.
9   *The Economist*, 23 June 1951, pp.1523-4.
10 *Annual Review* for 1950, op. cit.,
11 *The Economist*, 3 February 1951, p.252.
12 Nichols to Young, 16 January 1951, PRO FO 371/96100, file WN 1011/2, *letter* 1012/3/51.
13 Stikker, Dirk U., *Men of Responsibility*, London,1966, p.234.
14 Ibid., p.248.
15 *The Economist*, 3 February 1951, p.252.
16 Nichols to FO, 29 January 1951, PRO FO 371/96100, *despatch* no. 40, file WN1011.

17 Eisenhower, 31 January 1951, FRUS 1951, Vol III, p.452 Harry S Truman Library: Papers of George M Elsey, *Notes of a Meeting* at the White House.
18 Brouwer, J. W. L., 'De Stem van de Marine in de Ministeraad, Schout-bij-nacht H. C. W. Moorman als staatssecretaris van Marine in het Kabinet-Drees - Van Schaik, 1949-1951', *Politieke Opstellen* no. 9, Centrum voor Parlementaire Geschiedenis, Catholic University of Nijmegen, 1989, p.29.
19 Ibid., p.50.
20 Ibid., p.44.
21 Ibid., p.44.
22 Ibid., p.47.
23 Nichols to Atlee, 16 February 1951, PRO FO 371/96115. file WN 1011/1, *despatch* 62.
24 Kruls, General H. J., *Vrede of Oorlog*, Den Haag, 1952, p.193.
25 Nichols to Bevin, 21 July 1949, PRO FO 371/79600, file no. 1194, *letter* no. 248, 75/33/49, enclosing translated text of Kruls' speech of 16 June to the East Brabant Sector of the Netherlands Corporation for Industry and Commerce.
26 Chancery, British Embassy, to Western Department, FO, 21 October 1949, *letter* no. 421/11/49, enclosing translated text of Kruls' interview by *De Volkskrant* of 14 October.
27 Nichols to FO, 24 January 1951, PRO FO 371/96115, file WN 1192/5, *savingram* 13.
28 Nichols to Attlee, op. cit., *Annual Review for 1950*.
29 M. D. Butler, February 1951, PRO FO 371/96115, file no. WN 1011/1, *comment on file jacket*.
30 The word 'very' is frowned upon by the Diplomatic Service, as being unnecessarily strong.
31 Nichols to Young, 16 January 1951, PRO FO 371/96100, file no. WN 1015/2, *letter*.
32 Nichols to Bevin, 23 January 1951, PRO FO 371/96115, file WN 1192/1, *despatch 29*.
33 Nichols to Young, 16 January 1951 PRO FO 371/96100, file WN 1015/2, *letter*.
34 Dutch Council of Ministers, 22 January 1951, Dutch State Archives. MR 395, *minutes*.
35 Ibid.,
36 Nichols to Young, 16 January 1951, PRO FO 371/96100, file WN 1015/2, *letter*.
37 Dutch Council of Ministers, 21 August 1950, Dutch State Archives, MR 394, *minutes*.

38 Van der Harst, Jan, *European Union and Atlantic Partnership: Political, Military and Eonomic Aspects of Dutch Defence 1948 – 1954, and the Impact of the European Defence Community,* European University Institute, Florence, 1987, p.48.
39 Eisenhower to Chapin, 13 January 1951, FRUS, vol III, part 1, 740.5/1 -1951, *telegram,* p.416.
40 Ibid., p.417.
41 Chapin to US Embassy Lisbon (for Eisenhower), 16 January 1951, FRUS, vol III, pt. 1, 756.00/1-1651, *telegram,* p.425.
42 Chapin to Secretary of State, 19 January 1951, FRUS vol. III, pt. 1, 740.5/1-1951, *telegram,* p.436.
43 Van der Harst, Jan, op. cit., p.53.
44 Ibid., p.57.
45 Dutch Council of Ministers, 22 January 1951, op. cit., *minutes.*
46 Nichols to Young, 20 February 1951, PRO FO 371/96101, file WN 1015/24, *letter* 1015/36/51.
47 Nichols to Young, 27 February 1951, PRO FO 371/96101, file WN 1015/27, *letter* 1015/41/51.
48 Dutch Council of Ministers 22 January 1951, op. cit., *minutes.*
49 Butler to Eden, 13 February 1952, PRO FO 371/101898, file WN 1011/1, *Annual Review for 1951.*
50 Nichols to Young, 16 January 1951, PRO FO 371/96100, file WN 1011/2, *letter* 1012/3/51.
51 Nichols to Morrison, 27 March 1951, PRO FO 371/96102, file WN 1015/40, *letter* 102.
52 Nichols to FO, 5 February 1951, PRO FO 371/96115, file WN/1011/4, *savingram* 18.
53 Nichols to FO, 9 February 1951, PRO FO 371/96101, file WN/1015/19, *savingram* 23.
54 Nichols to FO, 15 February 1951, PRO FO 371/96101, file WN 1015/20, *savingram* 26.
55 Nichols to FO 26 February 1951 PRO F0 371 96101, file WN 1015/26, *savingram* 30.
56 Nichols to FO, 7 February 1951, PRO FO 371/96101, file WN 1015/18, *savingram* 22.
57 Nichols to FO, 10 March 1951, PRO FO 371/96115, file WN 1011/10, *savingram* 36.
58 Nichols to FO, 20 March 1951, PRO FO 371/96102, file WN 1015/35, *savingram* 42.
59 Nichols to FO, 17 March 1951, PRO FO 371/96102, file WN1015/34, *savingram* 40.

NOTES 267

60 Nichols to FO, undated, PRO FO 371/96102, file WN 1015/38, *savingram*.
61 Nichols to Morrison, 27 March 1951, PRO FO 371/96102, file WN 1015/40, *letter* 102.
62 Butler to Eden 1952 op. cit., *Annual Review for 1951*.
63 Dutch Council of Ministers 26 October 1951, MR 395, *minutes*.
64 Butler to Eden, op. cit., *Annual Review for 1951*.
65 Butler to Eden, 5 February 1952, PRO FO 371/101931 file WN 1201/1, *despatch* 42, enclosing Military Attachés (Col T C Williamson) *report* for 1951 on the Netherlands Army.
66 Ibid., Naval Attaché's report - *comment on file jacket* - signature illegible.
67 Butler to Eden op. cit., *Annual Review for 1951*.
68 *The Economist*, 19 May 1951, p.1142.
69 Nichols to Morrison, 27 March 1951, PRO FO 371/96117, file WN 1194/1, *despatch* 103.
70 Ibid., Butler, *comment on file jacket*.
71 Butler to Eden, op. cit., *Annual Review for 1951*.
72 Nichols to Morrison, 21 March 1951, PRO FO 371/96116, file WN 1193/2, *despatch* 101.
73 Nichols to Eden, 7 November 1951, PRO FO 371/95117, file WN 1194/3, *despatch* 360.
74 De Beus, 26 July 1951, MBZ file 912.1 - NL-US Verhouding en diplomatieke betrekkingen, deel 1+11, Doos 294, *article* in *Denver Post*.
75 Nichols to Eden, undated, PRO FO 371/96102, file WN 1015/47, *letter* 381.
76 Nichols to Morrison, 12 July 1951, PRO FO 371/96104, file WN 1021/1, *despatch* 228.
77 Stikker to MFA, 5 January 1952, MBZ file 999.4A - NATO -EDG, 1952, *telegram*.
78 Nichols to FO, 17 December 1951, PRO FO 371/96103, file W 1016/10, *despatch*. 407.

Chapter 9

1 Butler to Eden 13 February 1952, PRO FO 371/101898, file WN 1011/1, *Annual review for 1951*.
2 Van der Harst, Jan, European and Atlantic Partnership: Political, Military and *Economic Aspects of Dutch Defence, 1948 – 54, and the Impact of the European Defence Community*, Florence, July 1937, p.250.
3 Ibid., p.250.
4 *Annual Review for 1951*, op. cit.,
5 Kersten, Albert E., Niederlaendische Regierung, Bewaffung Westdeutschlands und EVG in *Die Europaeische Verteidigungsgemeinschaft. Stand und Probleme*

der Forschung, Militargeschichtliches Forschungsamt (ed.), (MGFA) Boppar-am-Rhein, 1985 p.209.
6 Ibid., p.209.
7 Ibid., p.210.
8 Ibid., p.210.
9 Van der Harst, op. cit., p.252.
10 Fursdon, Edward, *The European Defence Community: a History*, London 1980, p.134.
11 Warner to Eden, 14 February 1953, PRO FO 371/107307, file WB 1011/1, *letter* no. 60.
12 Kersten, op. cit., p.214.
13 Bruce to Department of State, 3 January 1952, FRUS 1952-1954, vol. V, part 1, *telegram* 740.5/1-352, pp.572-573.
14 Ibid., p.212.
15 Ibid., p.212.
16 Spits, F.C., *Naar een Europees Leger* 'Nederlandse Raad der Europese Beweging', The Hague, 1954, p.134.
17 Fursdon, op. cit., p.137.
18 Kersten, op. cit., p.216.
19 Ibid., p.216.
20 MFA to de Booy, 15 April 1952, MBZ file 921.311, Europese Defensie Gemeenschap 1951–3, *telegram* 6612-G.
21 Ibid.,
22 Kersten, op. cit., p.215.
23 MFA to de Booy, 15 April 1952, op. cit.,
24 Stikker to de Booy, 7 June 1952, MBZ file 921.311, Europese Defensie Gemeenschap 1951-3, *telegram* 9789-G.
25 Kersten, op. cit., p.216.
26 Fursdon, op. cit., p.185.
27 Oskam, B. P., *Twee Kapiteins op een Schip, De Nederlandse delegatie bij de onderhandelingen over de Europese Defensie Gemeenschup in Parijs (1951 – 1954)*, Utrecht 1989, p.88 (Doctoraalscriptie supervised by Dr. ☐.☐.☐. Volten).
28 Ibid., p.63.
29 Monnet, Jean, Memoires, London, 1978, p.357.
30 Oskam, op. cit., p.68.
31 Ibid., p.73.
32 Stikker, Dirk U., *Men of Responsibility*, London, 1966, p.302.
33 Fursdon, op. cit., p.145.
34 Stikker, op. cit., p.302.
35 Kersten, op. cit., pp.214-215.

36 Ibid., p.202.
37 De Booy to Stikker, 25 October 1951, MBZ file 921.1 part 1 - Duitsland (West) Militaire Aangelegenheden 1946-54, *letter* 17665-G/3549.
38 Ibid.,
39 MFA to Minister President, 6 November 1951, enclosing note by Minister President, MBZ file 921.1, part 1 - Duitsland (West) Militaire Aangelegenheden 1946 – 54, *Note* 109720-8635 GS.
40 De Booy to MFA, 9 February 1952, MBZ file 921.311 - Europese Defensie Gemenschap 1951-3, *telegram* 2665-G.
41 De Booy to Stikker, 5 March 1952, MBZ file 921.311 - Europese Defensie Gemeenschap 1951-3, *letter* 4125-G/941.
42 Fursdon, op. cit., p.137.
43 Spits, op. cit., p.155.
44 Ibid., p.156.
45 Butler to Eden 1 January 1953, PRO FO 371/107598, file WN1011/1, *Annual Review for 1952*.
46 Ibid.,
47 *The Economist*, 5 July 1952.
48 *Annual Review for 1952*, op. cit.,
49 Eden to Churchill, 18 March 1952, *Documents on British Policy Overseas Series II, vol I*, 'The Schuman Plan, the Council of Europe and Western European Integration', Bullen, Roger and Pelly, M. E. (eds.) assisted by Yasamee, H. J. and Bennett, G., no.439, p.847, file PM/52126 (PREM 11/153), *minute*.
50 Harvey to Foreign Office, ibid., 20 March 1952, file WU 10733/30, no. 441, p.855, *telegram* 164.
51 Ibid.,*Calendars* to no. 467, p.905.
52 Young, John W., 'The Schuman Plan and British Association in Young, John W.(ed.), *The Foreign Policy of Churchill's Peacetime Administration 1951–1955*, Leicester University Press 1988, p.130.
53 Yasamee, H. J., 'Anthony Eden and Europe' in 'Valid Evidence' (Seminar), November 1951, Occasional Papers no. 1, London November 1987, p.40.
54 Roberts, 17 July 1952, DBPO, Series II, Volume I, file M412/118, No 470, p.910, record.
55 Ibid., calendar to no. 470, 5 August 1952, file M412/118, *note*.
56 Bullen, Roger 'Britain and Europe 1950 – 1957' in Serra, Enrico (ed.) *The Relaunching of Europe and the Treaties of Rome*, European Community Liaison Committee of Historians, vol. 3, Brussels, Milan and Baden-Baden, 1987, p.328.
57 Beyen, K. H., 6 January 1990, The Hague, *telephone Interview*.
58 Dr. H. N. Boon, 5 January 1990, The Hague, *interview*.

59 Dilks, David, 'Britain and Europe, 1948–1950: the Prime Minister, the Foreign Secretary and the Cabinet' in Poidevin, Raymond (ed.), *Origins of European Integration, March 1948 – May 1950*, Actes du colloque de Stasbourg, 20-30 March 1984, Brussels, Milan, Paris, Baden Baden 1984, p.417.
60 *Annual Review for 1952*, op. cit.,
61 Fursdon, op. cit., p.213.
62 Stikker, op. cit., p.200.
63 British Ambassador, Rome, to Dixon, 4 February 1953, PRO FO 371/107604, *letter* no. 1037/1/53.
64 Ibid.,
65 *Annual Review for 1952*, op. cit.,
66 Butler to Harrison, 30 July 1952, PRO FO 371/10194, file WN 1051/1, *letter.*
67 Nichols to Eden, undated, probably October 1951, PRO FO 371/96102, file WN 1015/47, *letter* 381.
68 *Annual Review for 1952*, op. cit.,
69 Foreign Office (Western Department), *summary*, 10 March 1952, PRO FO 371/107611, file WN1151/12.
70 Foreign Office (Western Department), *brief*, 30 September 1952, enclosing *note* on Drees, PRO FO 371/101904, file WN 1051/3.
71 Sir Pierson Dixon, 8 April 1953, record of conversation, PRO FO 371/107612, file WN 1153/2.
72 *Yearbook* of the Royal Netherland Ministry of Foreign Affairs, 1951/2, p.90.
73 Ibid., 1952/3, p.68.
74 Ibid., 1951/2, p.84.
75 *Annual Review for 1952*, op. cit.,
76 Butler to Eden, 25 March1953, *despatch* enclosing Military Attaché's annual report on the Netherlands army, of 23 December 1952, PRO FO 371/107614, file WN 1201/1.
77 Alison, B.M.E., 19 May 1953, *comment on jacket*, PRO FO 371/107615, file WN1213/1.
78 *Annual Review for 1952*, op. cit.,
79 Bullen, Roger, *Britain and Europe 1950 – 1957*, op. cit., p.320.
80 It is possible that some non-specialist readers will not be aware of the 'Hallstein doctrine', which essentially advocated the idea that the reunification of Germany would best be achieved by West Germany sticking to the West.

Chapter 10

1 Butler to Eden, 1 January 1954, PRO FO 371/112957, file WN1011/1, *Annual Review for 1953*.
2 Ibid.,

NOTES

3 Ibid.,
4 *Yearbook* of the Netherlands Foreign Ministry for 1953/54, pp.71-2.
5 *Annual Review for 1953*, op. cit.,
6 Ibid.,
7 Lamping to Beyen, 25 March 1953, MBZ file 921.311 A - EDG 1951-3, *letter* 5525-G/914.
8 *Yearbook* of the Netherlands Foreign Ministry for 1952/3, p.66.
9 *Annual Review for 1953*, op. cit.,
10 Ibid.,
11 Strang, Sir William, 10 March 1953, PRO FO 371/107611, file WN 1151/11, *record of conversation*.
12 Foreign Office *summary* 10 March 1953, PRO FO 371/107611, file WN 1151/12.
13 Butler to Cheetham 9 October 1953, PRO FO 371/107614, file WN 1201/3, *letter* 1201/81/53.
14 Selby to Butler, 20 October 1953, PRO FO 371/107614, file WN 1201/4, *letter*.
15 Selby to Willan, 1 December 1953, PRO FO 371/107614, file WN 1201/5, *letter*.
16 Chancery, the Hague to Foreign Office, 14 July 1953, PRO FO 371/107608, *letter* 10316/3/53.
17 Ibid., *comment on file jacket* - signature illegible.
18 Boon, Dr. H. N., 5 January 1990, The Hague, *interview*
19 Coulson to Butler, 12 January 1953, PRO FO 371/107612, file WN 1153/1, *letter*.
20 Robey, 10 April 1953, PRO FO 371/107612, file WN 1153/2, *minute*.
21 Harrison, ibid., *comment*.
22 Beyen, J.W., Over de Europese integratie in Nederland en de Europese eenwording, Hommes, P. M.(ed.) , p.171, inOskam, B.P., *Twee Kapiteins op ein Schip: De Nederlandse delegatie bij de onderhandeiingen over de Europese Defensie Gemeenschap in Parijs, (1951 - 1954)*, doctoraalscriptie under supervision of Volten, Dr. P. M. E., Utrecht, 1989, p.57.
23 Van der Beugel, Ernst, 8 January 1990, The Hague, *interview*.
24 *Annual Review for 1953*, op. cit.,
25 Stikker to Beyen, 19 November 1952, MBZ file 912.1 - NL-UK Verhouding en Diplomatieke Betrekkingen, deel 1 + 2, MAP 2346, *telegram* 13507.
26 Confidential source (unknown) to Foreign Minister, 4 July 1952, MBZ file 999.0, Frankrijk, Algemene Beschouwing 1952-53 (EDG Archief), *letter*, U45326A - C42 - P1/PS6.
27 *NRC*, 7 July 1953 - author's translation.

28 Confidential Source (unknown) to Foreign Minister, 7 August 1952, MBZ file 999.0 - Duitsland West Algemene Beschouwingen 1952, (EDG Archief), *letter* U46705a - C42 - P1/PS.
29 May, Ernest R., 'The American Commitment to Germany 1949-55', *Diplomatic History*, vol. 13, no. 4, Fall 1989, Washington and Delaware, p.450.
30 Edward Fursdon, *The European Defence Community: a History*, MacMillan, London 1980, pp.207-8.
31 Stikker to Dutch Foreign Ministry, 30 January 1953, MBZ file 921.311 A - EDG 1954, *telegram* 2168.
32 Canadian Ministry of Foreign Affairs' Annual Review of Soviet Affairs for 1953 (Circular Document No A 87/54) on MBZ file 911.0- Sovjet Rusland Algemene Rapporten, deel I, 1947-54. Although it is not known how this secret Canadian document came to be on a Dutch Foreign Ministry file, co-operation between the Dutch and Canadians was known to be close.
33 Spits, F. C., *Naar een Europees Leger*, The Hague 1954, p.194.
34 Fursdon, op. cit., p.210.
35 Truman, 10 March 1953, FRUS 1952-4, volume V, 740.5/3-1153, p.761, *Memorandum of Conversation*.
36 Selwyn Lloyd, to Prime Minister, 20 June 1953, PRO FO 371, file WN 1153/14, *record of conversation*.
37 Ibid.,
38 *The Economist*, 20 June 1953.
39 Chapin to Beyen, 24 July 1953, MBZ file 999.1, - Nederland, ratificatie 1952-54, EDG Archief 1950-54, Omslag 55, 1/52-4/54, doos II, *letter*.
40 Teixeira de Mattos to Dutch Foreign Ministry, 27 July 1953, MBZ file, ibid., *letter* 2274/407.
41 *Annual Review for 1953*, op. cit.,
42 Fursdon, op. cit., p.222.
43 Ibid.,
44 *Annual Review for 1953*, op. cit.,
45 Ibid.,
46 *The Economist*, 25 July 1953.
47 Van der Harst, Jan, *The Netherlands and the European Defence Community*, European University Institute Working paper no. 86 / 252, Florence, undated, p.35.
48 Beyen to Stikker, 11 March 1953, Dutch Royal Archives Collection 357, 221.183, E.H. van der Beugel, *letter*.
49 Beyen, K. H., 6 January 1990, The Hague, *interview*.
50 Stikker, Dirk, 13 March 1953, Dutch Royal Archives Collection 194, 221.156, Stikker, *Address* on Modern Europe, Ashridge, Course no. 13.

51 Van der Beugel, Ernst, 8 January 1990, *interview*.
52 Ibid.,
53 Beyen, K. H., op. cit., *interview*.
54 Dixon, Sir Pierson, 8 April 1953, PRO FO 371/107612, file WN 1153/2, *record of conversation*.
55 Spalding, 11 March 1953, FRUS 1952-54, Vol VI, 740.5/3-1153, p.763, *memorandum of conversation*.
56 Butler to Dixon, 27 May 1953, PRO FO 371/107612, file WN 1153/7, *letter.*
57 Dixon, Sir Pierson, *record of conversation*, op. cit.,
58 Ibid.,
59 Ibid.,
60 Alison, B. M. E, .6 February 1953, PRO FO 371/107599, file WN 1015/1, *note on file jacket*.
61 B. A. (perhaps Alison, op. cit.,) 19 March 1953, PRO FO 371/107599, file WN 1015/4, *comment on jacket.*
62 Butler to Cheetham, 9 May 1953, PRO FO 371/107599, file WN 1015/5, *letter* 1-12/4/53.
63 Ibid.,
64 *Annual Review for 1953*, op. cit.,
65 Van der Beugel, Ernst, 8 January 1990, The Hague, *interview*.
66 Beyen, K. H., 6 January 1990, The Hague, *telephone interview*.
67 Luns, Joseph, 11 January 1990, Brussels, *interview*.
68 Van der Beugel, Ernst, op. cit., *interview*
69 Ibid.,
70 Spalding, op. cit., FRUS 1952-4, vol VI.
71 FRUS 1952-54, vol VI, 11 September 1953, OCB files, lot 61D385, 'Prestige Project', p.1504, *Special Report* by the Psychological Strategy Board.
72 Ibid., the Americans were worried about their image, which they felt was suffering because of a declining fear of the Soviet Union, and because of 'McCarthyism'.

Chapter 11

1 Fursdon, Edward, *The European Defence Community: A History*, London, 1980, p.242.
2 Ibid., p.252.
3 Ibid., p.296.
4 Ibid., p.273.
5 *The Economist*, 16 April 1954.
6 Beyen, J. W., *Het Spel en de Knikkers - Een KroniEk van Vijitig Jaren*, Amsterdam, 1968, p.206.

7   Stikker, Dirk U., *Men of Responsibility*, London 1966, p.254.
8   Beyen, J. W., 'L'Influence de l'Esprit Latin sur un Pays Nordique', discours prononcé à l'occasion du cinquantieme anniversaire de la Chambre de Commerce Néerlandaise en France, N V Lettergieterij 'Amsterdam', Vorheen N. Tetterode, 1953, p.26.
9   Mason to Eden, 24 September 1954 PRO FO 371/109480, file CN 1015/1 (WD), *despatch*.
10 Mason to Eden, 1 January 1955, PRO FO 371/118487, file WN 1011/1, *Annual Review for 1954*. See also Griffiths, R. T., 'The Abortive Dutch Assault on European Tariffs, 1950-2', in Wintle, Michael(ed.) and Vincent, Paul (co-ed.), *Modern Dutch Studies*, London, 1988, p.207, who wrote:'[...] Beyen's plan to form a European customs union among the six ECSC members had also foundered on the French refusal to ratify the EDC treaty.'
11 Van der Harst, Jan, *European Union and Atlantic Partnership; Political, Military and Economic Aspects of Dutch Defence, 1948 - 1954, and the Impact of the European Defence Community*, European University Institute, Florence, 1987, p.277.
12 Ibid., p.271.
13 Dutch Council of Ministers, 14 June 1954, Dutch State Archives, MR 399, *record*.
14 Beyen, J. W., *Het Spel en de Knikkers*, op. cit., p.233.
15 Acheson, Dean, *Sketches from Life*, London, 1961, p.57.
16 Butler to Eden, 1 January 1954, PRO FO 371/112957, file WN 1011/1, *Annual Review for 1953*.
17 Stikker to Eschanzier, 17 June 1954, MBZ file 912.1 NL-UK Verhouding en Diplomatieke Betrekkingen, deel 1 + 11, Map 2346, *letter* 10560.
18 Kohnstamm, Max, 'The European Community and its Rôle in the World', *John Findlay Green Foundation Lectures*, University of Missouri Press, 1964.
19 Willis, F. Roy, *France, Germany and the New Europe 1945-67*, Stanford, California and London (OUP) 1968, p.242.
20 Ibid., p.242.
21 *Yearbook* of the Royal Netherlands Foreign Ministry 1954–55, p.1. See also Warnecke, Steven J., *The European Community in the 1970's*, New York, 1971, chapter entitled 'The Failure of Foreign Relations between the United States and a united Europe: the European perspective', reprinted in *Internationale Spectator*, vol. XXVI, no. 13, 8 July 1972, p.1321. Warnecke wrote: 'The Dutch Minister of Foreign Affairs at that time, Dr Beyen, together with his Belgian colleague, Paul-Henri Spaak, played a prominent role with regard to the preparation of the [Messina] conference. The experience with the disillusionment caused by the abortive EDC negotiations in 1954 apparently put their mark on the negotiations leading to the Treaty of Rome. The issue now was eco-

NOTES

nomic co-operation instead of the previous efforts directed towards political and defence co-operation.'

22 Lamping to Beyen, 10 September 1954, MBZ file 921.311A - Ambassade Bonn 1949-54, deel 1, EDG: Multilaterale Problemen, *letter* 13159-G/2339.
23 MBZ file 912.13 - Duitsland West-Duitse Readies op Nederlandse eisen tot grenscorrecties, Deel V, 1953-4, Map 1964, *note*.
24 Van Tuyll van Serooskerken, 17 May 1954 MBZ file 912.1 - Duitsland West Verhouding, Deel II, 1951-54, Map 1884, *memorandum* 488.
25 Ibid., German Embassy, *note* 700-08/1447 of 24 May 1954.
26 Ibid., MFA *minute* 68477 of 3 June 1954.
27 Dutch Council of Ministers 31 May 1954, MR 399, *minutes*.
28 Chancery to Foreign Office, 11 June 1954, PRO FO 371/112960, file WN 10318/2, *letter*.
29 Lamping to MFA, 18 August 1954, MBZ file 912.1 Duitsland West-Verhouding, op. cit., *letter* 12118/2155.
30 Ibid., 14 September 1954, *letter*.
31 Lamping to Beyen and Luns, 18 June 1954, *letter* 8921-G/1591.
32 Wielenga, Friso, *West Duitsland: partner uit noodzak, Nederland en de Bondsrepubliek 1949–1955*, The Hague, 1989.
33 Beyen, 21 May 1954, MBZ file 912.1, Duitsland West Verhouding, op. cit., *memorandum*.
34 'since then' simply refers to a previous German note about the border problems.
35 Lamping to Beyen and Luns, 18 June 1954, *enclosure to letter* 8921-G/1591.
36 Ibid.,
37 Chancery to Foreign Office, 7 December 1954, PRO FO 371/109484, file CN 1081/2, *letter*.
38 *Yearbook* of the Royal Netherlands Foreign Ministry 1953/54, p.71.
39 Several Dutch friends of the writer told him that up to fairly recently, German tourists were still knocking on doors, asking to look around the houses where they were once billeted. I have not heard of this happening in Greece, where I now live…
40 *Annual Review for 1954*, op. cit.,
41 *Yearbook* of the Royal Netherlands Foreign Ministry for 1954/55, p.62.
42 *Annual Review for 1954*, op. cit.,
43 Ibid.,
44 Fursdon, op. cit., p.235.
45 Chapin to Beyen, 24 July 1954, MBZ file 999.1 - EDG Archief 1950-54, Nederland ratificatie, omslag 55, 1952-54, *letter*.
46 Ibid., Teixeira de Mattos to MFA, 27 July 1953, *letter* 2274/407.

47 Van der Harst, 'Jan, The Netherlands and the European Defence Community', *EUI Working Paper* no 86/252, Florence, undated, p.38.
48 *Annual Review* of Soviet Affairs for 1953 (Canadian Foreign Ministry) □. 7-MBZ file 911.0 - Sovjet-Rusland - Algemeen rapporten.
49 Mason to Foreign Office, 31 December 1954, PRO FO 371/118490, file WN 1022/1, *despatch* no. 373.
50 Van der Harst, Jan, 'The Netherlands and the European Defence Community', op. cit., The Richards Amendment in the US House of Representatives suggested reducing military aid to a value of $1000 million if the EDC did not come into force. Congress linked the amendment to the Military Security Programme for 1953-4. Half of the funds provided for European military aid could be made available only to the EDC or its member countries. Were the EDC treaty to fail to enter into force, the funds could not be made available by the Executive unless Congress changed this provision on the recommendation of the President.
51 May, Ernest R., 'The American Commitment to Germany 1949 – 55', *Diplomatic History*, vol. 13, no 4, Fall 1989, Washington and Delaware, p.453.
52 Fursdon, op. cit., p.256.
53 Nutting, Anthony, *Europe will not wait - a warning and a way out*, London, 1960, p.63
54 Fursdon, op. cit., p.257.
55 Ibid., p.269.
56 Dutch Council of Ministers, 14 June 1954, Dutch State Archives, MR 399, *minutes*.
57 *NRC*, 28 June 1954.
58 Chapin to Department of State, 8 July 1953, FRUS 1952-54, vol. V, *telegram* 740.5/7-853, p.795.
59 Nutting, op. cit., p.67.
60 Lamping to MFA, 24 August 1954, MBZ file 921.311A - Ambassade Bonn, 1949-54, Deel 1, EDG Multilateral Problemen, *telegram* 12412-G.
61 Fursdon, op. cit., p.304.
62 Mallet to Geiner, 30 October 1950, *Documents on British Policy Overseas*, series II, vol. I – 'The Schuman Plan, the Council of Europe and Western European Integration 1950-1952, no.177, p.333, file WF1023/36, *memorandum*.
63 Warner, Geoffrey, The United States and the Rearmament of West Germany, 1950–4 in *International Affairs*, vol. V, no. 2, Spring 1985, Royal Institute of International Affairs, London 1987, p.285.
64 *De Volkskrant*, 24 August 1954.
65 Nutting, op. cit., p.68.
66 Ernst van der Beugel, 8 January 1990, *interview*.

67 Luns to Lamping, 1 September 1954, MBZ file 921.311 A - Ambassade Bonn, op. cit., *telegram* 12788-G.
68 *NRC*, 31 August 1954.
69 Fursdon, op. cit., p.304.
70 Hasselman to MFA, 2 September 1954, MBZ file 921.311A - Ambassade Bonn, op. cit., *telegram* 162977.
71 *Trouw*, 31 August 1954.
72 Beus to MFA, 7 September 1954, MBZ file 921.311A - Ambassade Bonn, op. cit., *telegram* 9191.
73 De Beus to MFA, 10 September 1954, ibid., *telegram* 9313.
74 Van Roijen to MFA 15 September 1954, ibid., *telegram* 9498.
75 Boon to MFA, 16 September 1953, ibid., *telegram* 9633.
76 Van Boetzelaer to Van Starkenborgh, 17 September 1954, ibid., *telegram* 9624.
77 Lamping to MFA 17 September 1954, ibid., *telegram* 13676-G.
78 Beyen to Lamping, 18 September 1954, ibid., *telegram* 13678-G.
79 Luns to MFA 23 September 1954, ibid., *telegram* 9882.
80 Fursdon, op. cit., p.318.
81 *NRC*, 18 September 1954.
82 Ibid.,
83 *Trouw*, 1 October 1954.
84 *NRC*, 30 September 1954.
85 Fursdon, op. cit., pp.334-5.
86 Stikker, op. cit., p.315.
87 Fursdon, op. cit., p.319.
88 Dutch Council of Ministers, 8 March 1948, Dutch State Archives, MR 390, *minutes*.
89 *Annual Review for 1954*, op. cit.,

Chapter 12

1 *The Economist*, 3 February 1990, 'Neutrality's Identity Crisis'.
2 Tamse, C. A., 'Een historisch element in het Nederlandse buitenlands - politieke denken', *Internationale Spectator*, vol. 28, no. 22, 22 December 1974.
3 Brierly, J. L, *The Law of Nations*, Oxford University Press, 1963, (sixth edition) pp, 136-137.
4 Kersten, Albert,'Neutraliteit politiek versus selfstandigheidspolitiek', *Internationale Spectator*, vol. 38, no. 2, February 1984.
5 Schoffer, Dr. I. 'Het Trauma van de Nederlandse nederlaag', *Tijdschrift voor Geschiedenis*, vol. 84, no. 4, 1971.
6 Schaper, H. A.,'Nederlandse annexatie plannen na 1945', *Internationale Spectator*, vol, 39, no. 5 May 1985.

7   Luns, H. E. Dr. J. M. A. H., 'Benelux in Europe', *Internationale Spectator*, vol. 23, no. 17, October 1969.
8   Stikker, Dirk, *Memoires*, The Hague 1966, pp.276-7.
9   Beyen, K. H., 6 January 1990, The Hague, *telephone Interview*.
10 Beyen, Dr. J. W., 'United Europe - federal or supranational?', *Internationale Spectator*, vol. 14, no 7, 8 April 1965.
11 Samkalden, Prof. Dr. I.'. A Dutch retropective view on European and Atlantic Co-operation', *Internationale Spectator*, ibid.,
12 Luns, Joseph, 11 January 1990, Brussels, *telephone interview*.
13 Dilks, David, 'Britain and Europe 1948 –1950: the Prime Minister, the Foreign Secretary and the Cabinet', Poidevin, Raymond (ed.), *Histoire des débuts de la Construction Européenne*, mars 1948 - Mai 1950, Brussels, Milan, Paris, Baden-Baden, 1988.
14 Van der Beugel, 'Ernst, The United States and European Unity', *Internationale Spectator*, vol.14, no.7, 8 April 1965.
15 Warnecke, Steven J., 'The future of foreign relations between the United States and a unified Europe: the European perspective', *Internationale Spectator*, vol. 27, no. 13, 8 July 1972.
16 Brugmans, H., 'The European Community at point zero', *Internationale Spectator*, vol. 28, no. 4, 22 February 1974.
17 When the author put it to Luns that he was an Atlantic man, while Beyen was a European, he replied: 'There's something in it' - Brussels, 11 January 1990, *telephone interview*.
18 Ibid.,
19 Luns, H. J. M. A., 'European and Atlantic Co-operation, the Dutch Attitude', (foreword), *Internationale Spectator*, op. cit., p.434.
20 Stikker, op. cit., p.347.

APPENDIX: LIST OF MISSING AND UNAVAILABLE FILES IN THE NATIONAL ARCHIVES

The following is a list of some of the Public Records Office files that are unavailable for public inspection. Only the first one is accompanied by a description, and it is difficult to guess what areas the others cover.

Year 1948	- 73282 (files 10408) - Evidence concerning conduct of clandestine operations in the Netherlands during the war. Allegations of treachery by certain Dutch and British officers.
Year 1949	- 79556 - 9
Year 1950	- 89333
Year 1951	- 96099, 96107, 96108, 96125
Year 1955	-112956

Although File series 73256 is available the following file jackets were found to be empty :-Z 4749, Z 4965, Z 5168, Z 5376, Z 5574 and Z 5868.

No explanation e.g. 'Retained under Section 3(4) of the Public Records Act of 1958' is given. A polite letter (of 10 March 1989) to an individual at the Public Records Office, and some friendly verbal questions to friendly staff have failed to unearth an answer. They concern the weekly political reports from the British Embassy, The Hague, for the period 28 May to 7 July 1948. One explanation is that somebody has removed them, which is a shame.

Defence is, quite understandably, a sensitive matter, particularly where the origins of NATO are concerned. Thus, the NATO Foreign Ministry files are still closed, in both Britain and the Netherlands. Should the Soviet Union open its archives to public inspection, this should encourage more PRO files to become available.

According to The Economist of 6 January 1990, a Mr J R Green, a Downing Street official, is the person who 'has got there first'. (B.U. 2048 A.D.)

ARCHIVALIA

1. The most relevant archives consulted were those of the Royal Netherlands Ministry of Foreign Affairs, particularly since the book concentrates on the diplomatic aspects of Dutch foreign policy. The main series of files examined were:
    European Defence Community
    Brussels Treaty Organisation
    German Rearmament
    Economic and Military Aid Programme
    Bonn Embassy
    Military Affairs Directorate
    Schuman Plan
    West Germany
    Paris Embassy

2. The General State Archives' Cabinet records were consulted. Although the records are clearly worded diplomatically, they nevertheless reflected reality. At the State Archives, the collections of Ernst van der Beugel, Dirk Stikker, Willem Drees and J □ van Roijen were also consulted.

3. The Archives of the Second Chamber of the Dutch States General were consulted on the border corrections (the General Committee of the First and Second Chambers) and the Schuman Plan (combined meetings of the Foreign Affairs and Trade policy committees).

4. Public Records Office (now the National Archives). Foreign Office files were consulted, series F0371 and F0953. They were interesting, in that they threw into relief the British perspective on develop-

ments in the Netherlands, which at times seemed to push the border between detachment and imagined patronage. The main files studied were those of the Embassy in The Hague, Western Department and Information Policy Department. Occasionally files are retained. As the file number of retained documents is only rarely given in the PRO reference books, one is left wondering what the file heading is.

5. Documents on British Policy Overseas – these published documents, based on extensive archival research, proved invaluable, as they group together Cabinet, as well as Foreign Office documents. The work of the late Dr Bullen is impressive. Foreign Relations of the United States – these published documents, also based on extensive archival research, proved invaluable, since they are particularly comprehensive, drawing on a wide range of sources.

INTERVIEWS

Dr. H. N. Boon, The Hague, 5 January 1990

Mr K. H. Beyen, The Hague, 6 January 1990,

Prof. Dr. E. H. van der Beugel, The Hague, 8 January 1990.

Drs. Jan Hoffenaar, The Hague, 8 January 1990.

Mr. J. M. Drees & W. Drees, The Hague, 9 January 1990.

Dr. Mr. J. M. A. H. Luns, Brussels, 11 January 1990.

BIBLIOGRAPHY

Published Material
Newspapers
Editorials from *Trouw, De Volkskrant, Nieuwe Rotterdamse Courant,* and *Het Vrije Volk* were consulted. The author is grateful to Dr. Friso Wielenga for access to his own copies.

Periodicals
Internationale Spectator
The Economist
Survey of International Affairs (Royal Institute of International Affairs)
The World Today (Royal Institute of International Affairs)
Journal of the Royal Institute of International Affairs
Tijdschrift voor Geschiedenis

Published Articles
Alting van Gausen, Dr. F. A. M., 'Europe beyond the Six', *Internationale Spectator*, vol. 39, no.7, 8 April 1965.

Beijen, Dr. J W 'United Europe: federal or supranational?, *Internationale Spectator*, vol.14, no.7, 8 April 1965.
------------, 'L'influence de l'esprit latin sur un pays nordique', Letterieterij 'Amsterdam'. Amsterdam, 1953.

Boogman, J. C., 'The Dutch Crisis in the Eighteen Forties, Britain and the Netherlands', J. S. Bromley and E. H. Kossman (eds.): *paper* delivered to the Oxford-Netherlands Historical Conference, London, 1960.

Brouwer, J.W.L., 'De stem van de Marine in de Ministerraad, Schout-bij-nacht H.C.W. Moormanals Staatsecretaris van Marine in het Kabinet Drees-Van Schaik, 1941-1951', *Politieke Opstellen*, no.9, Centrum voor Parlementaire Geschiedenis, Catholic University of Nijmegen, 1989.

Bullen, Roger, 'An Idea enters Diplomacy: the Schuman Plan, May 1950, Ideas into Politics: *Aspects of European History 1850-1950*, Bullen, R., van Standman, Pogge and Polonsky, A.B.(eds.), London 1984.

Bullen, Roger, 'Britain and Europe 1950 – 1957', *The Relaunching of Europe and the Treaties of Rome*, European Community Liaison Committee of Historians, vol.3, Brussels, Milan and Baden Baden, 1987.

Brugmans, H., 'De Europeese Gemeenschap op het Nulpunt, *Internationale Spectator*, vol.28, no.4, 22 February 1974.

D. B., 'The Inter-Allied Reparations Agency', *The World Today*, Royal Institute of InternationalAffairs, vol.5, no. 1, January to December 1949.

D.P.E., 'A Note on the Dutch Economic Situation', *The World Today*, Royal Insyitute of InternationalAffairs, vol. 4, January to December 1948.

Dilks, David, 'Britain and Europe 1948-1950: the Prime Minister, the Foreign Secretary and the Cabinet', in Raymond Poidevin, op. cit.

Eisen, Janet, 'Anglo Dutch Relations and European Unity 1940 – 1948', *Occasional Papers in Modern Dutch Studies*, Hull University, 1980.

Hawtrey, R. G., 'The European Arena - Western Europe and Germany', *Survey of International Affairs 1947-48*, Royal Institute of International Affairs, Oxford, 1952.

H. C. C, 'German Rearmament: Policies and Options', *The World Today*, Royal Institute of International Affairs, vol. 7, January – December 1951.

R.S, 'The West German Political Parties', *The World Today*, Royal Institute of International Affairs, vol. 9, January – December 1953.

Heldring, J. L., 'De invloed van de openbare mening op het buitenlands beleid', ibid.,

Kersten, A. E., 'Neutraliteitspolitiek versus Zelfstandigheidspolitiek', *Internationale Spectator*, vol. 38, no. 2, February 1984.

Kersten, Albert E., 'Niederlaendische Regierung, Bewaffnung Westdeutschlands und EVG', *Die Europaische Verteidigungsgemeinschaft. Stand und Probleme der Forschung* Militargeschliches Forschungsamt (ed.), Boppard-am-Rein, 1985.

Klein, P. W., and van der Plaat, G. N. 'Het Nederlandse Veiligheids beleid 1945 – 50', *Herrijzend Nederland - Opstellen over Nederland in de Periode 1945-50*, The Hague, 1981.

Kohnstamm, Max, 'The European Community and its Role in the World', *John Findley Green Foundation Lectures*, University of Missouri, 1964.

Kossman, E. H., 'In Praise of the Dutch Republic: some Seventeenth Century Attitudes', *Inaugural Lecture*, University College, London, 13 May 1963.

Luns, J. M. A. H., 'European and Atlantic Co-operation-The Dutch Attitude', *Internationale Spectator*, vol. 39, no. 7, 8 April 1965.

Luns, J. M. A. H.,' De Westeuropese Unie als Katalysator', *Internationale Spectator*, vol.18, no. 19, 8 May 1964.

Luns, His Excellency Dr. J. M. A. H., 'Benelux in Europa', *Internationale Spectator*, vo.l 23, no. 17, October 1969.

Mallinson, W.D.E., 'The Dutch, the British abd Anti-Communism in the Immediate Post-War Years', *Dutch Crossing*, no.41., Summer 1990, University College, London.

Manning, A. F., 'De buitenlandse politiek van de Nederlandse regering in London tot 1942', Tijdschrift voor Geschiedenis, volume 91, n.o 2, Groningen, 1978.

Manning, Adrien, 'Les Pays Bas face à l'Europe', in Raymond Poidevin, op.cit.

May, Ernest R., 'The American Commitment to Germany, 1949 – 55', *Diplomatic History*, vol. 13, no. 4, Washington and Delaware, Fall 1989.

Melandri, Pierre, 'Le role de l'unification Européenne dans la politique extérieure des Etats-Unis 1948 – 1950,' in Raymond Poidevin, op.cit.

Patijn, C. I.,' Nederlandse buitenlandse beleid', *Internationale Spectator*, vol. 24, no. 1, 8 Janaury 1970.

Pistone, Sergio,' II ruolo del movimento federalisto europeo negli anni 1948-1950', in Raymond Poidevin, op.cit.

Poidevin, Raymond, 'Histoire des Debuts de la Construction Européenne, Origins of the [sic] European Integration', March 1948 - May 1950, *Colloquium*, Strasbourg 28-30 November 1984, R. Poidevin, (ed.), Brussels, Milan, Paris, Baden-Baden, 1986.

Roberts, Michael, 'The New Forces in Western Europe', *International Affairs*, Royal Intstitute of International Affairs, vol. 21, 1945.

Rom Colthoff, A., 'The Dutch business community and European integration', *Internationale Spectator*, vol. 39, no. 7, 8 April 1965.

Russel, Prof. Dr. Robert W, The Atlantic Alliance in Dutch Foreign Policy', *Internationale Spectator*, vol. 23, no. 13, 8 July 1969.

Samkalden, Prof. Dr. I., 'A Dutch retrospective view on European and Atlantic Co-operation', *Internationale Spectator*, vol. 39, no. 7, 8 April 1965.

Schaper, H. A., 'Het Nederlandse veiligheidsbeleid in de jaren 1945 – 1948', *Internationale Spectator*, vol. 32, no. 5, May 1978.

Schlaim, Avi, 'Engeland op zoek voor zijn plaats in de Wereld', *Internationale Spectator*, vol. 29, no. 5, May 1975

Schoffer, Dr. I., 'Het trauma van de Nederlandsenederlag', *Tijdschrift voor Geschiedenis*, Volume 84, no. 4, Groningen, 1971.

Schokking, J. J. 'The Netherlands in a Changing World', *Journal of the Royal Institute of International Affairs*, vol. 23, 1947.

Schroder, Hans-Jurgen, 'Die Amerikanische Deutschland politiek und das Problem der Westeuropaischen Integration,, 1947/48 – 1950, in Raymond Poidevin, op.cit.

Schwabe, Klaus, 'Der Marshall Plan und Europa', in Poidevin, Raymond, op.cit.

Sked, Alan, 'Britain and the Council of Europe', unpublished *paper* given to the annual conference of the Association of Contemporary Historians, London School of Economics and Political Science, 1983.

Smith, Lyn, 'Covert British Propaganda: the Information Research Department, 1947 – 77', *Millenium: Journal of International Sutdies*, Spring 1980, vol. 9, no. 1.

Stengers, Jean, 'Paul-Henri Spaak et le Traité de Bruxelles de 1948', in Raymond Poidevin, op.cit.

Tamse, C. A., 'Een historisch element in het Nederlandse buitenlands - politieke denken', *Internationale Spectator*, vol. 28, no. 22, 22 December 1974.

Thorne, Christopher, 'Engeland, Australie en Nederlands Oost-Indie,1941-1945', *Internationale Spectator*, vol 29, no. 8, August 1975.

Van der Beugel, E. H., 'The United States and European Unity', *Internationale Spectator*, vol. 39, no. 7, 8 April 1965.

Van Campen, Dr. S. I. P., 'De Noordatlantische Verdragsorganisatie 1949-1964', *Internationale Spectator*, vol. 28, no. 9, 8 May 1964.

Van den Heuvel, Martin, 'Nederlandse gedachten over de sovjetdreiging: tussen hoop en vreze', Internationale Spectator, vol. 39, no. 1, January 1985.

Van de Vooren, Drs. F. W. C J., 'Het Duitse Vraagstuk', *Internationale Spectator*, vol. 24, No. 19, 8 November 1970.

Vlekke, B. H. M.,' A Dutch view of the World Situation', *Journal of the Royal Institute of international Affairs*, vol. 28, 1952.

Warnecke, Steven J., 'The future of foreign relations between the United States and a united Europe: the European perspective', *Internationale Spectator*, vol.26, no. 13, 8 July 1972.

Warner, Geoffrey, 'The Unites States and the Rearmament of West Germany, 1950 – 4', *International Affairs*, vol. 61, no. 2, Spring 1985.

Wesselring, H L., 'Vier eeuwen Frans-Nederlandse betrekkingen: het soortelijk gericht van de geschiedenis', *Internationale Spectator*, vol. 42, no. 12, December 1988.

Wiebes, Cees and Zeeman Bert, 'Opdoemende contouren van Noordatlantisch Verdrag-onderhandelingen in het Pentagon in maart 1948', *Internationale Spectator*, vol 36, no. 1, January 1982.
--------------------------------------- 'Het Verdrag van Duinkerken: speelbal van Britse Buitenlandse politiek', *Internationale Spectator*, vo.l 38, no. 8, August 1983.
--------------------------------------- Nederland, Belgie en de Sovjetdreiging (1942-1948), *Internationale Spectator*, Vol 41, No 9, September 1987.
--------------------------------------- 'Stikker: Indonesia en het Noordatlantisch Verdrag, of: hoe Nederland in de pompe ging', *Bijdragen en mededelingen betreffende de geschiedenis der Nederlanden, Nederlands Historisch Genootschap*, Deel 100, Aflevering 2, S. C. H. Blom et al (eds.), Zeist 1985.

Willcox, T., 'Towards a Ministry of Information', History, vol ., no.227, October 1984.

Yasamee H. J., 'Anthony Eden and Europe', *Occasional Papers*, no. 1, London 1987 (Seminar, Valid Evidence).

Young, John W.' 'The Schuman Plan and British Association', *The Foreign Policy of Churchill's Peacetime Administration 1951 – 1955*, John W. Young (ed.), Leicester University Press, 1988.

Background Reading

Acheson, Dean, *Present at the Creation*, London, 1969.

Acheson, Dean, *Sketches from Life*, London, 1961.

Adenauer, Konrad, *Memoirs*, London, 1966.

Bohlen, Charles E., *The Transformation of American Foreign Policy*, London, 1969.

Beyen, J. W., *Het Spel en de Knikkers, een Kroniek van Vijftig Jaren*, Amsterdam, 1968.

Bogaarts, M. D., 'De Periode van het Kabinet Beel, 3 Juli 1946 – 1 August 1948'. *Parlementaire Geschiedenis van Nederland*, Deel 3, Thesis defended 30 November 1989, Catholic University of Nijmegen, The Hague, 1989.

Boon, Dr. H. N., *Bagatellen uit de Diplomatieke Dienst*, Rotterdam, 1972.

Brierley, J. L., *The Law of Nations*, Oxford 1963, sixth Edition, revised by Sir Humphrey Waldock.

Bullock, Alan, *The Life and Times of Ernest Bevin*, vol. I, London, Melbourne and Toronto, 1960.

Charité, D.r J. (ed.), Biografisch Woordenboek van Nederland, part 1 (1979), 2 (1985), and 3 (1989), the Hague, 1989.

De Baena, Duke, *The Dutch Puzzle*, The Hague, 1975 (Fifth Edition).

Diebold, Jr, William, *The Schuman Plan - A Study in Economic Co-operation 1950 - 1959*, New York, 1959.

Dockrill, Michael and Young, John W. (eds.), *British Foreign Policy 1945 - 56*, London, 1989.

Drees, Willem, *Zestig Jaar Levenservaring*, Amsterdam, 1962.

Dulles, John Foster, *War or Peace*, New York, 1957.

Eden, Rt. Hon Sir Anthony, *Full Circle*, London,1960.

Fisher, H. A. L., *A History of Europe*, vols. 1 and 2, London, 1960.

Fursdon, Edward, *The European Defence Community - A History*, London, 1980.

Griffith, R. T., 'The Abortive Dutch Assault on European Tariffs, 1950 – 2', *Modern Dutch Studies*, Michael Wintle and Paul Vincent (eds.), London, 1988.

Henderson, Sir Nicholas, *The Birth of NATO*, London, 1982.

Hirschfeld, Dr. H. M., *Herinneringen uit de Jaren*, 1933 – 1939, Amsterdam, 1959.

Hirschfeld, Dr. H. M., *Herinneringen uit de Bezettingstijd*, Amsterdam, 1960.

Hopkins, Alan, *Holland*, London, 1988.

Ismay, Lord, NATO - *the First Five Years*, Utrecht, 1954.

Kahin, George McT., 'The United States and the Anti-Colonial Revolution in South-East Asia, 1945-50', The Origins of the Cold War, Yonosuke Nagai and Akiwa Iriye (eds.), New York, 1977.

Klinkenberg, Wim, *Prins Bernhard-een politieke biografie*, 1911 – 1986, Haarlem, 1979, revised 1986.

Knorr, Klaus (ed.), *NATO and American Security*, Princeton, 1959.

Kruls, General H. J., *Vrede of Oorlog*, The Hague, 1952.

Leurdijk, .J. H. (ed.), *The Foreign Policy of the Netherlands*, Baarn, 1978.

Massigli, René, *Sur Quelques Maladies de l'Etat*, Paris, 1978.

------------------ *Une Comedie des Erreurs*, 1943-1956, Paris, 1978.

Melandri, Pierre, *Les Etats Unis face a l'Unification de l'Europe 1945-1954*, Paris, 1980.

Milward, Alan S., The Reconstruction of Western Europe 1945-51, London, 1984.

Moch, Jules, *Histoire du Réarmament Allemand depuis 1950*, Paris, 1950.

BIBLIOGRAPHY 293

Monnet, Jean, *Memoirs*, London, 1978.

Nutting, Rt. Hon Sir Anthony, *Europe will not wait - a warning and a way out*, London, 1960.

Oskam, B. P., *Twee Kapiteins op een Schip, De Nederlandse delegatie bij de onderhandelingen over de Europese Defensie Germeenschap in Parijs (1951 – 1954)*, doctoraalscriptie under supervision of P. M. E. Volten, Utrecht, 1989.

Renier, G. J., *The Dutch Nation*, London, 1944.

Royal Netherlands Ministry of Foreign Affairs, Directorate General of Economic and Military Aid Programme, *The Road to Recovery - The Marshall Plan - its importance for the Netherlands and European Co-operation*, The Hague, 1954.

Sandberg, H W, *Duitsland 1945 – 55*: object en subject, academic thesis defended at Amsterdam University, 27 November, 1959.

Spaak, Paul-Henri, *Why NATO?*, London, 1959.

---------------------- *Combats Inachevés*, vols. 1 and 2, Paris, 1969.

Spits, F. C., *Naar een Europees Leger*, The Hague, 1954.

Stikker, Dirk U., *Men of Responsibility*, London, 1966.

Thorne, Christopher, *Allies of a Kind - The United States, Britain and the War against Japan, 1941 - 1945*, Oxford and New York, 1979.

Van der Beugel, Ernst H., *From Marshall Aid to Atlantic Partnership - European Integration as a Concern of American Foreign Policy*, Amsterdam, 1966.

Van den Bosch, Amry, *Dutch Foreign Policy since 1815 - a Study in Small Power Politics*, The Hague, 1959.

Van Campen, S. I. P., *The Quest for Security - Some Aspects of Netherlands Foreign Policy 1949 – 50*, The Hague, 1958.

Van der Harst, Jan, *European and Atlantic Partnership: Political, Military and Economic Aspects of Dutch Defence 1948 – 54, and the Impact of the European Defence Community*, Florence, July 1987 - (successful Ph.D., European University Institute).

Van der Harst, Jan, *The Netherlands and the European Defence Community*, European University Institute Working Paper, no. 86/252, Florence, 1986.

Von Albertini, Rudolf, *The Decolonisation of the Dutch East Indies, The End of the European Empire - Decolonisation after World War II*, Tony Smith (ed.), Lexington, 1975.

Voorhoeve, Joris J., *Peace, Profits and Principles - A Study of Dutch Foreign Policy*, The Hague, 1979.

Wetenschapelijk Raad voor het Regerings beleid, *Onder Jnvloed van Duitsland*, The Hague, 1982.

Wielenga, Friso, *West-Duitsland: partner uit noodzaak - Nederland en de Borderspubliek 1949-1955*, Utrecht, 1989.

Willis, F. Roy, France, *Germany and the New Europe 1945 – 67*, Stanford and London, 1968.

Young John W. (ed.), *The Foreign Policy of Churchill's Peacetime Administration 1951-1955*, Leicester University, 1988.

Young John W., *Britain, France and the Unity of Europe 1945 – 51*, Leicester University, 1984.

INDEX

A

Acheson, Dean 36–37, 76, 110–112, 123–126, 129, 135, 139, 140–141, 144, 166, 180–182, 212, 235, 239, 242, 257–258, 261, 274
Adenauer, Konrad 33, 52, 106, 109, 118, 124, 138, 145, 154, 181, 183–185, 187, 197, 202, 222
America 8, 44, 55, 65, 97, 102, 112–113, 157, 168, 201, 220, 222–223, 229
Anti-Revolution Party, ARP 94
Arnold, Karl 23, 216
Attlee, Clement 19, 27, 112, 121, 126, 156, 240, 244–246, 257, 261–265

B

Belgium 1, 5, 7, 9–10, 22–24, 35–36, 40, 59, 61–63, 68, 105, 121, 149, 177–178, 180, 225, 227
Benelux xiii, 2, 25, 35–36, 38–40, 43–44, 46, 48, 59–60, 62–64, 68, 70, 72, 75, 106, 108, 117, 125–126, 129, 134, 141, 145, 149, 158, 177–179, 206, 211, 213–214, 220, 227–229, 262, 278
Bevin, Ernest 30, 41–43, 62–64, 67–69, 72, 77–78, 88, 90, 94, 109–112, 120, 123–125, 127, 132, 135, 146, 152, 235–237, 239, 240, 241–245, 247, 249–253, 256–260, 262–263, 265
Beyen, Karel xi, xv, 92, 176, 186, 188–189, 191, 195, 197–199, 201–207, 211–216, 218–219, 222, 224, 228, 230–232, 243, 252, 269, 271–275, 277–278
Bismarck 11
Boetzelaer van Oosterhout 19–20, 33, 55, 62–64, 107, 239, 242, 245
Border Rectifications 17, 23–24
Brussels Treaty Organisation ix, xv, 54–66, 61, 70, 83, 86, 97, 156, 221,

223, 227, 281. *See herein* BTO
BTO. *See* Brussels Treaty Organisation

C

Catholic People's Party, KVP ix, 32, 94, 185–186
CEEC ix, 14, 39–41, 43. *See herein* Committee for European Economic Co-operation
Christian Historical Union, CHU 94
Churchill, Winston 8, 28, 77, 82, 109–110, 117–118, 121, 127, 138–139, 142, 144, 146, 151, 153–156, 158, 186, 188, 193, 199–200, 204, 219, 231, 237, 261, 263, 269
Clayton 36–38, 235, 242
Committee for European Economic Co-operation. *See* CEEC
Council of Europe vi, xv, 43, 52–53, 109, 111, 118–124, 128, 134, 138, 140, 142, 153–155, 178, 186, 213, 227, 257, 259, 263, 269, 276

D

de Gasperi, Alcide 33, 52, 118, 154, 188–189
de Geer, Dirk Jan 8, 32
de Witt, Johan 7, 32
Drees, Willem xi, 40, 57, 61, 64, 82–83, 89, 95–96, 100–110, 119, 144, 158, 161, 163, 164–170, 176, 185–186, 190–193, 196, 203, 205–207, 212, 228–229, 243, 246, 251, 253, 265, 270, 281, 283, 286, 291
Dulles, John Foster 58, 80, 83, 137, 156, 201, 218, 220, 222–223, 231, 246, 250
Dutch Labour Party 132. *See also* PvdA

E

ECA 39, 58, 75, 78, 167, 254, 258. *See also* Economic Co-operation Administration
Economic Co-operation Administration 39, 82, 104, 124. *See also* ECA
ECSC ix, 203, 207, 214, 274. *See also* European Coal and Steel Community
EDC vii, ix, 2, 144, 146, 149–151, 153, 156, 158, 177–183, 188, 190, 193–196, 199–214, 217–224, 229–232, 274, 276. *See also* European Defence Community
Eden, Anthony 151, 153, 155, 172, 186, 199, 221–224, 231, 263–264, 266–270, 274
Eden Plan 133, 155, 178, 186, 187, 188, 193

INDEX 297

England xiv, 6–7, 41, 120–121, 127–128, 150, 155, 189, 199, 201
EPU ix, 53, 160, 227. *See also* European Payments Union
European Coal and Steel Community ix, 140, 194. *See also* ECSC
European defence community 180. *See also* EDC

F

Foreign Office 38, 42, 47–48, 58, 67, 72, 77–78, 89–90, 92–93, 101, 108,
   120, 129, 133, 135, 146, 152, 163, 167–172, 187, 189–192, 197–199,
   206–207, 216, 220–221, 237, 240, 252, 269–271, 275–276, 281–282
France xiii, 7, 9–10, 22, 32, 37, 40–41, 46, 53–54, 62–64, 68–69, 85, 93,
   96–97, 102, 113–114, 120, 123–124, 126, 128, 132–137, 140–142,
   145–146, 149–150, 153, 156, 178–181, 183–185, 187–188, 192, 195,
   200–203, 210–214, 218–223, 226–227, 231, 247, 258, 262, 274
Fritalux 63
Fursdon, Edward 97, 111–112, 118, 139, 140, 143, 146–148, 151, 178, 185,
   200, 202, 218–219, 221, 223, 253, 255–264, 268–270, 272–273,
   275–277

G

Gerbrandy 28
Germany v–xiii, xv, 1–2, 7, 9–13, 15–19, 21–26, 33–34, 36, 38–41, 43–51,
   53–55, 59–65, 69–70, 81–82, 84–86, 89, 93, 97, 99, 102–103,
   105–117, 119–120, 124, 126, 128, 133–135, 137–141, 144–150,
   152–153, 158–160, 164, 177–181, 183–185, 190–191, 193–197,
   200–202, 208, 210–224, 226–227, 240, 242, 244, 251, 260, 262, 270,
   272, 274, 276, 281
Grotius, Hugo 32, 235

H

Hirschfeld, Hans 14–15, 19, 36, 39, 44–46, 134, 237–238, 244, 254
Hitler, Adolf 12, 22

I

Indo-China 141, 218–220, 231
Indonesia xi, xv, 26–28, 30–31, 34, 38, 44, 56–60, 65, 70, 75–82, 84–85,
   94–96, 98–99, 101, 103, 115–116, 137, 160, 174–175, 196, 228, 232,
   241, 245–246, 249–250
Italy xiii, 37, 39–40, 63, 71, 93, 96, 107, 141, 145, 150, 153, 178, 180, 218, 223

J

Jews 12, 13, 14, 15

K

Kohnstamm, Max 44, 149–150, 213, 263–264, 274
Kruls, H.S. 88–89, 95, 99, 115, 158, 160–165, 168, 174–175, 228–229, 251, 265

L

Luns, Joseph xi, 60, 186, 201, 206–208, 216, 221–222, 224, 227, 231–232, 246, 273, 275, 277–278
Luxembourg 9, 11, 22, 24, 35–36, 59, 63, 74, 96, 178, 180, 225

M

Marshall Aid 37–44, 63–65, 82, 130
Marshall, George 36–37, 41, 62, 69, 242–244
Marshall Plan v, xv, 38–39, 44, 58, 69, 78, 80
Mendes-France, Pierre 210, 212–213, 219–220, 222
Monnet, Jean 116, 118, 123, 125, 126, 148, 182, 187, 230, 257, 268
Mussert, Jan 14

N

NATO iii, vi–vii, 1, 70, 79–83, 86, 95–97, 99, 101, 103, 105–106, 110–112, 114–116, 139–140, 142, 144–149, 152, 156, 159, 163, 171–172, 174, 177, 179–185, 190, 193–194, 200–201, 204, 206–207, 210, 212, 218, 219–221, 223, 226, 229, 232, 247, 263, 267, 279. *See also* North Atlantic Treaty Organisation
Nichols, Philip 38, 92, 165, 167–168, 176, 198, 235–237, 239–240, 242–245, 247, 250–253, 255–257, 259–262, 264–267, 270
North Atlantic Treaty Organisation xv, 152, 173, 185, 210, 219. *See also* NATO
Nutting, Anthony 42, 109, 127, 135, 152, 155, 219, 221, 243, 258, 260, 263–264, 276

O

Occupation xv, 13, 15, 45, 47–48, 51, 83, 85, 93, 113–114, 149, 201
OEEC ix, 39, 41, 43, 44, 52–53, 64, 81, 114, 122, 125, 131, 133–134, 198,

INDEX 299

207–208, 227, 259. *See also* Organisation for European Economic Co-operation

Organisation for European Economic Co-operation ix, 36. *See also* OEEC

P

Party of Freedom and Democracy ix, 94. *See also* VVD
Pléven Plan xv, 136–138, 140–143, 145–146, 148, 150, 153, 155, 173, 200
Pléven, René 262–263
PvdA ix, 23. *See also* Dutch Labour Party

R

Russia 54, 61, 67, 69, 83, 88, 108, 113, 115, 162, 164, 202, 220

S

Saar 22, 185
Schokking, J.J. 89, 161, 237, 251
Schuman, Maurice vi, xv, 33, 52, 110, 112, 116–118, 120, 122–126, 128–135, 137, 139–142, 144, 146–147, 150–151, 153–156, 179, 181–182, 186–188, 193, 201, 213, 228, 231, 257–259, 261, 263, 269, 276, 281
Schuman Plan vi, xv, 123–125, 128–135, 137, 139, 140–142, 144, 146–147, 150–151, 153, 155, 186–187, 228, 231, 257, 259, 261, 263, 269, 276, 281
Soviet Union 31, 33, 42, 44, 59–62, 64, 69–71, 82, 90–92, 95–97, 106, 116, 135, 144, 147, 162, 181, 210, 218, 220, 228, 248, 273, 279
Spaak, Paul-Henri 61, 72, 118, 120-122, 153, 178, 188, 228, 231-232, 257, 274
State Department 24–25, 27, 37, 40–41, 56, 64, 68, 71–72, 76, 81, 101, 105, 129, 148, 239, 243, 245, 253–254, 257, 259
Stikker, Dirk vi–vii, xv, 2, 15–17, 21–23, 33, 40, 46, 51–52, 56–57, 64, 66, 70, 77–79, 81, 85, 99, 102, 106–107, 110–115, 118–119, 122–123, 125, 127, 128, 130–134, 137, 139, 143–147, 149, 151–152, 154, 156–158, 160, 162–164, 166, 168–170, 173–174, 176–178, 180–183, 186, 188–191, 193, 195, 197, 199–201, 203–206, 208–209, 211–213, 219, 221–222, 224–231, 233, 236, 238–242, 244–245, 247–248, 250, 254–256, 258–259, 261–264, 267–272, 274, 277–278, 281

U

UN ix, 33, 58, 76, 78, 82, 102, 241. *See also* United Nations
United Nations ix, 8, 28, 31, 55–58, 61, 66, 71, 75–80, 86, 100, 115, 246, 249, 253. *See also* UN
United Nations Relief and Recovery Agency ix. *See* UNRRA
UNRRA ix, 37–38. *See also* United Nations Relief and Recovery Agency
US xiii, 24–25, 28, 31, 37, 57–58, 68, 71, 73, 78, 80, 82, 89–90, 101, 103, 104, 135, 141, 167, 180, 240, 242–243, 247–251, 254–255, 261–262, 264, 266–267, 276. *See also* USA
USA 2, 71–72, 114, 137. *See also* US

V

van Kleffens, Eeclo 8, 14, 17, 19, 28, 33, 55, 69, 73–74, 78, 81, 96, 241, 254
Van Reuchlin, Otto 73, 75
van Starkenborgh Stachouwer, A. W. L. Tjarda 19
van Verduynen, Michiels 19, 47, 238, 244, 258
van Voorst tot Voorst, Baron 21, 254
VVD ix, 131

W

Western European Union ix, 87, 135, 221, 223. *See also* WEU
WEU ix, 236, 247. *See also* Western European Union

Lightning Source UK Ltd.
Milton Keynes UK
UKHW020759250620
365503UK00006B/192